034406

DATE DUE		
RECEIVED NOV 2 0 1995	Apr 26/07	
RECEIVED NOV 2 2 1995		
FEB 0 2 1996		
RECEIVED FEB 0 8 1996		
NOV 2 1 1996	1 5 JUN 2002	
APR 2 3 1999	DEC 1 2 2003	
2 4 APR 2001		
2 1 JUN 2001		
0 8 APR 2002		

mill woods

Empirical studies of
alcoholism.

Empirical Studies
of Alcoholism

Empirical Studies
of Alcoholism

edited by
Gerald Goldstein
and
Charles Neuringer

Ballinger Publishing Company ● Cambridge, Mass.
A Subsidiary of J.B. Lippincott Company

International Standard Book Number: 0-88410-127-4

Library of Congress Catalog Card Number: 76-17285

Printed in the United States of America

Library of Congress Cataloging in Publication Data
Main entry under title:

Empirical studies of alcoholism.

    Includes index.
    1. Alcoholism—Addresses, essays, lectures.
2. Alcohol—Physiological effect—Addresses, essays, lectures. 3. Alcoholism—
Treatment—Addresses, essays, lectures. I. Goldstein, Gerald, 1931-
II. Neuringer, Charles, 1931-
HV5035.E47   616.8'61   76-17285
ISBN 0-88410-127-4

Dedication
To our Carolyns

✳ Contents

✳ List of Figures

❋ List of Tables

Empirical Studies
of Alcoholism

Chapter One

Introduction

Charles Neuringer and
Gerald Goldstein

Most people have some first-hand knowledge of alcoholism. Either a friend or relative is an alcoholic, there is a personal problem with possible excessive use of alcohol, or some acquaintanceship with the problem is made on the basis of information contained in the communications media. The association between alcoholism and violence, crime, deterioration of the individual, dismemberment of the family, and other personal and social ills are well documented in fiction as well as in the daily newspapers. Attempts to control alcohol consumption through law and social custom are seen throughout the world. The constant exposure to the consequences of excessive alcohol use has made most of us aware of it as a "problem." We confront the drunken driver, see the "skid-row" alcoholic on the street, watch the celebrity talk about his alcoholism on television. While this visibility has clearly had positive effects, it has also had the somewhat unfortunate consequence of providing a superficial knowledge about alcoholism that sometimes tends to block further inquiry.

One result of this situation is that the field of alcoholism appears to have become characterized by dogma, in which varying views are presented with an air of certainty and emotionality. In the history of medicine, this sort of situation is seen during the early stages of understanding some disease. We may recall the controversy surrounding the nature and treatment of poliomyelitis before Salk's development of the virus theory and poliomyelitis vaccine. Following that scientific breakthrough, the emotionality seems to have cooled. The breakthrough in alcoholism has not occurred as yet, despite the enthusiasm of proponents of various views concerning the condition.

Our relative lack of understanding of the nature of alcoholism can be easily exposed by asking a number of questions. The first question is, "What is alcoholism?" A currently popular view is that it is a disease. But not everybody concurs with that idea. Nor has alcoholism always been viewed as a disease. Many of us still recall the days when alcoholism (better known then as drunkeness) was viewed as willful and immoral conduct. This opinion no doubt continues to be maintained in some quarters. If, however, alcoholism is a disease, is it a disease of some organ system of the body, or is it what some would call a mental illness? Is it a problem for internal medicine or for psychiatry? As is well known, this issue is far from resolved. In recent years, and in conjunction with emerging criticisms of the illness model of mental and emotional disorders, other concepts have emerged regarding the nature of alcoholism. It has been described with such rubrics as a bad habit, a behavior disorder, a life style, a way of being-in-the-world and a problem in living. Disagreement also continues to exist on the very basic issue of whether alcoholism is a condition that victimizes the individual, or whether people become alcoholics on the basis of some kind of personal choice.

Considering the variety of hypotheses, theories, and beliefs suggested above, it is clear that there is no definite agreement concerning the nature of alcoholism. One important aspect of this lack of agreement has to do with the definition of alcoholism in individual cases. What criteria does one use to call another individual an alcoholic? There is obviously no laboratory procedure or diagnostic test that is definitive. Within a medical framework, we would say that only a clinical diagnosis is possible, based on the patient's history, mental status, and other examinational findings.

The ambiguities concerning the nature of alcoholism may be revealed further by asking our second question, "What causes alcoholism?" If one accepts the premise that there is no agreement concerning the nature of alcoholism, then this question is particularly difficult to answer because we do not know where to look for the answer. The general practice seems to be to look within the framework of one's own discipline or system of biases. Physiologists may look for it in the metabolism, neurologists in the brain, geneticists in the genes, psychologists in behavior, sociologists in the culture, etc. We are not resorting to hyperbole here for dramatic effect. It would be possible to document, although we will not do so here, that all of these disciplines and others have postulated a "cause of alcoholism." To list some of these "causes"—we have a metabolic disorder, a genetic defect, a fixation at the oral stage of psychosexual development, a rejecting-rigid-family, a set of learned responses, and limited psychological differentiation. Within this variety of postulated causes, there appear to be certain polarizations, i.e., organically biased individuals wholly reject psychological explanations and vice versa. At the present time, however, neither side appears to have sufficient evidence to convince the other.

If one accepts these views concerning gaps in our knowledge of the nature and causes of alcoholism, then the third question becomes an exceedingly difficult one to answer. "What is the cure for alcoholism?" Some believe that alcoholism is an incurable condition, and express their view in the form of the well-known maxim, "Once an alcoholic, always an alcoholic." However, advocates of this view tend not to be totally pessimistic, maintaining the belief that while the disease will always be there, the alcoholic can find ways of controlling his drinking. Others claim there are cures, but again they tend to follow more or less discipline-oriented lines. Thus, varying therapies including medication, psychotherapy, group psychotherapy, sensitivity training, behavior modification, and numerous other procedures have been used in the treatment of alcholism. Almost twenty years ago, Wallerstein and his associates at the Topeka VA Hospital and the Menninger Foundation (Wallerstein, 1957) published a volume containing the results of a study in which a variety of treatment modalities were compared. Since that time the variety of treatment methods has increased substantially. Again without providing the necessary documentation, it can be said that despite the proliferation of new treatment methods, alcoholism remains an exceedingly recalcitrant clinical problem, and the cure rate by any objective standard remains relatively low. It is, however, no worse than we would expect in the case of a condition for which the cause is not known. Such conditions frequently can be treated for symptomatic relief, but not cured in any definitive sense.

It would appear that an examination of the three questions posed above makes it clear that we really do not know a great deal about alcoholism, despite the enthusiasm of many workers in the field. While some may question this conclusion, we feel that it will ring true to the clinician "in the trenches," who every day experiences the hopes and frustrations that come with treating the alcoholic patient. It also seems obvious that if there were some straightforward and well-known procedures for diagnosing and curing alcoholism, we would not have millions of active alcoholics currently living in the United States and elsewhere.

In view of these considerations, the contributors to this volume share the general belief that the most promising opportunity for adding to our ability to understand and assist the alcoholic lies in scientific research. While the research to be reported here covers a variety of areas, and while there may not be agreement regarding certain issues, there is strong agreement that the most productive way to proceed in this emotionalized, controversial area is through the martialing of objectively obtained evidence. A major theme running through the book can be described as an attempt to understand the individual alcoholic through objective methods. In other words, the emphasis will be on what constitutes alcoholism. The question of the possible causes of alcoholism are not dealt with in detail, except with regard to distinguishing between cause and consequence.

Another trend or emphasis in the book is on the relatively new area of neuropsychology. Neuropsychology has given us a number of new tools and concepts with which to do alcoholism research. Several of the contributing authors hold the view that many of the behavioral manifestations of chronic alcoholism can be explained on the basis of alcoholism-produced damage to the central nervous system. These authors have utilized objective tests to demonstrate some of the behavioral deficits associated with alcoholism, and are in the process of attempting to bridge the gap between observed behavior and events taking place in the neural substrate. Clinical neuropsychological methods appear to be replacing the more casual "mental status examination" of the past, and clinical neuropsychologists appear to have a preference for objective experimental research over anecdotal observation. It would thus appear that this field has introduced something of a "new broom" into alcoholism research. Neuropsychological studies of alcoholism, while in an early stage, have already pointed out some rather significant phenomena related to alcohol addiction. While detailed information is provided in various chapters, we can anticipate conclusions reached a bit by saying that the long-term alcoholic tends to be a significantly impaired individual. Drs. Tarter and Goldstein document many of these deficits as found in the chronic alcoholic, while Drs. Butters and Cermak focus their attention on the deficits seen in the alcoholic patient with Korsakoff's syndrome. The clinical implications arising from these data concerning psychological deficit in alcoholics have barely begun to be explored.

Another trend noted in this book has to do with the attempt to bring concepts and techniques from the experimental laboratory into alcoholism research. Thus, Drs. Butters and Cermak work with some of the classical concepts, designs, and materials associated with experimental studies of human memory. Dr. Denney deals with concepts of conditioning and reinforcement that were originally developed in the learning laboratory. Drs. Tarter and Goldstein utilize techniques to study motor function, perception, concept learning, and related areas that have a long history in the field of experimental psychology. Congruent with this trend is that of Drs. Clopton and Neuringer's emphasis on research documentation in the use of psychological tests in the diagnosis of alcoholism. While many of these methods are old, the use of them to study clinical phenomena is relatively new in the alcoholism field. There now seems to be a productive interaction between the clinician and the experimentalist that will hopefully continue to produce significant findings in alcoholism research.

In his chapter, Dr. Higgins presents a thorough examination of one major theory concerning the nature of alcoholism; the tension reduction hypothesis. He reviews an extensive amount of literature revolving around the theory that alcoholism is maintained because alcohol consumption provides relief from unpleasant affective states. The question of subtypes of alcoholics is taken up by Ms. Shelly and Dr. Goldstein, who have written a chapter that presents a new objective approach to discovering types of alcoholics, and that also presents some preliminary evidence for the usefulness of a new typology.

Each chapter in this book is characterized by a tendency to weigh the evidence available and to report both success and failure. If anything, the book as a whole provides a precaution against maintaining the superficial under-standings so prevalent in the field of alcoholism. While many advances in knowledge are reported here, numerous questions are left unanswered. Disagree-ment remains concerning the consequences of alcoholism for the neural substrate. The locus of alcoholism-produced brain damage is still a matter of vigorous controversy. The reasons for the relative modesty of the results of behavior modification therapy remain to be explored, and, as Drs. Neuringer and Clopton conclude, the usefulness of psychological tests in alcoholism diagnosis remains equivocal. Dr. Higgins points out, in his conclusions, that there are substantial difficulties remaining with tension-reduction theory. The Shelly and Goldstein typology needs further documentation and refinement. Several of the authors are continuing their investigations along lines described in their chapters and many of the research programs described are ongoing. This volume may therefore be taken as a progress report of innovative research in a number of alcoholism related areas.

REFERENCES

Wallerstein, R.S., and Chotlos, J.W. *Hospital Treatment of Alcoholism.* New York: Basic Books, 1957.

Chapter Two

The Use of Psychological Tests for the Study of the Identification, Prediction and Treatment of Alcoholism

Charles Neuringer and
James R. Clopton

Psychological tests have been used for studying alcoholism with varying success. Much of the utility of any test depends upon (a) the context of usage and (b) specificity or generality of the device's measurement capacities, as well as (c) the conceptualization of the test's unique features which would make it useful for the diagnostic task. Aside from problems of correct administration, scoring, and interpretation of psychological tests, the greatest stumbling block to successful diagnosis of alcoholism has been injudicious use of these tests for tasks in contexts for which they were not designed.

Psychological tests as diagnostic tools for the assessment of alcoholism have traditionally been restricted to three areas. They were first used for simple diagnosis of the presence or absence of an alcholic problem. The assessment of extent of alcoholic dependency was a corollary development of this simple diagnostic task. Later on, psychological tests were utilized to assess alcoholic typologies (e.g., essential vs. reactive drinker.) Finally they have been utilized to discover and identify enduring personality constellations that were thought to be related to excessive alcoholic intake. This last type of diagnostic test usage has been directed towards the hunt for an "alcoholic personality."

Psychological tests have been used extensively in alcoholism research in areas other than diagnosis. Their use is extensive in the evaluation of particular problems or hypotheses dealing with the functional sequalae of alcoholic intake. In these circumstances, the psychological test is chosen more for its specific measurement potential rather than for its general differential diagnostic capacity. A good example of this would be the use of a "memory" or a "manual dexterity" test to measure changes in psychomotor and cognitive functioning under specific levels of alcohol in the blood. The utilization of psychological tests in these ways has been extensive, but basically they have not been called upon for diagnostic purposes.

It may be said at this time that psychological tests (with the major exception of the MMPI) have proved to be of little value for diagnosing alcoholism. The failure of standard psychological tests has led to the development of a whole series of specific alcoholism detection scales. Two examples of such procedures are the 18-item scale developed by Mortimer et al (1973), and The Michigan Alcoholism Screening Test (Moore, 1972). This type of highly specific inventory will not be discussed in this review and concentration will be focused on the standard, well-known, easily-available-to-user type of psychological tests.

As mentioned previously, the earliest use of psychological tests was for the diagnosis of the presence or absence of alcoholism. Later on, the added question of extent of alcoholism (if present) was also appraised. The diagnostic question of presence or absence of excess alcoholic dependency is one that rarely needs the use of a psychological test in order to arrive at an answer. The same is true (but to a lesser degree) for the corollary problem of extent of the alcoholism. The identification of whether a person has a serious drinking problem is best answered by an assessment of drinking habits, alcoholic intake, disruptive social relations, employment history, intellectual deterioration, etc. These social history factors are more than adequate for the sheer identification of the existence of excessive alcoholic intake. It should be noted that some psychological diagnosticians can diagnose alcoholism by merely asking an individual if he has a drinking problem. The degree of alcoholic intake (i.e., how serious is the alcoholic problem) is also best analyzed by inspection of social history data.

Psychological tests have been more useful in assessing types of alcoholism. The movement away from the concept of alcoholism as a single unitary disorder has been one of the major conceptual steps taken by researchers and clinicians interested in alcohol dependency. Walton (1968), using Cattell's 16 PF test, was able to investigate Jellinek's hypothesis about gamma and delta types of alcoholics, demonstrating that the former (who are compulsive drinkers) were more intropunitive and afraid of their impulses than the latter (who are drinkers who are unable to abstain.) Schafer's (1948) study of what he terms "essential" and "reactive" drinkers was able to uncover various personality characteristics differentiating the two types of alcoholics. Mortimer, Filkins, Kerlan, and Lower (1973) have been attempting to discriminate between "problem" drinkers and "social drinkers."

The possible existence of a cohesive constellation of traits and characteristics associated exclusively with alcoholism have led many people to conceptualize the existence of a highly specific "alcoholic personality." Psychological tests have been used in this search since it was thought that they had the capacity to simultaneously measure a wide variety of personality characteristics. One of the earliest forms of an alcoholic personality that was thought to exist was modeled on psychoanalytic theory, which emphasized oral fixation and consequent dependency as one of its main features. Examples are Wittman's (1939) use of the Chassell Inventory to evaluate whether alcoholism was the outcome of a doting mother, and Bertrand and Masling's (1969) use of the Rorschach in order to investigate the level of oral responses among alcoholics and nonalcoholics. The conclusions drawn from these and other studies about excessive oral dependency in alcoholics has been inconclusive.

As opposed to attempting to validate already existing hypotheses about the mediating processes underlying a possible alcoholic personality, attempts have been made to discover sets of interrelated traits that might exist in alcoholics from empirical test data constellations. Typically the approach has been to administer a wide variety of psychological tests to alcoholics and nonalcoholics and then to draw up a list of test response differences. Further analysis (either intuitive or via factor analysis) of these differences led to the construction of sets of personality characteristics and traits which were thought to be the essence of the alcoholic character. Unfortunately, the mass of results from these attempts has been so equivocal that it is impossible to conclude that there is (or is not) an "alcoholic personality." Support for the existence of such exclusive alcoholic character trait organization from psychological test data has been found by Bertrand and Masling (1969), Billig and Sullivan (1942), Button (1956), Halpern (1946), Hampton (1947), Harris and Ives (1947), Hewitt (1943), Jones (1938), Klebanoff (1947), Marshall (1947), McCord and McCord (1960, 1962), Modlin (1956), Morrow (1950), Murphy (1956), Quaranta (1949), Robins, Bates, and O'Neal (1962), Rubin (1948), and Sanford (1968). On the negative side of the controversy can be found the data of Brown and Lacey (1954), Kelley and Barrera (1941), Korman and Stubblefield (1961), Seliger and Cranford (1945), Singer (1950), Tremper (1972), and Zucker and Van Horn (1972). In their reviews of the alcoholic personality literature Sutherland, Schroeder, and Tordella (1950), Syme (1957), and Zwerling and Rosenbaum (1956) all raised serious doubts about the existence of an alcoholic personality.

Before discussing the tests in detail, it may be of interest to note that it was early discovered that there were little or no differentiating general intelligence potentials between alcoholics and nonalcoholics (Halpern, 1946; Moore, 1941; Roe, 1944) and that the variable could not be used for differential diagnostic purposes. Differences in intellectual functioning between alcoholics and nonalcoholics seem to be more a consequence of the effect of the alcohol on the brain tissue, than due to any innate dispositional tendency.

PROJECTIVE PERSONALITY TESTS

The first projective personality tests were developed in the early 1930s under the influence of psychoanalysis. Their popularity sprang from their being thought of as meeting a need which had not been satisfied by the then existing psychometric tests. It was felt that the psychometric devices of the time (item surveys requiring a "yes" or "no" response) produced a single quantitative score, which limited interpretation. In addition, there were severe criticisms about whether the name of the test (or what the test purported to measure) was in any way related to the test score. Few of these tests yielded anything other than a single test score, which was only thought to be related to one single dimension of personality. For these reasons, psychometric tests were considered to be narrow, restricted, fragmentary, and misleading.

The projective test was considered to be (especially by its developers) global and multidimensional, and could therefore yield a great deal of information about all aspects of the personality and their interactions. The major format of most projective tests hinges on a set of ambiguous stimuli which are presented to the examinee. Instead of a discrete verbal item, formless inkblots or hazy photographs are presented to the person and he is asked to free associate to the stimuli. There is no specific "right" or "wrong" answer, and all verbal responses are legitimate. It was felt that this freedom of response would allow a person to project his emotions, needs, drives, wishes, etc., onto the test stimulus to a much greater degree than when constrained to give a "yes" or "no" response to a psychometric test.

Another stated advantage of projective techniques was that fabrication was severely curtailed. The examinee could not figure out what was the "correct" response, as he could often do for psychometric test items. Psychometric test items were so transparent that an individual, if he chose to hide his psychopathology, could easily do so. Because of the opaqueness of projective tests, the examinee was bound to reveal himself since the stimuli provided no clues as to the implications of any answer. It was also thought that projective techniques tap "deeper" levels of the personality (i.e., the unconscious) while psychometric devices deal only with manifest or superficial behavior and attitudes. Another advantage to the projective device concerned the complexity of response. The response to projective tests must of necessity be a complex construction. The individual, in order to frame his response to the projective test stimuli, has to utilize a wide variety of resources, capacities, associations, etc., to construct the response. These complex responses allow the person doing the response interpretation to examine the underlying cognitive and emotional structure of the response in order to evaluate the interactive patterns of various aspects of the personality. It was correctly argued that this evaluative "richness" was lacking in psychometric quantitative test scores.

The major drawback to projective tests is an outcome of their virtues. Responses can be so complicated that their clear interpretation is difficult. In addition, since there are no clear inferential markers, interpretations tend to vary from examiner to examiner. Indeed, there is also a great deal of intra-examiner variability of interpretation. Without stable and valid interpretation points, the inferential process tends to be intuitive. The history of projective techniques is strewn with attempts to supply stable and valid interpretative markers (i.e., attempts to objectify the test results).

It is also probably true that projective tests yield data that reflect the deeper and more critically central aspects of personality. It is also true that the response to these tests is a complex interactive construction that reflects the functioning of the "whole" personality. However, these advantages have made interpretation more difficult and less trustworthy. The responses to projective tests are certainly more "relevant" than those of psychometric devices, but the price to be paid is diminished interpretative precision.

The Rorschach Inkblot Test

The Rorschach Inkblot is composed of ten ambiguous inkblots. The examinee is requested to peruse each inkblot and to describe what the blot represents or "what it might be." Any number of responses may be given to each blot. The responses are scored both in terms of formal (shape, form, movement, shading, etc.) and content criteria. The Rorschach was used extensively in the identification and diagnosis of alcoholism during the years from 1940 to 1960. Since that time its utilization by workers in the field of alcoholism diagnosis has diminished. Schafer (1948), influenced by psychoanalytic theory, linked orality to alcoholism and predicted that alcoholics could be diagnosed by their excessive use of food, eating, and mouth content responses on the Rorschach. Klopfer and Spiegelman (1956) argued for responses in which shading was ignored as the key for identifying alcoholics. A large number of empirical studies utilizing the Rorschach for alcoholism identification and diagnosis have been carried out (Bertrand and Masling, 1969; Billig and Sullivan, 1942, 1943; Buhler and Lefever, 1947; Button, 1956; Griffith and Dimmick, 1949; Halpern, 1946; Harris and Ives, 1947; Jastak, 1940; Karlan and Heller, 1946; Kelley and Barrera, 1941; Roe, 1946; Rosenwald, 1947; Schnadt, 1951; Seliger and Cranford, 1945; Sherehevski-Shere and Gottesfeld, 1953; Sherehevski-Shere and Lasser, 1952; Singer, 1950; and Weiss and Masling, 1970).

Klopfer and Kelley (1942) in their Rorschach manual raised doubts about the efficacy of the test for diagnosing alcoholism. On the basis of their clinical experience, they felt that "in general alcoholics show no typical Rorschach patterns" (p. 399). The empirical studies with the Rorschach have tended to support their contention. The results of the Rorschach literature pertaining to identification and diagnoses is extremely contradictory and equivocal. An examination of these studies reveals an excessive amount of variability of results. One example will suffice: Jastak (1940) reported that alcoholics give (on the average) about 14.2 responses to the Rorschach. Billig and Sullivan (1943), on the other hand, found that they give about 34 responses on the average. The same variability is found for all the other Rorschach formal and content categories. These wide discrepancies in results have led to a great deal of distrust of the Rorschach's capacity to identify and diagnose alcoholism. However, in defense of the Rorschach, it should be mentioned that many of the studies were poorly designed and executed. A fair number of the studies did not even use comparison control groups. When comparison controls were used they tended to differ from study to study. This has led various critics and reviewers to come to a negative conclusion about the efficiency of the Rorschach Test as a diagnostic procedure for alcoholism identification (Franks, 1970; Gibbon, 1953; Nathan and Harris, 1975; Syme, 1957; Sutherland, Schroeder, and Tordella, 1950; Tremper, 1972, Zucker and Van Horn, 1972).

However, the reader may be interested in the conclusions about the alcoholic personality drawn from the various studies that showed positive results. The reader is cautioned to remember that many of these characteristics have been resistant to validation. The alcoholism-specific characteristics derived from the Rorschach studies are: (1) Alcoholics are more psychopathic in nature than neurotics. (2) They show an incapacity to tolerate stress. (3) They lack the perseverance to overcome difficulties. (4) They are grandiose in their plans but do not have the patience or the concentration ability to reach their goals. (5) Alcoholics have a higher level of guilt and anxiety than does the psychopath but they show fewer of these feelings than do neurotics. (6) They are egocentric and lack emotional depth and warmth. (7) Alcoholics have poor or superficial interpersonal relationships. (8) They tend to be constricted, think in stereotypes and are pedantic. (9) Alcoholics use regression as their major defense mechanism.

Other Projective Tests

The Rorschach has led the list of projective test usage for diagnosing alcoholism. The next most utilized projective test is the Thematic Apperception Test (TAT). The TAT is composed of a series of twenty drawings on which figures appear either singularly or in groups. The figures themselves are not ambiguous, but the situations in which they appear or the relationships between figures is unclear. The examinee is asked to tell a story about the figures in each card. It is assumed that the themes produced arise out of the fantasy levels of the unconscious which are regulated by the person's unconscious needs, wishes, and drives. Thus TAT stories are purported to reveal unconscious content events.

Klebanoff (1947) analyzed the fantasy levels of 17 alcoholic patients and reported that they evinced a great deal of emotional tension concerning their drinking habits, and that frustrations led to passive withdrawal responses. Roe (1946), after comparing the TATs of alcoholics and nonalcoholics, reported that there were no basic differences in fantasy themes between the two groups. Singer (1950) also found no significant TAT differences between alcoholics and nonalcoholic patients. Knehr, Vickery, and Guy's (1953) results using the TAT were also essentially negative. However, Fisher and Fisher (1955) did conclude from their analysis of the TATs of alcoholics and hospital aide applicants that the former were less flexible and adaptable in the face of stress than the latter group. There have not been as many TAT studies as there have been Rorschach investigations, and it may be too early to draw any conclusions about the test's utility for diagnosing alcoholism, but the general indications are that the test show equivocal promise as an alcoholism-diagnostic assessment measure.

The Rosenzweig Picture-Frustration Test (P-F) consists of a set of cartoons depicting individuals in frustrating situations. The examinees are asked to indicate how they think the frustrated cartoon character will react to the frustration. The P-F was developed specifically to assess reactions to frustration, and since data from other tests have hinted that alcoholics have difficulty handling frustration, the results of this test should be very useful for validating this hypothesized characteristic of the alcoholic's personality. Unfortunately, the results of the few studies using the P-F test have been for the most part negative. Brown and Lacey (1954) gave the P-F to 36 alcoholics, 36 paranoid schizophrenics, and 36 normal individuals, and could report no useful differential response features. Murphy (1956) did find differences but they were of minimal utility.

The Bender-Gestalt test is basically not a projective personality test, but was designed to assess the psychomotor sequalae of brain damage. However, the test has been used as a projective test device, and various inferences about personality have been drawn from its data. The examinee is presented with a series of drawings ranging from initial simple ones to concluding complex designs. He is asked to copy them from models in front of him and/or from memory. Bender (1938) reported that alcoholics with severe encephalitis generally produce incomplete figures and perseveration of line strokes, and that patients suffering from chronic alcoholic hallucinatory states produce figures with hazy outlines. Curnutt (1953) claims to have found twenty differences between the Bender-Gestalt drawings of alcoholics and nonalcoholics. Farmer (1973) has also used the Bender-Gestalt test, but only to evaluate changes during periods of abstinence from alcohol. It should be pointed out that it is quite possible that the Bender-Gestalt test is picking up reflections of brain dysfunction that are consequences of alcoholism, and not the personality attributes of alcoholism itself. A critical test of the usefulness of the Bender-Gestalt for diagnosing alcoholism (and not the brain damage arising from the use of alcohol) would be a study where alcoholics without brain dysfunction were compared to nonalcoholic brain damaged individuals.

The last projective test to be mentioned here is the Word-Association Test. Schafer (1948) has suggested that the alcoholic will show conspicuous disturbances in reaction to words with oral connotations (breast, drink, suck, etc.) Disturbances would be in the nature of delayed reactions, affective outbursts, and false recall. No known research with the Word-Association Test has been conducted either to evaluate Schafer's contention or in any other alcoholism diagnosis context.

Psychometric Personality Tests

The earliest psychometric devices appeared in the late nineteenth century and were of the self-report type, i.e., a list of items purporting to reflect some area of psychological functioning to which an individual either assented to or denied as being true for him. The items generally dealt with the presence or absence of certain internal feelings about personal problems, symptoms, grievances, fears, etc. These tests were extremely crude and transparent, and could only yield a single score which would indicate only the sheer presence or absence of the purported measured variable. Greater variety was introduced by grouping the items into sets which seemed to be measuring the same variable. Such a multiscale test could yield several scores which were thought to be measuring several different variables. Regardless of the number of scales, scores for the most part still yielded crude dichotomous distinctions. It was the failings of these kinds of psychometric devices which led to the projective test movement.

The psychometric devices described above were also criticized by the behaviorists because they dealt with inner feelings rather than actual behavior. Their psychometric device items emphasized behavior (e.g., "I often wet my bed.") as opposed to feelings (e.g., "I feel lonely."). In addition, the behaviorists grouped sets of response patterns into what they called "traits." The various behavior patterns that individuals showed were categorized as "friendliness types of behavior," "confidence types of behavior," "perseverance types of behavior," etc. In time these behavior patterns came to be called "friendliness," "confidence," "perseverance," etc. (i.e., traits). The strength of any particular trait was dependent upon the frequency of agreeing to items about the behaviors that seemed to be related to these traits. The organizing of the trait behaviors was at first done on an inferential or suface validity basis, i.e., the item behaviors "seemed" to be measuring a particular trait. Later on factor analysis was used to determine the clustering of items. However, trait naming, which represents hypotheses about what is being measured, was in both instances done on the basis of surface validity.

One other approach to the utilization of psychometric devices needs to be mentioned here. The criterion-oriented test differs from trait tests in one important respect. These tests do not need to be validated because their validation is defined during their construction. Trait tests need the usual validation and reliability studies before they can be utilized with any degree of confidence. The criterion-oriented tests are valid by definition. These kinds of tests are of great interest to the reader since the Minnesota Multiphasic Personality Inventory, which is the most often used psychometric device for the diagnosis of alcoholism, is a criterion-oriented type.

The criterion-oriented test is developed by first locating and identifying a group that irrefutably evidences the behavior that is to be measured. If one wanted to develop a criterion-oriented test to measure schizophrenia, the test developers would first find a group of individuals that had been diagnosed as schizophrenic. It would be incumbent upon the constructors of the test to locate schizophrenics about which there was no question of the diagnosis. A set of items would be administered to the criterion group and their responses noted. A nonschizophrenic comparison group would also be subjected to the items. Those items which differentiate the schizophrenics from the nonschizophrenics would become the hallmarks of schizophrenia, i.e., the measurement scale.

After the test has been developed, and administered to a particular person, it is determined whether his responses are more similar to those of the schizophrenic criterion group or the nonschizophrenic comparison group. If it is found that he answers items in a manner similar to the criterion group schizophrenics, it is concluded that he is more like the schizophrenics than the nonschizophrenics. Thus if a person responds on a test of this sort in the same way as known alcoholics, it is concluded that he has a drinking problem. These kinds of tests have been found to be remarkable in their diagnostic power. They are rather rare because their construction is much more costly in terms of time, effort, and resources than trait tests. In addition, their validity is based upon the selection of truly adequate criterion populations which is a development strategy that is not often easily accomplished.

A criterion-oriented test such as the MMPI avoids the problem of "item transparency," since it is not necessary for items to deal directly with particular content areas. It is the pattern of responding that is crucial and not the response content. Thus, if alcoholics were found to almost universally enjoy reading detective stories, and all nonalcoholics were discovered to abhor such literature, the reader of such fiction could legitimately be considered as an alcoholic. It is difficult to arrive at the motivational basis of such a discriminating item. Only its empirical discriminatory power needs to be considered. The MMPI is essentially atheoretical and empirical.

MMPI Alcoholism Scales

A number of special MMPI scales to identify alcohol abuse have been developed. The most common method used in developing an MMPI alcoholism scale has been to compare the response frequencies (number of True answers and number of False answers) of an alcoholic group with those of a comparison group for each MMPI item. All MMPI items discriminating significantly between the two groups then become items of the new alcoholism scale.

Hampton (1953) developed an MMPI alcoholism scale by comparing the response frequencies of Alcoholics Anonymous members with those of university vocational guidance bureau clients matched on intelligence and age. Holmes (cf. Button, 1956) constructed an alcoholism scale by comparing the MMPI response frequencies of alcoholics committed to a state institution with those of the normative sample for the MMPI (Dahlstrom and Welsh, 1960). Similarly, Hoyt and Sedlacek's (1958) alcoholism scale was developed by comparing the MMPI responses of hospitalized alcoholics with the responses of the MMPI normative sample.

Although each of these three scales differentiated alcoholics from a normal comparison group, validity research has examined the possibility of using these three scales in psychiatric settings to identify patients who abuse alcohol. The results have been mixed. With the exception of one study done in an inpatient setting (Vega, 1971), the Hampton scale has been found not to identify alcoholism in psychiatric patients (MacAndrew and Geertsma, 1964; Rotman and Vestre, 1964; Uecker, Kish, and Ball, 1969). Rotman and Vestre (1964) found the Hoyt and Sedlacek scale to have some value in differentiating psychiatric hospital admissions with alcoholic problems from those admissions without alcoholic problems. However, three other studies (MacAndrew and Geertsma, 1964; Uecker, Kish, and Ball, 1969; Vega, 1971) have not found the Hoyt and Sedlacek scale to have validity with psychiatric patients. Although MacAndrew and Geertsma (1964) reported the Holmes scale to be unable to discriminate outpatient alcoholics from nonalcoholic psychiatric outpatients, other research has consistently shown this scale to differentiate inpatient alcoholics from nonalcoholic psychiatric inpatients (Apfeldorf and Hunley, 1975; Rich and Davis, 1969; Rotman and Vestre, 1964; Uecker, Kish, and Ball, 1969; Vega, 1971).

When MacAndrew and Geertsma (1964) found the Hampton scale, the Holmes scale, and the Hoyt and Sedlacek scale all unable to discriminate outpatient alcoholics from nonalcoholic psychiatric outpatients, they speculated that these three scales were measures of general maladjustment, not measures of alcoholism. This conclusion is not supported by the nonsignificant and negative correlations often found between the three scales (e.g., Rotman and Vestre, 1964). Furthermore, other research has shown the three scales to measure different aspects of personality (Korman, 1960; Rosenberg, 1972).

MacAndrew (1965) developed an alcoholism scale consisting of those MMPI items that differentiated between outpatient alcoholics and nonalcoholic psychiatric outpatients. After removing two MMPI items (215 and 460) which refer directly to alcohol use, the final scale consisted of 49 items. Using a cutting score of 24 to identify alcoholism, the MacAndrew scale correctly classified 81.5 percent of a cross-validation sample of outpatient alcoholics and nonalcoholic psychiatric outpatients. High scores on the MacAndrew scale have been found to come from uninhibited sociable people who appear to use repression and religion in controlling rebellious, delinquent impulses (Finney et al, 1971). Validation research has shown the MacAndrew scale to differentiate alcoholics and nonalcoholic patients in a variety of treatment settings (Apfeldorf and Hunley, 1975; DeGroot and Adamson, 1973; Kranitz, 1972; Rhodes, 1969; Rich and Davis, 1969; Vega, 1971; Whisler and Cantor, 1966; Williams, McCourt, and Schneider, 1971). Although Uecker (1970) discovered that more than half of the nonalcoholic psychiatric inpatients in his study were misdiagnosed as alcoholics by the MacAndrew scale, the percentage of correct classification found in all other available studies has varied between 60 percent and 80 percent. The cutting score of 24 suggested by MacAndrew (1965) certainly may need to be changed when the MacAndrew scale is used in a particular treatment setting.

Research (to be reviewed below) indicates that several distinct personality patterns are found among alcoholics and that there are no appreciable personality characteristics unique to alcoholics. In contrast, studies employing the MacAndrew scale provide evidence that alcoholics do have substantive personality characteristics different from those of other psychiatric patients and that alcoholism is not merely a symptom but a major disorder (Apfeldorf, 1974). An MMPI scale developed by Atsaides, Neuringer, and Davis (1975) seems to show promise of greater precision in discriminating alcoholics from psychiatric patients than the MacAndrew Alcoholism scale.

In summary, the MacAndrew alcoholism scale of the MMPI was developed in an outpatient treatment setting but has been shown to have value when used with various treatment populations. The usefulness of the Holmes alcoholism scale has been established only in inpatient treatment settings. Mental health professionals should be cautious in using the Holmes scale in other settings or in using either of the other two MMPI alcoholism scales.

Predicting Future Alcoholism and Response to Treatment

A series of three studies examined the MMPI scores of college freshman males who were later hospitalized as alcoholics at either a residential treatment center or a state hospital (Hoffmann, Loper, and Kammeier, 1974; Kammeier, Hoffmann, and Loper, 1973; Loper, Kammeier, and Hoffmann, 1973). The average time between college admission and time of hospitalization for alcoholism was 13 years. The college-entrance MMPI profiles from men later hospitalized for alcoholism were compared with MMPI profiles from a comparison group of male college classmates and with the MMPI profiles of the alcoholic men upon entering treatment. The prealcoholic men had significantly higher scores than the comparison group on MMPI scales F, 4 (Pd), and 9 (Ma). However, there was no significant difference between the two groups' mean scores on the Kleinmuntz MMPI College Maladjustment Scale and there were few signs of gross maladjustment in the MMPI profiles of the prealcoholic men. The MacAndrew alcoholism scale significantly differentiated both the prealcoholic group and the treatment group from the comparison group. With a cutting score of 26, the MacAndrew scale classified as alcoholics 72 percent of the prealcoholic sample, 28 percent of the comparison group, and 72 percent of the alcoholics at the time of treatment. Comparing the alcoholics at the time of college admission and at treatment, six of the thirteen Wiggins (1966) content scales were significantly different. At the time of treatment, the alcoholic men had increased scores on the Social Maladjustment, Depression, and Poor Morale scales. There were also changes indicating that the alcoholics had more interest in "feminine" pursuits (Feminine Interests scale), complained more about an unpleasant home life (Family Problems scale), and had less interest in religious activities (Religious Fundamentalism scale) than they did as college freshmen.

Moderate test-retest correlations demonstrated some stability of personality characteristics. Hoffmann, Loper, and Kammeier (1974) concluded that at the time of college admission there were already certain personality characteristics associated with the men who later developed alcoholism, and that between admission to college and the time of hospitalization for alcoholism, excessive drinking accompanied an increase in neurotic sysmptoms, depression, and environmental conflict.

Pretreatment to posttreatment changes in the personality test scores of alcoholics have been explored in a number of studies. Soskin (1970) examined changes in 16PF scores for two different inpatient treatment programs and found both programs produced significant changes in factors F, H, O, M, and Q_2, while Hoy (1969) reported that a decrease in tension (factor Q_4) was the only significant change in the 16PF scores resulting from inpatient treatment. MMPI studies have consistently shown treatment for alcoholism to produce a decrease in clinical scale scores (Ends and Page, 1959; Frankel and Murphy, 1974; Kraft and Wijesinghe, 1970; Kurland, Unger, and Shaffer, 1967; Rohan, 1969; Rohan, Tatro, and Rotman, 1969; Shaffer, et al., 1962; Sikes, Faibish, and Valles, 1965; Soskin, 1970; Wilkinson, et al., 1971). A significant decrease in MMPI scale 2(D) scores during treatment has been found in all studies, and when changes in Taylor Manifest Anxiety Scale scores have been reported they have always been significantly lower after treatment. Significant decreases in the scores of MMPI scales 1 (Hs) and 7 (Pt) during treatment are also nearly always found. MMPI research thus shows that treatment for alcoholism leads to less physical discomfort and fewer feelings of depression, anxiety, and guilt. The diversity of other changes in MMPI scores reported in the various studies may be related to differences in the type and length of treatment provided by various alcoholism treatment programs.

There are some indications that despite the significant changes in personality test scores produced by treatment for alcoholism, the personality test results obtained from alcoholics are relatively stable during treatment. The statistically significant pretreatment to posttreatment changes have often been of such small magnitude that they are clinically insignificant (e.g., Snibbe, 1970). Despite significant changes in scale scores, there is sometimes little or no change for central personality traits (Kraft and Wijesinghe, 1970) or for the overall personality test pattern (Hoffman, 1971; Rohan, Tatro, and Rotman, 1969).

Length of stay in treatment has been the most popular variable in studies using objective personality test data to predict the response of alcoholics to treatment. Most investigators who have studied the difference between alcoholics who leave treatment prematurely and alcoholics who remain in treatment have found either few differences in objective personality test scores or no differences at all (Fitzgerald, Pasewark, and Tanner, 1967; Gross and Nerviano, 1973; Hoy, 1969; Miller, Pokorny, and Hanson, 1968; Pryer and Distefano, 1970; Sinnett, 1961; Wilkinson, et al., 1971). Allen and Dootjes (1968) reported the number of visits by male alcoholics to an outpatient clinic to correlate significantly with only the Autonomy (−0.34) and Deference (0.46) scores from the Gough Adjective Check List. Similarly, Wilkinson, et al. (1971) found that of the 16 EPPS measures, only scores for Deference correlated significantly (0.17) with successful completion of an inpatient treatment program by male alcoholics. Mozdzierz, et al. (1973) compared the MMPI results of male alcoholics who completed a six-week inpatient program with those who left the treatment program against medical advice. Although there were no significant differences for the ten MMPI clinical scales, significant differences were found between the two groups for MMPI measures of denial (Dn scale), defensiveness (K scale), dependency (Dy scale), and admission of psychological symptoms (Ad scale). The direction of differences between the two groups indicated that alcoholics who left the treatment program against medical advice were more defensive about admitting interpersonal problems and denied dependency needs and conflicts. A discriminant function analysis showed the MMPI Dependency Scale by itself to be as effective as all four scales combined in discriminating AMA alcoholics from alcoholics who completed the treatment program. Thus, some research suggests that alcoholics who remain in treatment are more deferent and more open in admitting their dependency needs.

Only a handful of studies have attempted to use objective personality test scores to predict improvement during treatment or drinking behavior after treatment. Demographic variables were found more closely related than objective personality test data to ratings of improvement during treatment at one state hospital alcoholism treatment program (Hoffman and Jansen, 1973) and to adjustment ratings made at least 18 months after discharge from another state hospital treatment program (Trice, Roman and Belasco, 1969). The MMPI was reported by Muzekari (1965) to be unable to differentiate male alcoholics who had abstained from drinking alcohol for at least one year following treatment at an alcohol rehabilitation center from male alcoholics who had continued drinking after treatment. Sikes, Faibish, and Valles (1965) discovered that highly significant changes in MMPI scale scores occurred during an inpatient alcoholism program, but that there were no significant relationships between these changes and later drinking behavior. The only study to indicate that objective personality test data are capable of predicting the results of alcoholism treatment was that of Hedberg, et al. (1975). They investigated the use of the Mini-Mult form of the MMPI in predicting the success or failure of male alcoholics in a behavioral outpatient treatment program. The Mini-Mult was administered at the start of treatment and again after an average of 12 treatment sessions. Evaluation of each alcoholic's drinking behavior was made six months after the termination of treatment. A discriminant function analysis showed that using L scale scores obtained at the start of treatment and scale 6 (Pa) scores obtained during treatment, 73 percent of the failures and 71 percent of the successes could be correctly classified.

There is a clear need for more research looking for relationships between objective personality test scores and the outcome of treatment for alcoholism. It is important to learn whether or not personality test results obtained prior to treatment can predict the response of alcoholics to treatment. Given the diverse personality patterns found among alcoholics, two related questions are suggested for future research. First, are alcoholics of a certain personality type more likely to profit from alcoholism treatment programs than alcoholics with other personality patterns? Second, can an alcoholic's personality test scores be used to indicate which type of treatment will be of most benefit to him?

Characteristics of Alcoholics Identified by Objective Personality Tests

Research using objective personality tests with alcoholics has been dominated by the Minnesota Multiphasic Personality Inventory (MMPI). However, studies of alcoholism have also employed the Edwards Personal Preference Schedule (EPPS; Edwards, 1959), the Sixteen Personality Factor Questionnaire (16PF; Cattell, Ebner, and Tatsuoka, 1970), the Eysenck Personality Inventory (Eysenck and Eysenck, 1964) the Tennessee Self-Concept Scale (Fitts, 1965), the Personality Research Form (Jackson, 1967), and the Gough Adjective Check List (Gough & Heibrun, 1965).

Some studies have used objective personality test data to investigate a single characteristic in alcoholics. Tarter (1970) found inpatient alcoholics to have a significantly higher mean score on an MMPI acquiescence scale than either nonalcoholic male psychiatric patients or nonpsychiatric males. Scale 5 (Mf) of the MMPI was administered by Machover, et al. (1959) to male alcoholics who had stopped drinking and to male alcoholics who were still drinking. After comparing the scores of these two groups with male homosexuals and a group of nonpsychiatric males, they concluded that feminine interests were more marked in alcoholics who had stopped drinking than in alcoholics who had not stopped drinking. This suggested to the authors that alcoholism served as a defense against the threat of underlying homosexual trends.

There are numerous contradictions in studies using objective personality tests to identify the personality characteristics of alcoholics. There is contradictory evidence regarding whether alcoholics are dependent and whether they have a generally good or poor opinion of themselves. The MMPI Dependency (Dy) scale, the EPPS Dependency scale, and two other paper-and-pencil measures of dependency were used by Snibbe (1970) in a comparison of male outpatient alcoholics and a comparison group. Alcoholics were found to be significantly more dependent than average males. Likewise, the pattern of Personality Research Form scores collected by Hoffmann (1970) from male inpatient alcoholics revealed them to be more dependent than comparison group males. However, Goldstein, et al. (1968) examined a number of objective personality measures of dependency obtained from male inpatient alcoholics and found that the alcoholics were not particularly dependent when compared with average males. With regard to self-concept, some studies find that alcoholics see themselves as being inadequate and lacking personal worth (Connor, 1961; Gross and Alder, 1970; Vanderpool, 1969), while others present evidence that alcoholics are outgoing and self-confident (MacAndrew, 1967), or self-accepting (Reinehr, 1969).

Studies with the 16PF (Cattell, Ebner, and Tatsuoka, 1970; DePalma and Clayton, 1958; Fuller, 1966; Gross and Carpenter, 1971; Kirchner and Marzolf, 1974) have found male alcoholics to score higher than the general population on factors indicating less emotional stability (Factor C), more shyness (H), more apprehension (O), and more tension (Q_4). Results for the other 16 PF scales have not been in agreement in all studies. Gross and Carpenter (1971) found male alcoholics to be more outgoing (Factor A) than average males, while Kirchner and Marzolf (1974) found male alcoholics to be less outgoing. While two studies of second-order factors among the 16PF responses of alcoholics have presented different results (Kear-Colwell, 1972; Nerviano, 1974), both have found a large negative loading for Factor G (expediency versus conscientiousness) on the second-order anxiety factor. Nerviano (1974) has suggested on this basis that some behaviors exhibited by male alcoholics, such as self-indulgence and undependability, that are commonly assumed to indicate an asocial character disorder may actually be self-protective manuevers to cope with high anxiety.

Two comparisons of the MMPI data obtained from alcoholics and illicit drug users have demonstrated a marked similarity of group-average profiles for the two groups (Black and Heald, 1975; Hill, Haertzen, and Davis, 1962). Both studies reported some significant differences in the MMPI scale scores of alcoholics and those of illicit drug users, but the similarities in the composite MMPI profiles of the two groups far outweighed any differences. This result suggests that alcoholics and illicit drug users have essentialy similar personality patterns. However, the results of a study by Overall (1973) reported that if MMPI scales 4 (Pd) and 9 (Ma) are elevated relative to scales 3 (Hy) and 7 (Pt) then the MMPI profile suggests illicit drug abuse, but if scales 3 and 7 are elevated in addition to scales 4 and 9 then the profile suggests alcohol abuse.

The group average MMPI profile obtained in studies of alcoholics has most frequently had scales 2 (D) and 4 (Pd) as the two clinical scales with the highest scores (Curlee, 1970; Kammeier, Hoffmann and Loper, 1973; Overall, 1973; Paige, LaPointe, and Krueger, 1971; Rae and Forbes, 1966; Rohan, 1972; Soskin, 1970; Spiegel, Hadley, and Hadley, 1970). Although the 2–4 high point pair has often been found to be the dominant MMPI code type among alcoholics (e.g., Goss and Morosko, 1969), a variety of other high-point pairs have also been obtained from alcoholics (Kristianson, 1974; McLachlan, 1975; Paige and Zappella, 1969). Nearly all of the frequently occurring high-point pairs contain either scale 2 or scale 4 as one of the high points.

The group average MMPI profiles from different types of alcoholism treatment have been found to differ (English and Curtin, 1975; Pattison, Coe, and Doerr, 1973; Rosen, 1960; Zelen, et al., 1966). Of special interest is Rosen's (1960) discovery that the MMPI profiles of general psychiatric outpatients did not differ from the profiles of outpatient alcoholics, but that the group average MMPI profiles obtained from different alcoholism treatment populations did differ significantly.

Several studies have identified diverse profile types among the MMPI profiles of alcoholics. Neale (1963) discovered six distinct MMPI profile types of alcoholics. The MMPI profiles of state hospital alcoholics were sorted by Mogar, Wilson, and Helm (1970) into mutually exclusive and exhaustive types. Five profile types were found among female alcoholics and four profile types among male alcoholics. Only two of the male profile types were similar to any of the female profile types. Using a factor-analytic strategy, Skinner, Jackson, and Hoffmann (1974) found eight types of MMPI profiles among male inpatient alcoholics. These eight types were similar to MMPI profile types found elsewhere for alcoholics (Goldstein and Linden, 1969; Whitelock, Overall, and Patrick, 1971) and for general psychiatric patients (Gilberstadt and Duker, 1965; Marks and Seeman, 1963). For example, profile type 1 in the Skinner, Jackson, and Hoffman (1974) study was described as a pattern having elevations on scales 2 (D), 7 (Pt), and 4 (Pd). This profile type was quite similar to type 3 from Whitelock, Overall, and Patrick (1974), to type 2 from Goldstein and Linden (1969), and to the 2-7-4 profile type described both by Marks and Seeman (1963) and by Gilberstadt and Duker (1965).

Distinct and reliable profile types have also been found in a study using the 16PF profiles of alcoholics (Lawlis and Rubin, 1971). Two separate cluster analyses were performed with 16PF profiles obtained from state hospital alcoholics. In both analyses the same three types were found: a psychopathic pattern, an unsocialized aggressive pattern, and an inhibited, conflicted pattern. A third cluster analysis performed with the 16PF records of inpatient alcoholics at a vocational rehabilitation center also produced three types. Two were close approximations to the last two types in the other two analysis, and the other type was a schizoid pattern.

Because distinct MMPI profile types have been identified for alcoholics, studies employing only a group average MMPI profile may easily obscure important relationships. As an illustration of this, Whitelock, Overall, and Patrick (1974) would have found a 2-4 profile code type if they had obtained an average MMPI profile for their alcoholic population. Instead, they found four profile code types: one with an elevation for scale 2 (D), one with an elevation for scale 4 (Pd), and two with elevations on scales 2, 4, and 7 (Pt). The level of reported alcohol abuse among these four groups of alcoholics was significantly different. The group having prominent scale 4 (Pd) scores was low in reported level of alcohol use, and the predominant factors associated with the highest levels of alcohol abuse appeared to be subjective discomfort and depression. This suggested to Whitelock, Overall, and Patrick (1974) that there were two basic groups of alcoholics in their treatment population. One group of alcoholics would consist of psychopathic persons with poor impulse control whose moderate drinking led to antisocial behavior and hence brought them quickly to the attention of psychiatry. The other group of alcoholics would be characterized by neurotic depressive persons who abuse alcohol to a considerably greater extent without running into problems with society because of better impulse control and less underlying hostility.

It is now obvious that while there are some common patterns among the objective personality test data obtained from alcoholics, no one character type or personality pattern is shared by all alcoholics. The results of studies presented here support the view that alcoholism is a symptom associated with various problems in living. The personality dynamics associated with various alcoholic personality types suggest that such diverse people would benefit from different treatment programs designed for specific types of alcoholics rather than a general program for the treatment of all persons who abuse alcohol. There is a definite need to match the philosophy and treatment methods of treatment facilities with the specific needs of commonly occurring alcoholic personality types.

Studies using group average MMPI profiles have usually found highly similar profiles for male alcoholics and female alcoholics, with few significant differences (Curleee, 1970; Zelen et al., 1966) or significant differences of such small magnitude as to lack clinical significance (Jansen and Hoffmann, 1973). However, McLachlan (1975) examined the MMPI scale scores of male and female inpatient alcoholics and found several differences in the frequency of various high-point pairs. A greater proportion of female than male alcoholics had scale 4 (Pd) as one of the two most elevated scales, while more males than females had scale 5 (Mf) as one of the two most elevated scales. McLachlan's (1975) results and other evidence of different profile types for male and female alcoholics (Mogar, Wilson, and Helm, 1970) suggest that sex is an important factor producing differences in the objective personality test patterns of alcoholics.

Objective personality test scores also vary depending on the alcoholic's age and race. Significant differences in the test scores obtained from different age groups have been found for the MMPI (Hoffmann and Nelson, 1971; McGinnis and Ryan, 1965), the EPPS (Hoffmann and Nelson, 1971), the Eysenck Personality Inventory (Rosenberg, 1969), and the Personality Research Form (Hoffmann, 1970). There is a tendency for older alcoholics to have a greater need for order, to have less need for change and dominance, and to show fewer indications of impulsivity, anxiety, and feelings of inferiority. Two studies (Epstein, 1970; Hugo, 1970) have found significant differences in the MMPI scale scores of black and white alcoholics, although in both studies the group average profiles for the two races were quite similar.

Mental health professionals should also be aware of the possible effects of recent excessive drinking, or of withdrawal from alcohol, on psychological test results. Libb and Taulbee (1971) found psychotic-appearing MMPI profiles were frequently obtained from excessive drinkers who were newly admitted to a psychiatric hospital. A group of alcoholics and a schizophrenic comparison group were tested upon admission and then retested three weeks after admission. The decrease in the scores of MMPI scales indicating possible psychosis was found to be significantly greater for the alcoholics than for the schizophrenics.

Marital Interaction and Alcoholism

A number of studies have examined the wives of alcoholics or have focused on the marital relationships of male alcoholics. A central question in these studies has frequently been the degree and type of personality maladjustment in wives of alcoholics. Ballard (1959) examined the MMPI profiles from couples seen in marriage counseling. For approximately half of the couples marital conflict was accompanied by alcohol abuse by the husband but not by the wife. The other couples had marital conflict but no alcoholism. A comparison of the two groups of husbands revealed the alcoholic husbands to have significantly higher scores than nonalcoholic husbands for MMPI scales 1 (Hs), 3 (Hy), 4 (Pd), 7 (Pt), 8 (Sc), and 9 (Ma). Differences between the mean profiles for the two groups of wives were minimal, and there was no significant difference for any MMPI scale. Comparing the group average profiles of alcoholic husbands and wives, Ballard (1959) found both to have a high point for scale 4 and found alcoholic husbands scoring significantly higher than their wives on scale 9 while the wives of alcoholics had significantly higher Repression Scale (Welsh, 1956) scores than their husbands. The similarities and differences between MMPI profiles of alcoholic husbands and their wives provided an indication that the wives of alcoholics had repressed psychopathic tendencies which were vicariously expressed in their husbands' irresponsible and impulsive behavior.

Drewery and Rae (1969) studied the EPPS responses of male alcoholic inpatients and their wives, and compared them with EPPS results from nonpsychiatric couples. Each person in the study completed the EPPS from three different points of view: "myself as I am," "my spouse as I see him/her," and "myself as I think my spouse sees me." Overall the alcoholic couples were not markedly inferior to the nonalcoholic couples on measures of mutual understanding. However, there was a striking difference between the two groups of couples in the wives' descriptions of their husbands. The wives of nonalcoholic men described their husbands in a way that agreed well with the husbands' self-descriptions, while there was a marked disparity between the self-descriptions of alcoholic men and their wives' descriptions of them. This difference was partially explained by the presence in the nonalcoholic couples of a stereotype of masculinity (enduring, dominant, achieving, etc.) which they shared, and by the lack of this shared stereotype in the marriages of alcoholic husbands and their wives. The relationship between the alcoholic and his wife was characterized by sex-role confusion and by conflicting dependence-independence needs. Both partners in the alcoholic marriage described themselves as dependent and gave a description of their spouses in which a strong need for succorance coexisted with definite needs for autonomy and aggression. The evidence that wives of alcoholics were more accurate in their interpersonal perceptions than the wives of nonalcoholics, as well as other indications of the perceptiveness of wives of alcoholics, led Drewery and Rae (1969) to conclude that it was the alcoholic husband's own difficulties and incompatible needs, rather than any personality maladjustment in the wife, which led to troubles in their marriage.

Kogan and Jackson (1965) compared the wives of alcoholics who had achieved at least one year of sobriety with wives of active alcoholics and wives of nonalcoholic men. The two groups of wives of alcoholics did not differ significantly from each other as to the rate of personality disturbance on several MMPI indices which did differentiate between wives of active alcoholics and wives of nonalcoholic men. Wives of abstinent alcoholics were no more maladjusted than the wives of active alcoholics, and thus there was no support for a popular myth that wives of alcoholics have pathological personality needs such that their adjustment is jeopardized if their husbands stop drinking.

The MMPI profiles of wives of alcoholics have sometimes been found to be in the normal range (Corder, Hendricks, and Corder, 1964; Kogan, Fordyce, and Jackson, 1963; Paige, LaPointe, and Krueger, 1971). Other studies have reported several personality types among MMPI profiles obtained from wives of alcoholics (Kogan, Fordyce, and Jackson, 1963; Rae and Forbes, 1966). Two distinct MMPI profile types were found by Rae and Forbes (1966): one characterized by elevations of scales 4 (Pd), 3 (Hy) and 9 (Ma); the other with elevations on scales 2 (D), 7 (Pt), and 3 (Hy). The authors suggested that the first group of wives utilized alcoholic husbands as a defense against awareness of their own maladjustment and conflicts, but that the second group of wives were essentially normal personalities reacting to the stress of their husbands' alcohol abuse. Although there are some common patterns in alcoholic marriages, the evidence presently available suggests that women with different personality types and varying degrees of maladjustment are married to alcoholic men with diverse personality patterns.

THE PROBLEMS OF ALCOHOLISM
PSYCHOLOGICAL TEST RESEARCH

The research reviewed in the preceeding sections constitutes a mass of activity which has yielded bewildering results. There are some useful results among them, but they are far outweighted by the equivocal and contradictory findings of other studies. One would think that all that effort should have yielded more tangible and utilitarian outcomes.

Marconi (1967) found that scientists differed among themselves as to how to conceptualize and define alcoholism. Social and moral overtones were not absent from their attitudes and there was disagreement as to whether alcoholism was a symptom or a disease. One stumbling block to adequate diagnosis has only been partially overcome, i.e., there is less adherence to the view that alcoholism is a single "disorder." Marconi's findings about moral attitudes indicate that there may be other impediments to adequately identifying people with drinking problems, and therefore studying their particular psychological functioning and prescribing therapeutic strategies.

The diagnostician most certainly enters the evaluation arena with some concept of alcoholism. This definition determines how he approaches the identification problem, what data he seeks, and how he interprets them when he does discover them. The investigator who feels that alcoholism is related to a "deep" unconscious motivational system will also tend to irresistibly think about the presence of an "alcoholic personality" configuration. He will feel more comfortable using projective techniques (which to him assess the layers of personality wherein he thinks alcoholism dwells) than psychometric tests. He will also identify and interpret responses in terms of his definitional set. If alcoholism is thought to be a symptom, or related to "superficial" layers of the personality, or considered as only a behavioral habit, then the investigator is drawn towards the psychometric tests. His interpretation of results will also be determined by his ideas about the nature of alcoholism. The choice of psychological test research approach seems to be dictated by the researcher's conceptualization of what excessive drinking means to him. If one adds in the ingredient of moral approbation then the problems associated with adequate diagnosis of alcoholism become even more complex and confounded.

It may well be that the equivocalities found in alcoholism diagnosis research is an outcome of the investigators' own internal concept of alcoholism. This compounded with poor methodology and naive research designs had led to the difficulties that hinder successful identification, diagnosis, study, and prognosis of alcoholism. If the nature of alcoholism were somehow to suddenly be truly understood, then adequate diagnosis should be an easy task. It is interesting to note in relationship to the problems discussed above that whatever success has occurred in this field seems to be associated with empirical objective tests such as the MMPI, which are essentially atheoretical.

REFERENCES

Allen, L.R., and Dootjes, I. "Some Personality Considerations of an Alcoholic Population." *Perceptual and Motor Skills*, 27 (1968): 707–712.

Apfeldorf, M. "Contrasting Assumptions and Directions in MMPI Research on Alcoholism." *Quarterly Journal of Studies on Alcohol*, 35 (1974): 1375–1379.

Apfeldorf, M., and Hunley, P.J. "Application of MMPI Alcoholism Scales to Older Alcoholics and Problem Drinkers." *Journal of Studies on Alcohol*, 36 (1975): 645–653.

Atsaides, J.P.; Neuringer, C.; and Davis, K.L. "Development of an Institutionalized Chronic Alcoholism Scale." Unpublished manuscript, University of Kansas, 1975.

Ballard, R.G. "The Interrelatedness of Alcoholism and Marital Conflict: III. The Interaction Between Marital Conflict and Alcoholism as Seen through

MMPIs of Marriage Partners." Symposium, 1958, *American Journal of Orthopsychiatry*, 29 (1959): 528–545.

Bender, L. "A Visual Motor Gestalt Test and Its Clinical Use." *Research Monograph of the American Orthopsychiatric Association*, No. 3 (1938),

Bertrand, S., and Masling, J. "Oral Imagery and Alcoholism." *Journal of Abnormal Psychology*, 74 (1969): 50–127.

Billig, O. and Sullivan, D.J. "Personality Structure and the Prognosis of Alcoholic Addiction: A Rorschach Study." *Quarterly Journal of Studies on Alcohol*, 3 (1943): 554–573.

Black, F.W., and Heald, A. "MMPI Characteristics of Alcohol-/and Illicit Drug-Abusers Enrolled in a Rehabilitation Program." *Journal of Clinical Psychology*, 31 (1975): 572–575.

Brown, R., and Lacey, O.L. "The Diagnostic Value of the Rosenzweig Picture Frustration Test." *Journal of Clinical Psychology*, 10 (1954): 72–75.

Buhler, C., and Lefever, D.W. "A Rorschach Study on the Psychological Characteristics of Alcoholics." *Quarterly Journal of Studies on Alcohol*, 8 (1947): 197–260.

Button, A.D. "A Rorschach Study of 67 Alcoholics." *Quarterly Journal of Studies on Alcohol*, 17 (1956): 35–52.

Button, A.D. "A Study of Alcoholics with the Minnesota Multiphasic Personality Inventory." *Quarterly Journal of Studies on Alcohol*, 17 (1956): 263–281.

Cattell, R.B.; Ebner, H.W.; and Tatsuoka, M.M. *Handbook for the Sixteen Personality Factor Questionnaire (16PF)*. Champaign, Ill.: Institute for Personality and Ability Testing, 1970.

Connor, R.G. "The Self-Concept of Alcoholics." Ph.D. dissertation, University of Washington, 1961.

Corder, B.F.; Hendricks, A.; and Corder, R.F. "An MMPI Study of a Group of Wives of Alcoholics." *Quarterly Journal of Studies on Alcohol*, 25 (1964): 1–4.

Curlee, J.E. "A Comparison of Male and Female Patients at an Alcoholism Treatment Center." *Journal of Psychology*, 74 (1970): 239–247.

Curnutt, R. "The Use of the Bender-Gestalt with an Alcoholic and Non-Alcoholic Population." *Journal of Clinical Psychology*, 9 (1953): 287–290.

Dahlstrom, W.G., and Welsh, G.S. *An MMPI Handbook*. Minneapolis: University of Minnesota Press, 1960.

DeGroot, G.W., and Adamson, J.D. "Responses of Psychiatric Inpatients to the MacAndrew Alcoholism Scale." *Quarterly Journal of Studies on Alcohol*, 34 (1973): 1133–1139.

DePalma, N., and Clayton, H.D. "Scores of Alcoholics on the Sixteen Personality Factor Questionnaire." *Journal of Clinical Psychology*, 14 (1958): 390–392.

Drewery, J., and Rae, J.B. "A Group Comparison of Alcoholic and Non-Alcoholic Marriages Using the Interpersonal Perception Technique." *British Journal of Psychiatry*, 115 (1969): 287–300.

Edwards, A.L. *Edwards Personal Preference Schedule Manual*. New York: Psychological Corporation, 1959.

Ends, E.J., and Page, C.W. "Group Psychotherapy and Concomitant

Psychological Change." *Psychological Monographs*, 73, 10 (1959): 1–31.

English, G.E., and Curtin, M.E. "Personality Differences in Patients at Three Alcoholism Treatment Agencies." *Journal of Studies on Alcohol*, 36 (1975): 52–61.

Epstein, P.E. "Personality Characteristics of Skid Row Negro and White Chronic Alcoholics as Identified by the MMPI." Master's thesis, George Washington University, 1970.

Eysenck, H.J., and Eysenck, S.B.G. *Manual of the Eysenck Personality Inventory*. London: University of London Press, 1964.

Farmer, R.H. "Functional Changes During Early Weeks of Abstinence as Measured by the Bender-Gestalt." *Quarterly Journal of Studies on Alcohol*, 34 (1973): 786–796.

Finney, J.C.; Smith, D.F.; Skeeters, D.E.; and Auvenshine, C.D. "MMPI Alcoholism Scales; Factor Structure and Content Analysis." *Quarterly Journal of Studies on Alcohol*, 32 (1971): 1055–1060.

Fisher, S., and Fisher, R.L. "Application of Rigidity Principles to the Measurement of Personality Disturbances." *Journal of Personality*, 24 (1955): 86–93.

Fitts, W.H. *The Tennessee Department of Mental Health Self-Concept Scale*. Nashville: Tennessee Department of Mental Health, 1965.

Fitzgerald, B.J.; Pasewark, R.A.; and Tanner, C.E. "Use of the Edwards Personal Preference Schedule with Hospitalized Alcoholics." *Journal of Clinical Psychology*, 23 (1967): 194–195.

Frankel, A., and Murphy, J. "Physical Fitness and Personality in Alcoholism: Canonical Analysis of Measures Before and After Treatment." *Quarterly Journal of Studies on Alcohol*, 35 (1974): 1272–1278.

Franks, C.M. *Alcoholism*. In C.G. Costello (ed.), *Symptoms of Psychopathology*. New York: Wiley, 1970.

Fuller, G.B. *Research in Alcoholism with the 16PF Test*. (IPAT Information Bulletin No. 12.) Champaign, Ill.: Institute for Personality and Ability Testing, 1966.

Gibbon, R.J. *Chronic Alcoholism*. Toronto: Toronto University Press, 1953.

Gilberstadt, H., and Duker, J. *A Handbook for Clinical and Actuarial MMPI Interpretation*. Philadelphia: W.B. Saunders Co., 1965.

Goldstein, G.; Neuringer, C.; Reiff, C.; and Shelly, C.H. "Generalizability of Field Dependency in Alcoholics." *Journal of Consulting and Clinical Psychology*, 32 (1968): 560–564.

Goldstein, S.G., and Linden, J.D. "Multivariate Classification of Alcoholics by Means of the MMPI." *Journal of Abnormal Psychology*, 74 (1969): 661–669.

Goss, A., and Morosko, T.E. "Alcoholism and Clinical Symptoms." *Journal of Abnormal Psychology*, 74 (1969): 682–684.

Gough, H.G., and Heilbrun, A.B. *Manual for the Adjective Check List*. Palo Alto, Calif.: Consulting Psychologist Press, 1965.

Griffith, R.M., and Dimmick, G.B. "Differentiating Rorschach Responses of Alcoholics." *Quarterly Journal of Studies on Alcohol*, 10 (1949): 430–433.

Gross, W.F., and Alder, L.O. "Aspects of Alcoholics' Self-Concepts as Measured by the Tennessee Self-Concept Scale." *Psychological Reports*, 27 (1970): 431–434.

Gross, W.F., and Carpenter, L.L. "Alcoholic Personality: Reality or Fiction?" *Psychological Reports,* 28 (1971): 375–378.

Gross, W.F., and Nerviano, V.J. "The Prediction of Dropouts from an Inpatient Alcoholism Program by Objective Personality Inventories." *Quarterly Journal of Studies on Alcohol,* 34 (1973): 514–515.

Halpern, F. "Psychological Test Results." Part II of Studies of Compulsive Drinkers. *Quarterly Journal of Studies on Alcohol,* 6 (1946): 468–479.

Hampton, P.J. "The MMPI as a Psychometric Tool for Diagnosing Personality Disorders Among College Students." *Journal of Social Psychology,* 26 (1947): 99–108.

Hampton, P.J. "The Development of a Personality Questionnaire for Drinkers." *Genetic Psychology Monograph,* 48 (1953): 55–115.

Harris, R.E., and Ives, V.M. "A Study of the Personality of Alcoholics." *American Psychologist,* 2 (1947): 405.

Hedberg, A.G.; Campbell, L.M.; Weeks, S.R.; and Powell, J.A. "The Use of the MMPI (Mini-Mult) to Predict Alcoholics' Response to a Behavioral Treatment Program." *Journal of Clinical Psychology,* 31 (1975): 271–274.

Hewitt, C.C. "A Personality Study of Alcohol Addiction." *Quarterly Journal of Studies on Alcohol,* 4 (1943): 368–386.

Hill, H.E.; Haertzen, C.A.; and Davis, H. "An MMPI Factor Analytic Study of Alcoholics, Narcotic Addicts, and Criminals." *Quarterly Journal of Studies on Alcohol,* 23 (1962): 411–431.

Hoffmann, H. "Personality Characteristics of Alcoholics in Relation to Age." *Psychological Reports,* 27 (1970): 167–171.

Hoffmann, H. "Personality Changes of Hospitalized Alcoholics After Treatment." *Psychological Reports,* 29 (1971): 948–950.

Hoffmann, H., and Jansen, D.G. "Relationships Among Discharge Variables and MMPI Scale Scores of Hospitalized Alcoholics." *Journal of Clinical Psychology,* 29 (1973): 475–477.

Hoffmann, H.; Loper, R.G.; and Kammeier, M.L. "Identifying Future Alcoholics with MMPI Alcoholism Scales." *Quarterly Journal of Studies on Alcohol,* 35 (1974): 490–498.

Hoffmann, H., and Nelson, P.C. "Personality Characteristics of Alcoholics in Relation to Age and Intelligence." *Psychological Reports,* 29 (1971): 143–146.

Hoy, R.M. "The Personality of Inpatient Alcoholics in Relation to Group Psychotherapy as Measured by the 16PF." *Quarterly Journal of Studies on Alcohol,* 30 (1969): 401–407.

Hoyt, D.P., and Sedlacek, G.M. "Differentiating Alcoholics from Normals and Abnormals with the MMPI." *Journal of Clinical Psychology,* 14 (1958): 69–74.

Hugo, J.A., II. "A Comparison of Responses of Negro and White Outpatient Alcoholics on the Minnesota Multiphasic Personality Inventory." Master's thesis, Alabama University, 1970.

Jackson, D.N. *Personality Research Form Manual.* New York: Goshen, 1967.

Jansen, D.G., and Hoffmann, H. "Demographic and MMPI Characteristics of Male and Female State Hospital Alcoholic Patients." *Psychological Reports,* 33 (1973): 561–562.

Jastak, J. "Rorschach Performance of Alcoholic Inpatients." *Delaware State Medical Journal,* 12 (1940): 120–123.

Jones, H.E. "The California Adolescent Growth Study." *Journal of Educational Research,* 31 (1938): 561–567.

Kammeier, M.L.; Hoffmann, H.; and Loper, R.G. "Personality Characteristics of Alcoholics as College Freshmen and at Time of Treatment." *Quarterly Journal of Studies on Alcohol,* 34 (1973): 390–399.

Karlan, S.C., and Heller, E. "Chronic Alcoholism: Psychiatric and Rorschach Evaluation." *Journal of Clinical Psychopathology,* 8 (1946): 291–300.

Kear-Colwell, J.J. "Second Stratum Personality Factors Found in Psychiatric Patients' Responses to the 16PF." *Journal of Clinical Psychology* 28 (1972): 362–365.

Kelley, D.M., and Barrera, S.E. "Rorschach Studies in Acute Experimental Alcoholic Intoxication." *American Journal of Psychiatry,* 97 (1941): 1341–1364.

Kirchner, J.H., and Marzolf, S.S. "Personality of Alcoholics as Measured by Sixteen Personality Factor Questionnaire and House-Tree-Person Color-Choice Characteristics." *Psychological Reports,* 35 (1974): 627–642.

Klebanoff, S.G. "Personality Factors in Symptomatic Chronic Alcoholism as Indicated by the Thematic Apperception Test." *Journal of Consulting Psychology,* 11 (1947): 111–119.

Klopfer, B., and Kelley, D.M. *The Rorschach Technique.* Yonkers: World Press, 1942.

Klopfer, B., and Spiegelman, M. "Differential Diagnosis." In B. Klopfer (ed.), *Developments in the Rorschach Technique,* Vol. II. Yonkers: World, 1956.

Knehr, C.A.; Vickery, A.; and Guy, M. "Problem-Action Responses and Emotions in TAT Stories Recounted by Alcoholic Patients." *Journal of Psychology,* 61 (1953): 201–226.

Kogan, K.L.; Fordyce, W.E.; and Jackson, J.K. "Personality Disturbance in Wives of Alcoholics." *Quarterly Journal of Studies on Alcohol,* 24 (1963): 227–238.

Kogan, K.L., and Jackson, J.K. "Stress, Personality and Emotional Disturbance in Wives of Alcoholics." *Quarterly Journal of Studies on Alcohol,* 26 (1965): 486–495.

Korman, M. "Two MMPI Scales for Alcoholism: What Do They Measure?" *Journal of Clinical Psychology,* 16 (1960): 296–298.

Korman, M., and Stubblefield, R.L. "Definition of Alcoholism." *Journal of the American Medical Association,* 178 (1961): 1184–1186.

Kraft, T., and Wijesinghe, B. "Systematic Desensitization of Social Anxiety in the Treatment of Alcoholism: A Psychometric Evaluation of Change." *British Journal of Psychiatry,* 117 (1970): 443–444.

Kranitz, L. "Alcoholics, Heroin Addicts and Nonaddicts: Comparison on the MacAndrew Alcoholism Scale of the MMPI." *Quarterly Journal of Studies on Alcohol,* 33 (1972): 807–809.

Kristianson, P. "The Personality in Psychomotor Epilepsy Compared with the Explosive and Aggressive Personality." *British Journal of Psychiatry,* 125 (1974): 221–229.

Kurland, A.A.; Unger, S.; and Shaffer, J.W. "The Psychedelic Procedure in the Treatment of the Alcoholic Patient." In H.A. Abramson (ed.), *The Use of LSD in Psychotherapy and Alcoholism.* New York: Bobbs-Merrill, 1967.

Lanyon, R.I. *A Handbook of MMPI Group Profiles*. Minneapolis: University of Minnesota, 1968.

Lawlis, G.F., and Rubin, S.E. "16PF Study of Personality Patterns in Alcoholics." *Quarterly Journal of Studies on Alcohol*, 32 (1971): 318–327.

Libb, J.W., and Taulbee, E.S. "Psychotic-Appearing MMPI Profiles Among Alcoholics." *Journal of Clinical Psychology*, 27 (1971): 101–102.

Loper, R.G.; Kammeier, M.L.; and Hoffmann, H. "MMPI Characteristics of College Freshman Males Who Later Became Alcoholics." *Journal of Abnormal Psychology*, 82 (1973): 159–162.

MacAndrew, C. "The Differentiation of Male Alcoholic Outpatients from Nonalcoholic Psychiatric Outpatients by Means of the MMPI." *Quarterly Journal of Studies on Alcohol*, 26 (1965): 238–246.

MacAndrew, C. "Self-Reports of Male Alcoholics: A Dimensional Analysis of Certain Differences from Nonalcoholic Male Psychiatric Outpatients." *Quarterly Journal of Studies on Alcohol*, 28 (1967): 43–51.

MacAndrew, C., and Geertsma, R.H. "A Critique of Alcoholism Scales Derived from the MMPI." *Quarterly Journal of Studies on Alcohol*, 25 (1964): 68–76.

McCord, W., and McCord, J. *Origins of Alcoholism*. Stanford, California: Stanford University Press, 1960.

McCord, W., and McCord, J. "A Longitudinal Study of the Personality of Alcoholics." In D.P. Pitman and C.R. Snyder (eds.). *Society, Culture, and Drinking Patterns*. New York: Wiley, 1962.

McGinnis, C.A., and Ryan, C.W. "The Influence of Age on MMPI Scores of Chronic Alcoholics." *Journal of Clinical Psychology*, 21 (1965): 271–272.

McLachlan, J.F.C. "Classification of Alcoholics by an MMPI Actuarial System." *Journal of Clinical Psychology*, 31 (1975): 145–147.

Machover, S.; Puzzo, F.S.; Machover, K.; and Plumeau, F. "Clinical and Objective Studies of Personality Variables in Alcoholism: III, An Objective Study of Homosexuality in Alcoholism." *Quarterly Journal of Studies on Alcohol*, 20 (1959): 528–542.

Marconi, J. "Scientific Theory and Operational Definitions in Psychopathology with Special Reference to Alcoholism." *Quarterly Journal of Studies on Alcohol*, 28 (1967): 631–640.

Marks, P.A., and Seeman, W. *Actuarial Descriptions of Abnormal Personalities*. Baltimore: Williams & Wilkins, 1963.

Marshall, H. "A Study of Personality of Alcoholic Males." *American Psychologist*, 2 (1947): 289.

Miller, B.A.; Pokorny, A.D.; and Hanson, P.G. "A Study of Dropouts in an Inpatient Alcoholism Treatment Program." *Diseases of the Nervous System*, 29 (1968): 91–99.

Modlin, H.C. "A Study of the MMPI in Clinical Practice." In G.S. Welsh and W.G. Dahlstrom (eds.), *Basic Readings on the MMPI in Psychology and Medicine*. Minneapolis: University of Minnesota Press, 1956.

Mogar, R.E.; Wilson, W.M.; and Helm, S.T. "Personality Subtypes of Male and Female Alcoholic Patients." *International Journal of the Addictions*, 5 (1970): 99–113.

Moore, M. "Alcoholism: Some Contemporary Opinions." *American Journal of Psychiatry*, 97 (1941): 1455–1469.

Moore, R.A. "The Diagnosis of Alcoholism in a Psychiatric Hospital." *American Journal of Psychiatry*, 128 (1972): 1565–1569.

Morrow, M.A. "Alcoholic Profiles on the Minnesota Multiphasic." *Journal of Clinical Psychology*, 6 (1950): 266–269.

Mortimor, R.G.; Filkins, L.D.; Kerlan, M.W.; and Lower, J.S. "Psychometric Identification of Problem Drinkers." *Quarterly Journal of Studies on Alcohol*, 34 (1973): 1132–1335.

Mozdzierz, G.J.; Macchitelli, F.J.; Conway, J.A.; and Krauss, H.H. "Personality Characteristic Differences Between Alcoholics Who Leave Treatment Against Medical Advice and Those Who Don't." *Journal of Clinical Psychology*, 29 (1973): 78–82.

Murphy, M.M. "Social Class Difference in Frustration Patterns of Alcoholics." *Quarterly Journal of Studies on Alcohol*, 17 (1956): 255–262.

Muzekari, L.H. "The MMPI in Predicting Treatment Outcome in Alcoholism." *Journal of Consulting Psychology*, 29 (1965): 281.

Nathan, P.E., and Harris, S.L. *Psychopathology and Society*, New York: McGraw-Hill, 1975.

Neale, C.R., Jr. "An Investigation of Perception of Visual Space Among Alcoholics (Ph.D. dissertation, University of Utah, 1963). *Dissertation Abstracts*, 24 (1963): 1702.

Nerviano, V.J. "The Second Stratum Factor Structure of the 16PF for Alcoholic Males." *Journal of Clinical Psychology*, 30 (1974): 83–85.

Overall, J.E. "MMPI Personality Patterns of Alcoholics and Narcotics Addicts." *Quarterly Journal of Studies on Alcohol*, 34 (1973): 104–111.

Paige, P.E.; LaPointe, W.; and Krueger, A. "The Marital Dyad as a Diagnostic and Treatment Variable in Alcohol Addiction." *Psychology*, 8 (1971): 64–73.

Paige, P.E., and Zappella, D.G. "The Incidence of MMPI Code High Combinations and Extreme Scores of a Select Group of Male Alcoholic Patients." *Psychology*, 6 (1969): 13–21.

Pattison, E.M.; Coe, R.; and Doerr, H.C. "Population Variation Between Alcoholism Treatment Facilities." *International Journal of the Addictions*, 8 (1973): 199–229.

Pryer, M.W., and Distefano, M.K., Jr. "Further Evaluation of the EPPS with Hospitalized Alcoholics." *Journal of Clinical Psychology*, 26 (1970): 205.

Quaranta, J.V. "Alcoholism: A Study of Emotional Maturity and Homosexuality as Related Factors in Compulsive Drinking." *Quarterly Journal of Studies on Alcohol*, 10 (1949): 354.

Rae, J.B., and Forbes, A.R. "Clinical Psychometric Characteristics of the Wives of Alcoholics." *British Journal of Psychiatry*, 112 (1966): 197–200.

Reinehr, R.C. "Therapist and Patient Perceptions of Hospitalized Alcoholics." *Journal of Clinical Psychology*, 25 (1969): 443–445.

Rhodes, R.J. "The MacAndrew Alcoholism Scale: A Replication." *Journal of Clinical Psychology*, 25 (1969): 189–191.

Rich, C.C., and Davis, H.G. "Concurrent Validity of MMPI Alcoholism Scales." *Journal of Clinical Psychology*, 25 (1969): 425–426.

Robins, N.; Bates, W.M.; and O'Neal, P. "Adult Drinking Patterns of Former Problem Children." In D. Pittman and C.R. Snyder (eds.). *Society, Culture, and Drinking Patterns.* New York: Wiley, 1962.

Roe, A. "The Adult Adjustment of Children of Alcoholic Parents Raised in Foster Homes." *Quarterly Journal of Studies on Alcohol,* 5 (1944): 378–393.

Roe, A. "Alcohol and Creative Work; Part I: Painters." *Quarterly Journal of Studies on Alcohol,* 6 (1946): 415–467.

Rohan, W.P. "MMPI Changes in Hospitalized Alcoholics: A Second Study." *Quarterly Journal of Studies on Alcohol,* 33 (1972): 65–76.

Rohan, W.P.; Tatro, R.L.; and Rotman, S.R. "MMPI Changes in Alcoholics During Hospitalization." *Quarterly Journal of Studies on Alcohol,* 30 (1969): 389–400.

Rosen, A.C. "A Comparative Study of Alcoholic and Psychiatric Patients with the MMPI." *Quarterly Journal of Studies on Alcohol,* 21 (1960): 253–266.

Rosenberg, C.M. "Young Alcoholics." *British Journal of Psychiatry,* 115 (1969): 181–188.

Rosenberg, N. "MMPI Alcoholism Scales." *Journal of Clinical Psychology,* 28 (1972): 515–522.

Rosenwald, A.K. "A Comparison of Rorschach and Behn Rorschach Tests Based on a Study of Chronic Alcoholic Subjects." *American Psychologist,* 2 (1947): 270.

Rotman, S.R., and Vestre, N.D. "The Use of the MMPI in Identifying Problem Drinkers Among Psychiatric Hospital Admissions." *Journal of Clinical Psychology,* 20 (1964): 526–530.

Rubin, H. "The MMPI as a Diagnostic Aid in a Veterans Hospital." *Journal of Consulting Psychology,* 12 (1948): 251–254.

Sanford, N. "Personality and Patterns of Alcohol Consumption." *Journal of Consulting and Clinical Psychology,* 32 (1968): 13–17.

Schafer, R. *The Clinical Application of Psychological Tests.* New York: International Universities Press, 1948.

Schnadt, F.W. "A Study of Alcoholic Personality." *Quarterly Journal of Studies on Alcohol,* 12 (1951): 552–553.

Seliger, R.V., and Cranford, V. "The Rorschach Analyses in the Treatment of Alcoholism." *Medical Records of New York,* 158 (1945): 32–38.

Shaffer, J.W.; Hanlon, T.E., Wolf, S.; Foxwell, N.H.; and Kurland, A.A. "Nialamide in the Treatment of Alcoholism." *Journal of Nervous and Mental Disease,* 135 (1962): 222–232.

Sherehevski-Shere, E., and Gottesfeld, B. "An Evaluation of Anatomy Content and F+ Percentage in Rorschachs of Alcoholics, Schizophrenics and Normals." *Journal of Projective Techniques,* 17 (1953): 229–233.

Sherehevski-Shere, E., and Lasser, L.M. "An Evaluation of the Motor Responses in the Rorschachs of Alcoholics." *Journal of Projective Techniques,* 16 (1952): 489–495.

Sikes, M.P.; Faibish, G.; and Valles, J. "Evaluation of an Intensive Alcoholic Treatment Program." *Proceedings of the 73rd Annual Convention of the American Psychological Association,* 73 (1965): 275–275.

Singer, E. "Personality Structure of Chronic Alcoholism." *American Psychologist,* 5 (1950): 323.

Sinnett, E.R. "The Prediction of Irregular Discharge Among Alcoholic Patients." *Journals of Social Psychology,* 55 (1961): 231–235.

Skinner, H.A.; Jackson, D.N.; and Hoffmann, H. "Alcoholic Personality Types: Identification and Correlates." *Journal of Abnormal Psychology,* 83 (1974): 658–666.

Snibbe, J.R. "The Effects of Various Therapeutic Episodes on Dependency Feelings in Alcoholics as Measured by Four Tests," (Ph.D. dissertation, University of Utah, 1970). *Dissertation Abstracts International,* 31 (1970): 4345B.

Soskin, R.A. "Personality and Attitude Change After Two Alcoholism Treatment Programs: Comparative Contributions of Lysergide and Human Relations Training." *Quarterly Journal of Studies on Alcohol,* 31 (1970): 920–931.

Spiegel, D.; Hadley, P.A.; and Hadley, R.G. "Personality Test Patterns of Rehabilitation Center Alcoholics, Psychiatric Inpatients and Normals." *Journal of Clinical Psychology,* 26 (1970): 366–371.

Sutherland, E.H.; Schroeder, H.G.; and Tordella, C.L. "Personality Traits and the Alcoholic." *Quarterly Journal of Studies on Alcoholism,* 11 (1950): 547–561.

Syme, L. "Personality Characteristics and the Alcoholic." *Quarterly Journal of Studies on Alcohol,* 18 (1957): 288–302.

Tarter, R.E. "Acquiescence in Chronic Alcoholics." *Journal of Clinical Psychology,* 26 (1970): 301–302.

Tremper, M. "Dependency in Alcoholics.: A Sociological View." *Quarterly Journal of Studies on Alcohol,* 33 (1972): 186–190.

Trice, H.M.; Roman, P.M.; and Belasco, J.A. "Selection for Treatment: A Predictive Evaluation of an Alcoholism Treatment Regimen." *International Journal of the Addictions,* 4 (1969): 303–317.

Uecker, A.E. "Differentiating Male Alcoholics from Other Psychiatric Inpatients." *Quarterly Journal of Studies on Alcohol,* 31 (1970): 379–393.

Uecker, A.E.; Kish, G.B.; and Ball, M.E. "Differentiation of Alcoholism from General Psychopathology by Means of Two MMPI Scales." *Journal of Clinical Psychology,* 25 (1969): 287–289.

Vanderpool, J.A. "Alcoholism and the Self-Concept." *Quarterly Journal of Studies on Alcohol,* 30 (1969): 59–77.

Vega, A. "Cross-Validation of Four MMPI Scales for Alcoholism" *Quarterly Journal of Studies on Alcohol,* 32 (1971): 791–797.

Walton, H.J. "Personality as a Determinant of the Form of Alcoholism." *British Journal of Psychiatry,* 114 (1968): 761–766.

Weiss, L., and Masling, J. "Further Validation of a Rorschach Measure of Oral Imagery: A Study of Six Clinical Groups." *Journal of Abnormal Psychology,* 76 (1970): 83–87.

Welsh, G.S. "Factor Dimensions A and R." In G.S. Welsh and W.G. Dahlstrom (eds.), *Basic Readings on the MMPI in Psychology and Medicine.* Minneapolis: University of Minnesota Press, 1956.

Whisler, R.H., and Cantor, J.M. "The MacAndrew Alcoholism Scale: A Cross-Validation in a Domiciliary Setting." *Journal of Clinical Psychology,* 22 (1966): 311–312.

Whitelock, P.R.; Overall, J.E., and Patrick, J.H. "Personality Patterns and Alcohol Abuse in a State Hospital Population." *Journal of Abnormal Psychology,* 78 (1971): 9–16.

Wiggins, J.S. "Substantive Dimensions of Self-Report in the MMPI Item Pool." *Psychological Monographs,* 80, 22 (Whole No. 630), (1966).

Wilkinson, A.E.; Prado, W.M.; Williams, W.O.; and Schnadt, F.W. "Psychological Test Characteristics and Length of Stay in Alcoholism Treatment. *Quarterly Journal of Studies on Alcohol,* 32 (1971): 60–65.

Williams, A.F.; McCourt, W.F.; and Schneider, L. "Personality Self-Descriptions of Alcoholics and Heavy Drinkers." *Quarterly Journal of Studies on Alcohol,* 32 (1971): 310–317.

Wittman, M.P. "Developmental Characteristics and Personality of Chronic Alcoholics." *Journal of Abnormal and Social Psychology,* 34 (1939): 316–377.

Zelen, S.L.; Fox, J.; Gould, E.; and Olson, R.W. "Sex-Contingent Differences Between Male and Female Alcoholics." *Journal of Clinical Psychology,* 22 (1966): 160–165.

Zucker, R.A., and Van Horn, H. "Sibling Social Structure and Oral Behavior: Drinking and Smoking in Adolescence." *Quarterly Journal of Studies on Alcohol,* 33 (1972): 193–197.

Zwerling, I., and Rosenbaum, M. "Alcoholic Addiction and Personality (Non-Psychotic Conditions)." In S. Arieti (ed.), *American Handbook of Psychiatry,* Vol. I. New York: Basic Books, 1956.

※ Chapter Three

Experimental Investigations of Tension Reduction Models of Alcoholism

Raymond L. Higgins

The delineation of the forces underlying the etiology and maintenance of alcoholism is one of the most sought-after, yet elusive, goals in the mental health field. Although the public is regularly assailed through the mass media with the assertion that the nature of alcoholism is understood (as a disease) and that the effectiveness of its treatment is a matter of public record, these claims lack convincing empirical support. Because many hypotheses regarding the nature of problem drinking have proved unusually resistant to either proof or disproof, attempting to gain a comprehensive understanding of the problem of alcoholism is sometimes a bewildering undertaking. Fortunately, some hypotheses have proved to be more seminal than others. This chapter will be devoted to an in-depth examination of one of these—the tension-reduction hypothesis (TRH).

Historically, the idea that alcoholics drink in order to "escape reality" or to "forget their problems" has held wide popular sway. It remained only for Conger (1956) to systematically apply learning principles to this folk notion. Following an earlier observation by Masserman and Yum (1946) that the ingestion of alcohol enabled cats to resume a previously punished eating response, Conger (1951) demonstrated that alcohol allowed the resolution of a similar approach-avoidance conflict in rats. He was further able to demonstrate that the conflict resolution occurred primarily because the alcohol reduced the fear-motivated avoidance response. Based on this early work, Conger (1956) suggested that, over a course of repeated exposures to the effects of alcohol, an organism may come to learn that alcohol acts as a reinforcer. Accordingly, an

The preparation of this chapter was supported through funds from a Kansas University Bio-Medical Sciences Research Award.

organism might develop a pattern of increased alcohol consumption in response to heightened levels of tension or conflict.

Subsequent to Conger's work, a number of other learning theorists (e.g., Bandura, 1969; Coopersmith and Woodrow, 1967; Kepner, 1964; Kingham, 1958; Reinert, 1968; Ullman, 1952) have endorsed this "tension-reduction hypothesis" in one form or another. Although the various theories differ in specific details, the unifying notion is that alcohol consumption, through its ameliorative effects on unpleasant affective states, is reinforced and strengthened. The conceptual model most frequently advanced to account for this relationship is an escape-learning model with alcohol consumption allowing the organism to "escape" from unpleasant affective states. The theory predicts that, over time, with repeated exposures, this pattern of tension-induced drinking may gain sufficient "habit strength" or autonomy so that when the organism is faced with even minimal increases in tension a drinking sequence will ensue.

Clearly, the tenability of this theory depends directly upon the demonstration that alcohol does have tension-reducing effects. It is in a close examination of the evidence on this issue that the full complexity of the problems involved in validating this theoretical approach to alcoholism becomes clear. For that reason, this chapter will focus on what has been learned about the tension-reducing effects of alcohol, and under what conditions tension-reduction conceptions of problem drinking may be of assistance in understanding alcoholic behavior.

EXPERIMENTAL STUDIES OF THE TENSION-REDUCTION HYPOTHESIS

Although the present discussion will focus on studies using human subjects, the experimental work which provided the impetus for the development of drive-reduction theories of alcoholism was conducted with animals. In their comprehensive review of the animal literature relating to the TRH Cappell and Herman (1972) concluded that, with the exceptions of conflict resolution and the alleviation of experimentally-induced neuroses, the scientific support for the TRH is generally weak and contradictory. It seems fitting that this conclusion should serve as the jumping-off point for an examination of the research that has been conducted with humans.

The Effects of Alcohol on Anxiety

Throughout the last few decades there have been numerous attempts to identify and define an "alcoholic personality." These efforts have been singularly unsuccessful (e.g., Sutherland, Schroeder, and Tordella, 1950; Syme, 1957; Walton, 1968), and many investigators have concluded that such global personality types *do not* exist (e.g., Bandura, 1969). However, alcoholics have been found to score consistently higher on a variety of measures of "trait" anxiety than normals (e.g., Menaker, 1967; Okulitch and Marlatt, 1972; Parke and Walters, 1966; Walton, 1968; Williams, 1950; Williams, 1966). Although these higher levels of trait anxiety may be a consequence of a previously-existing alcohol problem, they do lend credence to the possibility that anxiety reduction plays a role in the development of pathological drinking. They do not, however, illuminate the effects of alcohol consumption on anxiety. Nor do they suggest a specific mechanism by which trait anxiety may be related to the development of problem drinking.

A study by Korman, Knopf, and Austin (1960) does suggest a means by which alcohol may serve the purposes of problem drinkers. They reasoned that, if alcohol does have anxiety-reducing effects, the ingestion of small amounts of alcohol should "facilitate psychological functions by permitting increased control over the disrupting effect of intruding emotional factors" (p. 219). They did demonstrate that, under stress in a serial-learning task, nonalcoholic subjects who were given small amounts of alcohol were able to perform more adequately than a control group. Goddard (1958) found that preflight administration of alcohol to men who were training to become glider pilots significantly reduced the postflight concentrations of noradrenaline in their urine. This was interpreted to mean that the alcohol had acted on the sympathetic adrenergic system in a stress-reducing fashion. Unfortunately, Goddard did not control for expectancy effects.

Studies using other physiological measures have also found evidence for the anxiety-mitigating effects of alcohol. Carpenter (1957) tested the hypothesis that the tension-reducing effects of alcohol would be reflected in measures of galvanic skin response and skin conductance. He compared the effects of three forms of alcohol (wine, whiskey, and an aqueous alcohol solution) and two alcohol doses (50 or 350 ml.) on male social drinkers. He found a significant inverse relationship between the dose of alcohol administered and the magnitude of GSR responses to a loud horn. Wine was slightly more effective than the alcohol solution in reducing the magnitude of the GSR response. Although the alcohol solution was more effective at lowering skin conductance levels than wine at the 50 ml. dose, this relationship was reversed at the 350 ml. dose level. This changing relationship was attributed to the varying absorption rates of the two dose forms and the poorer palatability of the alcohol solution. Greenberg and Carpenter (1957) found essentially the same relationship between the two dose forms. It should be pointed out, however, that neither of the above two studies controlled for expectancy effects. In a study which did use an appropriate placebo control group, Lienert and Traxel (1959) examined the effects of alcohol on GSR reactivity to 16 emotionally-laden sentences. Compared to the placebo group, the alcohol subjects showed significantly lowered GSR reactivity to the sentences.

While the studies reviewed above appear to confirm the anxiety-reducing potential of alcohol, a number of studies have reported that the effects of alcohol may be more complex. Coopersmith (1964) found that, while moderate doses of alcohol administered to social drinkers tended to increase overall GSR reactivity to affect-laden words, the mean recognition threshold differences for high- and low-affect words were smaller for alcohol than for nonalcohol subjects. They suggested that moderate doses of alcohol may have the combined effects of increasing responsivity to stimuli and decreasing subjective distress. In a study of social drinking in a fraternity party setting, Williams (1966) found that consumption of up to six ounces of whisky reduced anxiety as measured by an adjective check list. However, with consumption beyond six ounces, anxiety tended to regress towards the original levels. He also observed that alcohol tended to normalize people on measures of anxiety and depression, raising subjects who were low on those measures and lowering those who were high. This suggestion of a "normalizing" effect is supported by the findings from a study by Kissin and Hankoff (1959). Using a group of male alcoholics as subjects, Kissin and Hankoff studied the effects of alcohol on the Funkenstein Mecholyl response, assumed to be a measure of central sympathetic reactivity (CSR). They found that, rather than having any uniform stimulating or depressing effect on CSR, alcohol showed a significant tendency to reduce extremes of CSR to an intermediate degree of reactivity. Again, however, there was no control for expectancy effects.

In a study with somewhat parallel results Mayfield and Allen (1967) studied the effects of intravenously administered alcohol on affective states in three groups of subjects; alcoholics, clinically depressed psychiatric patients, and normal social drinkers. Using the Clyde Mood Scale, they found that, relative to normal controls and alcoholics, the depressed patients showed significantly greater improvement on measures of friendliness, energy levels, jitteriness, and depression. They concluded that alcohol tends to have a more profound effect on populations with disordered affects than on normals or alcoholics. However, their failure to statistically control for the initial group differences in scores on the above measures, as well as their failure to control for expectancy or for the possibility of increased tolerance on the part of the alcoholics makes these results difficult to interpret. In a follow-up article, Mayfield (1968) reports two experiments designed to further examine several questions raised by the 1967 study. In the first experiment, the effects of alcohol on two groups of clinically depressed patients (normal drinkers vs. excessive drinkers) were examined in essentially the same experimental procedure described above. The results demonstrated greater affective improvement following intoxication in the "nondrinker" group than in the excessive drinking group. The second experiment contrasted the effects of alcohol on a group of 12 clinically depressed subjects during the acute phase of their depression and following "remission" of the depression. The results indicated that the affective improvements associated with alcohol intoxication were more pronounced in the acute phase than following remission. As in the 1967 article, however, Mayfield failed to control for the possibility of increased behavioral tolerance to alcohol in the abusive drinking group (expt. I), and also to control statistically for the effects of different preintoxication scores in the second experiment (i.e., the preintoxication scores for "depression" and "jittery" were higher in the acute stage than in the remission stage, and the scores for "friendly," "energetic," "clear-thinking," and "aggressive" were lower). The interpretation of these results is, therefore, problematic.

Aside from the interpretational problems mentioned, these studies have produced results generally in accord with the tension-reduction hypothesis (i.e., alcohol intoxication tends to be accompanied by improvements in affective states). A number of studies, in contrast, have failed to find any relationship between unpleasant affect and alcohol intoxication. Smith, Parker, and Noble (1975) studied the affective consequences of alcohol consumptions in nonalcoholic subjects who were involved in dyadic social interactions. Subjects were 18 male-female couples. The members of each couple had been acquainted for a period of at least several months prior to the study. Each couple participated in both a low-dose experimental session and a control (placebo) session. Alcohol was presented in the form of 80-proof vodka in a peppermint-flavored cocktail. In the placebo condition, subjects received only the flavored cocktail. On the basis of self-report and observer ratings of the taped interactions, it was found that the alcohol produced significant increases in elation and emotional expression. However, the alcohol had no significant effect on an overall measure of total anxiety (the Gottschalk-Glesser Scale), on ratings of anxiety from the taped interactions, or on subjective responses about anxiety. In reference to the previously reviewed studies by Mayfield (1968) and Mayfield and Allen (1967), it is interesting to note that Smith, Parker, and Noble (1975) did find a significant effect for drinking history on emotional responsiveness to alcohol (i.e., tolerance effects).

In another study which failed to find any relationship between alcohol consumption and anxiety levels in subjects, McDonnell and Carpenter (1959) observed the effects of alcohol on the skin conductance of normal subjects interacting in groups. Subjects served as their own controls in a counterbalanced design and were seen for a total of two sessions. They were randomly divided into groups of four for the purpose of engaging in a card game. During the card game subjects were required to drink what appeared to be two ordinary bottles of beer. In fact, they drank either a commercially available "near" beer (not more than 0.05 percent alcohol by volume) or a fortified version of the same beverage (4.8 percent alcohol by volume). Continuous measures of skin conductance were taken. There was no significant relationship between alcohol consumption and the measure of skin conductance. The authors suggest that this may have been due to the relatively small amount of alcohol consumed.

To this point, the reviewed studies have been of the effects of relatively acute administrations of alcohol. Perhaps the most intriguing findings regarding the relationship of alcohol consumption to anxiety levels are found in studies of the effects of long-term intoxication. Contrary to predictions derived from the tension-reduction hypothesis these studies tend to show that alcohol consumption may actually result in *increased* levels of anxiety and dysphoria in human subjects. This unexpected finding was first reported by Mendelson and his colleagues (i.e., Mendelson, 1964), and grew out of a research strategy which involved studying the drinking patterns of alcoholics over periods of several days or weeks in a research ward setting. In this original study, ten alcoholics were observed while undergoing a 24-day period of continuous intoxication. Mendelson reported that, "The outstanding psychiatric finding was an increase rather than a decrease in feelings of anxiety among the men as drinking progressed" (p. 119).

In a later study, McNamee, Mello, and Mendelson (1968) studied a group of 12 male alcoholics who were given access to alcohol over a 7-day period. On the basis of psychiatric interviews and behavioral observations, the authors report that feelings of anxiety and depression showed marked *increases* as the length of intoxication and the amounts of alcohol consumed increased, beginning with the second or third day of drinking. They also noted that as drinking progressed, there seemed to be a greater expression of previously absent emotions—primarily hostility, guilt, and resentment. This particular pattern of findings (i.e., increasing dysphoria as intoxication progresses) has been reported in a number of studies. In a study of ten alcoholic subjects undergoing a 14-day experimental intoxication, Mendelson, La Dou, and Solomon (1964) observed that, as intoxication progressed, so did feelings of anxiety and depression. They also observed a general deterioration of behavioral controls along with the emergence of "psychopathic" behavior patterns in the specific areas of aggression and sexuality. Similarly, Tamerin and Mendelson (1969) studied the reactions of four alcoholics during a 21-day period of free-access drinking. They observed a pattern of increasing depression, guilt, and psychic pain as drinking progressed. This occurred despite an initial period of "elation" at the beginning of the study.

In contrast to the findings reported above, a study by McGuire, Stein, and Mendelson (1966) found little evidence of anxiety among four alcoholics undergoing a 4-day experimental intoxication. Of four alcoholics studied, three predicted that the alcohol would have little effect on them. In fact, those three subjects showed no clear anxiety response to the alcohol—neither decreasing nor increasing in anxiety during the study. The fourth subject did appear to experience heightened anxiety as the drinking phase of the study progressed. The authors noted that *all* of the four nonalcoholic subjects studied reported heightened levels of anxiety as the drinking progressed. This latter finding is interesting in light of an investigation reported by Nathan and O'Brien (1971). Nathan and O'Brien studied the reactions of four skid row alcoholics and four matched nonalcoholics undergoing an 18-day period of programmed drinking. Their results indicated that, rather than reducing levels of anxiety or depression, "most alcoholic subjects showed heightened depression, anxiety, and hostility and more symptoms of psychopathology during drinking. Nonalcoholics, by comparison, demonstrated essentially no change in affect with alcohol and only a mild increase in psychopathology" (pp. 472–473).

The findings of these long-term intoxication studies have been summed up by Mello (1972) in an extensive review: "Alcoholics most frequently show an increase in anxiety and depression and further impairment of an already fragile self-esteem during the course of a drinking episode" (p. 282). It appears, then, that while there is no firm consensus regarding the affective consequences of acute administrations of alcohol in either alcoholic or nonalcoholic populations, findings from studies of long-term intoxication appear to be both fairly consistent and contrary to the TRH. It should be noted, however, that the studies of long-term intoxication have generally failed to contrast the later stages of intoxication with the initial stages. Tamerin and Mendelson (1969) did note that subjects evidenced an initial period of "elation" shortly following the beginning of the intoxication phase of their study. There may be important differences in the affective consequences of short-term and long-term intoxication.

THE EFFECTS OF ALCOHOL ON MOOD, SELF-CONCEPT, AND SOCIAL INTERACTION

Clearly, the negative reinforcing effects of alcohol on anxiety and its correlates are directly relevant to the tension-reduction hypothesis. The effects of alcohol on other areas of personal functioning may also relate to the TRH. For this reason, this section will briefly review findings of the effects of alcohol on mood, self-concept, and social interaction. Although many of the findings reported in this section might easily have been reported in the previous section, they are generally somewhat broader in focus and are, therefore, presented here separately.

As was the case with the previously reviewed studies, the literature on the effects of alcohol on mood and self-concept presents an intriguing array of findings. It is possible to amass evidence that alcohol has either negative, positive, or variable effects. In a study using nonalcoholic subjects, Kastl (1969) assessed the effects of a range of alcohol dosages on a variety of dependent measures. His results indicated a significant linear increase of reported happiness by his subjects with higher doses. Berg (1971, study 3) also investigated the effects of alcohol on the self-concepts of nonalcoholic subjects. At a mean blood-alcohol level of 0.08 percent, Berg's subjects showed significant shifts in self-concept in a *negative* direction on the basis of Q-sort and adjective checklist measures.

Findings from studies using alcoholic subjects are no less enigmatic. Berg (1971, study 2) examined the effects of alcohol on the self-concepts of twenty alcoholics. Subjects were administered alcohol to a mean blood-alcohol level of 0.132 percent and were then administered Q-sort and adjective checklist measures. Compared to preintoxication levels, the alcoholics' ratings showed significant *increases* in positive self-esteem. In another study, Vanderpool (1969) examined the self-ratings of intoxicated alcoholics (blood-alcohol levels ranged from 0.097 percent to 0.133 percent) on the Adjective Check List and the Tennessee Self-Concept Scale. The results indicated that alcoholics reported a more *negative* self-concept compared to their predrinking levels. Finally, Gottheil et al. (1972) examined the reactions of alcoholics to alcohol in a fixed-interval drinking decisions program. The subjects were afforded access to alcohol at fixed intervals during a 20-day program, but were allowed the choice of whether or not to drink. According to the individual drinking patterns which emerged, subjects were classified as either nondrinkers, moderate drinkers, or heavy drinkers. Based on subjects's self-ratings, "The non-, moderate and heavy drinkers did not differ significantly in the predrinking week. The mean self-esteem scores of the nondrinkers and moderate drinkers increased significantly from the first to the last week, while those of the heavy drinkers did not change" (p. 333).

Another potential source of information regarding the validity of the TRH is the effect of alcohol on social interaction. Alcoholics have frequently been described as social isolates having little ability to sustain meaningful interpersonal relationships (e.g., Mowrer and Mowrer, 1965; Zwerling and Rosenbaum, 1959). In fact, many alcoholics report using alcohol in order to feel more comfortable in social interactions. McGuire, Stein, and Mendelson (1966) found that alcoholic subjects predicted becoming intoxicated would help them to achieve pleasurable social relationships with others—presumably because of the anxiety-reducing effects of the alcohol. The studies reviewed below investigated the effects of alcohol intoxication on social interaction.

In the McGuire, Stein, and Mendelson (1966) study, four alcoholic and four nonalcoholic subjects were observed before, during and following a four-day experimental intoxication period. As noted above, the alcoholic subjects predicted that intoxication would facilitate their social relationships. The nonalcoholic subjects reported no such expectations. The authors report that during the first three days of drinking the amount and variety of social interaction evidenced by the alcoholics increased. However, it was not judged to be serious interaction. Instead, the authors report it was characterized by a quality of "acting." During the fourth (last) day of drinking the alcoholics became more socially withdrawn. By comparison, the nonalcoholic subjects tended to increase the intimacy and quality of their social interactions as the drinking progressed. McNamee, Mello, and Mendelson (1968) studied the reactions of 12 alcoholic subjects undergoing a 7-day free-access drinking period and reported that the subjects generally maintained good levels of interaction throughout the drinking period. The only times at which they noted a tendency for their subjects to withdraw socially were during periods of maximum alcohol consumption. Similarly, Doctor and Bernal (1964) did a physiological study of two male alcoholics undergoing a 14-day drinking period. They report that, whereas both subjects were quiet and withdrawn while sober, they became much more talkative, assertive, and demanding when intoxicated. On the basis of the information presented, it is not possible to evaluate the quality of the heightened social interactions.

Judging from the results of these three studies, it would appear that there may be some justification in assuming that alcoholics drink in order to facilitate social interaction. However, findings from a previously cited study (i.e., Nathan and O'Brien, 1971) are much less optimistic—at least with reference to skid row alcoholics. In their 18-day study of programmed intoxication by four skid row alcoholics and four skid row nonalcoholics, Nathan and O'Brien observed that the most striking and consistent difference between their two groups was in the area of social interaction. The alcoholic group was not only characterized by social isolation before the onset of drinking, they became even more socially withdrawn during drinking. The nonalcoholic group, on the other hand, showed high rates of social interaction both while sober and intoxicated. Nathan and O'Brien comment that, "If one concludes from these data that the skid-row alcoholic is a social isolate, drunk or sober, and that his isolation serves the purpose of helping him drink longer and harder, one must also recognize that this conclusion obviates the common view of alcoholic drinking behavior as a social facilitator—a view shared by many alcoholics themselves" (p. 472).

If the various indices of arousal considered thus far are taken as legitimate measures of the tension-reducing effects of alcohol, we are left with a complex problem indeed. On the basis of the evidence considered it is difficult to evaluate the relevance of the TRH to the etiology and/or maintenance of problem drinking. Of course, it is the case that there are many factors which make it difficult to truly evaluate the experimental evidence. It is to a consideration of some of these factors that we will now turn our attention.

Problems and Issues in Evaluating the Evidence on the TRH

Perhaps one of the major problems contributing to the confused pattern of findings in the tension-reduction literature is the inconsistency with which the concept of "tension" has been operationalized. As we have seen, studies of the TRH have variously defined tension in terms of conflict reduction (Conger, 1956), biochemical indicators of stress (Goddard, 1958), psychophysiological indicators of arousal (Carpenter, 1957), behavioral performance under pressure (Korman, Knopf, and Austin, 1960), self-report on adjective checklists (Williams, 1966), indirect measures of central sympathetic reactivity (Kissin and Hankoff, 1959), findings from psychiatric interviews (McNamee, Mello, and Mendelson, 1968), observed behaviors (Nathan and O'Brien, 1971), Q-sorts

(Berg, 1971), etc. Given this array of operational definitions, it is little wonder that any attempt to synthesize the resulting findings becomes a considerable undertaking.

The process of discerning consistency in the data would be simplified if more were known about the interrelationships among the various measures of tension. Unfortunately, studies which report more than one type of measure are exceptional. When direct comparisons between different types of measures within a single study are possible, the results are often disarming. For example, Steffen, Nathan, and Taylor (1974) studied the responses of four chronic alcoholics undergoing a 12-day period of self-programmed intoxication. Throughout the drinking period, the interrelationships of measures of muscular tension (physiological recordings of tension in the frontalis muscle), blood-alcohol levels, and subjective distress were examined. The results indicated that there was a significant inverse correlation between blood-alcohol levels and muscular tension—a finding consistent with the TRH. However, there was a significant *positive* relationship between blood-alcohol levels and subjective distress—a finding inconsistent with the TRH. In addition, there was no significant relationship between the measures of muscle tension and subjective reports of distress. The authors speculate that, while the results generally support the tension-reducing effects of alcohol, there is probably no simple relationship between the various measures of tension.

A methodological problem which may contribute substantially to the confusion in the reviewed studies is their nearly uniform failure to include appropriate placebo groups. In view of the mounting evidence that expectancy can substantially influence drug effects (e.g., Ray, 1972), this must be considered a serious flaw. A recent study of the effects of alcohol consumption on aggression (Lang et al., 1975) is instructive in this regard. In a study which fully controlled for the effects of expectancy, Lang et al. instructed alternate halves of their subjects that they would be consuming either an alcoholic (vodka and tonic) or a nonalcoholic beverage. Following the beverage administration, half of the subjects were provoked to anger by an experimental confederate while the other half experienced a neutral interaction. On the basis of measures of the intensity and duration of shocks supposedly administered by the subjects to the experimental confederate following the above manipulations, the authors report that the only independent variables which were significantly related to increased aggression were the anger provocation manipulation and the *expectancy* of having consumed alcohol. Subjects who believed they had consumed alcohol were more aggressive than subjects who believed they had consumed a nonalcoholic beverage. This effect occurred regardless of the alcoholic content of the drink actually received.

In another instructive study, Marlatt, Demming, and Reid (1973) investigated the concept of loss-of-control drinking in alcoholics. Equal numbers of alcoholics and nonalcoholics were engaged in a taste-rating task in which they were led to believe they were either rating alcoholic (tonic and vodka) or nonalcoholic beverages (tonic). As in the study by Lang et al., the beverage subjects actually consumed was varied independently of their expectation. The results dramatically indicated that the only factors significantly related to consumption rates in the taste-rating task were the subject population (alcoholics drank more than nonalcoholics) and the expectancy condition (both alcoholic and nonalcoholic subjects who believed they were drinking alcohol drank more than subjects who believed they were drinking tonic). The actual beverage consumed bore no apparent relationship to the consumption rates. The authors also found that some of the alcoholics in the "expected alcohol-received tonic" condition reported feeling some of the initial signs of intoxication (i.e., getting a "buzz" etc.). Obviously there is considerable reason to suspect that at least some of the puzzling findings from the previously reviewed studies may have resulted from their failure to control for the expectancy effects associated with the belief of having consumed alcohol.

Expectational sets associated with the specific experimental settings and procedures used to investigate the effects of alcohol may also influence affective reactions to the drug. The conclusion that the experienced effects of a drug are inextricably bound up in the conditions surrounding its use now seems inescapable (cf. Schachter, 1964). A recent study by Pliner and Cappell (1974) focused on the importance of the experimental setting in determining affective reactions to alcohol.

Pliner and Cappell compared the effects of alcohol on mood in subjects who experienced the effects of alcohol or a placebo under either solitary or social conditions. The subjects were sixty male and sixty female social drinkers. After completing the Clyde Mood Scale, alcohol subjects consumed a peppermint-flavored cocktail containing 80-proof ethanol. Placebo subjects consumed only the peppermint cocktail. Subjects were asked to rate their level of intoxication and then listened to a humorous recording either alone or in groups of three. Following the recording, solitary subjects were asked to compose captions for 22 different cartoons. Subjects in the group condition devised captions for the same cartoons, but did so as a group. After twenty minutes of devising captions, subjects were again asked to rate their intoxication levels and to complete the Clyde Mood Scale. When compared to their placebo controls, alcohol subjects in the group condition reported feeling significantly more friendly, less unhappy, less bored, and more euphoric. There were no differences between the solitary-alcohol and solitary-placebo subjects on these same measures. On the other hand, when compared to their placebo controls, solitary drinkers reported feeling significantly less clear thinking, and dizzier. There were no significant differences between the group drinkers and their placebo controls on these measures. There were no significant differences between the group and solitary drinkers on their estimates of intoxication levels. The authors appropriately conclude that ". . . the cognitive context represented by the social manipulation had clear consequences for the intoxicated experience" (p.423).

It is unclear how this line of research should specifically affect our assessment of the tension-reduction literature. It does appear highly probable, however, that the importance of situational and expectational factors may be considerable. How are we to determine the relevance of the numerous studies which have taken great pains to eliminate the effects of "extraneous" variables from their findings at the price of studying the effects of alcohol in highly artificial and sterile conditions? When faced with the current diversity of findings regarding the TRH and with the diversity of settings in which these findings have been generated—from the pleasant party settings devised by Williams (1966), to the very different setting provided by the psychophysiological laboratory (e.g., Greenberg and Carpenter, 1957), to the hospital setting of the long-term intoxication studies (e.g., Mendelson, 1964)—one can only conclude that we need to know more than is now available to us.

Another potentially important aspect of the experimental setting which may significantly influence expectation has received very little attention to date. Simply stated, it is the manner and form in which alcohol is administered. Greenberg and Carpenter (1957) have observed different responses to equivalent doses of alcohol administered in different forms—that is wine vs. whisky vs. an alcohol solution. Even when the form of the alcohol is held constant, the manner in which it is administered may have important consequences. Mello and Mendelson (1970) observed that, when compared to subjects who are involved in programmed drinking, subjects who are allowed to drink spontaneously are able to drink more alcohol with fewer adverse reactions. In a study reported by Davis (1971), it was found that greater mood changes occurred with free-choice drinking than with programmed drinking, even though blood-alcohol levels were comparable. One can only begin to speculate about the affective consequences of administration procedures such as the intravenous infusions employed in the studies by Mayfield (1968) and Mayfield and Allen (1967). The situational-expectational determinants of reactions to alcohol must be more precisely delineated before the TRH can be fully evaluated.

There are obviously serious limitations to how effectively one can control for the combined effects of "set" and "setting" in drug research. It appears that appropriate controls can be most easily applied in studies of the effects of acute administrations of alcohol. In studies of longer-term intoxication, the problem will be less amenable to clever experimental manipulations. Electing to ignore these important sources of information, however, would appear to be a poor choice. One of the most perplexing problems facing the alcohol researcher is the question of why alcoholics persist in drinking abusively in the face of punishing social, physical, and affective consequences. Even though they may be plagued by unavoidable interpretational problems, studies of long-term intoxication in controlled environments may be instrumental in furthering our understanding of how the alcoholic's expectancies towards alcohol consumption and reactions to situational variables may serve to either perpetuate or terminate drinking episodes.

To this point, the discussion of complicating factors in the tension-reduction literature has centered on expectancy and its determinants. There is an additional topic which deserves attention before leaving this general area. There is a body of evidence which suggests that the stimuli associated with alcohol may be a source of considerable ambivalence for alcoholics. On the theoretical level, this notion has a considerable history. Ullman (1952), for example, suggested that one factor which may predispose an individual towards becoming an alcoholic is the amount of conflict he feels about drinking. In indirect support of this notion, Jackson and Connor (1953) found that the drinking habits of the parents of alcoholics were more discrepant than those of the parents of moderate drinkers. Similarly, McGonegal (1972) found evidence that attitudes and behaviors towards alcohol among parents of alcoholics were more inconsistent with operating social sanctions than were those of parents of nonalcoholics. More direct evidence of ambivalence towards alcohol among problem drinkers has been produced, but whether it represents a lingering effect of parental or social proscriptions regarding drinking, or whether it derives from the experienced consequences of abusive drinking has yet to be determined.

Menaker (1967) reported a study in which baseline anxiety scores of alcoholics (as measured by the Nowlis-Green Mood Adjective Check List) were compared with scores obtained either immediately preceding or shortly following consumption of an alcoholic beverage. He found significant increases in anxiety in alcoholics who were anticipating a drink of alcohol, but no change in alcoholics who were assessed shortly following a drink. Nonalcoholic subjects showed no significant changes in anxiety under either of these conditions. In a study of long-term intoxication by alcoholics, Davis (1971) examined alternations in mood immediately preceding the 11 A.M. drink each day for subjects undergoing either programmed or free-choice drinking. Although there was considerable variation in responses, Davis observed tendencies for measures of depression and anxiety to increase in anticipation of the drink.

There is, then, some evidence to support the possibility that alcoholics' attitudes towards alcohol may be different from those of nonalcoholics. There is no systematic research on the effects which attitudes towards alcohol might have on the affective consequences of drinking. However, in a theoretical paper, Heilizer (1964) develops the argument that different attitudes towards alcohol should logically lead to very different drinking *patterns*. He suggests that, "while alcohol represents something intrinsically positive for the positive-attitude drinker, the need for alcohol is largely occasioned by the occurrence of anxiety, fear, or fatigue; while alcohol represents something intrinsically negative for the negative-attitude drinker, the need for alcohol is occasioned by the recurrence of a context which was previously highly rewarding" (pp. 470–471).

Heilizer's analysis suggests that what would be a "high-risk" situation for an individual with a positive attitude towards alcohol (in terms of increasing the probability of alcohol consumption) would not necessarily be a "high-risk" situation for a negative-attitude drinker, and vice versa. One might expect that the specific effects of alcohol sought and expected by these two "types" of drinkers would also vary. A study reported by Vannicelli (1972, study 1) illustrates the possible importance of such individual differences in determining the outcome of studies of the effects of alcohol. She reports that of thirty alcoholics who were given alcohol up to a mean blood-alcohol level of 0.158 percent, 15 showed anxiety increases, and 15 showed anxiety decreases. In addition, while the final blood-alcohol level was achieved by using a series of alcoholic drinks, the subjects' affective reactions to the first drink of the series were highly predictive of their subsequent reactions. In other words, if a subject either increased or decreased in anxiety following the first drink, the tendency was to show similar changes following subsequent drinks. While this pattern of findings led Vannicelli to suggest that there may be two distinct "types" of alcoholics, the important point in terms of the present discussion is that affective reactions to alcohol may be largely a function of the individual subject's attitudes towards alcohol—even when subjects are taken from the same "population." To what degree these differences in affective reactions may result from or contribute to different anticipational sets towards alcohol is uncertain at this time. It is certain, though, that until we can gain some means of understanding these individual differences and predicting their consequences, definitive studies of the effects of alcohol will be hampered.

Aside from problems surrounding the issue of expectancy, there are at least three additional problems which must be dealt with in attempting to synthesize the tension-reduction literature. First, the specific population one is dealing with appears to have important consequences. Whatever the reasons, it no longer appears feasible to expect parallel, or even similar, responses to alcohol by alcoholics and nonalcoholics under all conditions. More specifically, it may not only be important to differentiate social drinkers from alcoholics, it may also be important to differentiate experienced from inexperienced social drinkers (cf., Smith, Parker, and Noble, 1975), and, perhaps, to differentiate "types" of alcoholics (cf. Vannicelli, 1972). Among other things, this suggests the possibility that responses to the effects of alcohol may undergo an "evolution" such that they may be identifiable only in mutated forms in the various stages of a person's drinking history. This is an interesting possibility which itself deserves intensive investigation.

A second important issue has to do with the theoretical sophistication of the tension-reduction hypothesis itself. As previously indicated, the original basis for the TRH was the finding that alcohol ingestion facilitated the resolution of approach-avoidance conflict in experimental animals (e.g., Masserman and Yum, 1946) and the subsequent finding that the conflict resolution was based on alcohol's ameliorative effects on the fear-motivated avoidance response (i.e., Conger, 1951). Dating from the original statement of the TRH by Conger (1956), it appears to have been generally assumed that findings of increased tension in response to alcohol ingestion are necessarily at odds with what would be predicted from the theory. A recent provocative theoretical reanalysis of the consequences of alcohol-facilitated conflict resolution by Brown and Crowell (1974), casts doubt on the validity of this assumption. They argue that, in an approach avoidance conflict situation, the fear-reducing effects of alcohol might actually result in *increased* levels of tension. In the words of Brown and Crowell, "It is concluded that, while alcohol may weaken fear-motivated avoidance and thereby produce closer approach to the goal, goalward movements are always accompanied by progressively increasing conflict; that conflict will be more intense at stopping places near the goal than at more remote locations; and that even when the goal is actually reached, conflict may be either more or less severe than at pregoal stopping positions" (p. 84).

This apparently simple conceptual "twist" can be readily seen to add a whole new dimension of complexity to the TRH literature. For example, in those studies which have found anxiety increases in response to alcohol consumption, one might ask whether they were a function of alcohol's tension-enhancing actions, or whether they were an indirect result of its tension-reducing properties. There are experimental indications that the latter possibility may be a viable one. Pollack (1966) found that, when compared with their sober performance on a sentence-completion task, inebriated alcoholics showed significant decreases in coping behaviors. Although Pollack did not directly test this possibility, it is conceivable that the reduction in coping resulted from the tension-reducing effects of alcohol. In line with this speculation, Pollack did suggest that "The complex nature of initial relief of anxiety and tension due to alcohol, followed by entry into previously avoided situations, probably leads to a secondary increase in anxiety" (p. 419). It appears likely, then, that interpretations of experimental results as being either concordant or discordant with the TRH must be based on an analysis of the possible consequences of tension-reduction in each particular experimental setting. If one consequence of decreased "social" anxiety, for example, were an increase in aggression or assertiveness, it might be expected that additional tension-producing social consequences might accrue to the intoxicated individual. In this context, it will be recalled that, in the account of the results of a long-term intoxication study, Mendelson, La Dou, and Solomon (1964) observed the emergence of "psychopathic" behavior patterns in the areas of aggression and sexuality, in conjunction with self-reports of increased dysphoria. Their application of the term "psychopathic" to the emerging behaviors strongly suggests the manner in which the staff in question reacted to their expression. As a result, the possibility that the reported anxiety increases may have been secondary rather than primary results of the intoxication cannot be lightly dismissed.

A study reported by Martorano (1974) drives this latter point home rather forceably. Martorano studied the combined effects of intoxication and assertiveness training in a group of hospitalized alcoholics. While assertiveness training with nonintoxicated alcoholics was observed to enhance staff ratings of their social desirability, combining the assertiveness training with intoxication resulted in the alcoholics' being perceived as less socially desirable. Apparently the effect of the alcohol was to potentiate the assertiveness training to such a degree that the overall result was increasing social censure. The affective responses of the alcoholics in this study to the alcohol could not be properly understood without reference to the social consequences produced by the behaviors which emerged. The same argument logically applies to the other studies which have been reviewed.

The final point to be discussed with regard to problems involved in the interpretation of the TRH literature has to do with the effects of alcohol at different dose levels. It is now widely acknowledged that all central nervous system depressants have a biphasic effect on the nervous system. Although it has been suggested that alcohol is a "stimulant" at low doses and a "depressant" at higher doses, the biphasic nature of the effects of alcohol may be more properly understood with regard to the central nervous system functions being depressed at various dose levels. The initial "euphoria" producing effects of alcohol result from its depressant effects on cortical inhibitory functions (Ray, 1972). In other words, rather than being stimulated at lower dose levels, certain behaviors and affects are "disinhibited." Depending on the circumstances and the individual being studied, the disinhibited thoughts, fantasies, feelings, or behaviors may have very different consequences. For example, it is conceivable that, for a conflict-ridden alcoholic, the disinhibition provided by low doses of alcohol might be so aversive that higher, more uniformly depressing doses of the drug are sought. For the normal drinker, the pleasure associated with the early disinhibiting effects of alcohol may be the primary motivation for maintaining consistently lower levels of intoxication. Although it might be argued that this could account for the fact that many alcoholics rarely terminate consumption at low to moderate levels of intoxication, this is not an argument that I have either the necessary data nor desire to push in this forum.

Fanciful speculation aside, it most likely is the case that the biphasic nature of the physiological response to alcohol has contributed to confusion in the TRH literature. Subjects may experience very different reactions at different levels of intoxication. In addition, what may be a merely "disinhibiting" dose for an alcoholic may be frankly depressant for a normal drinker. Some investigators have attempted to compensate for the "tolerance" of alcoholics by studying the affective consequences of different (presumably) comparable dose levels in alcoholics and nonalcoholics. One strategy has been to administer alcohol to the subjects until certain indices of intoxication (sweating, flushing, slurring of speech, loss of coordination) were achieved (e.g., Berg, 1971). In Berg's studies, this procedure resulted in mean blood-alcohol levels of 0.132 percent in his alcoholic group and 0.08 percent in his nonalcoholic group. Given that the nature of tolerance is only incompletely understood and that there are no guidelines as to what might be comparable levels of intoxication in alcoholics and nonalcoholics, Berg's attempt to draw comparisons between the affective reactions of his two groups is highly suspect. By the same token, however, it is no more acceptable to administer uniform doses to alcoholic and nonalcoholic subjects (e.g., Mayfield and Allen, 1967) and to make direct comparisons of the effects of alcohol on the two populations.

Closely related to the above issue has been the general failure of researchers to control for the influence of "rising" versus "falling" blood-alcohol levels. That the point on the blood-alcohol level curve at which dependent measures are taken may be important is suggested by the work of Jones and Vega (1972). They found differential effects of rising and falling blood-alcohol levels on cognitive states even though absolute blood-alcohol levels were comparable.

Perhaps the major conclusion to be drawn from the discussion thus far is that it is not yet possible to state with any degree of confidence the particular ways in which the available evidence supports or contradicts the TRH. There is certainly enough confirmatory evidence to justify keeping the concept on the "front burner," but much remains to be discovered regarding the manner in which tension reduction may contribute to the development of problem drinking. As we have seen, the complications involved in assessing the viability of the TRH by studying the affective consequences of alcohol consumption are so great that no definitive understanding of its importance may be at hand for some time. Fortunately, there is an alternative method of studying the role of tension reduction. The basis of this method lies in the fact that there are *two* basic assumptions at the heart of the TRH. The first assumption, that alcohol *does* reduce tension, we have discussed at some length. The second assumption, that increased levels of tension will result in increased alcohol consumption, remains to be examined. Smart (1964) has observed that even though certain doses of alcohol may always lead to anxiety reduction, it does not necessarily follow that increases in tension will result in increased or excessive alcohol use. Following Smart's lead, we will now turn our attention to the few studies which have examined the relationship between stress and alcohol consumption in human subjects.

EXPERIMENTAL INVESTIGATIONS OF STRESS-INDUCED DRINKING

In the review of studies on the tension-reducing effects of alcohol, the conclusions of a comprehensive review of the animal literature on the TRH (i.e., Cappell and Herman, 1972) were noted. In effect, the conclusion was that the experimental evidence was too problem-ridden and inconsistent to permit final judgment. In a recent review of the animal literature bearing on the question of stress-induced alcohol consumption, Cappell (1975) arrived at a similar conclusion. It was his opinion that "even though it has been possible to show stress-induced increases in alcohol intake in highly restricted circumstances, there is no way to be certain whether reinforcement by stress *reduction* was the reason for the increase" (p. 199).

There has been a very limited body of research generated regarding the issue of stress-induced drinking in human subjects. The lack of activity in this important area is partly a function of the difficulties involved in manipulating levels of stress within an experimental context which permits reasonably precise yet *unobtrusive* measures of consequent alcohol consumption. It is by no means clear that measures of drinking obtained within the context of a laboratory study will be free of contamination from demand characteristics built into the artificial setting. The constraints operating in a controlled study may render findings meaningless in terms of their generalizability to "in vivo" drinking behavior. However, the ethical and practical difficulties involved in manipulating levels of stress and measuring resulting consumption in natural settings makes laboratory study of this behavior an attractive alternative at this time.

The immediate problem facing the interested researcher is the development of an experimental task which (a) lends itself to the manipulation of levels of stress, and (b) permits *valid* and *unobtrusive* measures of drinking behavior to be obtained. The strategy employed by the present author was inspired by a procedure originally used by Schachter, Goldman, and Gordon (1968) in a study of stress-induced eating in obese subjects. The procedure, as adapted to the study of drinking behavior, involves engaging subjects in an ostensible "taste-rating" study in which they are informed that various parameters of the sense of taste are being explored. The tasting materials for the study are alcoholic beverages. Subjects are asked to sample the beverages and to make comparative ratings of them on a variety of adjectives. They are told to sample as much or as little of each beverage as is required to make accurate taste ratings. The measure of alcohol consumption is then derived by subtracting the amount of alcohol remaining at the end of the taste-ratings from the amount originally presented. It has been possible to incorporate a considerable variety of stress manipulations within the context provided by the taste-rating task.

The original study based on this format was a study of the effects of threat of shock on alcohol consumption (Higgins and Marlatt, 1973). In this study, nonabstinent alcoholics and matched social drinkers were engaged in what they believed to be a study of the effects of tactile stimulation on the sense of taste. Subjects were assigned to either high- or low-threat-of-shock conditions. In the high-threat conditions, subjects were connected to a large complex of electrical gadgetry by means of electrodes attached to their ankles, and were led to believe that they would receive a severe and painful shock midway through the alcohol taste-rating task. Subjects in the low-threat condition were similarly attached to a small box containing two size-D flashlight batteries and were told that midway through the taste-rating task they would be receiving a slight, probably imperceptible, shock. The taste materials in this study included a beer, a fortified wine, and a brandy. All subjects took part in a 15-minute taste-rating task in which they sampled and rated the three beverages. At the end of the taste-ratings, the subjects were informed that they were in a control group which would not be receiving the expected shocks. The results indicated that the only variable significantly affecting consumption rates was the subject population factor—alcoholics consumed significantly more alcohol than the social drinkers. Consumption did not appear to be affected by the threat-of-shock variable.

Following completion of this study, several hypotheses were entertained. On the basis of observational and self-report information, the possibility that the threat-of-shock conditions had failed to elicit different degrees of arousal was deemed unlikely. A second possibility, that threat of shock may be a particularly poor arousal manipulation when studying stress-induced drinking seemed more plausible. Subjects may not have expected to experience the tension-reducing effects of alcohol under those specific conditions. If stress reduction is involved in learning to drink, it may be that "escape" drinking will occur only under conditions reasonably similar to those in which the stress-reducing effects of alcohol have been experienced and have come to be expected.

A more meaningful type of arousal (in terms of consumption-eliciting potential) was suggested by a study conducted by Williams (1965). Using college social drinkers as subjects, Williams found that problem drinking was significantly related to self-critical tendencies and low self-acceptance. It was also the case that many of the alcoholics in the study by Higgins and Marlatt (1973) reported drinking in situations in which they experienced social anxiety. Both of these findings seemed to indicate that situations involving elements of interpersonal evaluation might be relatively high-probability elicitors of drinking. Higgins and Marlatt (1975), therefore, studied the effects on drinking of threats of interpersonal evaluation.

For this study, male heavy social drinkers were selected from a college population on the basis of their responses to an alcohol consumption inventory developed by Cahalan, Cisin, and Crossley (1969). Subjects were introduced to the alcohol taste-rating task (they rated three different types of wine) with the explanation that the study was an investigation of the effects of different "psychological states" on the sense of taste. They were randomly assigned to either low- or high-threat of evaluation conditions. High-threat subjects were told that, in preparation for a subsequent experiment in which their attractiveness would be rated, their performance during the taste-rating task was being monitored by a group of female peers. Following the first and second 5-minute intervals of the 15-minute taste-rating task, the subjects were asked to orally respond to personal questions about themselves (supposedly as a means of inducing altered psychological states). It was these oral responses that the female peers were to monitor over an intercom. Low-threat subjects were led only to expect a second experiment in which they would be asked to rate the attractiveness of pictures of females. They also responded to the personal questions, but did not believe that their responses were being monitored by anyone other than the experimenter and his assistants. Under these conditions, high-threat subjects consumed significantly more wine than low-threat subjects. If, as the results of this study suggest, the increased consumption resulted from a motivation to obtain the tension-reducing effects of the alcohol, it should be possible to demonstrate that consumption rates can be reduced by providing subjects with alternate means of reducing tension in a stressful situation.

Marlatt, Kosturn, and Lang (1975) conducted an investigation in which subjects were aroused and then given various alternatives for reducing their arousal. Both male and female heavy social drinkers were told that they were participating in a study to determine the relationship of intelligence to the ability to make fine taste discriminations. The subjects were randomly assigned to either an insulted condition; an insulted with opportunity to retaliate condition; or a no-insult, no-retaliation control condition.

Prior to participating in the taste-rating task, subjects in the insulted conditions had their performance on a difficult anagrams task (ostensibly a measure of intelligence) harshly criticized by an experimental confederate. Control subjects were exposed to a neutral confederate. In the retaliation condition, subjects were given the opportunity to deliver a set number of punishing shocks to the offending confederate while he purportedly attempted to learn and recall a list of paired-associates. Subjects were then engaged in the alcohol taste-rating task and asked to rate three different types of rosé wine. Insulted subjects with no chance to retaliate consumed significantly more wine than the no-insult control subjects. Also, the insulted subjects who were allowed to retaliate consumed significantly less wine than the insulted subjects with no chance to retaliate. Their consumption was not, however, significantly different from that of the no-insult control group. It is apparent that allowing the offended subjects to retaliate reduced their consumption. Whether or not this was a function of lowered levels of arousal or tension is not certain. However, this would appear to be a likely explanation.

Whereas Marlatt, Kosturn, and Lang (1975) studied the effects of inter-polating an alternate stress-reducing activity between an arousal manipulation and the drinking task, Higgins (1975), in an unpublished investigation, examined the effects on drinking of giving subjects direct control over a threatened situation. The impetus for this investigation grew out of a large body of evidence (reviewed by Averill, 1973) which indicates that the amount of anxiety experienced in a potentially stressful situation is largely a function of the degree of control which the subject feels he can exercise over the stressful event. The subjects were told that they were participating in a study of the effects of different psychological states on the perception of taste (two wines and a nonalcoholic grape drink were rated). Prior to the taste rating task, they were told that they were to participate in a second experiment which would closely follow completion of the taste ratings. The nature of the second experience was to be an interaction with a group of female peers, on the basis of which the female peers would rate their attractiveness. Half of the subjects were told that they had the option of whether or not to be included in the second experiment and that they could get out of it by simply telling the experimenter that they did not wish to participate. The other half were not given this instruction. In addition to anticipating the second experiment, the subjects were told that their oral responses to two personal questions (at 5-minute intervals during the 15-minute taste rating task) were to be recorded for later use. They were told that, in order to insure that quality recordings were obtained, they would receive immediate feedback during their answers (by means of signal lights) regarding how well their responses were coming across on the recording apparatus. Half of the subjects were given fixed negative feedback (that the recordings were not coming across well) and half were given fixed-positive feedback (that the recordings were coming across well).

In keeping with the predictions for the study, the subjects who received negative feedback regarding their oral responses consumed significantly more wine (but not significantly more fruit drink) than positive-feedback subjects. Contrary to the predictions, however, subjects who were told they could choose whether or not to be in the second experiment did not consume less wine than the low-control subjects. In fact, there was a substantial tendency for them to drink more. Although the reason for this is not clear, subject reactions strongly suggested that having control over the second experiment was somehow aversive. Perhaps making their control over participation in the second experiment explicit sensitized them to the future need to assert themselves vis-á-vis the experimenter. This possibility is consistent with the findings of a study reported by Miller et al. (1974).

Miller et al. investigated the possibility that situations involving the need to be assertive are high-risk situations for alcoholics in that they are stressful and may precipitate increased consumption. Alcoholics and nonalcoholics were required to make role-played responses to a series of difficult social situations calling for assertiveness. Subjects were then given harshly negative feedback regarding the adequacy of their responses. Tendencies to drink more following exposure to these conditions were assessed by recording the number of operant responses subsequently made to procure alcohol from an alcohol-dispensing machine. While there were no significant differences between the alcoholics and social drinkers in the amount of physiological arousal induced by the manipulations, there were differing patterns of alcohol consumption. Compared to their consumption rates under no-stress conditions, the alcoholics showed significantly greater consumption under the stress condition. The consumption rates of the nonalcoholics, did not differ under the stress and no-stress conditions. The authors concluded that alcoholics, but not nonalcoholics, drink more following situations requiring assertive behavior. In light of the fact that subjects also recieved negative social evaluations, however, it is not clear that the increased consumption was specifically in response to the role-played assertive behaviors. There are some additional aspects of this study which warrant attention.

It is interesting to question why the alcoholics, but not the nonalcoholics, increased their consumption under the stress condition. With the exception of the study by Higgins and Marlatt (1973), the studies thus far reviewed have consistently found nonalcoholic social drinkers to respond to social stress with increased consumption. One possibility is that the social drinker controls in the Miller et al. study were not sufficiently experienced to have learned the stress-reducing actions of alcohol. Those studies which have found stress-induced drinking in social drinkers have used only heavy social drinkers. It may be that drinking to reduce stress is a relatively late development in the process of learning to drink. This would be consonant with tension-reduction theories of alcoholism since they imply that stress-induced drinking is a "habit" which gradually builds in strength as experience with alcohol is acquired. Another possible explanation for the discrepancy is that the social drinkers may have been "inhibited" by the method used to assess consumption.

In introducing this section on stress-induced drinking, the importance of having unobtrusive measures of alcohol consumption was emphasized. The use of an operant assessment task in the study by Miller et al. (1974) may have served to focus subjects' attention on the fact that their consumption was of central concern. As a result, it is possible that the social drinkers "suppressed" their tendency to drink more under the stress conditions. Although resolving this issue is of importance in clarifying the relationship of Miller's study to those previously reviewed, the findings are still interpretable within the framework of tension-reduction theories. In that these theories imply the role of increasing "habit strength" with increasing experience, it is logical to expect that alcoholics would be less likely than nonalcoholics to control their tendency to drink in the face of obtrusive assessment.

The studies reviewed appear to have firmly established the fact that certain conditions will increase the likelihood of alcohol consumption. The manner in which these findings should most appropriately be interpreted is somewhat less clear. One problem, for example, derives from the failure of Higgins and Marlatt (1973) to find increased alcohol consumption in alcoholics and social drinkers anticipating painful shocks. While there is no question that the majority of tension-reduction theorists have focused their attentions on "social anxiety" as the prime motivator in learning escape drinking (cf. Kraft, 1971), there is nothing inherent in these drive-reduction theories which suggests that escape drinking should occur *only* in response to social stress. While the Higgins and Marlatt (1973) study is the only one reported to date which has failed to find stress-induced consumption (and its findings certainly bear replicating) it does strongly intimate that tension-reduction notions of alcohol consumption need to be stated more precisely in order to account for those specific types of stress which might be expected to result in increased drinking. This speculation is strengthened by the fact that *all* of the studies to date which have demonstrated "escape" drinking have employed strong social-evaluation components. It seems reasonable to expect that certain types or sources of arousal would be more relevant to the learning and elicitation of escape drinking than others. As suggested by Higgins and Marlatt (1975), it may be that fear of electric shock is not a meaningful source of tension as it relates to alcohol consumption. Drinking may increase only in those situations which are defined as stressful by the individual and in which he expects alcohol to reduce his experience of tension or stress.

It needs to be stressed that it is premature to draw firm conclusions regarding the nature of alcoholic drinking from this body of literature. The number and scope of studies bearing on the question of stress-induced drinking is very small. In addition, only one study to date (e.g., Miller et al., 1974) has demonstrated stress-induced drinking by alcoholics. What we may have, therefore, is a developing description of the drinking behavior of social drinkers (albeit heavy social drinkers). It cannot be automatically assumed that principles of behavior derived from the evidence to date will also apply the drinking behavior of alcoholics. It is also the case that, however consistent the findings from studies of stress-induced drinking might be with the TRH, the data regarding the tension-reducing effects of alcohol (as has been extensively developed) is by no means clearly supportive of that position. It seems prudent, then, to consider alternative theoretical explanations of the reviewed findings.

One important finding which has not been addressed thus far is that reported by Caudill and Marlatt (1975). They found that when social drinkers were engaged in an alcohol taste-rating task under nonstressful conditions and in the presence of an experimental confederate, they tended to model the drinking behavior of the confederate. Even though the confederate made no attempt to call attention to himself, those subjects exposed to a light-drinking model consumed less than no-model controls, while subjects exposed to a heavy-drinking model consumed more. This finding focuses attention on the potentially powerful influences of observational learning and/or positive social reinforcement on drinking behavior. Although it is not immediately apparent how these influences could be made to account for the findings reviewed above, they do serve notice that motives to reduce tension are not the only (or even necessarily the most important) factors governing drinking behavior. Attempting to construct a theoretical description of the development of problem drinking solely on the basis of drive-reduction mechanisms, then, may be dangerously myopic.

An important theory of alcoholism which may bear a more direct relationship to the findings of stress-induced drinking has been proposed by McClelland et al (1972). They report a number of investigations which aim at exploring the motivations underlying alcohol consumption. Based on studies using a variety of investigative techniques (ranging from examining the effects of alcohol on fantasy to analyzing the thematic content of folktales from heavy and light drinking societies), these authors have suggested that people drink in order to enhance their feelings of "power." Using Thematic Apperception Test (TAT) protocols obtained from social drinkers at various stages of intoxication, McClelland et al. report that after two or three drinks, social power thoughts (nonaggressive and for social good) predominate; after six or more drinks, themes of social power and inhibition decrease and thoughts of personal power (impulsive and without concern for others) emerge most strongly. Consonant with this are findings that the folktales of heavy-drinking societies are characterized by a high-power low-inhibition (personal power) *themes.* These authors also cite evidence which suggests that excessive drinkers in North American culture may be characterized by a high-power low-inhibition personality pattern. This evidence, McClelland asserts, indicates that "men drink primarily to feel stronger. Those for whom personalized power is a particular concern drink more heavily." (p. 334). In support of this conclusion, McClelland et al. report a study by Davis which found that experimentally stimulating feelings of power in social drinkers tended to increase alcohol consumption.

The theoretical position of McClelland et al. could be construed to account for the findings of studies of stress-induced drinking. For example, it is possible that Higgins and Marlatt (1975) found increased consumption by subjects who were led to anticipate a stressful evaluation because the perceived inevitability of the evaluation threatened their feelings of personal power, and thereby, resulted in increased consumption. On the other hand, in the study by Marlatt, Kosturn, and Lang (1975), allowing angered subjects to retaliate against the offending confederate may have reduced their subsequent consumption by providing them with an alternate means of satisfying their aroused power motives. From the perspective afforded by McClelland's theory, however, it is not clear why subjects in the retaliation condition did not consume *more* alcohol. This outcome would appear to be more consistent with the findings of the study by Davis in which stimulating subjects' sense of "power" led to increased consumption. Pending clarification of McClelland et al.'s theoretical position, it must be concluded that this study bears an equivocal relationship to the theory.

McClelland's theory might provide an explanation for the somewhat paradoxical finding by Higgins (1975). In this study, subjects who believed they would be able to decide whether or not to participate in a subsequent evaluation tended to increase their level of alcohol consumption. In accordance with McClelland's notion, this may have tended to stimulate their feelings of power with resulting increase in consumption.

Given the current lack of precision which characterizes both the TRH and McClelland's "power" hypothesis, it is difficult to determine which provides the better "fit" with the evidence. The theoretical contrast between these two positions is assisted somewhat, however, by the findings of a study by Cutter et al. (1973). These authors reasoned that McClelland's "need-power-drinking" model predicts that the size of a second drink of alcohol selected by a subject should be a direct function of the size of the first. In other words, if a large amount of alcohol stimulates the need for personal power, and if stimulating the need for personal power increases alcohol consumption, then subjects given an initial large dose of alcohol should tend to choose larger second drinks than subjects given initial small doses. Contrary to this predicted effect, Cutter et al. found no evidence of a relationship between the size of the initial dose and the size of subsequently chosen drinks. They concluded that, although increased power needs may be a result of alcohol consumption, these needs may exercise little or no control over actual drinking behavior. This conclusion is supported by the findings of an earlier study by Cutter, Schwaab, and Nathan (1970). They found that a prior drink of alcohol administered to alcoholics and nonalcoholics had no effect on the subsequent drink-earning strategies adopted in a probability learning task. It would appear, then, that until there is further development of the "power hypothesis" and the means with which to assess its ramifications, the TRH probably provides the more parsimonious accounting of the findings from studies of stress-induced drinking.

Another alternative to the TRH has recently been advanced by Marlatt (1975). In developing his model, Marlatt attempted to synthesize and extend the findings of a variety of investigators. Most important, perhaps, are the findings of a biphasic response to alcohol, the previously reviewed findings of McClelland et al., and those of Sells (1970). Sells suggested that when an individual is called upon to respond in a stressful situation, this stress will be experienced as a loss of personal control if (a) he has no adequate response available, and (b) if the consequences of not responding are important to the individual. Based on these, and other findings, Marlatt proposes the following model:

> The probability of drinking will vary in a particular situation as a function of (a) the degree of perceived stress in the situation, (b) the degree of perceived personal control the individual experiences, (c) the availability of an "adequate" coping response to the stressful situation and the availability of alcohol; and (d) the individual's expectations about the effectiveness of alcohol as an alternative coping response in the situation. If the drinker experiences a loss of personal control in a stressful situation (and has no other adequate coping response available), the probability of drinking will increase. Alcohol consumption, under these conditions serves to restore the individual's sense of personal control because of its enhancing effects on arousal and thoughts of "personal power" or control (pp. 24–25).

Marlatt illustrates the possible functioning of this group of hypothetical principles by noting the findings of the above-mentioned studies of stress-induced drinking. Marlatt, Kosturn, and Lang (1975), it will be recalled, found that subjects who were provoked by an abusive confederate consumed more alcohol in a subsequent taste-rating task than either unprovoked control subjects or provoked subjects who were allowed to "retaliate." Marlatt suggests that the provoked subjects who could retaliate may have consumed less because the opportunity to retaliate served to restore their sense of control over their experimental involvement—something that the subjects who were provoked but could not retaliate accomplished by consuming more alcohol. By the same token, Marlatt suggests that the findings of increased consumption by social drinkers anticipating an interpersonal evaluation experience (i.e., Higgins and Marlatt, 1975) may have resulted from those subjects' attempts to recover from their sense of powerlessness over the impending social threat. This model would account for the failure to find increased drinking in response to a threat of shock (i.e., Higgins and Marlatt, 1973) on the basis that those subjects probably had no expectation that alcohol consumption would be an effective alternative response in that specific situation.

Quite apart from abandoning notions of tension-reduction, the model proposed by Marlatt appears to make the tension-reducing effects of alcohol secondary to a primary function of enhancing feelings of personal control or "power." While this model might significantly enhance our understanding of the immediate motivations underlying drinking behavior, Marlatt himself observes that "inferring the motivation for a particular behavior from a study of its effects or consequences is always a hazardous endeavor" (p. 24). The fact that it is difficult to imagine a set of conditions under which the predictions derived from Marlatt's model would differ from those derived from a more direct tension-reduction model serves only to compound the problem. There may be, nevertheless, a way of evaluating the utility of Marlatt's proposal. As previously noted, the evidence regarding the functional relationship between perceived control and the experience of situational stress tends to substantiate the theoretical position that the two are intimately related (cf. Averill, 1973). However, Averill observes that the relationship is a complex one in which the effects of having control depend upon the specific natures of the stressful situation and the control being exercised. While the ability to exercise control in most stressful circumstances may tend to reduce stress, in certain types of situations, the ability to exercise control may actually result in *increased*, rather than decreased stress.

An interesting example of a situation in which increased control apparently resulted in increased stress has been reported by Corah and Boffa (1970). Corah and Boffa contrived a situation in which subjects believed they could either terminate (escape) or not terminate (no escape) an aversive loud noise. Half the subjects in both the escape and no-escape conditions were given instructions emphasizing that it was entirely up to them (i.e., decisional control) whether they terminated the noise (escape condition) or endured the noise (no escape condition). The other half of the subjects were similarly told to either escape or not escape in the respective conditions (i.e., no decisional control). Looking only at subject reactions in the no-choice condition, the results clearly indicated that subjects who felt they had behavioral control (i.e., could escape by terminating the noise) experienced less stress than subjects who did not feel they could escape. When looking only at subjects in the no-escape condition, it was equally clear that subjects who felt they had some degree of choice experienced significantly less stress than no-choice subjects. In terms of the present discussion, the most interesting result was in the case of subjects who felt they had access to *both* types of control—escape was possible and they were free to choose. On the basis of self-reports of discomfort, this condition was judged to be *equally* stressful to the no-choice, no-escape condition, and to be significantly *more* stressful than either the behavioral or decisional control conditions separately.

The type of situation described by Corah and Boffa (1970) appears to be one instance in which the model proposed by Marlatt (1975) and the TRH would make distinctly different predictions regarding resulting consumption rates. The TRH would predict that alcohol consumption would evidence a direct relationship to the amount of stress experienced, regardless of the amount of control subjects could exercise. Marlatt's model, on the other hand, would suggest that consumption should vary inversely with the amount of control afforded subjects.

To date, there is only one study which may provide a more or less direct contrast of the predictions generated from the two models. In the study by Higgins (1975), subjects were led to anticipate a stressful social evaluation experience following their completion of an alcohol taste-rating task. Half of the subjects were told that they could decide whether or not to be in the second experiment and that they could get out of it by simply telling the experimenter of their decision. The other half were given no such instructions. In other words, half of the subjects were given the expectation that they had *both* behavioral and decisional control over the aversive event (a situation similar to that described by Corah and Boffa, 1970), while the other half could be considered comparable to their no-choice, no-escape condition. Briefly, it will be recalled that the subjects in the no-choice, no-escape condition consumed *less* wine than subjects given both behavioral and decisional control. Although this difference was not statistically significant, it was strongly in the direction *opposite* that which would be predicted by Marlatt's model. In support of the assertion that the finding is more consistent with what would be expected from a TRH-based analysis of the situation, when subjects were asked to rate how concerned they were about the second experiment, those who had both behavioral and decisional control rated themselves as slightly (but not significantly) more concerned.

It should be pointed out that Marlatt qualified his proposal that affording a subject with control over stress should tend to hold down consumption by stating that the alternative (to drinking) coping response should be "adequate." Although he does not elaborate on what an "adequate" response should be (and consequently it is not possible to determine if the control afforded subjects in the Higgins experiment fits this description), there is nothing in his statement of the model to suggest that providing a subject with a less than completely adequate coping response should increase his consumption above that of subjects with no control. An additional argument which could be raised regarding the appropriateness of the Higgins study as a test of Marlatt's hypothesis has to do with the consequences which subjects in this experiment might have anticipated from their exercise of control. Specifically, it has been previously suggested that subjects given both forms of control over the second experiment may have experienced increased concerns over being placed in a position of having to assert themselves in order to avoid the threatened evaluation. Some investigators (e.g., Miller et al., 1974) have directly implicated the role of situations which require assertive responses in increasing alcohol consumption. High-control subjects may have consumed more than low-control subjects owing to their feelings of limited control and/or adequacy regarding the need to assert themselves at a future point. Why this should outweight the impact of being able to control their involvement in the threatened evaluation is unclear, but it is a possibility which merits consideration.

Pending studies which illuminate the proper interpretation of the findings by Higgins (1975), the model of drinking proposed by Marlatt (1975) remains a viable alternative to direct tension-reduction models. However, from the perspective of the present writer, the usefulness of developing models of drinking which serve only to make the tension-reducing effects of alcohol secondary to the actions of an intervening variable is questionable at the present time. Attempts to determine the specific motivational states which underlie stress-induced drinking might more properly await more complete descriptions of those conditions which lead to escape-like drinking. Perhaps, given the current status of our knowledge, a more useful purpose could be served by developing more purely descriptive models which are directly based on drive-reduction mechanisms, which can successfully incorporate the current evidence, and which generate testable predictions.

One possible model could be stated in the following manner: Alcohol consumption may reduce the stress associated with life circumstances in which an individual experiences a need to act effectively or to exercise control but experiences uncertainty regarding his ability to do so. An inability to exercise control or to act effectively might result from either behavioral deficits or constraints (environmental or psychological) on behavior. The reinforcing properties of such stress reduction might lead to increased alcohol consumption (a) when alcohol is available, (b) when the individual feels a need to act effectively but is uncertain or doubtful about his ability to do so, (c) when the outcome of the individual's behavior or circumstance is highly valued, (d) when the resulting stress is sufficiently arousing, and (e) when there is a basis in the individual's experience to expect that the consumption of alcohol in that specific situation will serve a useful function (i.e., tension reduction).

One finding from studies of the effects of drinking which would appear to be consistent with the model being proposed is the apparent increase in anxiety experienced by alcoholics facing the possibility of drinking (e.g., Menaker, 1967). The model would suggest that, under appropriate circumstances, this type of arousal might, in itself, precipitate a drinking bout. Faced with the possibility of drinking, it may be that the alcoholic is in a state of arousal because of the interaction between his need to control his drinking and his perceived inability to do so. The research on this question remains to be conducted, but if the alcoholic's previous experience leads him to believe that drinking would alleviate the resulting tension, he may begin drinking as a means of reestablishing his sense of equilibrium.

The model would also appear to be consistent with the evidence generated from studies of stress-induced drinking. Subjects in the study by Higgins and Marlatt (1973) may have failed to drink more in response to threats of severe shock because they had no basis on which to expect that alcohol would meaningfully alter their dilemma. Subjects in the study by Higgins and Marlatt (1975) who were threatened with impending evaluation may have consumed more because, while they felt a need to control the outcome of the evaluation, they had doubts as to their ability to do so. Perhaps, in addition, they had a basis in experience to expect that the effects of alcohol would facilitate their effective functioning in the threatened situation. In the study by Marlatt et al. (1975), subjects who were angered and were not allowed to retaliate against the offending confederate may have consumed more in order to reduce the arousal generated because of their inability to effectively control the outcome of their performance on a task with far-reaching personal implications (i.e., an intelligence task). Allowing subjects to retaliate may have reduced their consumption because it served to reestablish their feelings of effectiveness and/or control in that situation. Similar observations could be made about the alcoholics in the study by Miller et al. (1974). They may have consumed more alcohol because of the stress they experienced as a result of their inability to deal effectively with role-played situations which revealed their personal inadequacies.

In the study by Higgins (1975), subjects who were given both behavioral and decisional control over their participation in an anticipated evaluation may have consumed more because being able to exercise control placed them in a "no-win" conflict situation. Agreeing to participate would expose them to an interpersonal stressor over which they would have uncertain control. On the other hand, refusing to participate would expose their anxiety regarding the anticipated experience, and/or require them to assert themselves vis-à-vis an experimenter who was asking a taxing "favor."

One advantage of simply describing the characteristics of high-risk drinking situations is that the biphasic physiological response to alcohol (i.e., initial disinhibition or "arousal" followed by more general physiological depression) may be seen as a meaningful component of the overall tension-reducing effects of alcohol. In addition to the tension reduction which may occur at higher (depressant) doses of alcohol, the behavioral, psychological, and/or physiological consequences of the initial disinhibitory (arousal) phase may serve to counteract the negative emotional consequences of experienced stress. By adopting the immediate strategy of simply describing high-risk drinking situations, a wider range of specific motivational states underlying increased drinking may be considered and contrasted. For example, the high-control subjects in the study of Higgins (1975) may have sought the tension reduction associated with the depressant effects of alcohol. On the other hand, they may have consumed more in order to reduce their level of inhibition regarding their felt need to assert themselves. In line with this latter possibility, it is interesting to recall the results of the study of the effects of alcohol on the expression of aggression which was reported by Lang et al. (1975). They found that the mere expectation of having consumed alcohol was sufficient to significantly increase the level of aggressive responding by subjects administering fake shocks to an offending experimental confederate. Understanding the relationship between the different forms of tension-reduction achieved at varying levels of intoxication may contribute substantially to our understanding of some apparently inconsistent findings from studies of the effects of alcohol.

Staying within the context provided by the TRH, then, it appears that it may be wise to entertain the possibility that alcohol consumption serves a variety of stress-reducing functions. As suggested above, one function might be the disinhibition of responses (behaviors or fantasies) which have been previously held in check by either situational or psychological factors. These "disinhibited" responses may significantly alter an organism's affective and/or behavioral reactions to a stressful situation. Another function might be to directly suppress the organism's affective or physiological arousal. In as much as it appears likely that these functions may predominate at different levels of intoxication, it may also be wise to entertain the hypothesis that experienced drinkers will discriminate among situations and alter their drinking behavior in such a way as to achieve the effects perceived to be most likely to produce a favorable outcome under those specific circumstances.

THE PROBLEM OF CONTINUED DRINKING
BY ALCOHOLICS IN THE FACE OF
AVERSIVE CONSEQUENCES

An important assumption which has been made throughout this chapter is that, to the extent that the TRH provides an adequate description of the learning of drinking behavior, it applies equally to alcoholics and nonalcoholics. It has been assumed that the mechanisms underlying the development of pathological drinking are not qualitatively different from those underlying the development of "normal" behavior. This assumption poses some important difficulties. The focus of the TRH is most specifically on the factors which may come to *precipitate* "escape" drinking by individuals who are knowledgeable regarding the effects of alcohol. Clearly, the TRH cannot be invoked as an explanation of the initial stages of learning to drink. At this level, it seems more reasonable to expect that other learning factors such as exposure to positive reinforcement for drinking or exposure to drinking models (e.g., Caudill and Marlatt, 1975) would be more important in governing drinking behavior.

The evidence reviewed thus far provides substantial support for the position that drive reduction may play a significant role in governing the short-term drinking behavior of both alcoholics and nonalcoholics. However, we have reviewed evidence which strongly suggests that drive-reduction mechanisms, by themselves, may not be sufficient to account for the protracted drinking episodes frequently engaged in by alcoholics. Far from indicating that the drive-reducing effects of alcohol operate uniformly throughout a period of chronic intoxication, most studies indicate that the opposite tends to occur—protracted drinking is likely to be accompanied by *increases* in anxiety and psychic pain (Mello, 1972). These findings are a definite problem for tension-reduction models of alcoholic behavior. It appears that these theories must either narrow their focus of attention to those specific factors which govern short-term consumption rates and serve to precipitate drinking, or they must find an internally consistent means of incorporating the findings of long-term intoxication studies into an overall tension-reduction model. It should be pointed out, however, that if future research verifies the role of tension-reduction motives in governing the onset of drinking and consumption rates in a short-term sense only, the TRH will still have contributed substantially to our knowledge of drinking behavior.

The remainder of this section will briefly introduce the reader to some hypotheses which may eventually allow us to understand the maintenance of prolonged intoxication within the framework of drive-reduction theory. The essential problem encountered in attempting to integrate tension-reduction models of drinking behavior with what we have learned about the effects of prolonged intoxication is that of explaining why drinking does not stop at the point at which it ceases to have overall tension-reducing effects.

Menaker (1967) found that following a drink of alcohol, alcoholics showed an almost immediate reduction in self-reported anxiety. The strength of the anxiety reduction and its immediacy following the alcohol consumption led him to believe that the lowered anxiety represented a conditioned response to the alcohol rather than its actual tension-reducing effects. It is possible that a conditioned response to alcohol which is acquired at low levels of intoxication might persist in relatively unaltered form at higher levels of intoxication. By this means, an overall increase in anxiety might be observed, but the immediate response to any one drink of alcohol might still be a short-term decrease in tension. One long-term intoxication study which examined the effects of individual drinks on anxiety levels in alcoholics has been reported by Davis (1971). He studied the effects of drinking on alcoholics undergoing prolonged periods of either programmed or free-choice drinking. As part of his investigation, he regularly took measures of mood both before and after the 11 A.M. dose of alcohol. Comparing the measures taken before and after this drink, it appeared that there was a trend for subjects to show increases in "carefree" scores and decreases in measures of depression and anxiety following the drink. This finding contrasts with Davis' overall conclusion "that anxiety reduction is not an effect of the alcohol except in very low doses" (p. 617), and lends some plausibility to the above speculation. However, until more definitive evidence can be generated, this possibility must be viewed with caution.

A related question has to do with why alcoholics, in spite of a history of experiencing the aversive consequences of prolonged intoxication, continue to report that they drink in order to experience the tension-reducing effects of alcohol and to predict that future intoxications will result in reduced anxiety. One might assume that the alcoholic would come to realize that prolonged drinking results in aversive rather than positive consequences. In their study of prolonged intoxication, Tamerin, Weiner, and Mendelson (1970) asked alcoholics to predict their response to alcoholic intoxication over the course of a period of intoxication. The subjects predicted that intoxication would be accompanied by increases in aggression, irresponsibility, and passivity, and by decreases in both sexuality and dysphoria. Based on Q-sorts administered at various points during the study, it was determined that they were correct only in their predictions of increased aggressiveness, irresponsibility and, in the later stages of intoxication, passivity. Following the intoxication phase of the study, when subjects were asked to recall what had happened to them, they found a general failure to recall the increases in sexuality, dysphoria, and initial activity levels that actually occurred during intoxication. This, along with similar observations, has led some investigators to speculate that the continued belief by sober alcoholics that alcohol has tension-reducing effects is based on their inability to remember what has happened to them while drunk; a sort of state-dependent learning (cf. Nathan and O'Brien, 1971). In other words, while sober, the alcoholic may remember and anticipate the tension-reducing effects of alcohol previously experienced at low to moderate levels of intoxication, but be relatively unable to remember the unpleasant consequences of later stages of intoxication. There is some experimental evidence to support this possibility.

In a study by Goodwin et al. (1969), four groups of 12 nonalcoholic subjects performed learning tasks on two successive days. One group was intoxicated on both days, one group was intoxicated on day 1 and sober on day 2, one group was sober on day 1 and intoxicated on day 2, and one group was sober on both days. Their findings confirmed that learning which takes place while intoxicated may be more available to recall while intoxicated than while sober. A similar but less powerful effect was found for sober states. This line of investigation leads to the logical hypothesis that whereas drinking by alcoholics may develop as a legitimate operant response to reduce anxiety, it may later be maintained long after the drinking response has ceased to be adaptive through the interplay of expectation and state-dependent learning.

Although the ideas presented above have important implications, they have only been briefly developed; partly because of space limitations, and partly because there is little evidence available to firmly establish or refute their validity. The delineation of the factors which are responsible for the maintenance of pathological drinking is an area of investigation which is badly in need of attention. It is hoped that this brief discussion has served to highlight areas for further research and to indicate that the factors which govern short-term or "acute" drinking may be both considerably different from and closely related to those which govern the prolonged maintenance of alcohol intoxication. Before we can achieve an understanding of alcoholic behavior in its many forms, it will be necessary to gain an appreciation for the situational and motivational determinants of both.

OVERVIEW AND CONCLUSIONS

An attempt has been made in this chapter to outline in a constructive form the experimental evidence which is currently available regarding the heuristic and practical utility of tension-reduction theories of alcoholism. Despite an extensive and complex body of research, it must be concluded that the specific role of tension-reduction in the etiology of either normal or abusive drinking remains obscure. The research aimed at delineating the tension-reducing effects of alcohol is currently so entangled in a host of methodological and interpretational problems that very few generalizations are warranted. Perhaps the most that can be concluded is that, with the exception of the effects of long-term intoxication, the preponderance of the evidence is generally supportive of the proposition that alcohol does have tension-reducing effects. However, the specific tension-reducing actions of alcohol and the determinants of those actions remain to be fully described. As the review of this literature suggests this is a challenging area in which to do research and it will take extraordinary efforts before the issues raised can be resolved. However, given the importance of the questions involved, both in individual and social terms, extraordinary efforts are warranted.

Perhaps the most optimistic evidence on the TRH to date has been generated by studies of the ability of manipulated levels of stress to influence alcohol consumption. Continued work in this area appears to have considerable potential for describing not only the situational determinants of increased alcohol consumption, but also for revealing the subtle motivational states which underlie alcohol-seeking behavior. Although the results of the studies of stress-induced drinking appear to be consonant with tension-reduction formulations, the specific determinants of drinking in these studies are not so well defined that they "demand" tension-reduction interpretations. Studies of this nature appear, however, to present a unique potential for successive refinements of tension-reduction models of drinking behavior. As the methods of conducting controlled investigations into the nature of drinking behavior become more refined, we may finally arrive at the point of asking those critical questions which will reveal the nature of both "normal" and "abusive" drinking.

REFERENCES

Averill, J.R. "Personal Control Over Aversive Stimuli and Its Relationship to Stress." *Psychological Bulletin*, 80 (1973): 286–303.

Bandura, A. *Principles of Behavior Modification*. New York: Holt, Rinehart, and Winston, 1969.

Berg, N.L. "Effects of Alcohol Intoxication on Self-Concept." *Quarterly Journal of Studies on Alcohol*, 32 (1971): 442–453.

Brown, J.S., and Crowell, C.R. "Alcohol and Conflict Resolution: A Theoretical Analysis." *Quarterly Journal of Studies on Alcohol*, 35 (1974): 66–85.

Cahalan, D.; Cisin, I.H.; and Crossley, H.M. *American Drinking Practices: A National Study of Drinking Behavior and Patterns*. Monograph No. 6, New Brunswick, N.J.: Rutgers Center at Alcohol Studies, 1969.

Cappell, H. "An Evaluation of Tension Models of Alcohol Consumption." In R.J. Gibbins, Y. Israel, H. Kalant, R.E. Popham, W. Schmidt, and R.G. Smart (eds.), *Research Advances in Alcohol and Drug Problems*. Vol. 2. New York: Wiley, 1975.

Cappell, H., and Herman, C.P. "Alcohol and Tension Reduction: A Review. *Quarterly Journal of Studies on Alcohol*, 33 (1972): 33–64.

Carpenter, J.A. "Effects of Alcoholic Beverages on Skin Conductance: An Exploratory Study." *Quarterly Journal of Studies on Alcohol*, 18 (1957): 1–18.

Caudill, B.D., and Marlatt, G.A. "Modeling Influences in Social Drinking: An Experimental Analogue." *Journal of Consulting and Clinical Psychology*, 43 (1975): 405–415.

Conger, J.J. "The Effects of Alcohol on Conflict Behavior in the Albino Rat." *Quarterly Journal of Studies on Alcohol*, 12 (1951): 1–29.

Conger, J.J. "Alcoholism: Theory, Problem and Challenge. II. Reinforcement Theory and the Dynamics of Alcoholism." *Quarterly Journal of Studies on Alcohol*, 17 (1956): 296–305.

Coopersmith, S. "The Effects of Alcohol on Reactions to Affective Stimuli." *Quarterly Journal of Studies on Alcohol*, 25 (1964): 459–475.

Coopersmith, S., and Woodrow, K. "Basal Conductance Levels of Normals and Alcoholics." *Quarterly Journal of Studies on Alcohol,* 28 (1967): 27–32.

Corah, N., and Boffa, J. "Perceived Control, Self-Observation, and Response to Aversive Stimulation." *Journal of Personality & Social Psychology,* 16 (1970): 1–4.

Cutter, H.S.G.; Key, J.C.; Rothstein, E.; and Jones, W.C. "Alcohol, Power and Inhibition." *Quarterly Journal of Studies on Alcohol,* 34 (1973): 381–389.

Cutter, H.S.G.; Schwaab, E.L.; and Nathan, P.E. "Effects of Alcohol on Its Utility for Alcoholics and Nonalcoholics." *Quarterly Journal of Studies on Alcohol.* 31 (1970): 369–378.

Davis, D. "Mood Changes in Alcoholic Subjects with Programmed and Free-Choice Experimental Drinking." In N.K. Mello and J.H. Mendelson (eds.), *Recent Advances in Studies of Alcoholism: An Interdisciplinary Symposium.* Washington, D.C.: U.S. Government Printing Office, 1971.

Doctor, R.F., and Bernal, M.E. "Immediate and Prolonged Psychophysiological Effects of Sustained Alcohol Intake in Alcoholics." *Quarterly Journal of Studies on Alcohol,* 25 (1964): 438–450.

Goddard, P.J. "Effect of Alcohol on Excretion of Catecholamines in Conditions Giving Rise to Anxiety." *Journal of Applied Physiology,* 13 (1958): 118–120.

Goodwin, D.W.; Powell, B.; Bremer, D.; Hoine, H.; and Stern, J. "Alcohol and Recall: State-Dependent Effects in Man." *Science,* 163 (1969): 1358–1360.

Gottheil, E.; Murphy, B.F.; Skoloda, T.E.; and Corbett, L.O. "Fixed Interval Drinking Decisions: II. Drinking and Discomfort in 25 Alcoholics." *Quarterly Journal of Studies on Alcohol,* 33 (1972): 325–340.

Greenberg, L.A., and Carpenter, J.A. "The Effect of Alcoholic Beverages on Skin Conductance and Emotional Tension. I. Wine, Whiskey and Alcohol." *Quarterly Journal of Studies on Alcohol,* 18 (1957): 190–204.

Heilizer, F.H. "Conflict Models, Alcohol, and Drinking Patterns." *Journal of Psychology,* 57 (1964): 457–473.

Higgins, R.L. "Fear of Interpersonal Evaluation, Situational Control, and Perception of Behavioral Effectiveness as Determinants of Alcohol Consumption in Social Drinkers." Unpublished manuscript, University of Kansas, 1975.

Higgins, R.L., and Marlatt, G.A. "The Effects of Anxiety Arousal Upon the Consumption of Alcohol by Alcoholics and Social Drinkers." *Journal of Consulting and Clinical Psychology,* 41 (1973): 426–433.

Higgins, R.L., and Marlatt, G.A. "Fear of Interpersonal Evaluation as a Determinant of Alcohol Consumption in Male Social Drinkers." *Journal of Abnormal Psychology,* 84 (1975): 644–651.

Jackson, J.K., and Connor, R. "Attitudes of the Parents of Alcoholics, Moderate Drinkers and Nondrinkers Toward Drinking." *Quarterly Journal of Studies on Alcohol,* 14 (1953): 596–613.

Jones, B.M., and Vega, A. "Cognitive Performance Measured on the Ascending and Descending Limb of the Blood Alcohol Curve." *Psychopharmacologia,* 23 (1972): 99–114.

Kastl, A.J. "Changes in Ego Functioning Under Alcohol." *Quarterly Journal of Studies on Alcohol,* 30 (1969): 371–383.

Kepner, E. "Application of Learning Theory to the Etiology and Treatment of Alcoholism." *Quarterly Journal of Studies on Alcohol,* 25 (1964): 279–291.

Kingham, R.J. "Alcoholism and the Reinforcement Theory of Learning." *Quarterly Journal of Studies on Alcohol,* 19 (1958): 320–330.

Kissin, B., and Hankoff, L. "The Acute Effects of Ethyl Alcohol on the Funkenstein Mecholyl Response in Male Alcoholics." *Quarterly Journal of Studies on Alcohol,* 20 (1959): 696–703.

Korman, M.; Knopf, I.J.; and Austin, R.B. "Effects of Alcohol on Serial Learning Under Stress Conditions." *Psychological Reports,* 7 (1960): 217–220.

Kraft, T. "Social Anxiety Model of Alcoholism." *Perceptual and Motor Skills,* 33 (1971): 797–798.

Lang, A.R.; Goeckner, D.J.; Adesso, V.J.; and Marlatt, G.A. "Effects of Alcohol on Aggression in Male Social Drinkers." *Journal of Abnormal Psychology,* 84 (1975): 508–518.

Lienert, G.A., and Traxel, W. "The Effects of Meprobamate and Alcohol on Galvanic Skin Response. *Journal of Psychology,* 48 (1959): 329–334.

McClelland, D.C.; Davis, W.N.; Kalin, R.; and Wanner, E. *The Drinking Man.* New York: Free Press, 1972.

McDonnell, G.J., and Carpenter, J.A. "Anxiety, Skin Conductance and Alcohol. A Study of the Relation Between Anxiety and Skin Conductance and the Effect of Alcohol on the Conductance of Subjects in a Group." *Quarterly Journal of Studies on Alcohol,* 20 (1959): 38–52.

McGonegal, J. "The Role of Sanction in Drinking Behavior." *Quarterly Journal of Studies on Alcohol,* 33 (1972): 692–697.

McGuire, M.T.; Stein, S.; and Mendelson, J.H. "Comparative Psychosocial Studies of Alcoholic and Nonalcoholic Subjects Undergoing Experimentally Induced Ethanol Intoxication." *Psychosomatic Medicine,* 28 (1966): 13–26.

McNamee, B.; Mello, N.K.; and Mendelson, J.H. "Experimental Analysis of Drinking Patterns of Alcoholics: Concurrent Psychiatric Observations." *American Journal of Psychiatry,* 124 (1968): 1063–1069.

Marlatt, G.A. "Alcohol, Stress, and Cognitive Control." Paper presented at the NATO-sponsored International Conference on Dimensions of Stress and Anxiety in Oslo, Norway, June 29–July 3, 1975.

Marlatt, G.A.; Demming, B.; and Reid, J.B. "Loss of Control Drinking in Alcoholics: An Experimental Analogue." *Journal of Abnormal Psychology,* 81 (1973): 233–241.

Marlatt, G.A.; Kosturn, C.F.; and Lang, A.R. "Provocation to Anger and Opportunity for Retaliation as Determinants of Alcohol Consumption in Social Drinkers." *Journal of Abnormal Psychology,* 84 (1975): 652–659.

Martorano, R.D. "Mood and Social Perception in Four Alcoholics: Effects of Drinking and Assertion Training." *Quarterly Journal of Studies on Alcohol,* 35 (1974): 445–457.

Masserman, J.H., and Yum, K.S. "An Analysis of the Influence of Alcohol on Experimental Neurosis in Cats." *Psychosomatic Medicine,* 8 (1946): 36–52.

Mayfield, D.G. "Psychopharmacology of Alcohol. I. Affective Change with Intoxication, Drinking Behavior and Affective State." *Journal of Nervous and Mental Disease,* 146 (1968): 314–327.

Mayfield, D.G., and Allen, D. "Alcohol and Affect: A Psychopharmacological Study." *American Journal of Psychiatry,* 123 (1967): 1346–1351.

Mello, N.K. "Behavioral Studies of Alcoholism." In B. Kissin and H. Begliefer (eds.), *The Biology of Alcoholism.* Vol. 2. New York: Plenum, 1972.

Mello, N.K., and Mendelson, J.H. "Experimentally Induced Intoxication in Alcoholics: A Comparison Between Programmed and Spontaneous Drinking." *Journal of Pharmacology and Experimental Therapeutics,* 173 (1970): 101–116.

Menaker, T. "Anxiety About Drinking in Alcoholics." *Journal of Abnormal Psychology,* 72 (1967): 43–49.

Mendelson, J.H. (ed.). "Experimentally Induced Chronic Intoxication and Withdrawal in Alcoholics." *Quarterly Journal of Studies on Alcohol,* Supplement No. 2 (1964).

Mendelson, J.H.; La Dou, J.; and Solomon, P. "Experimentally Induced Chronic Intoxication and Withdrawal in Alcoholics. Part 3. Psychiatric Findings." *Quarterly Journal of Studies on Alcohol.* Supplement No. 2 (1964): 40–52.

Miller, P.M.; Hersen, M.; Eisler, R.M.; and Hillsman, G. "Effects of Social Stress on Operant Drinking of Alcoholics and Social Drinkers." *Behavior Research and Therapy,* 12 (1974): 67–72.

Mowrer, H.R., and Mowrer, E.R. "Ecological and Familial Factors Associated with Inebriety. *Quarterly Journal of Studies on Alcohol,* 6 (1965): 36–44.

Nathan, P.E., and O'Brien, J.S. "An Experimental Analysis of the Behavior of Alcoholics and Nonalcoholics During Prolonged Experimental Drinking: A Necessary Precursor of Behavior Therapy?" *Behavior Therapy,* 2 (1971): 455–476.

Okulitch, P.V., and Marlatt, G.A. "The Effects of Varied Extinction Conditions with Alcoholics and Social Drinkers. *Journal of Abnormal Psychology,* 74 (1972): 205–211.

Parke, R.D., and Walters, R.H. "Alcoholism, Avoidance Learning and Emotional Responsiveness." *British Journal of Social and Clinical Psychology,* 5 (1966): 276–289.

Pliner, P., and Cappell, H. "Modification of Affective Consequences of Alcohol: A Comparison of Social and Solitary Drinking." *Journal of Abnormal Psychology,* 83 (1974): 418–425.

Pollack, D. "Coping and Avoidance in Inebriated Alcoholics and Normals." *Journal of Abnormal Psychology,* 71 (1966): 417–419.

Ray, O.S. *Drugs, Society, and Human Behavior.* St. Louis, Mo.: The C.V. Mosby Company, 1972.

Reinert, R.E. "The Concept of Alcoholism as a Bad Habit." *Bulletin of the Menninger Clinic,* 32 (1968): 35–46.

Schachter, S. "The Interaction of Cognitive and Physiological Determinants of Emotional State." In L. Berkowitz (ed.), *Advances in Experimental Social Psychology.* Vol. 1. New York: Academic Press, 1964.

Schachter, S.; Goldman, R.; and Gordon, A. "Effects of Fear, Food Deprivation, and Obesity on Eating." *Journal of Personality and Social Psychology,* 10 (1968): 91–97.

Sells, S.B. "On the Nature of Stress." In J.E. McGrath (ed.), *Social and Psychological Factors in Stress.* New York: Holt, Rinehart & Winston, 1970.

Smart, R.G. "Some Difficulties with Current Learning Concepts of Alcoholism" *Ontario Psychological Association Quarterly* (Winter, 1964).

Smith, R.C.; Parker, E.S.; and Noble, E.P. "Alcohol and Affect in Dyadic Social Interaction." *Psychosomatic Medicine*, 37 (1975): 25–40.

Steffen, J.J.; Nathan, P.E.; and Taylor, H.A. "Tension-Reducing Effects of Alcohol: Further Evidence and Some Methodological Considerations." *Journal of Abnormal Psychology*, 83 (1974): 542–547.

Sutherland, E.A.; Schroeder, H.G.; and Tordella, C.L. "Personality Traits and the Alcoholic. A Critique of Existing Studies." *Quarterly Journal of Studies on Alcohol*, 11 (1950): 547–561.

Syme, L. "Personality Characteristics and the Alcoholic." *Quarterly Journal of Studies on Alcohol*, 18 (1957): 288–302.

Tamerin, J.S., and Mendelson, J.H. "The Psychodynamics of Chronic Inebriation: Observation of Alcoholics During the Process of Drinking in an Experimental Group Setting." *American Journal of Psychiatry*, 125 (1969): 886–899.

Tamerin, J.S.; Weiner, S.; and Mendelson, J.H. "Alcoholics' Expectancies and Recall of Experiences During Drinking." *American Journal of Psychiatry*, 126 (1970): 1697–1704.

Ullman, A.D. "The Psychological Mechanism of Alcohol Addiction." *Quarterly Journal of Studies on Alcohol*, 13 (1952): 602–608.

Vanderpool, J.A. "Alcoholism and Self-Concept." *Quarterly Journal of Studies on Alcohol*, 30 (1969): 59–77.

Vannicelli, M. "Mood and Self-Perception of Alcoholics When Sober and Intoxicated. I. Mood Change." *Quarterly Journal of Studies on Alcohol*, 33 (1972): 341–357.

Walton, H.J. "Personality as a Determinant of the Form of Alcoholism." *British Journal of Psychiatry*, 114 (1968): 761–766.

Williams, A.F. "Self-Concepts of College Problem Drinkers: I. A Comparison with Alcoholics." *Quarterly Journal of Studies on Alcohol*, 26 (1965): 586–594.

Williams, A.F. "Social Drinking, Anxiety, and Depression." *Journal of Personality and Social Psychology*, 3 (1966): 689–693.

Williams, E.Y. "The Anxiety-Syndrome in Alcoholism." *Psychiatric Quarterly*, 24 (1950): 782–787.

Zwerling, I., and Rosenbaum, M. "Alcohol Addiction and Personality (Non-Psychopathic Conditions)." In S. Arieti (ed.), *American Handbook of Psychiatry*. New York: Basic Books, 1959.

Chapter Four

Behavioral Approaches to the Treatment of Alcoholism

Douglas R. Denney

A variety of psychotherapeutic techniques have been employed in the treatment of alcoholism, including psychodynamic therapies (Brunner-Orne, 1958; Freytag, 1967; Silber, 1959), psychodrama (Weiner, 1967), transactional analysis (Steiner, 1969), and milieu therapy (Kendell, 1967). Exhaustive reviews of the psychotherapy litarature relevant to the treatment of alcoholism have been prepared by Hill and Blane (1967), Voegtlin and Lemere (1942), and Wallgren and Barry (1970). The same conclusion has been reached in all three of these reviews: the value of psychotherapeutic methods in the treatment of alcoholism has yet to be demonstrated conclusively. Furthermore, the relapse rate for patients receiving various conventional hospital procedures (e.g., didactic therapy, Antabuse therapy, AA meetings, tranquilizing and antidepressant medication, conventional group therapy) is discouragingly high. For example, Gerard, Saenger, and Wile (1962) reported that only 19 percent of 399 patients exposed to a variety of conventional alcoholic treatment programs were able to remain abstinent for one year following treatment.

The lack of success achieved by conventional methods has undoubtedly served to encourage behavioral approaches to the treatment of alcoholism. How much greater success has been brought about by the advent of behavioral approaches is a central issue in the current chapter.

Clearly another factor which served to encourage the advent of behavioral approaches was the apparent simplicity of the problem. It was easy to conceptualize alcoholism as a deviant approach response and to view alcohol as a

The preparation of this chapter was supported through funds from a Kansas University General Research Award. The author gratefully acknowledges the assistance of Carol Lowery and Raymond Higgins during various stages in the development of this chapter.

stimulus which had acquired excessively strong reinforcing properties. From there, one could readily formulate behaviorally based treatments for reducing the positive valance of alcohol and decreasing the frequency of the drinking response. As we shall see, our conceptualization of alcoholism has grown in complexity since the first behavioral treatments were introduced.

One of the major points of this chapter is that studies directed toward the treatment of alcoholism and studies directed toward understanding the nature of alcoholism are intimately intertwined. It is clear that new behavioral approaches have evolved from changes in our understanding of the nature of alcoholism. It is equally apparent that the treatment studies reviewed in the present chapter have contributed to the alterations in our view of alcoholism. The preceding chapter by Ray Higgins presents much of the behavioral research dealing with the nature of alcoholism, while the present chapter is concerned with behavioral approaches to treatment. Given the coordination between these two research areas, this division is somewhat artificial. Thus, in the present chapter, we can not avoid mentioning changes in the conceptualization of alcoholism—changes which have both evolved from and contributed to the treatment of this disorder.

The behavioral approaches reviewed in this chapter are divided into three major categories: aversion conditioning procedures, operant procedures, and broad-spectrum procedures. The aversion conditioning procedures include chemical aversion therapy, electrical aversion therapy, and verbal aversion therapy. In general, these techniques are directed toward changing the valence of alcohol and alcohol-related stimuli. By way of contrast, operant procedures are directed more explicitly toward the drinking response. Contingent punishment is used to discourage this response, and contingent reinforcement is supplied to encourage incompatible, nondrinking behavior. The shift from aversion conditioning procedures to operant conditioning procedures reflects a fundamental change in treatment orientation. The earlier aversion conditioning procedures were directed toward abstinence, and abstinence figures are commonly found as the outcome measure in studies of these procedures. Operant procedures are more often predicated upon moderate drinking as a legitimate treatment goal for at least some alcoholics. One commonly finds alcohol consumption figures as the outcome measure in studies of operant procedures.

The broad spectrum procedures represent a fairly recent development in the treatment of alcoholism. These procedures stem from the recognition that a variety of factors can serve to bring about and maintain excessive drinking, and that alcohol can serve a variety of functions for the individual. Several techniques are combined within broad spectrum treatment packages, including training behaviors incompatible with drinking, teaching alternative ways of handling situations which might precipitate drinking, altering the environment of the alcoholic so that it supports nondrinking behavior, as well as bringing about direct aversions toward alcohol. As various views concerning the nature of alcoholism have grown toward greater complexity, it is only natural that more complex treatment approaches would be developed. It is also true that part of this development resulted from the inconclusive evidence concerning the effectiveness of single behavioral approaches. The review begins with a consideration of these single behavioral approaches.

AVERSION CONDITIONING PROCEDURES

Rimm and Masters (1974) have drawn an important distinction between procedures aimed at reducing the likelihood or frequency of a particular behavior and procedures aimed at reducing the attractiveness of a particular behavior and the stimuli which elicit that behavior. The term "punishment" will be applied to the former and the term "aversion conditioning" to the latter type of procedure. Punishment is conceptualized within an operant conditioning paradigm and may be defined as the withdrawal of a positive reinforcer or the presentation of a negative reinforcer *following* the occurrence of a particular behavior. Therapies which employ punishment, as well as some which employ reinforcement, are discussed in a later section under the heading of operant procedures.

The present section is concerned with aversion conditioning, which is more closely aligned with a respondent conditioning paradigm. The emphasis is placed upon changing the valence of alcohol-related stimuli by contiguous pairings of these stimuli (the conditioned stimuli) with an aversive event (the unconditioned stimuli). Eventually the discomfort and/or anxiety responses formerly elicited by the aversive event come to be elicited by the conditioned stimuli alone.

Unfortunately tidy distinctions between punishment and aversion conditioning begin to dissolve when considering two additional procedures, escape conditioning and aversion-relief. Both of these procedures are involved when the aversive stimulus (or negative reinforcer) is terminated. The removal of an aversive stimulus is reinforcing. Any behavior occurring at the time of termination of an aversive stimulus is reinforced, and any stimulus present at this time is enhanced in terms of positive valence. For example, a patient sips (but does not swallow) a mouthful of alcoholic beverage and receives a painful electrical shock. The shock is terminated only after the patient has spit out the mouthful of alcohol, and the act of spitting out the drink is thus reinforced (escape conditioning). The termination of the shock is immediately followed by the presentation of fruit juice which the patient sees, smells, and tastes. The feelings of relief are paired with the fruit juice stimuli, and these stimuli consequently acquire a greater positive valence (aversion-relief). Escape conditioning and aversion-relief procedures are often added to both punishment and aversion conditioning therapies. Nonetheless, it seems possible to distinguish between these two types of therapy.

Chemical Aversion Therapy

The most extensive program employing chemical aversion therapy was conducted by Voegtlin and his associates (Lemere and Voegtlin, 1940, 1950;

Voegtlin, 1940). Their procedure was administered during four to seven sessions ranging over a 2-week period. Each 45-minute session consisted of two or three aversion trials conducted in a darkened soundproof room free from distracting stimuli. At the start of the trial, emetine was administered both orally and by injection. The patient was then given an ounce of whiskey and told to focus his attention on its sight and smell as feelings of nausea continued. He was told to taste and swallow the alcohol, and, when necessary, additional mixtures of whiskey and warm water were ingested until vomiting occurred. Afterwards the patient drank a mixture of beer and tarter emetic which prolonged his feelings of nausea.

Whiskey was used in the initial conditioning trials because it provided a maximum of gastric irritation. However, the aversion conditioning process was found to be highly specific, and aversions established to whiskey did not readily generalize to other alcoholic beverages. Both Lemere and Voegtlin (1940) and Quinn and Henbest (1967) reported instances in which an aversion was established to one alcoholic beverage used in the conditioning trials, but the patient subsequently changed his preference to another alcoholic beverage. Thus other beverages have to be introduced during later therapy sessions, with particular attention being paid to the patient's favorite alcoholic beverage.

In evaluating the effectiveness of Voegtlin's procedure, it is important to note that the aversion therapy was embedded within a complex treatment program which included hospitalization, Alcoholics Anonymous type supportive groups, and for some patients, booster sessions after discharge. Since there were no control groups in Voegtlin's studies, it is impossible to evaluate the contribution that chemical aversion therapy made to the effectiveness of the total treatment program.

The instructions which accompanied the aversion therapy are also note-worthy. A patient was told that the injections he received had sensitized his nervous system to alcohol so that it would continued to react adversely to alcohol. Accordingly he must remain abstinent and never experiment with liquor after the aversion therapy. Such instructions clearly implied that nausea and vomiting would commonly occur in response to alcohol even after the conditioning sessions had been discontinued. It is impossible to assess the contribution made by these instructions, but some speculations are in order. On the one hand, patients may have followed the advice and thus were less likely to attempt drinking after the treatment. On the other hand, patients who did experiment with drinking and discovered that nausea and vomiting did not occur may have viewed the therapy as a total failure and thus returned more readily to their prior drinking patterns.

Lemere and Voegtlin (1950) surveyed 4,468 patients treated over a 13-year period and obtained data from 4,096 of these. They found 44 percent of their patients had remained totally abstinent (and 51 percent had remained abstinent after one relapse and retreatment) over a follow-up period ranging from one to

13 years. The results showed 60 percent of their patients were totally abstinent after one to two years, 51 percent after two to five years, 38 percent after five to ten years, and 23 percent after ten to 13 years. These figures are conservative estimates of treatment success since patients who failed to remain totally abstinent but who nonetheless maintained moderate, nonalcoholic drinking patterns were counted as treatment failures.

Voegtlin et al. (1941) also evaluated the contribution made by booster sessions administered at thirty, sixty, and then every ninety days after the regular treatment sessions. Follow-up evaluations conducted one year after the treatment sessions revealed that 90 percent of the patients who received booster sessions were abstinent, compared with 72 percent of the patients who refused booster sessions and 70 percent who were not offered such sessions. Since the patients who received booster sessions were self-selected rather than randomly assigned, the differences in abstinence rates may be attributed to motivational differences between the samples rather than valid contributions resulting from the booster sessions themselves. Although booster sessions are frequently recommended in the behavioral treatment of alcoholism, the effectiveness of such sessions remains to be demonstrated.

The clients included in Voegtlin's treatment program were unselected, except for those who refused treatment (5 percent) and those for whom treatment was contraindicated on medical grounds (4 percent). The heterogeneous nature of his sample made it possible for Voegtlin to examine factors contributory to long-term treatment success. A more favorable response to treatment occurred for older patients (above age 25 from upper-middle or middle class backgrounds and with histories of stable employment. The approximately 100 charity cases which had been treated showed an especially poor response to the treatment, only 20 percent of these remaining abstinent from one to 13 years after treatment. Patients who participated in abstinence organizations after therapy showed a higher level of abstinence (87 percent) than those who did not (40 percent) (Lemere and Voegtlin, 1950).

Chemical aversion therapy using emetic drugs has also been administered to groups of alcoholics (Miller, Dvorak, and Turner, 1960). The group procedure not only provides greater efficiency but also may encourage continued participation in the conditioning sessions and maintenance of sobriety after treatment through group support. Miller et al. were able to locate only ten of twenty patients who had received group aversion therapy eight months earlier. Of these, five were totally abstinent, three were drinking occasionally, and two had returned to their pretreatment alcoholic patterns.

A variety of other studies have been reported involving chemical aversion therapy using emetic drugs. These studies employ procedures very similar to those of Voegtlin, and like Voegtlin's studies, none of these studies employ appropriate untreated or placebo control groups. Either emetine (Edlin et al. 1945; Kent, 1944, 1945; Shanahan and Hornick, 1946; Thimann, 1949;

Wallace, 1949) or apromorphine (DeMorsier and Feldmann, 1950; Mestrallet and Lang, 1959; Ruck, 1956) has been employed as the aversive stimulus. In general, the abstinence rates reported in these studies average slightly higher than 50 percent. As one might expect, abstinence figures are quite high when examined shortly after treatment, tending to decline very sharply during the first 12 months after treatment and continuing to decline more gradually thereafter.

Another form of chemical aversion therapy involves the use of succinyl-choline chloride dyhydrate (anectine) to bring about a temporary respiratory arrest in the patient. In the application of this procedure to the treatment of alcoholism, the patient receives a continuous intravenous injection of saline solution from a drip bottle while he looks at, smells, and tastes a sample of his favorite alcoholic beverage. This sequence is repeated several times at one minute intervals without the administration of anectine. Next, anectine is introduced into the drip, and the alcoholic beverage is again handed to the patient. The respiratory paralysis occurs just as the patient raises the glass to his lips and sips the alcohol. The therapist continues to hold the glass to the patient's lips and to pour a few drops of the alcohol in his mouth while the paralysis ensues. The glass is withdrawn just as regular breathing begins to return, an interval of from sixty to ninety seconds after the cessation of breathing (Campbell, Sanderson, and Laverty, 1964; Sanderson, Campbell, and Laverty, 1963).

Initially, the use of anectine instead of emetic drugs in chemical aversion therapy seemed advisable for several reasons. The onset and termination of anectine's effect was much more tightly controllable and predictable, thereby allowing a closer association of the conditioned and unconditioned stimuli and also permitting the use of aversion-relief procedures as the effect subsided. Furthermore, the aversive event was more traumatic, some patients feeling as if they were about to die during the procedure (!). In spite of these "advantages," the procedure is considerably more dangerous than the use of emetic drugs, and the results with respiratory paralysis do not seem to justify this greater danger. Sanderson, Campbell, and Laverty (1963) administered a single conditioning session to 15 lower class alcoholics and examined abstinence figures one year after treatment. Of the 12 patients who could be located, six were abstinent and six had returned to their former alcoholic patterns. More recent studies have reported far less success. For example, Holzinger, Mortimer, and Van Dusen (1967) found 81 percent of their patients had returned to heavy drinking after only four months, and Farrar, Powell, and Martin (1968) reported that 77 percent of their patients were drinking after a one year follow-up.

It also appears that pseudoconditioning procedures bring about as great a reduction in drinking as does the regular conditioning procedure involving respiratory paralysis. Madill. et al. (1966) compared the effectiveness of aversion conditioning, pseudoconditioning, and sham conditioning procedures. Patients in the aversion conditioning procedure received a single conditioning trial pairing the sight, smell, and taste of an alcoholic drink with the administration of anectine. Patients in the pseudoconditioning procedure received a single administration of anectine without its being paired with alcoholic stimuli. Patients in the sham conditioning procedure were presented with the alcoholic stimuli but received no anectine injection. Pre-treatment and posttreatment physiological measures were obtained and drinking behaviors were monitored for three months following treatment. On most measures the aversion conditioning and the pseudoconditioning groups differed significantly from the sham conditioning group. However, in no instance did these first two groups differ from each other in terms of either posttreatment physiological responses to alcoholic stimuli or follow-up measures of drinking behavior.

In a similar study, Clancy, Vanderhoff, and Campbell (1967) examined the aversion conditioning procedure and the sham conditioning procedure described above in relation to regular hospital care and no treatment controls. On several measures of drinking behavior, patients who received the aversion conditioning or the sham conditioning procedures showed substantial improvements beyond the other two groups. However, patients who received aversion conditioning did not improve more than those who received sham conditioning.

The preceding two studies employing various pseudoconditioning and placebo control groups illustrate basic experimental designs in outcome research. Without these control groups, one can not distinguish valid effects due to the conditioning procedure from those attributable to various nonspecific treatment factors such as attention, expectance, and demand. It is indeed noteworthy that in the few instances in which these controls were included in studying the respiratory paralysis procedure, no differences were found which could be attributable to aversion therapy. Unfortunately similar studies have not been conducted on aversion therapy using emetic drugs. This is an important weakness in the chemical aversion therapy literature. Without such studies, it is impossible to conclude that any of the chemical aversion therapies are effective.

Electrical Aversion Therapy

With one notable exception (Kantorovich, 1928), studies using electrical aversion procedures to treat alcoholism are more contemporary than those using chemical aversion. The principal advantages adhering to electric shock are (a) the onset, termination, and intensity of the electrical stimulus can be more tightly controlled, (b) a larger number of discrete trials can be administered during a treatment session, (c) the dangers of medical complications are fewer, (d) electrical aversion trials can be self-administered more easily, and (e) fewer staff members are needed in order to administer electrical aversion therapy (Davidson, 1974; Rachman and Teasdale, 1969).

One potential problem concerning the use of electrical aversion therapy in treating alcoholism was pointed out by Wilson and Davison (1969). They noted that the conditioning of aversive responses to gustatory and olfactory cues may be more easily accomplished with biologically allied drugs which produce nausea and vomiting than with painful electrical stimulation. In support of this notion, Garcia, McGowan, and Green (1972) have shown that taste aversions in rats can be more easily conditioned using chemical rather than electrical aversive stimuli. To date, no studies have been completed which directly compare chemical and electrical aversion therapies in the treatment of alcoholism. However, in general, outcome studies involving electrical aversion therapy report about the same levels of success as do those employing chemical aversion, and thus Wilson and Davison's concerns have been largely ignored.

Unlike the case for chemical aversion therapy, pseudoconditioning, placebo-control, and untreated control groups are much more frequently employed in studies evaluating the effectiveness of electrical aversion therapy. Furthermore, a wider variety of conditioning techniques, including aversion relief and escape and avoidance conditioning, have been incorporated in electrical aversion therapy. Undoubtedly these differences stem from the more contemporaneous nature of the research concerning electrical aversion therapy and the greater precision that can be exercised in the administration of electrical stimuli.

Kantorovich (1928) treated twenty alcoholics by pairing electrical shocks with the sight, smell, and taste of alcoholic beverages. These patients were compared with a placebo control group consisting of ten patients who received hypnotic suggestions and medication while hospitalized for the same period of time. Seventy percent of the experimental groups remained abstinent over a follow-up period ranging from three weeks to twenty months. Only 30 percent of the placebo control group were still abstinent a few days after release from the hospital.

A unique aversion therapy procedure was adapted by MacCulloch et al. (1966) from their work dealing with the treatment of homosexuality. In this escape-avoidance conditioning procedure, patients observed a hierarchy of increasingly more attractive alcoholic stimuli accompanied by a voice inviting the patients to have a drink. The patient was instructed to observe each stimulus as long as it continued to attract him but to press a button removing the stimulus whenever his attraction ceased. If the patient did not press the button within eight seconds of the stimulus onset, a shock was administered which remained until the patient did press the button. However, button presses occurring before the eight-second interval resulted in the patient's avoiding the shock and the replacement of the alcoholic stimulus with a "relief" stimulus—an orange drink. The procedure was attempted with four alcoholic patients and found to be ineffective with all four of them.

Hallam, Rachman, and Falkowski (1972) paired electrical shocks with (a) slides depicting a bar or bottles of alcoholic beverages and (b) the sight, smell, and taste of several favorite alcoholic beverages. Six middle class alcoholics with favorable prognoses and five lower class alcoholics with unfavorable prognoses were each administered a total of 15 conditioning sessions. A follow-up evaluation conducted four months after treatment revealed marked decreases in alcohol consumption for five of the six middle class patients and two of the five lower class patients, although across both groups only four patients had remained totally abstinent over the entire follow-up period. Treatment success was found to be related to positive expectations and to the absence of "tempting" fantasies about drinking during the treatment period. Without an untreated control group, it is impossible to evaluate the effectiveness of this electrical aversion treatment program.

By far the most extreme electrical aversion procedure was one employed by Hsu (1965) in which electrical shocks of 2 to 5 mA were administered to the patient's head for thirty seconds when he sipped alcoholic rather than nonalcoholic beverages. Treatments were administered daily for five days, and booster sessions were provided one month and six months following release from the hospital. As an indication of the aversiveness of Hsu's procedure, only 16 patients (out of a total of forty volunteers) completed the full treatment program. Of these, however, 90 percent were abstinent at the end of one year. This estimate of success may well be inflated because of the selected nature of the patients who completed treatment. Motivational differences between those who remained in this highly aversive procedure and those who withdrew could be quite pronounced.

Blake (1965, 1967) evaluated the effectiveness of electrical aversion therapy both alone and in combination with training in progressive muscle relaxation. In the electrical aversion procedure, the patient was instructed to mix himself a drink with his favorite liquor and to sip (but not swallow) the drink. The therapist observed the patient from behind a one-way mirror and, on a random schedule of 50 percent of the sips, administered a painful electrical shock to the patient's forearm. The patient terminated the shock by spitting the mouthful into a bowl. On nonshocked trials, a green light appeared and the patient again spit out the mouthful of alcohol. Aversion conditioning was administered over a period ranging from four to eight days and required a total of about five hours of the patient's time. Relaxation training consisted of the administration of Jacobson's (1938) deep muscle relaxation procedure in combating tension and bringing about the onset of sleep at night.

In Blake's first study (1965), electrical aversion therapy was combined with relaxation training and "motivation-arousal" procedures in which the patient was instructed to think about the negative effects of his drinking and other problems. Fifty-four percent of the patients who received this combined procedure were abstinent after a six-month follow-up, and 52 percent were abstinent after one year. In Blake's second study (1967), 37 patients who received both electrical aversion therapy and training in progressive relaxation were compared with 22 patients who received only electrical aversion therapy alone. Of the former group, 46 percent were totally abstinent, 13 percent were improved and were considered controlled social drinkers, 30 percent had relapsed, and 11 percent could not be located, one year after treatment.

Concerning the latter group, given only aversion therapy, the figures were 23 percent, 27 percent, 27 percent, and 23 percent respectively. Although these differences between the two groups were not significant, the trend in favor of the combined procedure is noteworthy in view of the broad spectrum approaches to alcoholic treatment to be considered in a later section.

Some caution must be exercised in attempting to generalize from Blake's results since his patients represented a rather select group. His patients were fee-paying, upper class individuals with above average intelligence, a group which would have a favorable prognosis under any type of treatment program. Similar levels of treatment success might not have been obtained with an unselected sample of alcoholics. The absence of any untreated control group selected from the same upper class sample makes these results even more difficult to interpret.

We turn now to a series of studies which have adopted more adequate experimental designs in evaluating the effectiveness of electrical aversion therapy. In a well-controlled study, Vogler et al. (1970) compared groups of patients who received aversion conditioning plus booster sessions, aversion conditioning alone, pseudoconditioning, sham conditioning, and routine hospital care. Patients in the first four groups received twenty 45-minute conditioning sessions conducted twice daily over a two-week period. In the aversion conditioning only group, patients were instructed to take a sip of alcoholic beverage and were shocked until they spit the mouthful into a bowl. Patients were required to take a minimum of twenty sips during each session. Shock was initially administered on a continuous schedule but was decreased to a 75 percent variable ratio schedule during the last ten sessions. Patients in the aversion conditioning plus booster group received the same twenty conditioning sessions and also returned for booster sessions starting two weeks after their discharge from the hospital. Patients in the pseudoconditioning group received the same number of shocks as those in the preceding two groups, but these shocks were programmed randomly over the sessions and were not contingent on the sipping of alcohol. Sham conditioning patients received twenty sessions in the preceding groups; however no shocks were administered. Patients in the routine hospital care group received no specialized conditioning sessions.

Of 73 patients who began the study, only 51 completed the treatment program. The majority of those who withdrew were in the two aversion conditioning groups. Thus the final subject samples may not have been comparable in motivation across the various groups. The percentages of patients within each group who were abstinent after an eight-month follow-up are as follows: aversion conditioning plus boosters, 70 percent; aversion conditioning alone, 46 percent; pseudoconditioning, 50 percent; sham conditioning, 13 percent; and routine hospital care, 42 percent. In terms of these abstinence figures, aversion conditioning therapy did not differ from pseudoconditioning therapy, an outcome that parallels that found by Clancy, Vanderhoff, and Campbell (1967) and Madill et al. (1966) with chemical aversion therapy using anectine. Vogler did claim that the two aversion conditioning procedures resulted in significantly longer time intervals before first relapses than was the case for the pooled control groups. This difference seems more clearly attributable to the booster sessions received by one of the aversion conditioning groups rather than to aversion conditioning per se. In all, Vogler's carefully executed study does not provide any evidence of the effectiveness of electrical aversion therapy.

A similar conclusion can be drawn from Regester's (1972) study comparing aversion conditioning and pseudoconditioning procedures. Sixty alcoholic patients were assigned to four treatment conditions. In the first condition, patients received electric shock contingent upon the ingestion of alcohol. In the second condition, the same aversion conditioning procedure was combined with additional information concerning the negative effects of alcohol. The third condition included the same negative information along with a pseudoconditioning procedure wherein noncontingent shocks were randomly administered. In the fourth condition, patients received only routine hospital care. A sixth-month follow-up evaluation showed all four groups having made a significant reduction in their alcohol intake, with no differences existing between the groups.

Marlatt (1973) compared simple aversion conditioning, escape conditioning, and avoidance conditioning procedures with pseudoconditioning and routine hospital care controls. Each of the first four procedures were administered during eight daily treatment sessions in a barroom treatment setting. Each session consisted of 24 conditioning trials. In the simple aversion conditioning procedure, patients (a) lifted a glass of their favorite alcoholic beverage, (b) touched the glass to their lips, (c) smelled the contents, (d) received a brief electrical shock, and (e) lowered the glass. In the escape conditioning procedure, the termination of the shock at point *d* was made contingent upon the patients' stating that he did not drink and pouring the alcohol into an ice bucket. In the avoidance conditioning procedure, the shocks could be avoided (after the third session) by the patient's stating he did not drink and pouring out the alcohol within three seconds after raising the glass to his lips. In the pseudoconditioning procedure, noncontingent shocks were randomly applied at various times during the raising or lowering of the glass.

Follow-up evaluations were conducted three months after treatment. No significant differences existed between any of the five groups in terms of total abstinence figures over the three month period. The abstinence rate was about 23 percent for each of the groups. However, when considering the percentage reduction in consumption of alcohol from pretreatment levels, significant differences among the groups did emerge. The percentage reduction figures were as follows: simple aversion conditioning, 94 percent; escape conditioning, 69 percent; avoidance conditioning, 65 percent; pseudoconditioning, 23 percent; routine hospital care, 42 percent. Clearly, the simple aversion conditioning procedure was the most effective, and each of the aversion conditioning procedures resulted in substantially greater reductions in alcohol consumption than pseudoconditioning.

Marlatt's study is the only investigation demonstrating aversion conditioning procedures to be better than pseudoconditioning. This unique finding may have resulted from the use of alcohol consumption figures. When abstinence rates were used as the measure of treatment success, no differences were found among the groups. Since previous studies have relied heavily upon abstinence measures, differences between aversion conditioning procedures and pseudoconditioning procedures may have been obscured. Reductions in alcohol consumption constitute a more sensitive measure of treatment effects than do abstinence figures. Furthermore, in most instances, abstinence figures are arrived at through patients' self-reports. Even when attempts are made to obtain corroborating evidence of these reports from arrest and hospital records or from significant others in the patient's environment, the accuracy of these reports remains doubtful. Although a similar argument could be raised about patient's self-reports of alcohol consumption, it may be possible to devise laboratory measures of consumption that are more objective, less sensitive to dissimulation, and more sensitive to treatment effects.

One such measure is the taste-rating task originally devised by Higgins and Marlatt (1973) and later employed as a measure of treatment effects by Miller et al. (1973). In this measurement procedure, the subject is required to rate different alcoholic and nonalcoholic beverages in terms of taste. Ratings are performed using a semantic differential, and these ratings constitute a measure of the subject's attitudes toward alcohol. However, the more critical measure is the amount of each alcoholic beverage sampled while the subject performs the taste rating task.

Miller et al. evaluated the effectiveness of electrical aversion therapy using attitudinal and behavioral data derived from the taste rating task. Thirty hospitalized alcoholics were assigned to three treatment conditions: electrical aversion conditioning, pseudoconditioning, and group psychotherapy. Patients in the electrical aversion conditioning group received painful shocks when they sipped alcoholic drinks; the shock was terminated when the patients spit out the drink. Twenty sessions of electrical aversion therapy consisting of a total of 500 shocked trials were administered. Patients in the pseudoconditioning group received the same procedure except that they were administered only very low level shocks that were barely detectable. Patients in the group psychotherapy condition met for six sessions during which they discussed some of the situations in which drinking was precipitated. The taste rating task was administered to all patients on each of three days preceding treatment and on each of three days following treatment. No significant differences were found in either the amounts of alcohol consumed or the patients' attitudes toward the alcoholic beverages in the test.

Another method of measuring treatment effects requires that alcoholics be allowed to drink unrestrictedly within a controlled environment where their alcohol consumption can be measured. A study by Wilson, Leaf, and Nathan (1975) was conducted under these conditions at the Alcohol Behavior Research Laboratory at Rutgers University. A total of six chronic alcoholics served as the subjects. A cross-over design was employed in which three baseline periods were interposed between two treatment periods. Each baseline period lasted three days during which patients could drink *ad libitum.* Each of the two treatment periods lasted four days during which time patients were allowed no alcohol. During the first treatment period, three of the patients were administered the escape-conditioning procedure devised by Blake (1965). Electric shocks were administered after the patient had raised a drink to his lips and had smelled and sipped its contents. The shock was terminated when the patient spit the mouthful into a bucket. The remaining three patients received a pseudo-conditioning procedure during the first treatment period. Shocks of equal intensity and duration were administered before the patient had touched the glass. After receiving a shock, the patient raised the glass, smelled and sipped its contents, and then spit out the mouthful. During the second treatment period, the procedures were reversed. The first three patients now received the pseudoconditioning procedure, and the latter three, the escape conditioning procedure. Comparisons of alcohol consumption during each of the baseline periods revealed that neither procedure had brought about decreases in consumption.

In conclusion, several of the earlier studies have revealed abstinence rates of approximately 50 percent following electrical aversion therapy. However, when appropriate pseudoconditioning and placebo control groups are employed, these treatment effects do not appear to be attributable to the electrical aversion conditioning procedure per se. Instead they probably are the result of nonspecific treatment factors such as expectancy, demand, attention, and motivating instructions.

One explanation for the failure to show treatment effects directly attributable to aversion conditioning is the gross nature of the abstinence measures typically employed in these controlled studies. Indeed, in the one instance in which effects attributable to aversion conditioning were found (Marlatt, 1973), these effects were shown in terms of alcohol consumption measures rather than abstinence figures. However, the last two studies reviewed in this section also employed these more sensitive consumption measures, and once again no effects were found.

Another explanation is the one offered by Wilson and Davison (1969) that electrical stimuli may not be biologically appropriate for effecting an aversion to the taste and smell of alcohol. However, when appropriate pseudoconditioning and placebo control groups were used in the case of chemical aversion therapy using anectine, once again no effects directly attributable to aversion conditioning per se were found (Clancy, Vanderhoff, and Campbell, 1967; Madill et al., 1966). Here again, one might argue that chemicals which bring about

·respiratory paralysis are also not biologically appropriate and what is needed are chemical aversive stimuli which produce internal malaise, nausea, and vomiting. This issue remains unresolved because appropriately controlled studies of the chemical aversion therapy using emetic drugs have not been performed.

Verbal Aversion Therapy

A third type of aversion therapy makes use of noxious imagery as the aversive stimuli. Although the best known form of verbal aversion therapy is covert sensitization (Cautela, 1967, 1970), similar procedures combining aversive imagery with hypnosis have been discussed in earlier papers (Gordova and Kovalev, 1961; Miller, 1959; Strel'chuk, 1957). In these earlier procedures, patients were first hypnotized and then were led to imagine scenes in which they became nauseated and began vomiting while engaging in drinking activities. Using this procedure, Miller (1959) reported that 83 percent of his 24 patients remained completely abstinent during a 9-month follow-up period.

The covert sensitization procedure does not employ hypnosis, although relaxation training is usually included during the initial treatment sessions. The patient is then instructed to imagine a scene in which he is about to drink an alcoholic beverage and he becomes nauseated and vomits profusely. A typical scene used in alcoholic treatment is presented below:

> You are walking into a bar. You decide to have a glass of beer. You are now walking toward the bar. As you are approaching the bar you have a funny feeling in the pit of your stomach. Your stomach feels all queasy and nauseous. Some liquid comes up your throat and it is very sour. You try to swallow it back down, but as you do this, food particles start coming up your throat to your mouth. You are now reaching the bar and you order a beer. As the bartender is pouring the beer, puke comes up into your mouth. You try to keep your mouth closed and swallow it back down. You reach for the glass of beer to wash it down. As soon as your hand touches the glass, you can't hold it down any longer. You have to open your mouth and you puke. It goes all over your hand, all over the glass and the beer. You can see it floating around in the beer. Snot and mucuous comes out of your nose. Your shirt and pants are all full of vomit. The bartender has some on his shirt. You notice people looking at you. You get sick again and you vomit some more and more. You turn away from the beer and immediately you start to feel better. As you run out of the bar room, you start to feel better and better. When you get out into the clean fresh air you feel wonderful. You go home and clean yourself up. (Cautela, 1970, p. 87).

After imagining the above "sensitizing" scene, the patient visualized a "relief" scene in which he imagines himself approaching a drinking setting, beginning to feel nauseated, turning away from the situation before vomiting, and feeling relief, pride, and relaxation. Cautela recommended that a total of ten sensitizing scenes and ten relief scenes be presented during each treatment session and that special care be taken to insure that the patient is imagining the scenes vividly and actually experiencing feelings of visceral malaise during the presentation of the scenes. Patients are instructed to practice the twenty scenes twice daily between treatment sessions. Cautela also recommended that covert sensitization therapy continue for six to twelve months, with two sessions per week. Over the course of this treatment period, the aversive images of nausea and vomiting are associated with increasingly earlier steps in the chain leading to the ingestion of alcohol. Ultimately the patient imagines scenes in which he becomes nauseated as a result of merely the urge to drink. As in the case of other types of aversion therapy, the effects of covert sensitization appear to be highly specific. Accordingly, Cautela emphasized that beer, wine, and hard liquor be incorporated within the scenes used in teating alcoholism. As we shall see, very few of Cautela's recommendations have been followed in studies examining the effectiveness of covert sensitization in the treatment of alcoholism.

The advantages of covert sensitization over other types of aversion therapy are readily apparent. Covert sensitization is easily administered, requires no specialized apparatus, does not employ physically aversive stimuli, usually results in small drop-out rates, and can be easily taught to the client for purposes of self-administration during home practice as well as during episodic urges to drink. Covert sensitization is often combined with other forms of treatment. Cautela (1970) discussed the combination of covert sensitization with desensitization, thought stopping, and relaxation procedures. Also, the aversive images in covert sensitization have been augmented by the use of electric shock (Cautela, 1970), noxious odors (Maletzky, 1974), and even false physiological feedback (Elliott and Denney, 1975).

Four studies have investigated the effectiveness of covert sensitization in the treatment of alcoholism. Anant (1967) employed from five to ten covert sensitization sessions to treat 26 chronic alcoholics. Eleven of these patients were treated individually, while 15 were treated in groups of four. During the initial sessions, patients were instructed to imagine themselves drinking their favorite drinks in their usual drinking places and then vomiting after a few drinks. In later sessions, patients imagined themselves becoming nauseated and vomiting after merely feeling a desire to drink and also imagined themselves surmounting these desires and feeling calm and relieved. The results of this study are unclear. Anant claimed that 25 of the 26 patients remained abstinent during a follow-up period ranging from 8 to 15 months. However, in a later report, Anant (1968) stated that only 3 of the 15 patients who received group treatment remained abstinent during a 6- to 23-month follow-up period. The results are reported in a very sketchy fashion with no indication of abstinence rates over various follow-up periods and no untreated control groups for comparison purposes. Accordingly, this study can only be considered as anecdotal evidence of the effectiveness of covert sensitization.

A somewhat better study was conducted by Ashem and Donner (1968). Twenty-three chronic alcoholic males were randomly assigned to covert sensitization—forward conditioning, covert sensitization—backward conditioning, or regular hospital care groups. Patients in each of the covert sensitization conditions received nine treatment sessions with a total of 35 sensitization and relief scenes. Patients in the forward conditioning group were instructed to first imagine alcoholic stimuli and then to imagine feeling nauseous and vomiting. For patients in the backward conditioning procedure, the order of these images was reversed, with the unpleasant images preceding the images of alcohol. However, Ashem and Donner noted that backward conditioning patients were making as strong an association between the conditioned stimuli and the unconditioned stimuli as were those in the forward conditioning procedure. Thus, although originally intended to be a pseudoconditioning control group, the backward conditioning patients were combined with the forward conditioning patients, and these combined covert sensitization patients were compared with the regular hospital care group. Six months after treatment, patients were questioned about their drinking, and their responses were checked against the reports of their wives or parents. Forty percent of the patients who received covert sensitization were totally abstinent while none of the control group patients had remained abstinent over the six month follow-up period.

Wisocki (1972) has reported a study conducted by Rohan (1970) in which the effectiveness of covert sensitization was compared with electrical aversion therapy. Patients in the covert sensitization condition received 22 treatment sessions in which they were to imagine a single sensitization scene. The scene was not altered throughout the treatment period, and patients were told to practice the scene twice daily as homework. Patients in the electrical aversion therapy condition received 11 treatment sessions during which they were instructed to ingest six drinks. Three of the drinks contained alcohol and their ingestion was followed by shock. No shock was administered in conjunction with the nonalcoholic drinks. After a three month follow-up period, 20 percent of the covert sensitization patients and 58 percent of the electrical aversion therapy patients were found to have remained totally abstinent.

Another study comparing covert sensitization and electrical aversion therapy was conducted by Wilson and Tracey (1974—reported by O'Leary and Wilson, 1975). Like the study by Wilson, Leaf, and Nathan (1975), the present study employed a cross-over design and was conducted in the Alcoholic Behavior Research Laboratory. Rather than abstinence figures, alcohol consumption measures collected during the baseline, *ad libitum* drinking periods constituted the primary dependent variable. Two patients were administered a covert sensitization procedure during the first treatment period and an escape conditioning electrical aversion procedure during the second treatment period. The remaining two subjects in the design received the same treatment procedures in reverse order. The decrease in alcohol consumption (from the initial baseline period) was 36 percent for the covert sensitization procedure and 41 percent for the electrical aversion procedure. O'Leary and Wilson describe these results as "distinctly unimpressive," since the patients were still drinking over ten ounces of alcohol per day while residing in a minimally stressful, conflict-free laboratory environment.

The studies concerning covert sensitization share many of the same methodological weaknesses that have plagued outcome studies of other aversion therapies. Untreated and placebo treatment control groups are frequently omitted. Abstinence measures predominate and the follow-up periods are usually too short to be of much practical significance in appraising the effectiveness of the procedure. However, the studies of covert sensitization also suffer from a second major weakness. None of the studies have followed Cautela's recommendations regarding the administration of covert sensitization to the treatment of alcoholism. Homework assignments are usually not included. Scenes are never presented for twenty times per session, as Cautela advised. And no studies have employed a six-month treatment period which Cautela stated was necessary in treating a long-standing habit such as alcoholism. In contrast to these recommendations, we have studies in which only one scene is presented per session (Rohan, 1970) and in which only five to ten treatment sessions are employed (Anant, 1967; Ashem and Donner, 1968). While the research does not indicate much effectiveness for covert sensitization, no conclusions can be drawn until the procedure as described by Cautela is actually subjected to empirical investigation.

OPERANT PROCEDURES

As noted earlier, the primary focus of the aversion conditioning procedures was one of decreasing the positive valence of alcohol and alcohol-related stimuli. By way of contrast, the operant procedures are directed more explicitly at the drinking response. One way in which this difference is manifested is in terms of the timing of the aversive stimulus. In the aversion therapies, the emphasis was upon the contiguous pairings of alcoholic stimuli (CS) and aversive stimuli (UCS). Thus, for example, in studies of electrical aversion therapy where the onset of the aversive stimulus could be tightly controlled, the aversive stimulus was usually introduced as the subject touched the glass to his lips or after sipping but not swallowing the drink. The idea here is to pair the aversive stimulus with the sight, smell, and taste of alcohol. In many of the operant therapies, the emphasis is upon the presentation of an aversive stimulus immediately after the completion of a drinking response, a procedure which we have called punishment. Presumably, the negative consequences following drinking decrease the likelihood of the drinking response reoccurring. This difference in terms of the timing of the aversive stimulus is inherent to the distinction between respondent and operant conditioning.

However, a more important distinction exists between aversion conditioning therapies and operant therapies, one which reflects a fundamental change in our conceptualization of alcoholism. The operant therapies have shown a much greater acceptance of the notion of moderate drinking rather than abstinence as a legitimate treatment goal. This greater acceptance is, in large part, a consequence of procedures which place emphasis upon reducing drinking responses rather than rendering a negative valence to alcoholic stimuli. Accordingly before examining the operant therapies, it is appropriate to review briefly the issue of abstinence versus moderate or controlled drinking.

Abstinence has long been the traditional goal of alcoholic treatment programs. This goal is predicated upon the assumption that an alcoholic is unable to ingest even a small amount of alcohol without having an uncontrollable compulsion to return to excessive drinking. Although widely accepted, this loss of control (or "one drink, then drunk") formulation of alcoholism has almost no empirical support. In opposition to this formulation, Marlatt, Demming, and Reid (1973) showed that alcoholics' belief about what they were drinking was a stronger determinant of their alcohol consumption during a taste-rating task than was the actual beverage they consumed. Those who believed they were drinking an alcoholic beverage drank twice as much as those who believed they were drinking a tonic water solution. However, whether they were actually given an alcoholic or nonalcoholic solution had no effect upon the taste-rating task measure.

Cohen et al. (1971) gave two chronic alcoholic subjects "priming" doses (six to ten ounces) of 47 percent alcohol and then offered them money not to drink the remainder of their 24-ounce allotment. The subjects stopped drinking when paid $7 and $12 respectively. Similarly, Sobell, Sobell, and Christelman (1972) allowed alcoholics to drink up to 16 ounces of an alcoholic beverage each day on an open ward, *ad libitum* drinking environment. More alcohol was freely available in a number of bars nearby the hospital. However, patients were told they would be placed on a locked ward and then discharged from the hospital if they were caught attempting to obtain more alcohol. Under these conditions, only seven of 214 patients made such an attempt. The results of these studies hardly coincide with the picture of an inevitable compulsion to drink triggered by small initial amounts of alcohol.

It is also clear that a small but significant proportion of patients treated in traditional, abstinence-oriented treatment programs acquire patterns of moderate drinking. Davis (1962) reported that seven of 93 patients who received psychotherapy for their alcoholism had developed moderate drinking patterns which they maintained for up to 11 years after treatment. A number of other articles indicate that from 4 to 10 percent of patients develop moderate drinking patterns following various traditional treatment programs (Bailey and Stewart, 1967; Gerard and Saenger, 1966; Kendell, 1965; Pattison, 1966; Pattison et al., 1968; Quirk, 1968). These figures are even more noteworthy when one recalls that they occurred in abstinence-oriented treatment programs which viewed controlled drinking as an impossibility and undoubtedly communicated that view to the patients.

When biases against controlled drinking are removed and moderate drinking is openly pursued as the treatment goal within an operant program, the evidence indicating this to be a realistic objective is even stronger. Mills, Sobell, and Schaefer (1971) attempted to teach alcoholics to drink like moderate social drinkers. A previous study (Schaefer, Sobell, and Mills, 1971) had shown that alcoholics differed from social drinkers in that they ordered more straight drinks, tended to gulp their drinks, and continued to drink well beyond the stage at which social drinkers would stop. Mills et al. established a barroom setting within a hospital and made alcohol freely available during 14 daily treatment sessions. Electric shocks were administered if a patient ordered a straight drink, if he gulped his drink, or if he ordered more than three drinks. Higher intensity shocks (30 percent above pain threshold) were administered when more than one rule was violated. As treatment proceeded, escalating social pressure was applied to impel the patient to order more than three drinks. Measures of the number of straight drinks ordered, the ratio of gulps to sips, and the numbers of orders exceeding three drinks were collected on 13 patients during the treatment sessions. Marked decreases occurred in all three measures by about the fifth treatment session. When compared to a group of 13 untreated control patients, two of the treated patients and none of the controls were found to be drinking "moderately" (i.e., "occasional consumption of alcohol without evidence of drunkenness") six weeks after treatment. In addition, three of the treated patients and two controls were abstinent, while none of the treated patients and four of the controls were reported drunk after six weeks.

A 12-month follow-up conducted by Schaefer (1972) revealed that 78 percent of the treated patients now were classified as abstinent or moderate drinkers, whereas only 25 percent of the controls fit these categories. These results suggest that operant procedures directed toward moderate drinking may have a self-sustaining quality which is lacking in abstinence treatment approaches.

Wilson, Leaf, and Nathan (1975) also demonstrated the effectiveness of an operant procedure for lowering alcohol consumption. Following a two-day *ad libitum* drinking baseline period, four alcoholics (patients #1–4) received a shock for every one-ounce drink which they consumed. The amount of alcohol dropped significantly during the two-day shock period but rose again when the shock contingency was removed. After a second two-day baseline period, the alcoholics were presented with another shock-contingent drinking period. During this second period, patients administered shocks to themselves and were allowed to decide whether each drink was to be followed by shock. Alcohol consumption again fell markedly below baseline and remained below ten ounces per day for three of the four patients during the entire ten-day, self-administered shock period. A final seven-day baseline period revealed that the decreases resulting from self-administered shock remained in effect even when all shocks were discontinued.

In order to show that these decreases were the result of the contingent shock rather than a placebo effect, Wilson, Leaf, and Nathan (1975) completed a second study using another four patients (patients #5–8). Following a two-day baseline period, patients #5 and #8 were given experimenter-administered contingent shocks on a 100 percent schedule, while patients #6 and #7 were given the same number of shocks on a noncontingent basis. After a second baseline period, the contingent and noncontingent conditions were reversed. The results indicated substantial decreases in alcohol consumption only during the periods of contingent shock.

Finally, Wilson, Leaf, and Nathan (1975) compared self-administered and experimenter-administered shock using the same four patients from the preceding study. Patients #5 and #7 now received self-administered shock after the first baseline and experimenter-administered shock after the second baseline. Patients #6 and #8 received experimenter-administered shock first, followed by self-administered shock. Both punishment procedures resulted in marked reductions in alcohol consumption for patients #6 and #8, but only the experimenter-administered procedure seemed effective for patients #5 and #7. Combining these results with those for the first four patients, it appears that self-administered shock may be more effective when it is preceded by an experimenter-administered shock period.

One of the most innovative studies aimed at training alcoholics in moderate drinking patterns was conducted by Lovibond and Caddy (1970). Their procedure included two phases. During the first, alcoholic patients were trained to discriminate differences in their own blood alcohol levels ranging between 0 and 0.08 percent. Subjective experiences were noted as the patient consumed alcoholic drinks, and blood alcohol levels were fed back by means of Breathalyzer readings. During the second phase, the patients were instructed to drink their favorite alcoholic drinks but not to allow their blood alcohol levels to increase above 0.065 percent. Breathalyzer readings were again available to the patient. Shocks were administered to the patient if he attempted to consume drinks when his blood alcohol level exceeded 0.065 percent. In addition, a strong emphasis was placed upon patients' learning self-control over their drinking, and family members were invited to view the treatment sessions and to cooperate in the program. Each conditioning session lasted about two hours. A total of six to 12 sessions were employed, depending upon each patient's progress.

Thirty-one patients were assigned to the above program. An additional 13 patients served as a pseudoconditioning control group and were exposed to all aspects of the program except that shocks were administered on a random basis. Twenty-eight patients completed the contingent treatment program; however only five patients remained for three or more sessions in the pseudoconditioning program. Alcohol consumption data recorded during the treatment sessions revealed a sharp decline for both experimental and pseudoconditioning groups during the first treatment session. However the experimental group stabilized at a low level of alcohol consumption during the remaining treatment sessions, while the control group quickly returned to significantly higher consumption levels during the second and later sessions. Data collected during a follow-up period ranging from 16 to 60 weeks indicated that 21 of the experimental patients were drinking in a controlled fashion with their blood alcohol levels very rarely exceeding 0.07 percent. Three additional patients were considered partially successful in that they were drinking less than before treatment and exceeded the 0.07 percent level only once or twice per week. The remaining four subjects were judged failures. No follow-up data were available for the pseudoconditioning patients.

A variety of other procedures have been used to encourage and shape moderate levels of drinking in alcoholics. Cohen and his colleagues (Bigelow et al., 1972; Cohen, Liebson, and Faillace, 1972) have reported on the use of positive reinforcement in the form of access to an enriched hospital environment contingent upon patients decreasing the amount of alcohol they drank. The enriched environment included opportunity to work in the hospital laundry for $1.00 per hour, use a private phone, socialize with nursing staff and other patients, participate in group therapy sessions, use a recreation room with a TV, pool table, and other games, receive visitors, have a bedside chair and reading materials in his room, eat a regular diet. The impoverished environment lacked all of these opportunities. Patients were given one ounce drinks of 95 proof alcohol upon request. A maximum of ten ounces was allowed during any one day. Patients who consumed no more than five ounces per day were permitted to remain in the enriched environment. Whenever a patient exceeded his five ounce limit, he was immediately removed from this environment and not allowed to return for a specified period of time (at least 24 hours, during which he had no access to alcohol).

Cohen, Liebson, and Faillace (1972) reported the results for five patients who were exposed to the contingent enrichment procedure on weeks 1, 3, and 5. During weeks 2 and 4, noncontingent procedures were in effect; alcohol was still freely available up to ten ounces, and patients were confined in the impoverished environment. Comparisons between alcohol consumption during contingent and noncontingent weeks revealed a significantly lower consumption level during the contingent weeks. Bigelow et al.'s (1972) report includes the results for 19 patients. Again patients' consumption levels were compared for contingent and noncontingent periods. While all patients drank excessively during the noncontingent period, excessive drinking beyond the five ounce limits occurred on only 9.7 percent of the days during the contingent period. During this period, patients remained abstinent on 13.7 percent of the days, and drank moderately on 76.5 percent of the days.

Miller (1972) has reported a case study illustrating the application of operant procedures to maintain controlled drinking patterns in an outpatient setting. Following recommendations by Cheek et al. (1971) and by Sulzer (1965) that significant persons in the alcoholic's environment be employed in behavioral treatment, Miller conducted a behavioral contracting procedure with an alcoholic patient and his wife. The patient was a 44-year-old man who had been drinking in excess of four pints of whiskey per week for over two years. The patient and his wife agreed that one to three drinks containing 1 1/2 ounces of alcohol each day was an acceptable limit for his drinking. A contract was established whereby the husband agreed to limit his drinking to three drinks consumed in his wife's presence before dinnertime. Drinking in any other context or in excess of three drinks was expressly forbidden and resulted in the patient's paying his wife a fine of $20 and in the wife's withdrawing her attention. The wife in turn agreed to refrain from making negative comments about the patient's drinking, and violations on her part also resulted in a $20 fine and withdrawal of her husband's attention. With the contract in effect, the husband's drinking rapidly declined from a baseline average of about eight drinks per day, eventually stabilizing at about two drinks per day after thirty days under the contract period. A six-month follow-up revealed that the moderate drinking pattern had persisted, with several abstinent days reported. Both parties reported a marked improvement in their marital relationship.

The studies involving operant procedures offer some very compelling evidence that alcoholics can learn controlled drinking patterns. However as outcome studies of treatment effectiveness the operant studies reviewed in this section leave much to be desired. When contingencies are arranged to support controlled drinking, these patterns are readily observed. However follow-up data after the termination of formal treatment were available in only three studies (Lovibond and Caddy, 1970; Miller, 1972; Schaefer, 1972), and control group data for comparison purposes were provided in only one of these follow-up studies (Schaefer, 1972). In this one study, substantially greater improvement was found for the group receiving the operant procedure. Nevertheless, it is clear that more studies employing follow-up procedures and adequate controls will be required to establish the viability of operant procedures.

BROAD SPECTRUM APPROACHES

Much of the field of psychopathology has been dominated by a prevailing myth, one which has its origins in the medical model. The myth holds that there is a single determinant or etiological factor associated with each disorder. The "single" determinant" myth has tended to persist even among the early proponents of behavioral approaches. The behaviorists leveled some telling criticisms at the medical model and redefined the nature of disorders in psychopathology, but until recently they did little to dispell this single determinant myth. In attempting to understand alcoholism behaviorists tended to make the same mistake that their medical model colleagues made in various other areas of psychopathology; they tended to seek out and ascribe a single determinant to alcoholism.

Early proponents of behavioral interpretations of alcoholism designated tension reduction as the single determinant of excessive drinking. Alcoholics continued to drink because the ingestion of alcohol was followed by the reduction of tension or stress. Several recent studies have raised serious objections to this singular view of alcoholism. A consideration of these studies is beyond the scope of this chapter. Cappell and Herman (1972) and Ray Higgins (see preceding chapter) have offered excellent reviews of this literature and have reached similar conclusions: little evidence exists to support the tension reduction model as an exclusive model of alcoholism.

A major consequence of the single determinant myth is that it leads to a search for the single solution (i.e., a single treatment procedure, or at best a single, inalterable combination of procedures) which will eradicate the problem. Only recently has there been a dawning recognition that even the more tightly circumscribed "behavioral" problems like insomnia, obesity, smoking, and alcoholism have multiple determinants and serve a multitude of purposes in the psychological and behavioral economy of the individual. In the wake of this recognition have come the broad spectrum treatment approaches.

In the area of alcoholism, these approaches begin with a careful analysis of the specific circumstances in which a particular individual engages in excessive drinking and of the behavioral deficits which he might have which prevent more appropriate responses under these circumstances. Treatment is individually tailored to the patient and aimed not only at directly reducing his drinking but also at providing him with skills with which to behave more effectively within these high risk settings. To implement such an approach it is important to have some understanding of behavioral deficits and the high-risk circumstances surrounding alcoholism. Unfortunately, having only recently put aside the tension reduction model as the exclusive determinant of alcoholism, investigators have devoted precious little attention to these topics (see preceding chapter by Higgins).

One study by Marlatt (1973) offers a beginning in this area. During an extensive follow-up of the patients who received electrical aversion treatment, Marlatt inquired about the circumstances under which the patients had returned to drinking. Responses were classified into the following six categories (the figures in parentheses indicate the percentage of nonabstinent patients whose answer conformed to that category): (a) inability to react to frustration and to express anger in a constructive fashion (29 percent); (b) inability to resist social pressures from others to resume drinking (23 percent); (c) inability to deal effectively with intrapersonal negative emotional states (10 percent); (d) inability to resist intrapersonal temptations to resume drinking (21 percent); (e) miscellaneous other reasons such as celebrations for successes and attempts to test ones ability to drink socially (10 percent); and (f) no reason given or inability to remember the circumstances (7 percent). Marlatt was encouraged by the finding that a fairly limited number of circumstances existed under which patients returned to drinking. He recommended that assertion training procedures should be combined with aversion conditioning procedures in the treatment of alcoholism. The assertion training might serve to immunize the patient to the frequently encountered circumstances under which a return to drinking is likely to occur, providing the patient with effective alternative behaviors with which to handle these circumstances. The aversion conditioning procedures were seen as useful in helping patients to control the amount of alcohol consumed should a return to drinking occur. Although a treatment program specifically formulated around Marlatt's suggestions has not yet been established, the broad spectrum treatment approaches that have been cited in the literature have often included both aversion conditioning and assertion training (along with anxiety management procedures). We turn now to a consideration of these programs.

The concept of broad spectrum behavioral treatment was introduced by Lazarus (1965), and it is noteworthy that one of the first illustrations of this concept dealt with the treatment of alcoholism. Lazarus successfully brought about moderate drinking in a chronic alcoholic patient using a broad spectrum treatment. After a careful functional analysis of the role played by alcohol in the patient's life, Lazarus incorporated the following procedures in the treatment program: (a) specific measures were taken toward physical rehabilitation of the patient; (b) aversion conditioning therapy was included to decrease the patient's urges to drink; (c) relaxation, desensitization, and assertion training procedures were employed to eliminate the patient's social anxiety; (d) alternative sources of reinforcement such as hobbies and sports were encouraged; (e) significant persons in the patient's environment, such as his wife, employers, and friends, were enlisted to support the patient's altered drinking patterns.

Another example of a broad spectrum treatment program was presented by McBrearty et al. (1968). Their program included the following procedures: (a) Didactic training for behavioral change. Patients were taught basic behavioral principles such as reinforcement shaping and extinction during group sessions held three times weekly. The patients were helped to formulate specific behavioral management programs around problems they themselves had, and homework assignments were made in order to put these programs into practice. (b) Aversive conditioning. Electric shocks were paired with the appearance of alcohol-related words projected onto a screen and with the smell, taste, and ingestion of alcoholic beverages. An aversion-relief procedure was employed in which a "relief" word or "relief" beverage (fruit juice) was occasionally interposed among the shocked trials. Also patients were taught thought-stopping techniques to eliminate ruminations about alcohol, depression, and anxiety. In a later stage in this general procedure, covert sensitization was substituted for the electrical aversion trials. (c) Relaxation and desensitization. Relaxation training sessions were conducted first with individuals and later with groups of patients. Where appropriate, anxiety-arousing thoughts and events which seemed to trigger drinking were incorporated into fear hierarchies, and desensitization sessions were used to reducing the associated anxiety. (d) Training in areas of behavioral deficit. Both behaviordrama within the treatment setting and *in vivo* training sessions were used to reduce or eliminate behavioral deficits in the patients. The type of deficits which were usually addressed in these sessions involved vocational behaviors, husband and father behaviors, general social behaviors, and specific behaviors for avoiding drinking (such as walking past bars and turning down drinks).

The entire treatment program was administered in an inpatient alcoholic treatment center at the Eagleville Hospital. The center was established as a token economy with points awarded for self-care and ward maintainance behaviors. Narrol (1967) had described a similar type of token economy ward for alcoholics, although his did not include the broad spectrum behavioral program adopted by McBrearty et al. Although McBrearty's program was interesting, no outcome data have been reported from this work, and thus it is impossible to evaluate its effectiveness. Only three broad spectrum programs have been evaluated, and these represent the most ambitious projects in the behavioral treatment of alcoholism.

Hunt and Azrin (1973) devised the Community Reinforcement approach "to rearrange the vocational, family, and social reinforcers of the alcoholic such that time out from these reinforcers would occur if he began to drink" (p. 93). This broad spectrum program included five general procedures. (a) Vocational counseling. The patients were shown how to prepare a resume, locate possible jobs through friends and newspapers, and conduct job interviews. As soon as a patient obtained a job or could return to a previous, satisfactory job, he was released from the hospital and the remainder of the program was administered on an outpatient basis. (b) Marital and family counseling. Behavioral contracting was illustrated during approximately five counseling sessions. Marital problems in areas such as money management, family relations, sex, social life, attention, and ideological differences were resolved through reciprocal contracting agreements. Unmarried patients were helped to formulate similar reciprocal contracting agreements with their parents, and synthetic or foster families were established for patients having no family relations. In all instances, marital and family benefits were always made contingent upon sobriety. (c) Social counseling. Patients were encouraged to schedule regular social contacts with friends and relatives who would not tolerate drinking and were discouraged from associating with former drinking partners. A self-supporting social club was formed through which a variety of social activities were scheduled. Business meetings were held, dues were collected, transportation to the club was provided whenever necessary, and all activities within the club were made contingent upon sobriety. (d) Reinforcer-access counseling. The objective here was to increase patients' access to various sources of reinforcement commonly available to nondrinkers. To accomplish this, patients were assisted in obtaining transportation, telephones, newspapers, radios, and television. These facilities might increase the attractiveness of the patient's home and increase his access to potential employers, friends, and social events. (e) Community maintenance. Counselors visited the patients periodically for several months after their discharge from the hospital. These visits served to remind the patient of the reinforcers attached to sobriety and to address any problems the patient was having in implementing the various programs.

Eight chronic alcoholics were assigned to the Community Reinforcement Program. Another eight alcoholics, matched for employment and drinking histories, family stability, age, and education, were assigned to a regular hospital treatment procedure which included 25 one-hour didactic lectures and audio-visual presentations dealing with various topics in alcoholism, along with other regular hospital services. Data collected during a six month follow-up session revealed a marked superiority for the Community Reinforcement program in terms of percentages of time patients spent sober, employed, living at home, and living away from institutions. Community Reinforcement patients were able to obtain substantially more reinforcers (social contacts, earnings, etc.) than control patients. There seemed to be no abatement of these changes over the six-month period. In general, Hunt and Azrin were led to conclude that social-cultural influences play a major role in the maintenance of alcoholism and that community-based treatments were necessary in order to alter these influences.

The second broad spectrum treatment program was developed and evaluated by Volger, Compton, and Weissbach (1975). This program included the following component procedures: (a) videotape recording and three sessions of videotape playback of the patient's drunken comportment; (b) three sessions devoted to education about alcohol including discussions focussed upon controlled drinking; (c) two training sessions for discriminating blood alcohol levels, similar to those employed by Lovibond and Caddy (1970); (d) five sessions of electrical aversion therapy, with shocks applied when blood alcohol levels exceeded 50 mg percent or when the patient displayed alcoholic drinking patterns such as gulping, drinking unmixed drinks, drinking too quickly, etc.; (e) behavioral counseling, assertion training, role playing, and contingency contracting to foster the development of competing responses incompatible with drinking; (f) counseling and assistance directed toward the patient's posthospital plans; and (g) regular monthly booster sessions for the first year following discharge. Two groups of chronic hospitalized alcoholics were included in this study. The first group, consisting of 23 patients, received all of the above component procedures. The second group, with 19 patients, received only the various counseling sessions (b, e, f, g) and were administered no alcohol during the treatment sessions.

Over a 12-month follow-up period, 62 percent of the patients remained abstinent or engaged only in controlled drinking. Alcoholic intake declined significantly from pretreatment levels. Patients in the first group decreased from an average of 14 to an average of three drinks per day, and those in the second group decreased from ten to five drinks per day during the first year. The difference in favor of the first group was significant. However, on all other outcome measures (changes in preferred beverage, drinking companions, drinking environment; the number of days of employment lost due to drinking), no differences were found between the two groups. On most of these additional outcome measures, both groups showed significant declines from pretreatment levels. Initial alcohol intake, preferred beverage, and drinking environment served as the best predictors of patients' response to the treatment program.

The "individualized behavior therapy program" devised by Sobell and Sobell (1973 a, b, c) represents the most carefully investigated broad spectrum approach to date. Chronic alcoholic patients were assigned either to controlled drinking or to nondrinking conditions, based on their own preference and the staff's decision as to which goal seemed most appropriate for the patient. Within each group, subjects were then assigned to either individualized behavior therapy (experimental) or regular hospital treatment (control). Thus the four groups in Sobell and Sobell's study were controlled drinking-experimental (CD-E), controlled drinking-control (CD-C), nondrinking-experimental (ND-E), and nondrinking-control (ND-C).

Regular hospital treatment included conventional group therapy, AA meetings, drug therapy, occupational and physical therapy. Individualized behavior therapy consisted of 17 treatment sessions with three general features: (a) self-exposure to videotaped replays of the client's own drunken behavior (Sobell and Sobell, 1973); (b) operant training of nondrinking or controlled drinking patterns using electric shocks; and (c) behavior change training sessions to teach patients skillful alternatives for handling situations which, in the past, might have led to drinking. The operant training procedures for controlled drinking subjects were similar to those devised by Schaefer, Sobell, and Mills (1971). Patients were shocked for ordering straight drinks, gulping their drinks, ordering drinks too frequently, and consuming more than three drinks per session. Patients in the nondrinking condition were shocked for ordering each drink and for each attempt to consume it. The behavior change training sessions emphasized the analysis of setting conditions for patients' drinking, the development of a number of possible alternative behaviors which might be employed in those settings, the evaluation of consequences that might result from the use of each alternative behavior, and finally, practice involving the most viable alternative. Extensive use of role playing techniques, assertion training, and other replication techniques were employed in these sessions.

Sobell and Sobell have been able to conduct a two year follow-up on the seventy subjects in their original study (Sobell and Sobell, 1973 b, c). The subjects themselves as well as collateral information sources were contacted every three or four weeks throughout the follow-up period. Subjects' drinking behaviors were categorized in terms of (a) drunk days, during which more than six ounces of alcohol were consumed, (b) controlled drinking days, during which less than six ounces were consumed, (c) abstinent days, and (d) incarcerated days. The controlled drinking and abstinent categories were combined to provide a general estimate of the percentage of days within a particular time interval during which a subject was functioning well. The percentages of abstinent or controlled drinking days for each six-month interval during the two-year follow-up are presented in table 4–1.

Table 4–1. Percentage of Days Spent in Abstinence or Controlled Drinking During Each Six-Month Interval Following Sobell and Sobell's Outcome Study

	First 6 months (1–6)		*Second 6 months (7–12)*		*Third 6 months (13–18)*		*Fourth 6 months (19–24)*	
Experimental Condition	%	N	%	N	%	N	%	N
CD-E	68.4	(20)	72.6	(20)	83.1	(20)	91.8	(19)
CD-C	38.6	(19)	31.9	(19)	43.3	(17)	46.9	(17)
ND-E	70.2	(15)	66.6	(15)	62.3	(14)	66.4	(13)
ND-C	34.2	(14)	42.8	(14)	42.2	(14)	48.2	(14)

Note: The four treatment groups were controlled drinking-experimental (CD-E), controlled drinking-control (CD-C), nondrinking experimental (ND-E), and nondrinking-control (ND-C).

The data in table 4–1 clearly indicate the superiority of the individualized behavior therapy procedure over that of regular hospital care. At the end of the first year, both the controlled drinking- and the nondrinking-experimental subjects showed significantly more improvement than their respective controls. At the end of the second year, the controlled drinking-experimental subjects were still showing significantly more improvement than their controls. A similar trend was also present for the nondrinking subjects at this time, but these differences were not significant.

Additional differences were found on a variety of other measures, including general adjustment, vocational status, job satisfaction, and residential status. In general, both controlled drinking- and nondrinking-experimental subjects scored significantly higher than their respective controls during the first year following treatment. During the second year, however, only the controlled drinking-experimental subjects achieved significantly higher scores than control subjects.

CONCLUSIONS

The survey of behavioral approaches to treatment offered in the preceding pages leads to a number of conclusions encompassing both methodological and substantive issues. Together these conclusions constitute an overview of the present status existing in the behavioral treatment of alcoholism.

Research Designs

Single-subject and single-group designs employing pretreatment and post-treatment assessments of patients' drinking predominate this area of research. These designs are vulnerable to such a vast number of potentially confounding variables that the effectiveness of the particular treatment procedure being evaluated is totally obscured (Campbell and Stanley, 1966).

The use of untreated control groups helps to control for some of these confounding variables, particularly effects due to the act of measurement and to the passage of time. In addition, most untreated control groups in the preceding studies are actually routine hospital care groups which control for additional confounding variables as well. Routine hospital care groups receive all of the procedures regularly administered to all patients in the particular alcoholic treatment program in which the research is being conducted. Experimental groups also receive these routine procedures, along with the specific treatment procedure under study. These routine hospital care groups control for extraneous procedures inherent to the alcoholic treatment program (e.g., drug therapy, information regarding alcohol, group counseling). Theoretically they also control for a host of nonspecific treatment factors adhering to any treatment program (e.g., attention, demand characteristics, subjects' expectancies). In practice, however, it is quite possible that patients receiving only routine hospital care have lower expectancies, experience less demand, receive less attention, and are subject to less pronounced Hawthorne effects than patients in the experimental group. The extent to which adequate control over these extraneous factors is attained by the use of a routine hospital care group is open to question and should be evaluated through the use of manipulation check measures of these extraneous factors during the course of any outcome study. Nevertheless, this practice has not been adopted in any of the research reviewed here.

Another problem typically encountered in controlled research stems from differential dropout rates among subjects in experimental and control groups. Particularly in the case of aversion conditioning studies (e.g., Hsu, 1965; Vogler et al., 1970), larger numbers of experimental subjects than control subjects tend to withdraw from the study, leading to possible differences in the levels of motivation between the groups at the conclusion of the study. To the extent that motivation is related to successful outcome, differential dropout rates can produce spuriously high estimates of treatment effectiveness. Again, manipulation check measures that evaluate subjects' levels of motivation should be included in any outcome study in order to insure that these levels are equated between experimental and regular hospital care control groups.

Subject Characteristics

Several authors (Davidson, 1974; Lunde and Vogler, 1970; Miller and Barlow, 1973) have noted that subject variables and their relationship to treatment outcome are frequently ignored in outcome studies. Lemere and Voegtlin (1950) found that patients' age, social class, and employment history were highly related to outcome in the case of chemical aversion therapy, and Vogler, Compton, and Weissbach (1975) reported several features pertaining to patients' drinking history which predicted outcome within their broad spectrum treatment program. While several other investigators have speculated about the results of various studies in terms of differences in subject characteristics, no other systematic examination of these variables are to be found. Lunde and Vogler (1970) have proposed a set of guidelines to be followed in describing alcoholic subject samples in published research. They recommend that, in addition to the usual features such as age, sex, marital status, IQ, chronicity, previous hospitalizations, and social class, descriptions should also include information regarding drinking environments, drinking associates, preferred drinks, drinking cycle, average time of abstinence after hospitalization, and circumstances which precipitate drinking. Clearly more reporting of these features and more investigation of their relationship to treatment outcome need to be done.

One particularly important issue for future study is the identification of characteristics which predict whether controlled drinking or abstinence is the more appropriate treatment goal. Initial results pertaining to this issue have been reported by Orford (1973). This study indicates that features of the patient's previous drinking patterns can be useful in deciding upon the appropriate treatment goal.

Dependent Measures

We have already noted an evolution in the behavioral treatment literature away from abstinence measures and toward alcohol consumption measures to reflect treatment outcome. Consumption figures offer far more sensitive indices of treatment effects as well as being more consistent with current thought regarding the possibility of teaching controlled drinking patterns to alcoholics. Unfortunately since both measures are often collected through patients' self-reports, they are subject to a great deal of distortion. The use of collateral information sources helps to correct for this distortion, but only to a limited extent.

Other more objective indices of treatment effectiveness are available in the form of choice tests (Morosko and Baer, 1970; Raymond, 1964), taste rating tasks (Higgins and Marlatt, 1973; Miller et al., 1973), and operant measures taken within *ad libitum* drinking settings (Wilson, Leaf, and Nathan, 1975). A problem common to all of these measures is that their relationships to actual drinking behavior in a natural setting have not yet been adequately established. Until these relationships have been demonstrated, outcome studies should not employ these measures exclusively.

The Evolution of Behavioral Approaches
to Treatment

A fundamental characteristic of the behavioral approach is that all procedures subsumed under this heading are supported by empirical investigation. The failure to find empirical support for a particular procedure leads to a withdrawal of interest and redirection of attention toward other procedures. Because of this strong commitment to empirical validation, behavioral approaches tend to evolve more quickly than other types of therapeutic approaches.

Our review of the controlled studies of chemical, electrical, and verbal aversion therapies offered little support for aversion conditioning procedures. A few of these studies (particularly in the area of electrical aversion therapy) employing untreated control or routine hospital care groups have found significantly greater changes for the aversion conditioning group. Nonetheless we are led to conclude, along with Regester (1972) and Hallam, Rachman, and Falkowski (1972), that any success achieved by aversion conditioning procedures results from nonspecific treatment factors rather than from conditioning processes per se.

This conclusion is predicated on four bases. First, as we have noted, routine hospital care groups probably do an incomplete job at controlling for nonspecific factors so that these factors may still be operating more strongly in the case of the aversion conditioning group. Second, with only one exception (Marlatt, 1973), those studies which have included pseudoconditioning control groups have never shown results favoring the aversion conditioning procedure over the pseudoconditioning procedure. Third, increases in autonomic arousal in response to alcoholic stimuli have generally not been found following aversion conditioning procedures (Hallam, Rachman, and Falkowski, 1972; Madill et al., 1966), thus raising questions concerning the conditioning model upon which these procedures are founded. And finally, differential success rates have been reported for different types of alcoholic patients. It is difficult for a simple respondent conditioning model to account for these subject differences, especially given that the factors which have been found to relate to success apparently have nothing to do with conditionability.

Grave ethical issues concerning aversion conditioning procedures combine with the lack of empirical support for these procedures. Many professionals feel that the application of aversive stimuli can only be justified when the aversive technique has a demonstrated effectiveness, when it is employed to correct a behavior which is substantially more harmful to the patient than the aversive stimuli themselves, and when no other, nonaversive procedure is viable. While few would argue with the harmfulness of excessive drinking, stronger empirical evidence of the effectiveness of aversion conditioning procedures and of their advantages over alternative procedures is certainly required before the ethical issues surrounding their administration could be put aside. Since this empirical evidence has not been forthcoming, there has been a general drift of interest away from aversion conditioning procedures in the treatment of alcoholism, to the extent that some writers (e.g., Hamburg, 1975) are currently questioning whether such procedures even need to be included within broad spectrum treatment approaches.

Replacing the aversion conditioning procedures are a variety of approaches which have two basic characteristics: (a) they are environmentally directed; and (b) they are "packaged" treatments combining several elemental procedures. Consideration of these two characteristics suggests some future directions in the behavioral approaches.

In order to attain the levels of control necessary to alter so strong a habit as excessive drinking, environmentally-directed treatments require extensive involvement and cooperation from the people who inhabit the alcoholic patient's environment. While such control is relatively easy to obtain in inpatient settings, the problem is to devise environmentally-directed outpatient treatments of alcoholism. More than one such approach has been thoroughly sabotaged through the neglect, indifference, or active obstruction of others who share the patient's environment. It may be wise to begin assessing patient's environments as homestatic systems in which alcohol plays a pathognomic but stabilizing functional role. We should ask (a) what repercussions might the removal of excessive drinking behavior on the part of the identified patient have on this system, and (b) what adjustments will need to be made in the system so that a new stability can be attained in the absence of alcohol? Only by resolving these issues can long-term alterations of drinking behaviors in natural settings be accomplished.

As packaged approaches continue to emerge, some ambiguity is discernable in the concept of broad spectrum treatment as envisioned by various investigators. In its original form, broad spectrum treatment referred to any approach that combined a variety of procedures to meet the specific needs of a particular individual. Since the combination of needs for one individual might differ from those of another, broad spectrum approaches were highly personalized (Lazarus, 1971). Given this high degree of specificity, the most appropriate form of research involved designs calling for intensive study of limited numbers of subjects.

The more recent package treatment programs which have been evaluated in group designed experiments (Hunt and Zarin, 1973; Sobell and Sobell, 1973a; Vogler, Compton, and Weissbach, 1975) seem to depart from the original concept of broad spectrum approaches. Rather than being individually personalized on the basis of a careful analysis of the specific roles that alcohol plays in the life of a particular individual, these later broad spectrum programs assume more of a "shot-gun" approach. Fairly large groups of patients receive essentially the same complex combination of procedures. Hopefully a broad enough range of procedures is encompassed so that the idiosyncractic needs of individual patients are met.

This erosion in the concept of broad spectrum approaches toward "shot-gun" programs may present a serious problem regarding the future development of behavioral appraoches. It seems clear that this development will depend upon greater understanding of the various functions which alcohol serves in the behavioral and psychological economy of the individual, the circumstances under which excessive drinking occurs, and the behavioral deficits typifying the alcoholic patient. In other words, advances in behavioral approaches to treatment will be tied to taxonomic discovery concerning the behaviors labeled alcoholism. There is a danger that the drift toward shot-gun approaches may delay this taxonomic discovery.

REFERENCES

Anant, S.S. "A Note on the Treatment of Alcoholics by a Verbal Aversion Technique." *Canadian Psychologist,* 8 (1967): 19–22.

Anant, S.S. "Treatment of Alcoholics and Drug Addicts by Verbal Aversion Techniques." *International Journal of the Addictions,* 3 (1968): 381–388.

Ashem, B., and Donner, L. "Covert Sensitization with Alcoholics: A Controlled Replication." *Behaviour Research and Therapy,* 6 (1968): 7–12.

Bailey, M.B., and Stewart, J. "Normal Drinking by Persons Reporting Previous Problem Drinking." *Quarterly Journal of Studies on Alcohol,* 28 (1967): 305–315.

Bigelow, G.; Cohen, M.; Liebson, I.; and Faillace, L.A. "Abstinence or Moderation? Choice by Alcoholics." *Behavior Research and Therapy,* 10 (1972): 209–214.

Blake, B.G. "The Application of Behaviour Therapy to the Treatment of Alcoholism." *Behaviour Research and Therapy,* 3 (1965): 75–85.

Blake, B.G. "A Follow-up of Alcoholics Teated by Behaviour Therapy." *Behaviour Research and Therapy,* 5 (1967): 89–94.

Brunner-Orne, M. "Group Therapy of Alcoholics: International Conference." *Quarterly Journal of Studies on Alcohol,* 19 (1958): 164–165.

Campbell, D.; Sanderson, R.E.; and Laverty, S.G. "Characteristics of a Conditioned Response in Human Subjects During Extinction Trials Following a Single Traumatic Conditioning Trial." *Journal of Abnormal and Social Psychology,* 68 (1964): 627–639.

Campbell, D.T., and Stanley, J.C. *Experimental and Quasi-Experimental Designs for Research.* Chicago: Rand McNally, 1966.

Cappell, H., and Herman, C.P."Alcohol and Tension Reduction." *Quarterly Journal of Studies on Alcohol,* 33 (1972): 33–64.

Cautela, J.R. "Covert Sensitization." *Psychological Reports,* 20 (1967): 459–468.

Cautela, J.R. "The Treatment of Alcoholism by Covert Sensitization." *Psychotherapy: Theory, Research, and Practice,* 7 (1970): 86–90.

Cheek, F.E.; Franks, C.M.; Laucius, J.; and Burtle, V. "Behavior Modification Training for Wives of Alcoholics." *Quarterly Journal of Studies on Alcohol,* 32 (1971): 456–461.

Clancy, J.; Vanderhoff, E.; and Campbell, P. "Evaluation of an Aversive Technique as a Treatment of Alcoholism: Controlled Trial with Succinyl-choline-Induced Apnea." *Quarterly Journal of Studies on Alcohol,* 28 (1967): 476–485.

Cohen, M.C.; Liebson, I.A.; and Faillace, L.A. "A Technique for Establishing Controlled Drinking in Chronic Alcoholics." *Diseases of the Nervous System,* 33 (1972): 46–49.

Cohen, M.C.; Liebson, I.A.; Faillace, L.A.; and Speers, W. "Alcoholism: Controlled Drinking and Incentives for Abstinence." *Psychological Reports,* 28 (1971): 575–580.

Davidson, W.S. "Studies of Aversive Conditioning for Alcoholics: A Critical Review of Theory and Research Methodology." *Psychological Bulletin,* 81 (1974): 571–581.

Davies, D.L. "Normal Drinking in Recovered Alcohol Addicts." *Quarterly Journal of Studies on Alcohol,* 23 (1962): 94–104.

DeMorsier, G., and Feldmann, H. "Le traitment biologique de l'alcoolisme chronique par l'apomorphine. Etude de 200 cas." ("The Biological Treatment of Chronic Alcoholism with Apomorphine. Study of 200 cases.") *Schweizer Archiv fur Neurologie und Psychiatrie,* 65 (1950): 472–473.

Edlin, J.V.; Johnson, R.H.; Hletko, P.; and Heilbrunn, G. "The Conditioned Aversion Treatment of Chronic Alcoholism. Preliminary Report." *Archives of Neurology and Psychiatry,* 53 (1945): 85–87.

Elliott, C.H., and Denney, D.R. "Weight Control Through Covert Sensitization and False Feedback." *Journal of Consulting and Clinical Psychology,* 43 (1975): 842–850.

Farrar, C.H.; Powell, B.J.; and Martin, K.L. "Punishment of Alcohol Consumption by Apneic Paralysis." *Behaviour Research and Therapy,* 6 (1968): 13–16.

Freytag, F. "Psychodynamisms with Special Refernce to the Alcoholic." In R. Fox (ed.), *Alcoholism: Behavioral Research, Therapeutic Approaches.* New York: Springer, 1967.

Garcia, J.; McGowan, B.K.; and Green, K.F. "Biological Constraints on Conditioning." In A.H. Black and W.F. Prokasy (eds.), *Classical Conditioning II: Current Research and Theory.* New York: Appleton-Century-Crofts, 1972.

Gerard, D.L., and Saenger, G. *Outpatient Treatment of Alcoholism.* Toronto, Canada: University of Toronto Press, 1966.

Gerard, D.L.; Saenger, G.; and Wile, R. "The Abstinent Alcoholic." *Archives of General Psychiatry,* 6 (1962): 83–95.

Gordova, T.N., and Kovalev, N.K. "Unique Factors in the Hypnotic Treatment of Alcoholism." In R.B. Winn (ed.), *Psychotherapy in the Soviet Union.* New York: Philosophical Library, 1961, pp. 136–140.

Hallam, R.; Rachman, S.; and Falkowski, W. "Subjective, Attitudinal and Physiological Effects of Electrical Aversion Therapy." *Behaviour Research and Therapy,* 10 (1972): 1–13.

Hamburg, S. "Behavior Therapy in Alcoholism: A Critical Review of Broad Spectrum Approaches." *Journal of Studies on Alcohol,* 36 (1975): 69–87.

Higgins, R.L., and Marlatt, G.A. "The Effects of Anxiety Arousal on the Consumption of Alcohol by Alcoholics and Social Drinkers." *Journal of Consulting and Clinical Psyhology*, 41 (1973): 426–433.

Hill, M.J., and Blane, H.T. "Evaluation of Psychotherapy with Alcoholics: A Critical Review." *Quarterly Journal of Studies on Alcohol*, 28 (1967): 76–104.

Holzinger, R.; Mortimer, R.; and Van Dusen, W. "Aversion Conditioning Treatment of Alcoholism." *American Journal of Psychiatry*, 124 (1967): 246–247.

Hsu, J. "Electroconditioning Therapy of Alcoholics: A Preliminary Report." *Quarterly Journal of Studies on Alcohol*, 26 (1965): 449–459.

Hunt, G.M., and Azrin, N.H. "A Community-Reinforcement Approach to Alcoholism." *Behaviour Research and Therapy*, 11 (1973): 91–104.

Jacobson, E. *Progressive Relaxation*. Chicago: University of Chicago Press, 1938.

Kant, F. "Further Modifications in the Technique of Conditioned Reflex Treatment of Alcohol Addiction." *Quarterly Journal of Studies on Alcohol*, 5 (1944): 229–232.

Kant, F. "The Use of Conditioned Reflex in the Treatment of Alcohol Addicts." *Wisconsin Medical Journal*, 44 (1945): 217–221.

Kantorovich, N.V. "An Attempt of Curing Alcoholism by Associated Reflexes." *Novoye Refleksologii nervnoy i Fiziologii Sistemy*, 3 (1928): 436–445. Cited by G.H.S. Razran. "Conditioned Withdrawal Responses with Shock as the Conditioning Stimulus in Adult Human Subjects." *Psychological Bulletin,* 31 (1934): 111–143.

Kendell, L. "The Role of the Nurse in the Treatment of the Alcoholic Patient." In R. Fox. (ed.), *Alcoholism: Behavioral Research Therapeutic Approaches*. New York: Springer Publishing Co., Inc. 1967.

Kendell, R.E. "Normal Drinking by Former Alcohol Addicts." *Quarterly Journal of Studies on Alcohol*, 26 (1965): 247–257.

Lazarus, A.A. "Towards the Understanding and Effective Treatment of Alcoholism." *South African Medical Journal*, 39 (1965): 736–741.

Lazarus, A.A. *Behavior Therapy and Beyond*. New York: McGraw-Hill, 1971.

Lemere, F., and Voegtlin, W.L. "Conditioned Reflex Therapy of Alcoholic Addiction: Specificity of Conditioning Against Chronic Alcoholism." *California and Western Medicine*, 53 (1940): 268–269.

Lemere, F., and Voegtlin, W.L. "An Evaluation of the Aversion Treatment of Alcoholism." *Quarterly Journal of Studies on Alcoholism*, 11 (1950): 199–204.

Lovibond, S.H., and Caddy, G. "Discriminated Aversive Control in the Moderation of Alcoholics' Drinking." *Behavior Therapy*, 1 (1970): 437–444.

Lunde, S.E., and Vogler, R.E. "Generalization of Results in Studies of Aversion Conditioning with Alcoholics." *Behaviour Research and Therapy*, 8 (1970): 313–314.

McBrearty, J.F.; Dichter, M.; Garfield, Z.; and Heath. G. "A Behaviorally Oriented Treatment Program for Alcoholism." *Psychological Reports*, 22 (1968): 287–298.

MacCulloch, M.J.; Feldman, M.P.; Orford, J.F.; and MacCulloch, M.L. "Anticipatory Avoidance Learning in the Treatment of Alcoholism: A Record of Therapeutic Failure." *Behaviour Research and Therapy*, 4 (1966): 187–196.

Madill, M.F.; Campbell, D.; Laverty, S.G.; Sanderson, R.E.; and Vandewater, S.L. "Aversion Treatment of Alcoholics by Succinyl-Choline-Induced Apneic Paralysis." *Quarterly Journal of Studies on Alcoholism*, 27 (1966): 483–509.

Maletzky, B.M. "Assisted Covert Sensitization for Drug Abuse." *International Journal of the Addictions*, 9 (1974); 411–429.

Marlatt, G.A. "A Comparison of Aversive Conditioning Procedures in the Treatment of Alcoholism." Paper presented at the Western Psychological Association Annual Convention, Anaheim, California, April 1973.

Marlatt, G.A.; Demming, B.; and Reid, J.B. "Loss of Control Drinking in Alcoholics: An Experimental Analogue." *Journal of Abnormal Psychology*, 81 (1973): 233–241.

Mestrallet, A., and Lang, A. "Indications, techniques, et resultats du traitement par l'apormorphine de l'alcoolisme psychiatrique." ("Indications, technique, and results in apormorphine therapy of psychiatric alcoholism") *Le Journal de Medicine de Lyon*, 40 (1959): 279–285.

Miller, E.C.; Dvorak, B.A.; and Turner, D.W. "A Method of Creating Aversion to Alcohol by Reflex Conditioning in a Group Setting." *Quarterly Journal of Studies on Alcohol*, 21 (1960): 424–431.

Miller, M.M. "Treatment of Chronic Alcoholism by Hypnotic Aversion." *Journal of the American Medical Association*, 171 (1959): 1492–1495.

Miller, P.M. "The Use of Behavioral Contracting in the Treatment of Alcoholism: A Case Report." *Behavior Therapy*, 3 (1972): 593–596.

Miller, P.M., and Barlow, D.H. "Behavioral Approaches to the Treatment of Alcoholism." *Journal of Nervous and Mental Disease*, 157 (1973): 10–20.

Miller, P.M.; Hersen, M.; Eisler, R.M.; and Hemphill, D.P. "Effects of Faradic Aversion Therapy on Drinking by Alcoholics." *Behaviour Research and Therapy*, 11 (1973): 491–498.

Mills, K.C.; Sobell, M.B.; and Schaefer, H.H. "Training Social Drinking as an Alternative to Abstinence for Alcoholics." *Behavioral Therapy*, 2 (1971): 18–27.

Morosko, T.E., and Baer, P.E. "Avoidance Conditioning of Alcoholics." In R. Ulrich, T. Stachnich, and J. Mabry (eds.), *Control of Human Behavior, Vol. II*. Glenview, Illinois: Scott Foresman, 1970.

Narrol, H.G. "Experimental Application of Reinforcement Principles to the Analysis and Treatment of Hospitalized Alcoholics." *Quarterly Journal of Studies on Alcohol*, 28 (1967): 105–115.

O'Leary, K.D., and Wilson, G.T. *Behavior Therapy: Applications and Outcome*. Englewood Cliffs, N.J.: Prentice-Hall, 1975.

Orford, J. "A Comparison of Alcoholics Whose Drinking is Totally Uncontrolled and Those Whose Drinking Is Mainly Controlled." *Behaviour Research and Therapy*, 11 (1973): 565–576.

Pattison, E.M. "A Critique of Alcoholism Treatment Concepts with Special Reference to Abstinence." *Quarterly Journal of Studies on Alcohol*, 27 (1966): 49–71.

Pattison, E.M.; Headley, E.B.; Gleser, G.C.; and Gottschalk, L.A. "Abstinence and Normal Drinking: An Assessment of Drinking Patterns in Alcoholics After Treatment." *Quarterly Journal of Studies on Alcohol*, 29 (1968): 610–633.

Quinn, J.T., and Henbest, R. "Partial Failure of Generalization in Alcoholics Following Aversion Therapy." "*Quarterly Journal of Studies on Alcohol*, 28 (1967): 70–75.

Quirk, D.A. "Former Alcoholics and Social Drinking: An Additional Observation." *Canadian Psychologist*, 9 (1968): 498–499.

Rachman, S., and Teasdale, J. *Aversion Therapy and Behavior Disorders.* Coral Gables, Florida: University of Miami Press, 1969.

Raymond, M.J. "The Treatment of Addiction by Aversion Conditioning with Apomorphine." *Behaviour Research and Therapy*, 1 (1964): 287–291.

Regester, D.C. "Change in Autonomic Responsivity and Drinking Behavior of Alcoholics as a Function of Aversion Therapy." Paper presented at the American Psychological Association Annual Convention, Honolulu, Hawaii, September 2, 1972.

Rimm, D.C., and Masters, J.C. *Behavior Therapy: Techniques and Empirical Findings.* New York: Academic Press, 1974.

Rohan, W.A. "A Comparison of Two Aversive Conditioning Procedures for Problem Drinking." Unpublished Manuscript, 1970. Cited by P.A. Wisocki, "The Empirical Evidence of Covert Sensitization in the Treatment of Alcoholism: An Evaluation." In R.D. Rubin, J.D. Henderson, H. Fensterheim, and L.P. Ullmann (eds.), *Advances in Behavior Therapy.* New York: Academic Press, 1972.

Ruck, F. "Alkoholentziehungskur met hilfe eines bedingten reflexes." (Apmorphinentziehungskur). ("Conditioned reflex treatment of alcoholism.") *Psychiatrie, Neurologie, und Medizinische Psychologie*, 8 (1956): 88–92.

Sanderson, R.E.; Campbell, D.; and Laverty, S.G. "An Investigation of a New Aversive Conditioning Treatment for Alcoholism." *Quarterly Journal of Studies on Alcohol*, 24 (1963): 261–275.

Schaefer, H.H. "Twelve-Month Follow-up of Behaviorally Trained Ex-alcoholic Social Drinkers." *Behavior Therapy*, 3 (1972): 286–289.

Schaefer, H.H.; Sobell, M.B.; and Mills, K.C. "Baseline Drinking Behaviors in Alcoholics and Social Drinkers: Kinds of Drinks and Sip Magnitude." *Behaviour Research and Therapy*, 9 (1971): 23–27.

Shanahan, W.M., and Hornick, E.J. "Aversion Treatment of Alcoholism." *Hawaii Medical Journal*, 6 (1946): 19–21.

Silber, A. "Psychotherapy with Alcoholics." *Journal of Nervous and Mental Disease,* 129 (1959): 477–485.

Sobell, L.C., and Sobell, M.B. "A Self-Feedback Technique to Monitor Drinking Behavior in Alcoholics." *Behaviour Research and Therapy*, 11 (1973): 237–238.

Sobell, L.C.; Sobell, M.B.; and Christelman, W.C. "The Myth of 'One Drink'." *Behaviour Research and Therapy*, 10 (1972): 119–123.

Sobell, M.B., and Sobell, L.C. "Individualized Behavior Therapy for Alcoholics." *Behavior Therapy*, 4 (1973a): 49–72.

Sobell, M.B., and Sobell, L.C. "Alcoholics Treated by Individualized Behavior Therapy: One-Year Treatment Outcome." *Behaviour Research and Therapy*, 11 (1973b): 599–618.

Sobell, M.B., and Sobell, L.C. "Evidence of Controlled Drinking by Former Alcoholics: A Second Year Evaluation of Individualized Behavior Therapy." Paper presented at the American Psychological Association Annual Convention, Montreal, Canada, August 31, 1973(c).

Steiner, C.M. "The Alcoholic Game." *Quarterly Journal of Studies on Alcohol*, 30 (1969): 920–938.

Strel'chuck, I.V. "New Contemporary Methods of Treating Patients with Alcoholism." *Soviet Medicine*, 21 (1957): 26–33.

Sulzer, E.S. "Behavior Modification in Adult Psychiatric Patients." In L.P. Ullman and L. Krasner (eds.), *Case Studies in Behavior Modification*. New York: Holt, Rinehart, and Winston, 1965.

Thimann, J. "Conditioned Reflex Treatment of Alcoholism. II. The Risks of its Application, its Indication, Contraindications, and Psychotherapeutic Aspects." *New England Journal of Medicine*, 241 (1949): 406–410.

Voegtlin, W.L. "The Treatment of Alcoholism by Establishing a Conditioned Reflex." *American Journal of Medical Science*, 199 (1940): 802–810.

Voegtlin, W.L., and Lemere, F. "Treatment of Alcohol Addiction: A Review of the Literature." *Quarterly Journal of Studies on Alcohol*, 2 (1942): 717–803.

Voegtlin, W.L.; Lemere, F.; Broz, W.R.; and O'Hallaren, P. "Conditioned Reflex Therapy of Chronic Alcoholism. IV. A Preliminary Report on the Value of Reinforcement." *Quarterly Journal of Studies on Alcohol*, 2 (1941): 505–511.

Vogler, R.E.; Compton, J.V.; and Weissbach, T.A. "Integrated Behavior Change Techniques for Alcoholics." *Journal of Consulting and Clinical Psychology*, 43 (1975): 233–243.

Vogler, R.E.; Lunde, S.E.; Johnson, G.R.; and Martin, P.L. "Electrical Aversion Conditioning with Chronic Alcoholics." *Journal of Consulting and Clinical Psychology*, 34 (1970): 302–307.

Wallace, J.A. "The Treatment of Alcoholism by the Conditioned-Reflex Method." *Journal of the Tennessee Medical Association*, 42 (1949): 125–128.

Wallgren, H., and Barry, H. *Actions of Alcohol*, Vol. II. Amsterdam: Elsevier Publishing Company, 1970.

Weiner, H.B. "Psychodramatic Treatment for the Alcoholic." In R. Fox (ed.), *Alcoholism: Behavior Research, Therapeutic Approaches*. New York: Springer Publishing Company, Inc., 1967.

Wilson, G.T., and Davison, G.C. "Aversion Techniques in Behavior Therapy: Some Theoretical and Metatheoretical Considerations." *Journal of Consulting and Clinical Psychology*, 33 (1969): 327–329.

Wilson, G.T.; Leaf, R.C.; and Nathan, P.E. "The Aversive Control of Excessive Alcohol Consumption by Chronic Alcoholics in the Laboratory Setting. *Journal of Applied Behavior Analysis*, 8 (1975): 13–26.

Wilson, G.T., and Tracey, D.A. "The Effects of Imaginal Aversive Conditioning on Excessive Drinking by Chronic Alcoholics." Unpublished manuscript. Rutgers University, 1974. Cited in O'Leary, K.D., and Wilson, G.T. *Behavior Therapy: Applications and Outcome*. Englewood Cliffs, N.J.: Prentice-Hall, 1975.

Wisocki, P.A. "The Empirical Evidence of Covert Sensitization in the Treatment of Alcoholism: An Evaluation." In R.D. Rubin, J.D. Henderson, H. Fensterheim, and L.P. Ullmann (eds.), *Advances in Behavior Therapy*. New York: Academic Press, 1972.

Chapter Five

Perceptual and Cognitive Deficit in Alcoholics

Gerald Goldstein

The presence of psychological deficit in individuals with chronic alcoholism is readily observed. Many alcoholics cannot remember well, or become easily confused, or cannot control their gait and fine motor coordination. In cases of advanced alcoholism, these deficits are clearly seen in everyday behavior. In the earlier stages of chronic alcoholism, they are more subtle and sometimes require special tests to elicit. When the degree of impairment in the alcoholic patient becomes prominent, he may receive the diagnosis of "organic brain syndrome" or "alcoholic encephalopathy." Many researchers have attempted to specify in detail the nature of the alterations in behavior that appear to accompany advancing alcoholism, and to draw inferences concerning the relationship between these alterations and structural changes taking place in the brain. However, other investigators have focused their attention on the role certain perceptual and cognitive characteristics or styles play in the individual's becoming an alcoholic. Since these lines of investigation tend to take place independently of each other, situations have arisen in which the same behavioral phenomena are explainable on entirely different grounds. To the more organically oriented, the behavior is attributed to brain alterations consequent to alcoholism, while others may claim that the individual possessed the characteristic before he became an alcoholic, and indeed it was instrumental in making him one.

It is our purpose here to review some of the literature related to this controversy, and hopefully to draw some conclusions concerning the nature of psychological deficit in chronic alcoholics. We will not be dealing with the diagnostic or neurological aspects of the problem, which are covered elsewhere in this volume, but rather with the nature of the particular patterns of cognitive, perceptual, and motor behaviors that characterize the chronic alcoholic. In this review, we will emphasize programs of research carried on at the Veterans Administration Hospital, Topeka, Kansas, and the Center for Alcohol-Related Studies, University of Oklahoma, which address themselves to this specific question, but the context of research in which these programs developed will also be considered.

FIELD-DEPENDENCE-INDEPENDENCE

Many investigators have found that alcoholics tend to perceive the world in a way that is strongly dominated by the prevailing field. They rely more on the appearance of the perceptual environment than they do on internal cues in making judgments. The dimension of perception or of personality that has to do with reliance on internal or external sources of information has been studied in a wide variety of applications by Herman Witkin and his various collaborators (Witkin et al. 1954; Witkin et al., 1962). Individuals who tend to base their perceptions more on external cues are termed "field-dependent" while internal-ly-oriented perceivers are classed as "field-independent." The Witkin group's view is that degree of field dependence or independence reflects a dimension of personality termed "psychological differentiation." Greater differentiation is associated with field independence, while less differentiated people tend to be more field-dependent. While Witkin's entire theoretical framework cannot be presented here, there are two points that have particular reference to the problem of alcoholism. First, the establishment of field dependence/indepen-dence level in an individual takes place during childhood and remains stable during adulthood (Witkin, Goodenough, and Karp, 1967). Children tend to become increasingly field-independent up to age 17, but thereafter there is little change. Second, perceptual field dependency, or field dependency as measured by a series of perceptual-cognitive tests, is related to other aspects of behavior. Thus, the field-dependent person is psychologically dependent in other ways. He depends upon the social context to define himself, and has less of a sense of a separate identity than does the field-independent person. He responds in a more global, less differentiated way. For example, he uses more primitive defenses such as denial and repression, while field-independent people tend to use intellectualization and isolation. In other words, one can predict from level of perceptual dependency to more affective and social aspects of the personality.

The Witkin group has used a standard series of tests for assessing field dependency. They will be described briefly here. The first of them is the Rod and Frame Test (RFT). The subject sits in a darkened room and sees only a luminous rod surrounded by a frame. The frame is always tilted 28 degrees right or left, and the subject's task is to adjust the rod so that it is upright with the walls of the room. In doing so he must resist the distraction of the tilted frame. Sometimes the test is administered in a tilting chair, so that both the body of the subject and the frame may be tilted right or left. The test is scored in degrees of deviation of the adjusted rod from true vertical. The Body-Adjustment Test (BAT) is similar to the RFT, except that the person sits in a tilting room and must adjust his own body to true vertical. The Embedded Figures Test (EFT) consists of a series of simple geometric figures which the subject must find in more complex patterns. The EFT is scored in minutes of time to completion. Because of the elaborateness of the equipment involved in the BAT, investigators outside of Witkin's laboratory have tended to confine their studies to the RFT and EFT.

In a series of studies, the Witkin group explored the implications of field dependency for alcoholism. In the initial study (Witkin, Karp, and Goodenough, 1959) it was discovered that alcoholic males were extremely field-dependent as compared with the normal male. A subsequent study (Karp, Poster, and Goodman, 1963) indicated that alcoholic women also tend to be field-dependent. In additional studies, the Witkin group attempted to defend the view that this field dependence is not a product of the alcoholism itself, but rather, that it is there prior to acquisition of the alcoholism. Indeed, field dependence in a young person was suggested as a predictor of later development of alcoholism. Thus, to the Witkin group, the field dependence of the alcoholic is viewed like the field dependence of other groups; a manifestation of a broader dimension of personality that developed during childhood and adolescence. They reject the view that alcoholism is a special case in which the field dependence may be produced by brain damage or other nervous system impairment.

It is clear that the most direct way of defending this position would be through a longitudinal study in which it could be determined whether or not there is a higher incidence of alcoholism among individuals who were found to be field-dependent during young adulthood than among field-independent young adults. Since such a study was never accomplished, it has been necessary to take a more inferential approach. In one study (Karp, Witkin, and Goodenough, 1965a) it was hypothesized that if field dependence is directly related to the short-term effects of alcohol, then active alcoholics should be more field-dependent than recovered alcoholics. This situation was found not to be the case, supporting the view that field dependence is a consistent characteristic of alcoholics, and not simply a function of whether or not they are still engaging in excessive drinking. In another study (Karp and Konstadt, 1965) it was shown that degree of field dependence in alcoholics is unrelated to length of time drinking. A third study (Karp, Witkin, and Goodenough, 1965b) indicated no difference in degree of field dependence in alcoholics under conditions of sobriety or intoxication. These studies in combination suggest that the extreme field dependence of alcoholics is unrelated to the direct effect of the alcoholism, but rather reflects some stable, consistent trait that may antedate the acquisition of the alcoholism.

Numerous studies have been done in attempts to clarify the many issues raised by the Witkin group studies. In our own laboratory, we attempted to replicate the finding that alcoholics are more field-dependent than nonalcoholics as measured by the RFT (Goldstein and Chotlos, 1965). We were successful in doing so, in that we found highly significant differences on various conditions of the test between alcoholic subjects and a normal control group. Bailey, Hustmeyer, and Kristofferson (1961) also were able to document extreme field dependency in alcoholic subjects. Unpublished data collected over the years in Topeka from a large number of chronic alcoholic patients also reflect a high incidence of field-dependence, often of a very extreme degree. It now seems safe to say that the field dependence of the chronic alcoholic is a well-established finding, and although what it means is still unclear, it appears to be a frequently appearing perceptual-cognitive characteristic in alcoholics. In fact, it appears to be one among very few cognitive structure or personality characteristics alcoholics have in common, and which they exhibit as a relatively unique feature among psychopathological groups. In other words, field dependence has held up as a feature of alcoholism or the "alcoholic personality" more than have other traits or behaviors said to be commonly found among alcoholics. With regard to uniqueness, of all the psychopathological groups, only patients with brain damage tend to perform in the same range as alcoholics on tests of field dependence (Elliott, 1961).

We still lack the longitudinal study that could provide more definitive answers concerning the meaning of field dependence in alcoholics. The matter of whether it is an antecedent or a consequent is of particular importance because of the implications for our understanding of the etiology of alcoholism. Therefore, a number of investigators did follow-up investigations of the original Witkin group's research, in order to examine some of the conclusions reached on the basis of those studies. Much of this research was done by the Topeka group, and the following material contains a summary of what was hypothesized and concluded.

While Goldstein and Chotlos (1965) found that alcoholic males were significantly more field-dependent on the RFT than were normal controls, they also administered a number of tests that should have been field-dependence related, but that did not discriminate between alcoholics and normals. One of these measures was the Stroop Color-Word Interference Test. The test involves the rapid reading aloud of colors that are printed in the form of words. Each of the words is the name of a color, but the color name and the color in which the name is printed never correspond. For example, the word green may be printed in red ink. In this case the correct response would be red. Therefore the subject must name the color and ignore the interference provided by the word. The authors suggested that this task should be done poorly by field-dependent people, since it requires differentiation of a figure from an interfering context. For the same reason, delayed auditory feedback was also used. In this task, the subject reads a passage while listening to his own voice which is heard slightly delayed. In this case, the sound of one's own voice is the interfering stimulus.

Nonsignificant differences between alcoholics and normal controls were found for both of these procedures. Thus, the authors concluded that while alcoholics tend to be more field-dependent as measured by the RFT, other kinds of interference tasks do not discriminate between alcoholics and nonalcoholics.

This initial study apparently raised more questions than it answered, as attested to by the number of follow-ups done. One series of investigations related to whether or not there was something peculiar to the RFT itself that produced the discrimination between alcoholics and normals. Put another way, is there something about chronic alcoholism that engenders field-dependent performance on the RFT, but that is unrelated to developmentally acquired field dependence, and to other measures of field dependence? The Witkin group studies showed that RFT performance was unrelated to the direct effects of alcohol, since both active and recovered alcoholics were equally field-dependent, and ingestion of alcohol did not affect performance on tests of field dependence by alcoholic subjects. However, if one looks at the RFT situation, it is clear that accurate judgments require accurate knowledge of the position of the body in space. Judgments made while the subject is seated in a tilted position would seem to be particularly difficult to make without such knowledge. We generally think of the proprioceptive system in the cerebellum, and of the vestibular system, as the mediators of information concerning position in the absence of visual cues. It is well known that alcohol impairs, at least temporarily, the functioning of these mechanisms.

In a follow-up study (McCarthy, 1967; Goldstein et al., 1968) the issue of the role of proprioception was evaluated in the following way. A direct method of assessing proprioceptive skill was used, the Heath Railwalking Test (Heath, 1942). This procedure involves having the subject tandem walk along a series of rails of decreasing thickness. His score is based on the point at which he can no longer maintain his balance. A group of chronic alcoholics was administered this test and the RFT during the first week of a psychiatric treatment program. The only finding of relevance here involves the correlations between the two procedures. For the RFT tilted chair conditions, the correlations were statistically significant, but low. The Pearson r for the chair tilted left condition was -0.24 ($p<0.025/df = 70$), while for the chair tilted right position r was equal to -0.32 ($p<0.005/df = 70$). The correlation between railwalking and the seated upright condition was nonsignificant ($r = -0.15$; $p>0.05/df = 70$). These findings yield only weak support for the hypothesis that RFT performance is associated with level of proprioceptive skill. While there is some relationship, it only accounts for 6–10 percent of the variance. A great deal remains to be explained.

In a subsequent investigation, Goldstein, Neuringer, and Klappersack (1970) did a more extensive component analysis of the RFT task. They postulated that performance on the RFT requires a number of cognitive, perceptual and motor skills. These include the postural or proprioceptive abilities discussed above, but there is also the visual-postural skill of estimating the vertical while positioned in a tilted position, and the cognitive or analytic skills needed to deal with the distraction provided by the tilted frame, and in some conditions, the tilt of the body. Possibly, the difference between field dependent and field independent individuals has to do with differences in ability levels on one or more of these sets of skills. The authors also suggested that these differences may not be the same for alcoholics as they are for nonalcoholics. Measures of all of these component skills were selected. For postural orientation, the authors used the Heath Rails and a test in which the seated subject is slowly moved from a tilted position through an arc, and he indicates the point at which he feels that he is sitting exactly upright. The visual-postural measure involved judgment of the verticality of a luminous rod while seated in a tilted position; i.e., the Rod and Frame Test without the frame. The cognitive analytic measures were the Witkin Embedded Figures Test (EFT) and the Picture Completion, Block Design and Object Assembly subtests of the Wechsler Adult Intelligence Scale (Wechsler, 1955).

The design of the study constituted a four-group comparison; field-independent alcoholics, field-independent nonalcoholics, field-dependent alcoholics, and field-dependent nonalcoholics. Assignment as field-dependent or field-independent was based on performance on the RFT. Individuals with scores of 9 degrees or less deviation from verticality were classed as field-independent, while those with scores of 12 degrees or more were called field-dependent. The point of the study was to determine whether or not the differences found between field-dependent and field-independent alcoholics appear on the same tests as those that were found between field-dependent and field-independent nonalcoholics. In terms of the analysis of variance, this expectation translates to hypothesizing a significant interaction effect for certain of the measures. For example, if a significant interaction were found for railwalking in the expected direction it would mean that while field-independent and field-dependent alcoholics differ with regard to sense of balance, field-independent and field-dependent nonalcoholics do not differ from each other in this way.

The results of the study indicated that with one exception, the Wechsler Object Assembly subtest, the interactions hypothesized did not exist. Many differences were found between field-dependent and field-independent subjects, with a smaller number of differences between alcoholics and nonalcoholics regardless of field orientation. However, the abilities that separate field-independent alcoholics from field-dependent alcoholics appear to be the same ones that separate the corresponding nonalcoholic groups.

The findings of this study suggested that alcoholics were not field-dependent for some reason unique to them as a group, and more specifically tended to lend further disconfirmation to the explanation of alcoholic field dependence in terms of impaired proprioception. In essence, the studies reported thus far indicate (1) that while alcoholics tend to be field-dependent as measured by the RFT, they do not differ from normals on logically related interference tasks (the

Stroop Test and Delayed Auditory Feedback); and (2) the influence of proprioception in determining RFT performance is present but minimal. It was found that whether one is field-dependent or field-independent does seem to be related to level of ability on tasks of a cognitive-analytic nature, but this is as true for nonalcoholics as it is for alcoholics. Taking this into account, it would appear that there are two major possibilities. The first of them is since the cognitive and perceptual ability sources of field dependence are the same for alcoholics as they are for nonalcoholics, if field dependence/independence is a consistent stable style, then alcoholism can be seen as a form of psycho-pathology for which field dependence is a predisposing factor. This possibility is the one favored by the Witkin group. However, it is also possible that while the sources of field dependence in chronic alcoholics are essentially unrelated to impairment of proprioception, they may still be related to some other direct consequences of alcoholism.

In order to examine this question further, we will depart momentarily from studies of field dependence/independence done with alcoholics, and discuss two investigations of normal subjects. The first of them was done by Elliott (1961), who was interested in the relationship between field dependence on the one hand, and various abilities and personality characteristics on the other. Utilizing a battery of tests including the RFT, EFT, a block puzzle test, a finger maze which yielded an uncertainty measure, paper and pencil measures of psychologi-cal mindedness, self-concept differentiation and independence of judgment, and the ACE or SCAT Quantitative and Linguistic Scales, the investigator reached several conclusions of interest to us. First, he found that in normal subjects, field dependence as measured by the EFT is correlated with the ACE or SCAT measures of ability, but field dependence as measured by the RFT was uncorrelated with the ability measures. He also found that while the field-dependent person gave a more socially desirable picture of himself than did the field-independent person, none of the other measures of behavioral dependence was related to performance on the RFT or EFT. No relationship was found between degree of field dependence and measures of psychological mindedness, independence of judgment or self-concept differentiation. A third finding of interest was that the author's measures of uncertainty in unstructured situations were correlated with RFT performance, with more uncertain subjects being more field-dependent.

Elliott suggests that the correlates of field dependence are to be found more in the area of intellectual functioning than in that of personality. Indeed field dependence may be a form of intellectual deficit, and only secondarily related to the personality. In summarizing his study, Elliott concluded that field dependence appears to be associated with intellectual and emotional disruption as a response to situations that lack clear structure and instructions. The reason for citing this study is that if we think of the chronic alcoholic who may have sustained some degree of brain dysfunction, the Elliott formulation may be quite appropriate. That is, the alcoholic may not be field dependent because of some developmentally determined personality characteristic, but because his impaired intellectual abilities readily lead to disruption in situations of the type for which the RFT and EFT may be models.

Support for this view is offered by Reinking, Goldstein, and Houston (1974), who showed that RFT performance by normal subjects could be affected by the situational factors of induced stress and set, as well as by the cognitive-perceptual style of the individual taking test. Utilizing a complex analysis of variance design, these authors were able to separate out a number of factors that apparently influence the RFT performance of normal subjects. For example, inducing stress (threat of shock) was shown to make initially field-independent people more field-independent, and field-dependent people even more field-dependent. Thus, under stress conditions people appear to revert more deeply into their preferred cognitive styles. As a supplement to Elliott's proposition, it might be said that individuals who are field-independent and who are stressed when placed in an unstructured situation tend to become more extreme in their field orientation, as do field-dependent people. Reinking, Goldstein, and Houston also found that RFT performance can be influenced by the set given to the subject, with regard to whether he should focus on visual or body cues.

The point of reviewing these two papers is to show that performance on tests of field dependence/independence may be affected by a number of influences in addition to the individual perceptual-cognitive style. Now what does this have to do with the alcoholic? Simply that the field dependence of the alcoholic may be determined by numerous factors, and not only by his premorbid personality characteristics. The Elliott (1961) and Reinking, Goldstein, and Houston (1974) studies show how, in normal subjects, such factors as stress, uncertainty, set, and intellectual ability may all be affecting a subject's test performance at some particular time. Another implication coming from the Elliott study and from the Goldstein, Neuringer, and Klappersack (1970) study mentioned above is that performance on tests of field dependence/independence may be more related to cognitive than to personality variables. Tarter, Sheldon and Sugerman (1975) make this point even more clearly.

One of the Topeka studies took up the matter of the relationship between RFT performance and personality variables in alcoholic subjects (Goldstein et al. 1968). These investigators were interested in pursuing the Witkin group's view that field dependency in alcoholics is associated with more global aspects of dependency. The problem was approached directly by administering the RFT and a battery of objective tests of various aspects of dependency to a group of thirty chronic alcoholic inpatients. Essentially no relationship was found between RFT performance and measures of dependency. In this study, the measures used defined dependency in numerous ways. For example, the Edwards Personal Preference Schedule (Edwards, 1954) was used since it has measures of "deference" and "succorance." The MMPI Mf Scale was used as a measure of "femininity." Tests of "conformity" and "social acquiescence" were also used. In no case did degree of field dependence correlate with degree of dependency as measured by these tests. Indeed, a significant correlation was found between field dependence and a measure of dominance, a result that goes in the opposite direction to the hypothesis that field-dependent alcoholics are more interpersonally submissive individuals. Thus the Goldstein et al. (1968) study added a number of personality variables to the list of measures, also contributed to by Elliott (1961), with which RFT performance does not correlate.

To recapitulate, the finding that alcoholics tend to fall in the field-dependent range on several measures of perceptual-cognitive functioning appears to be well established. However, the explanation for this phenomenon is far from clear. To one group of investigators the field dependence in alcoholics is viewed as a predisposing factor present prior to acquisition of the alcohol addiction. To others, it is a manifestation of some specific consequence of alcoholism and/or situational variables that bear little relationship to the personality of the alcoholic or his cognitive style prior to his becoming an alcoholic. A longitudinal study that could provide some definitive resolution to this issue has not been accomplished. Thus, it has not been directly demonstrated that field-dependent individuals become alcoholics with greater frequency than do field-independent individuals, nor has this hypothesis been clearly refuted. Evidence can be found in a number of studies that used inferential methods in lieu of a longitudinal investigation to support either position.

One of the more viable alternatives to the Witkin group view involves a kind of toxicity hypothesis, in which perceptual-cognitive dependency is associated with the point in the alcoholic cycle at which the subject is tested. While the Witkin group demonstrated that level of field dependency remained stable despite differences in degree of sobriety, length of time drinking, and state of recovery, Goldstein and Chotlos (1966) found statistically significant changes in the direction of greater field independence in a group of chronic alcoholic inpatients who were administered the RFT before and after three months of hospitalization.

This finding was studied in greater detail by Chess, Neuringer, and Goldstein (1971) with a new group of alcoholic subjects and a normal control group. The RFT was administered weekly to both groups over a period of seven weeks. The initial mean score for the alcoholics was $12.7°$ deviation from vertical (SD = $8.6°$) while the equivalent score for the control group was $5.1°$ (SD = $2.3°$). Here again we see the greater amount of field dependence in the alcoholic group. However, for the seventh session the mean score for the alcoholics was $9.1°$ (SD = $8.7°$) while for the controls the mean was $4.5°$ (SD = $2.1°$). Thus, the alcoholics became more field-independent while the controls remained about the same. The change in the alcoholics as compared with the controls was statistically significant.

It would seem reasonable to infer that this change can be attributed to increasing detoxication. However, Jacobson (1968) was able to induce a significant change in alcoholic subjects on the RFT test following one hour of sensory isolation. Again the change was in the direction of reduction of field dependence. The author expressed the view that these results were produced by an increase in the availability and saliency of internal body sensation. Sensory deprivation is known to have the affect of altering body awareness. Jacobson's finding receives some verification from another result of the Chess, Neuringer, and Goldstein et al.(1971) study. These investigators found that as the RFT scores changed in the direction of reduced field dependence, there was a corresponding change on the Internal-External Locus of Control Scale (Rotter, 1966) in the direction of increased internal control. Thus, change in the direction of reduced field dependence appears to be associated with some change in perceived awareness and control of the self or body.

With regard to the detoxication hypothesis, three studies have shown that alcoholics can significantly alter their RFT performance over time, but the Jacobson (1968) study in which retesting was accomplished only an hour after the first testing casts some doubt on the view that the reduced field dependence can be attributed solely to maintenance of sobriety with gradual detoxication. It may be noted that patients were apparently not acutely intoxicated during any testing session in any of the three studies cited. Moreover, Karp, Witkin, and Goodenough (1965b) induced acute intoxication in their study, but obtained no change in RFT performance. The evidence would thus suggest that while alcoholics may exhibit reduced field dependence on serial testing with the RFT, it is unlikely that the change can be attributed to simple progressive detoxication. Certain changes in body awareness and/or perceived control over the body appear to be strongly contributing factors. It may be added that even if certain of the changes noted are simply manifestations of regression to the mean, they would still reflect relative instability of RFT performance in alcoholics.

Another related hypothesis concerning the nature of field dependence in alcoholics is also organically oriented, but views the matter in terms of chronic, structural brain damage. We will avoid the neuropsychological aspects of this hypothesis here as they will be dealt with in another chapter, but we will look at some studies involving the use of neuropsychological tests insofar as they are related to explicating the matter of field dependence. In its simplest form, the hypothesis is that alcoholics are field dependent because of the brain damage produced by some combination of excessive alcohol ingestion and malnutrition. The relative importance of malnutrition or vitamin deficiency as opposed to the effects of the alcohol itself, as well as the nature and location of the brain lesion remain basic research issues, but will not be dealt with here.

As mentioned previously, the extent of field dependence in the alcoholic is greater than in any other diagnostic group, with the one exception of patients with diffuse brain lesions. Teuber and Mishkin (1954) demonstrated that patients with focal brain lesions did more poorly at estimating verticality than did normals, and that subjects with frontal lobe lesions did more poorly than subjects with lesions in other brain loci, in the tilted chair situation. Welch,

Goldstein, and Shelly (1973) found that subjects with miscellaneous forms of brain damage showed more of a "starting position" effect than did normals or psychiatric patients. The "starting position" effect is the tendency to stop the rod in a different position depending on whether its movement begins from the right or left. Goldstein, Neuringer, and Klappersack (1970) included a brain damaged group in their study. This group performed in the clearly field dependent range on the RFT, and the authors noted that they were unable to acquire a group of field independent brain damaged subjects, apparently because of the extremely low incidence of field independence in brain damaged patients. Thus, the finding that both alcoholics and individuals with documented brain lesions tend to fall into an extreme range of field dependence has led some investigators to hypothesize that alcoholics are field dependent because they are brain damaged.

In an attempt to deal with this question, Goldstein and Shelly (1971) reasoned that if field dependence reflects the alcoholic's present mental status, then a measure of field dependence, the RFT, should correlate with scores derived from neuropsychological tests. If field dependence reflects a stable cognitive orientation, then there should be no correlation between RFT performance and performance on neuropsychological tests.

The essence of a good neuropsychological test is that it is sensitive to the present condition of the brain, such that performance levels fluctuate in correspondence with alterations in brain function. Tests that elicit stable performance levels despite alterations in brain function may be valuable for many purposes, but are not good diagnostic neuropsychological tests.

Goldstein and Shelly (1971) chose as their neuropsychological tests the battery of tests of biological intelligence devised by Halstead (1947) and modified and extensively researched by Reitan and various collaborators (Reitan, 1966; Reitan and Davison, 1974). This test battery is recognized as probably the most extensive and sensitive neuropsychological test battery in common use. This battery, the Wechsler Adult Intelligence Scale (WAIS) (Wechsler, 1955) and the RFT were administered to a group of 50 chronic alcoholic inpatients. The large number of variables generated were reduced through factor analysis, and the strategy of the study involved a determination of those factors upon which RFT loaded.

The findings can perhaps be best described as equivocal. The RFT loaded in a substantial way on only one of the five factors extracted. Only one neuropsychological test, the Trail Making Test, also had a substantial loading on this factor. In addition, a substantial loading was obtained on the factor by the Object Assembly Subtest of the WAIS. The major tests of the battery such as the Category and Tactual Performance Tests clearly did not load on the same factors as did the RFT. The investigators concluded that the RFT does not appear to be a test of biological intelligence, or put another way, is not correlated with many tests known to be sensitive to brain dysfunction.

The equivocality of findings in this study enters largely because the RFT does load on the same factor as the Trail Making Test. The Trail Making Test is a good neuropsychological test as defined above (Reitan, 1955, 1958) and is commonly used as a diagnostic test for brain dysfunction. For those unfamiliar with the test, it consists of two parts, A and B. In Part A the subject connects circled consecutive numbers randomly scattered over a sheet of paper. In Part B, there are circled numbers and letters on the sheet, and the subject must alternate between the two, going from number to letter to number, etc. Time to completion is the most commonly used score.

Why of all the measures of cognitive, perceptual and motor skill given in the study the Trail Making Test showed the strongest relationship with RFT is unclear. Nevertheless the commonality shared by the RFT and the Trail Making Test rules out the conclusion that the RFT is not associated with tests sensitive to brain dysfunction. It is not associated with large numbers of such tests, but the lack of association does not apply to all neuropsychological tests.

In a subsequent study done by Neuringer, Goldstein, and Gallaher (1975), a significant correlation between RFT performance and the Reitan modification of the Halstead Neuropsychological Test battery was found. In this study, the subjects were normals, and a single index derived from the total battery was correlated with the RFT score. Correlation coefficients were also computed for the RFT score against the various battery subtests. Interestingly, the Trail Making Test was not among the measures on which the correlation coefficient exceeded chance expectation.

These studies, among others cited previously, appear to reflect some tenuous connection between field dependence-independence and neuropsychological test performance. Based on this approach to the organic hypothesis, the view that alcoholics are field-dependent because of alcoholism induced brain damage cannot be unequivocally supported. It is possible that alcoholics are both brain damaged and field-dependent but that these dimensions are unrelated to each other. Thus, field dependence may be a relatively stable orientation that remains constant as various abilities progressively deteriorate in correspondence with the length and degree of alcoholism. On the other hand, the compelling finding that field dependence, often of an extreme degree, is commonly seen in individuals with many kinds of brain damage makes it difficult to give up on the organic hypothesis in the case of alcoholism. Furthermore, the evidence based on the studies reviewed above tends to be equivocal, sometimes favoring the premorbid disposition and sometimes the organic hypothesis.

The controversial and equivocal nature of the findings related to field dependence in alcoholics has tended to allow investigators having differing orientations to draw inferences derived from a number of theoretical bases. The one stable finding appears to involve the phenomenon itself. The predominance of field dependency among alcoholics has been independently demonstrated in at least three laboratories (Witkin, Karp, and Goodenough, 1959; Bailey, Hustmeyer, and Kristofferson, 1961; Goldstein and Chotlos, 1965). With regard to the stability of field dependency over time in alcoholics, the Topeka studies (Goldstein and Chotlos, 1966; Chess, Neuringer, and Goldstein, 1971) demonstrated reduction in field dependence following a period of sobriety, while Jacobson (1968) also demonstrated such a reduction following a period of sensory deprivation. On the other hand, the Witkin group has offered evidence to suggest that RFT performance remains stable over time in alcoholics (Karp, Witkin, and Goodenough, 1965a, b). With regard to generalizability of perceptual field dependence, Elliott (1961) found that it does not generalize to other personality variables in normal subjects, while Goldstein et al. (1968) found that it does not generalize to personality variables in alcoholics. Nevertheless the Witkin group reports that their evidence suggests that the perceptual dependency of the alcoholic reflects a global lack of differentiation in his entire personality structure.

Attempts to attribute the field dependence of alcoholics to neuropsychological or personality related phenomena have shared a similar fate. The explanation in terms of personality dynamics faces the absence of a longitudinal study and the lack of evidence for generalization of perceptual dependence to personality variables cited above, while the organic or neuropsychological hypothesis suffers from lack of substantial correlation between RFT performance and tests known to be sensitive to the condition of the brain. As pointed out above, field dependence and organic deficits may exist concurrently in alcoholics, but the available evidence does not rule out the possibility that these phenomena are unrelated.

An important implication of the failure to make a distinction between the organic and personality hypothesis is that we still do not know whether field dependence is an antecedent or consequent of the alcoholic process. A derivative of this implication is that if the personality or antecedent hypothesis is correct, then there may be an alcoholic or pre-alcoholic personality. Indeed, it would be possible to predict with some certainty whether or not a young adult may become an alcoholic on the basis of his field orientation. As is well known in the field, the search for an alcoholic personality has been discouraging, with little evidence that some particular personality configuration makes one alcoholism prone. On the other hand, the organic hypothesis makes no assumptions concerning an alcoholic personality, but rather assumes that the effects of the alcoholism process itself tends to make individuals who may have been quite disparate at one time, acquire increasingly more of those characteristics that identify him as an alcoholic.

At present, we are particularly impressed with the consistency with which RFT performance correlates with intellectual variables of a particular type. Indeed, Witkin uses an intellectual measure, the Embedded Figures Test, as an index of field orientation. Goldstein et al. (1968) obtained a substantial correlation between RFT score and general intelligence. High correlations between RFT and tests of the Block Design type have been found in numerous studies, (e.g., Witkin, 1960). Thus, from the point of view of what it correlates with and what it does not correlate with, it would appear that the RFT is more a test of nonverbal problem solving ability than of personality dynamics. Apparently, the RFT presents a problem to the subject in which he must take into account the position of the frame and of his body in order to determine where the rod must be to be vertical. Alcoholics apparently tend to be deficient in this type of ability. Earlier, the Topeka group thought that this may have been because of impairment of proprioception particularly with regard to the position of the body in space, but they later found that this factor appears to be relatively insignificant in comparison with the problem solving aspect of RFT performance. Alcoholics do have proprioceptive difficulties as is well known, but there seems to be only a minimal relationship between such phenomena as gait instability and perception of body position, and performance on the RFT (McCarthy, 1967; Goldstein, Neuringer, and Klappersack, 1970). If RFT performance does correlate with cognitive variables and does not correlate with personality variables it would appear to be reasonable to view the RFT as a measure of a particular kind of cognitive ability. It would follow from the evidence cited that the level of this ability does not necessarily covary with the degree to which the individual is a dependent person in social and interpersonal situations.

A difficulty with the above analysis is that it does not address itself to the issue of whether deficient nonverbal problem solving ability is an antecedent or consequent of alcoholism. While it is true that the way in which the deficiency is described resembles descriptions often made of individuals with brain lesions, it is also reasonable to hypothesize that young adults with poor problem solving ability are more likely to become alcoholics than are young adults with good problem solving ability. Dr. Tarter discusses this hypothesis in his chapter.

It is our current view that no amount of neurological speculation and no accumulation of inferential studies will answer this question in the absence of longitudinal data. In effect, it is our belief that field dependence in alcoholics is a form of cognitive deficit rather than a manifestation of some personality pattern characteristic of alcoholics. However, the many disparate and inconclusive findings in the research accomplished thus far has not answered the question of whether this cognitive deficit antedated acquisition of the alcoholism or is a consequence of the brain dysfunction produced by it.

While the material on reduction of field dependence on serial testing (Goldstein and Chotlos, 1966; Jacobson, 1968; Chess, Neuringer, and Goldstein, 1971) tends to favor the consequence hypothesis, Bailey, Hustmeyer, and Kristofferson (1961) and Jacobson, Pisani, and Berenbaum (1970) did not find such reduction with increasing sobriety. Even in the studies that obtained reduction in field dependence, the magnitude of change, though statistically significant, was relatively small, and the Chess, Neuringer, and Goldstein (1971) study found that even at the last session, the alcoholics were substantially more field dependent than were the controls at the first testing. The mean score for the alcoholics on the final testing was 9.1° (SD = 8.7°) while the mean for the controls was 5.1° (SD = 2.3°) on first testing. Thus, the changes found should not be taken to indicate that initially field dependent subjects were transformed into field independent subjects. While it is true that the difference between these mean values is not statistically significant ($t = 1.53$; $df = 24, p > 0.05$), the absence of significance can probably be attributed to the variability found in the alcoholic group. This high degree of variability relative to the controls suggests that alcoholics are not as uniformly field dependent as normal males are field independent. This variability can be seen as providing additional equivocality to field dependence in alcoholism research.

ABILITY CONFIGURATIONS

As indicated in the preceding section, a difficulty with the field dependence/independence research has been the lack of success in placing it into some context. The knowledge that alcoholics tend to be field-dependent could not be incorporated effectively into some larger body of knowledge about alcoholics. We suspect that comparable analysis of any single variable will have the same fate, and so an attempt will now be made to look at the research findings from the point of view of configurations rather than through the more traditional categories of general intelligence, cognitive processes, perception, memory, etc.

As a preliminary working hypothesis concerning perceptual and cognitive structure in alcoholics we would provide the following formulation. The alcoholic maintains those kinds of abilities that would contribute to the appearance of intactness in many of the situations of everyday living, but he also has more subtle deficits in complex abilities that may provide substantial difficulties in situations in which high level adaptive functioning is required. Situations of this type often involve such capacities as planning, foresight and the ability to make the appropriate decision on the basis of available evidence. This hypothesis would be consistent with Elliott's (1961) formulation of field dependence in terms of disruption as a response to unstructured situations. We believe it is also consistent with the material to be reviewed below.

One of the more seminal studies involving a configurational approach to psychological deficit in alcoholics was done by Fitzhugh, Fitzhugh, and Reitan (1960). These authors evaluated groups of alcoholic, brain damaged and control subjects with a large number of tests including the Wechsler-Bellevue Intelligence Scale, Form I, (Wechsler, 1944), seven of the Halstead biological intelligence measures and the Trail Making Test. Twenty-five measures derived from these tests were utilized in the data analyses. The investigators, like Halstead (1947) before them, made a distinction between tests of general or psychometric intelligence, and tests sensitive to the condition of the brain, which Halstead called tests of biological intelligence. Operationally, the Wechsler-Bellevue would be classed as a test of psychometric intelligence, while the Halstead tests and the Trail Making Test are defined as measures of biological intelligence. The results of the study appeared to bear out the utility of this distinction in that on the Wechsler-Bellevue, the performance of the alcoholic group was more like that of the controls than like that of the brain damaged group, while on the Halstead and Trail Making Tests, the performance level of the alcoholic group was more similar to that of the brain damaged group than it was to the control group. In order to verify these findings, this study was replicated with a larger group of subjects (Fitzhugh, Fitzhugh, and Reitan, 1965). Essentially the same results were obtained.

Evaluation of our working hypothesis in the light of these studies requires some examination of the individual tests. In general Halstead's concept of psychometric intelligence can be equated with what we have described as those abilities that would contribute to the appearance of intactness in everyday living situations. These tests tend to be verbal in content, related to past learning, and are largely measures of long-term memory. In clinical parlance, high level performance on tests of this type with relatively poor performance elsewhere is frequently described as a "good verbal facade." The verbal subtests of the Wechsler-Bellevue, most notably Information, Comprehension and Vocabulary, are good examples of such tests. The performance subtests of the Wechsler-Bellevue share this characteristic to a somewhat lesser extent, but examination of these so-called performance tests quickly reveals that several of them require extensive verbal mediation. For example, Picture Completion requires knowledge of the depicted object from past learning, and the most efficient way of identifying the missing part is by naming it. Similarly, Digit Symbol requires reading of numbers, a language related or verbal ability. In general, when tasks of this at least partially verbal, past-learning-dependent type are presented to the alcoholic, he tends to look very much like the normal person.

When we present the alcoholic with tests of biological intelligence, an entirely different picture is obtained. In general, there would be a correspondence between the biological intelligence concept and what we have referred to as the complex adaptive abilities of which planning, foresight, and decision-making are aspects. Unlike the preponderance of tests on the Wechsler-Bellevue Scales, the Halstead tests tend to be nonverbal and generally cannot be dealt with effectively by recourse to past learning and long-term memory. Several of the tests require that the subject solve problems of a novel type utilizing information provided in the test situation itself. On the one hand, all the information needed for solution is given, while on the other, information brought to the situation by the subject in the form of past memory and learning is of relatively little value for problem solution.

A good example of this kind of procedure is Halstead's Category Test. The Category Test utilizes sets of geometric forms that are related to each other by some principle or concept. The subject's task is that of learning the concept through a system whereby he is informed as to whether he got the right or wrong answer for each trial of the series. A chime sounds every time the answer is correct, and a buzzer sounds after a wrong answer. In this way, the subject may test hypotheses concerning the correct concept and evaluate them against the feedback received.

Goldstein and Scheerer (1941) identified the ability to perform this kind of task, calling it the abstract attitude. Essentially, it involves the capacity to derive a concept or principle that unites entities that may vary in many ways. Numerous studies have shown that alcoholics tend to be exceptionally poor abstract reasoners. It is interesting to note that in the Fitzhugh, Fitzhugh, and Reitan studies (1960, 1965) the alcoholic group not only did worse than the control group on the Category Test, but also did worse than the group of patients with established brain damage.

The impairment of abstraction ability in alcoholics has been examined in detail (Jones and Parsons, 1971, 1972, 1975; Tarter, 1971; Tarter and Parsons, 1971; Pishkin, Fishkin, and Stahl, 1972) utilizing the Halstead Cateory Test and other measures of abstraction ability, notably the Wisconsin Card Sorting Test (Grant and Berg, 1948). These investigators were able to document the impairment of abstract reasoning ability found in alcoholics by Fitzhugh, Fitzhugh, and Reitan (1960, 1965) but attempted to go further in eliciting the specific nature of the deficit. According to these investigators, the Card Sorting data indicated that the particular deficit that seemed to characterize the alcoholic was a disability in shifting from one concept to another. In these studies, this conceptual shifting defect was shown to be of greater significance than ther perseverative type of error making seen in some brain damaged patients (Milner, 1963), and the ability to acquire concepts, as seen in many kinds of brain damaged patients. The performance of alcoholic subjects in these studies was characterized by difficulties in flexibility and persistence in adhering to new strategies, but not in acquiring simple concepts or in perseveration of previously correct responses. These investigators also maintain that the abstraction deficit seen in alcoholics is specific to visual-spatial stimuli, and is not a generalized deficit (Jones and Parsons, 1972).

The impairment of abstraction ability is an example of a subtle cognitive deficit that may not be readily apparent, but that may have significant consequences for the life course of an inidividual. Another related ability is tapped by Halstead's Tactual Performance Test. The stimulus material for this test is a modified version of the Seguin-Goddard Formboard, which the subject must complete while blindfolded. After completing the task with the preferred hand, nonpreferred hand, and both hands, the subject must attempt to draw the board from memory, reproducing as many of the blocks as he can recall, if possible in their proper locations on the board. In the Fitzhugh, Fitzhugh, and Reitan studies (1960, 1965) the alcoholic group achieved a performance level that was about midway between the brain damaged and control groups. Thus, while the alcoholics showed deficit on this test, it was not of the magnitude shown on the Category Test.

The Tactual Performance Test is frequently described as a measure of psychomotor problem solving ability. The subject must plan an efficient strategy to deal with the task in the time available, and execute the plan in an efficient manner. For most people the task is a novel one, since it is unusual to solve a complex problem with tactile perception as the major source of information. The reason for alcoholics doing relatively better on this test than on the Category Test is unclear, and further analysis of this pattern would be of interest. In any event, alcoholics do poorly on this test relative to controls though not as poorly as individuals with documented brain lesions.

In contrast with the Category and Tactual Performance Tests, the performance of the alcoholic group on the Wechsler-Bellevue verbal subtests was much like that of the control group, and quite discrepant from that of the brain damaged group. The same can be said for the performance tests, but to a lesser extent. Inspection of the Fitzhugh, Fitzhugh, and Reitan (1965) data reveals different performance subtest patterns among the alcoholic, control, and brain damaged groups. While the reliability of these patterns would require further evaluation, they are of interest for purposes of preliminary discussion. Two features appear to be particularly striking. The alcoholics did slightly better than the controls on the Picture Arrangement subtest, but significantly ($p < 0.02$) less well than the controls on Block Design. Thus, while the Wechsler-Bellevue performance of alcoholics may be more like that of normals than like brain damaged subjects, the performance subtest pattern differs among the three groups studied. Most prominently, the alcoholics showed deficient performance on the Block Design subtest relative to the controls, although they did better than the brain damaged subjects on Block Design, along with the other subtests.

Returning to the neuropsychological tests, while the performance of the alcoholic group was generally more like that of the brain damaged group than like that of the controls, there was one notable exception; the finger tapping test. On finger tapping, the alcoholics not only did better than the brain damaged group, but they also did slightly better than the controls. Thus, the alcoholic performance on the Halstead tests and the Trail Making Test can be characterized in a relative way as exceptionally poor on the Category Test and mediocre on the remaining tests with the exception of the finger tapping test, which is done exceptionally well. Putting all of this information together, the results of the Fitzhugh, Fitzhugh, and Reitan (1960, 1965) studies indicate selective performance deficit in the alcoholic group. While the miscellaneous brain damaged group tended to show relative deficit in all areas tested, and the control group showed relative intactness in all areas, the alcoholics exhibited a performance pattern that differentiated them from both of the other groups.

To what extent does this pattern fit our distinction between abilities that create the appearance of intactness and complex adaptive abilities? On the basis of the Wechsler-Bellevue data, it could be inferred that the alcoholic would be indistinguishable from the normal person on the basis of ordinary verbal interchange. Parenthetically, it is just this characteristic that may be deceptive in assessing the capabilities of the alcoholic patient. On the basis of the finger tapping data, the alcoholic, at least while sober, would not display any detectable motor abnormality. Thus, he would not look like many brain damaged individuals who have gross, readily observable motor impairments. On the other hand, performance on tests of more complex abilities gives an entirely different picture. The alcoholic turns out to be an exceptionally poor abstract reasoner, and his capacity to solve complex problems approaches that of the brain damaged patient with regard to severity of deficit. It might be appropriate to point out here, as others have done, that the intelligence quotient (IQ) may be highly deceptive if used by itself as an index of cognitive functioning. In the studies being reviewed, the mean full scale IQ of the brain damaged group was 99.51; for the controls it was 113.34 and for the alcoholic, 109.26. Thus, on the basis of these scores all groups would be within the average range of intelligence. However, the neuropsychological tests revealed outstanding differences among these groups with regard to level and pattern of cognitive functioning.

To tie up some loose ends, we will return to the matter of the intergroup discrepancies in Picture Arrangement and Block Design. With regard to the high Picture Arrangement, while there is no direct empirical evidence to support this view, on a clinical basis Picture Arrangement is thought to be more a measure of knowledge of social conventions and expectations, than of visual-spatial problem solving ability. It apparently requires a good deal of verbal mediation. Factor analytic studies have supported this view (Goldstein and Shelly, 1971, 1972; Matarazzo, 1972) in that Picture Arrangement, Picture Completion and Digit Symbol have higher loadings on "verbal" or "language comprehension" factors than do Block Design and Object Assembly. The alcoholic is generally characterized clinically as having good, if superficial, knowledge of social conventions. The Block Design finding has more empirical backing. Numerous investigators (Grassi, 1953; Jonsson, Cronholm, and Izikowitz, 1962; Claeson and Carlsson, 1970; Goldstein, Neuringer, and Klappersack, 1970) have found alcoholics to be deficient on this task.

As a partial replication and extension of the Fitzhugh, Fitzhugh, and Reitan (1960, 1965) studies, Goldstein and Shelly (1971) administered the Wechsler Adult Intelligence Scale (WAIS), the Trail Making Test, the RFT, five of Halstead's neuropsychological tests, the Reitan-Heimburger aphasia screening test, and a test of various perceptual disorders developed by Reitan and his collaborators to a group of fifty chronic alcoholic inpatients. The part of this study related to the RFT was reviewed above. Here we will focus on the other tests. It should be noted that this study was not controlled, in that only alcoholic subjects were tested. However, some tentative comparisons with available norms were made through converting raw test scores to a five-point rating scale ranging from excellent and normal performance through mild and moderate impairment to severe impairment. Of course, the WAIS results could be compared with the published norms (Wechsler, 1955).

In general, the findings were consistent with those of the Fitzhugh, Fitzhugh, and Reitan studies. The IQ of the alcoholic group was in the average range, but impairment was found on the neuropsychological tests. Again, the Category Test was not done well by the subjects. Thus, there is evidence for impairment on this test coming from three sets of investigators (Fitzhugh, Fitzhugh, and Reitan, 1960, 1965; Jones and Parsons, 1971, 1972; Goldstein and Shelly, 1971). It appears to be a stable finding. Again in correspondence with the Fitzhugh et al. studies, Goldstein and Shelly (1971) found normal finger tapping speed, and in addition, normal performance on test of elementary perceptual skills. Thus, the alcoholic would be seen as having not only normal motor skill, but also no apparent impairment of sensory function. This finding would lend support to the part of our hypothesis having to do with the appearance of intactness. Aside from the Category Test, mild to moderate degrees of impairment were found for most of the other Halstead tests and the Trail Making Test. On the WAIS performance scales, Goldstein and Shelly (1971) did not find Picture Arrangement to be higher than Block Design, but it is possible that differences between the WAIS and the Wechsler-Bellevue may have contributed to this discrepancy. In general, however, there was generally good agreement among the studies.

Goldstein and Shelly (1971) went on to factor analyze their data, and obtained a five-factor structure. The factors were described as verbal, abstraction/problem solving, perceptual and motor skills, memory for spatial relations, and numerical. The subjects tended to do better at tasks loading on the verbal and numerical factors, and relatively worse on the other factors. The task the subjects did worst on, the Trail Making Test, loaded heavily on the same factor as did the Category Test, the Tactual Performance Test, Block Design, Object Assembly, and Perceptual Disorders. It is interesting to note that the distinction made between verbal, long-term memory dependent abilities as opposed to complex abstraction and problem solving abilities is a distinction also made by the quantitative method of factor analysis.

It would appear that the studies we have been reviewing provide a reasonably tenable perceptual-cognitive description of the alcoholic. His characteristics have some resemblance to that of the normal person and some resemblance to the brain damaged patient. There seems little question that alcoholism is associated with some form of cognitive deficit. The remaining problems involve describing its characteristics, discovering its specific etiology and attempting to understand the implications it has for such matters as treatment, course, recovery and related matters.

One additional study may shed some light on a finding that was consistent in the Fitzhugh, Fitzhugh, and Reitan (1960, 1965) and Goldstein and Shelly

(1971) studies. We have reference to the presence of normal finger tapping speed. This finding in isolation may appear to be of little consequence, but in combination with other findings may be of interest.

Vivian, Goldstein, and Shelly (1973) based a study on the finding that while tapping speed was normal in alcoholics, motor tasks that required perceptual guidance and coordination were not performed normally. Good examples of this latter type of task are the Trail Making Test and the Digit Symbol subtest of the Wechsler scales. While these tasks are perceptual-motor coordination measures, they also measure other functions of a more cognitive nature. Thus, the authors used simpler tests, a reaction time and a tracing task, as their indices of perceptual-motor function.

The findings were consistent with previous results. The alcoholics did not differ from the normal controls on tapping, but highly significant differences were found for reaction time and tracing. The authors suggested that a pattern that appears in the alcoholic is preserved motor function in association with impaired ability to integrate perceptual information with motor output.

It may be pointed out that not all studies done in this area arrived at the same conclusion. Tarter and Jones (1971) using the tapping test, a hand dynamometer and the Purdue Pegboard came to quite different conclusions. They, first of all, found slower tapping speed among their alcoholic subjects than among their controls. In this regard it is interesting to note that the mean right hand tapping speed found for alcoholics (47.7 taps/10 sec.) was quite close to what was found by Vivian, Goldstein, and Shelly (1973), (49.5). However, while the Vivian et al. normals obtained a mean of 50.8, Tarter and Jones' controls obtained a mean of 54.5. Thus, in the case of the Tarter and Jones study, a question may be raised regarding whether the alcoholics were unusually slow or the controls unusually fast.

In answering this question, it might be useful to look at normative studies of the finger tapping test. Klove (1974) reviews a number of such studies (Halstead, 1947; Vega and Parsons, 1967; Klove, 1974) which show that finger tapping with the dominant hand ranges from 54.9 to 43 taps in control subjects. The mean for Tarter and Jones' alcoholics was 47.7, which was significantly slower than their control group, but well within the range of control group scores reported by various normative studies. Assuming reasonable uniformity or procedure, it would appear that relative to the range of normal function, the alcoholic cannot be described as substantively impaired in the area of motor speed, as measured by Halstead's tapping test. More interesting perhaps was Tarter and Jones' (1971) finding that perceptual-motor coordination, as evaluated by the Purdue Pegboard, was intact in their alcoholic subjects following a period of detoxication. The improvement was not seen in tapping speed or in strength of grip. Thus, to these investigators, impairment of motor speed and muscle strength is a relatively stable consequence of alcoholism, while perceptual-motor coordination and speed impairment is transient in nature, and essentially disappears following detoxication.

This hypothesis is difficult to respond to since all of the studies cited thus far except that of Tarter and Jones (1971), (Fitzhugh, Fitzhugh, and Reitan, 1960; 1965; Goldstein and Shelly, 1971; Vivian, Goldstein, and Shelly, 1973) did not involve testing before and after detoxication. Furthermore, a variety of tests and procedures were used to evaluate perceptual motor coordination; tracing, reaction time, Digit Symbol, Purdue Pegboard, etc. It would have been interesting to see the results, had Vivian et al. retested their recently admitted alcoholics following a period of detoxication. In any event, the Tarter and Jones (1971) study again raises the issue of stability of function in the alcoholic, and reminds us that phenomena observed at some particular time and under certain conditions need not be static and immutable, but may vary from time to time and condition to condition. Numerous lines of evidence suggest that the behavioral correlates of alcoholism are frequently associated with the point in the alcoholic cycle at which the behavior sample is taken. Obviously, a great deal of further research is needed in order to differentiate between the relatively stable and the transient deficits associated with alcoholism. This issue will be returned to in a later section of this chapter.

In summarizing this discussion of ability configurations in alcoholics, it can be said that there appear to be certain relatively consistent patterns seen in alcoholics as a group. This pattern has a contemporary and a temporal dimension which differentiates it from what is seen in other diagnostic groups. There appears to be general agreement about the pattern of well-preserved "psychometric intelligence" in contrast with substantially impaired abstract reasoning and complex problem solving abilities. The status of various levels of motor function is somewhat controversial, but there is general agreement that there is some form of motor disorder. Whether pure motor speed and strength are implicated, or the disorder is restricted to higher level perceptual-motor function remains unresolved.

Contrasts have been made between the alcoholic and the non-alcoholic subject, and between alcoholics and subjects with documented brain damage from causes other than alcoholism. In general, the alcoholic falls in between, in that he does not show the uniform impairment seen in groups of subjects with miscellaneous forms of brain damage, but he does show distinct deficits when compared with the normal individual. The temporal dimension of the pattern suggests that characteristic behavior patterns in the alcoholic may be described as semipermanent in that some performance levels remain stable while others fluctuate in apparent correspondence with various positions in the alcoholism cycle.

Much research has been done with chronic alcoholics shortly after admission to the psychiatric unit of a hospital. However, as is well known, alcoholics are also seen on neurology services, general medical services, in the emergency room, and in the community. Generalizations made from the recent admission to a psychiatric program to alcoholics seen in these other settings is somewhat questionable. The following section briefly deals with this issue.

TEMPORAL STABILITY OF PERFORMANCE LEVELS

By its nature, alcoholism is a fluctuating process and is generally viewed as a cycle with poles of sobriety and acute intoxication. In this respect it is unlike many other neurological and/or psychiatric illnesses, since such illnesses are often characterized by stability, progressive deterioration or permanent recovery. Even within an alcoholic episode, behavior changes with changes in the blood level of alcohol (e.g., Tarter et al., 1971). It is apparent that overlaying these episodic cycles in the alcoholic is a slower-moving cycle covering large portions of the life span. Thus, the alcoholic has his relatively good and bad periods, but as long as the alcoholism is maintained the general course is in the direction of deterioration. The course seems to involve intoxication followed by recovery, but the recovery is never a complete return to the pre-intoxicated state. Thus, there is the acute deterioration associated with a drinking episode, but a slower deterioration that takes place across episodes and reflects the chronic, permanent component of the alcoholism process.

What is the evidence for this viewpoint? One line of evidence comes from the serial testing of alcoholics, generally before and after detoxication. We have just reviewed such a study (Tarter and Jones, 1971) in which it was shown that alcoholics improved on the Purdue Pegboard following a period of intoxication, but not on tests of motor speed or grip strength. In the section on field dependence-independence several studies were reviewed involving reduction of field dependence by alcoholics on retesting.

A third type of study involving a different modality will be reviewed here. The study was done in the Topeka VA Hospital laboratory by Goldstein et al. (1968). It involved the disturbance of gait frequently observed in intoxicated individuals, and utilized the Heath Railwalking Test, described above (cf., Heath, 1942). In this study, alcoholic subjects were found to have significantly impaired railwalking skill relative to controls. Following this initial testing, the alcoholic group was divided into two subgroups. One subgroup repeated the railwalking test every day for a period of twenty days, while the other subgroup only railwalked at the initial testing and on the twentieth day. The results were that at the end of twenty days both subgroups improved significantly, but the group that practiced railwalking improved significantly more than the group that did not. Indeed, the twentieth day performance level of the practice group was almost identical to that of the normal control group. Thus, practice plus detoxication brought the alcoholics up to a level obtained by nonalcoholics without such practice. Detoxication alone was associated with improvement, but not a return to normal level functioning. Tarter et al. (1971) also demonstrated that practice tends to overcome the adverse influence of alcohol on performance on a variety of cognitive and perceptual tests.

Findings from the field dependence, motor function, and railwalking studies all support the view that there is some recovery of function in alcoholics following a period of detoxication. In the case of the study by Chess, Neuringer, and Goldstein (1971) in which a control was run, it was shown that these changes could not be attributed to previous experience with the test; that is, the performance of the alcoholics changed on serial retesting, while that of the controls remained stable. The current issues seem to involve the extent of recovery, its nature, and the influence of practice. In the research literature, full recovery appears to be associated with absence of a significant difference from a control group, when such a difference appeared previously. This convention is similar to the one used in medical practice in the case in which a pathological laboratory finding changes from the abnormal range to within normal limits.

Granting the acceptability of this procedure, the studies reviewed would suggest that perceptual-motor function, as measured by the Purdue Pegboard, recovers fully following detoxication, but degree of field dependence following detoxication, while substantially reduced, does not approach the level of field independence found among controls. Railwalking performance only reaches a normal level with practice. It would be of great interest and import to do serial testing on a variety of cognitive and perceptual tests, in order to delineate the nature and extent of recovery.

There is evidence that the reason for recovery from behavioral deficits does not stem from detoxication alone. The finding of Jacobson (1968), who significantly reduced field dependence following one hour of sensory isolation, should be considered, as well as the data on the effects of practice. The Jacobson finding could hardly be attributed to one hour of detoxication, while the findings of Goldstein et al. (1968) suggest that practice interacts with detoxication in determining degree of improvement.

We can only draw the preliminary conclusion that recovery appears to involve the detoxication process, the organic condition of the subject at the time of detoxication, and certain behavioral changes related to learning and attitudinal variables. In some cases, the extent of recovery reaches the criterion of no significant difference from normal, while in other cases, degree of recovery is significant but does not reach the normal range.

In interpretation of this material, a cautionary note should be struck regarding generalization from acute studies involving administration of alcohol to normal subjects to the case of the chronic alcoholic. Preexisting organic and personality differences between the alcoholic and nonalcoholic acute experiment subject may produce qualitatively and quantitatively disparate responses. Noting this point, it still remains a matter of great interest to differentiate, in the alcoholic, between what may be called "state" symptoms associated with the more direct effects of intoxication and "trait" symptoms that have to do with stable personality dimensions or chronic consequences of the alcoholism process. The distinction between "state" and "trait" symptoms and methods for distinguishing between them, have been suggested by Zubin (1975) within the context of schizophrenia research.

THEORETICAL MODELS

Our review thus far suggests that alcoholism is associated with a series of partially reversible perceptual, motor, and cognitive deficits. The remaining problems tend to revolve around finding some generally acceptable explanation for this relationship. Since a definitive understanding has not yet been reached, it remains necessary to construct models or networks of hypothesis, and to martial evidence in support of these models. Some of the evidence for various models will be reviewed here.

In the light of current evidence, perhaps the most appealing explanation for psychological deficit in alcoholics revolves around some of the various organic or neuropsychological models. Tarter, in a recent publication (Tarter, 1975), and elsewhere in this book, reviews the evidence for the various neuropsychological models in detail. We would only emphasize here that the evidence for brain dysfunction in advanced alcoholics is impressive, although the specific areas and mechanisms of pathology have not yet been fully determined. Thus, there is more than one neuropsychological theory of alcoholism within the context of agreement concerning the responsibility of some form of neuropathology for the various impairments and deficits noted behaviorally.

One of the advantages of a neuropsychological model is that it can handle a great deal of the data. The field dependence, the impairment of abstract reasoning ability, the perceptual-motor disorders, and other related phenomena can all be attributed to the presence of brain dysfunction. There is hard and extensive evidence that individuals with documented brain damage demonstrate deficits of just these types. In studies contrasting alcoholics with normals and subjects with known brain damage, the alcoholics tend to perform more like the brain damaged subjects than like the normals on tests known to be sensitive to brain dysfunction. Similarly, it is well documented that brain damaged individuals, as a group, tend to be markedly field-dependent. Furthermore, numerous investigators of alcoholism have drawn convincing parallels between neuropathological findings and behavioral data.

As suggested above, one of the more fruitful research areas aimed at developing the organic model relates to a determination of "state" as opposed to "trait" dimensions of the alcoholism process. In our review of the literature, it was noted in several instances that under conditions of serial testing, ability levels changed in the direction of improvement. These changes appeared to be associated with periods of sustained abstinence and generally healthy living, but it was also pointed out that, in some instances, the change could not reasonably be attributed solely to detoxication. These changes provide a source of difficulty for the neuropsychological theories, in that behavioral phenomena said to be related to structural changes in the central nervous system should not change following, for example, an hour of sensory isolation. While it can be said that deficits that disappear involve "nonorganic" factors, such as motivation or degree of cooperation, the post hoc nature of such explanations often leave one less than convinced.

Other criticisms of the organic model relate to specific findings, particularly in regard to field dependence. We have already reviewed the position of the Witkin group, which in essence postulates that performance on tests of the rod and frame type reflect a personality dimension that antedates acquisition of alcoholism. These investigators apparently do not accept the organic-consequent explanations of field dependence in alcoholics. Pisani, Jacobson, and Berenbaum (1973) make the point that neither explanation may be completely correct, and suggest that alcoholics may have been predisposed to that condition by field dependence, but the effects of alcohol may make them even more field-dependent.

There is also a widely used criticism of neuropsychological explanations in general, when they are based on comparisons between some diagnostic group and a group of subjects with known brain damage. The criticism is that just because individuals in the diagnostic group in question perform like brain damaged individuals, that does not necessarily mean that they are brain damaged. For example, in the area of schizophrenia research, there are many studies in which the performance of schizophrenic patients cannot be distinguished from that of individuals with documented brain damage. The results of such studies are often unfortunately ambiguous, since one can conclude either that schizophrenics are brain damaged or schizophrenics demonstrate deficit owing to considerations other than what is producing the deficit in the brain damaged subjects; e.g., inattention, lack of motivation, unwillingness to cooperate, etc. These critics point out that tests are, after all, taken by persons and therefore performance level may be mediated by numerous influences, some of which may be described as "organic" and some as "nonorganic."

Another model related to the neuropsychological ones, but not necessarily coextensive with them, makes an analogy between alcoholism and aging. It is said that alcoholism is a condition of premature aging. Often this hypothesis is taken to mean that the alcoholic brain is like the brain of the old person, but aging is a broad concept that has to do with more than the anatomy and physiology of the brain. It is also related to sociocultural considerations, the affective life of the individual, capacity to communicate, and numerous other areas. If one were to review the literature on psychological deficit in aging and compare it with the literature in alcoholism and in brain damage, it would become apparent that old people, brain damaged patients, and alcoholics show many of the same cognitive, perceptual, and motor deficits. In his chapter, Dr. Tarter reviews some of the studies suggesting various resemblances between the aging process and alcoholism.

While the premature aging model may provide good working hypotheses, it also has its difficulties. We will address outselves to those difficulties that lie in the area of behavioral deficit, and that have to do with the proposition that the performance of alcoholics resembles that of brain damaged individuals which in turn resembles that of old people. The problem is that much of the research having to do with mental deterioration in the aged is felt by some (e.g., Schaie and Strother, 1968) to be fraught with artifact. The difficulty in interpreting such studies is attributed to a "cohort effect," here taken to mean that people of different ages are brought up under different sociocultural conditions. Thus, in a cross-sectional study of aging, one confounds the effect of age with possible differences among generations in educational systems, availability of information, and the like. The psychological test performance of old people may therefore look like that of individuals with known brain damage, but may in fact be largely determined not by the biological but by the cultural consequences of aging.

Furthermore, recent evidence suggests that the classical curve of mental deterioration (Wechsler, 1944) may be, at least in part, a statistical artifact. It now appears more likely that in the aging person who remains in reasonably good health, mental functioning remains relatively intact until shortly before death, when there is a rapid deterioration. Since there is an increasing number of people close to death as one goes up the age scale, group data give the impression of gradual deterioration. However, in the individual aging person, the deterioration may appear abruptly close to the time of death. Thus, if one views the changes of aging as a process of gradual mental deterioration primarily associated with progressive impairment of brain function, then one could say that alcoholism is like aging.

However, recent evidence suggests that these assumptions regarding aging do not necessarily tell the whole story. Another related area that requires extensive further study concerns the relationship between perceptual-cognitive functioning and the psychological depression that often accompanies aging. In summary, while viewing the alcoholic as a person who is old before his time is in many respects reasonable, caution should be exercised regarding accepting this analogy in an overly literal manner.

When one departs from the neuropsychological models of perceptual-cognitive deficit in alcoholics, one is confronted with a plethora of theories of alcohol addiction ranging in sophistication from folklore to highly scientific formulations. Many of these theories do not address themselves to the issue of perceptual-cognitive functioning, while others do so in only a casual or peripheral way. A theory that does address itself to this matter, but that differs in orientation, is that of the Witkin group. The research and views of this group have been reviewed above, but we can restate their basic position that field dependency in alcoholics is established early in life, primarily as a function of patterns of parent-child relations, and predisposes the individual to alcoholism. The performance of alcoholics on tests of field dependence/independence may be attributed to these considerations, and is not an epiphenomenon associated with toxicity or other organic consequences of excessive alcohol ingestion. The Witkin group's approach can perhaps be best characterized as a developmental model. It has been well researched, both by its proponents and its critics with, as we have pointed out, equivocal results.

The ultimate correctness of the Witkin group model is yet to be determined, since the much needed longitudinal study has not yet been done. If, in fact, more field-dependent young adults become alcoholics than do field-independent adults, the correctness of the theory would gain major support. If we could then predict the likelihood of an individual becoming an alcoholic on the basis of field orientation data, then we would have not only an excellent theory of alcoholism, but a highly valuable prognostic device as well.

In the absence of this research, and in the presence of the equivocal findings currently available, all we can really do is try to forecast how likely these longitudinal and predictive studies are to come out in a positive direction. On the one hand, there are the hopeful looking original studies of the Witkin group (Witkin, Karp, and Goodenough, 1959; Karp, Witkin, and Goodenough, 1965a, 1965b), but on the other are numerous other studies that suggest that level of field dependence is not stable in alcoholics, and that it does not generalize to other personality variables. Despite the difficulties noted, there are also several studies that provide reasonably compelling evidence that the performance of alcoholics on tests of field dependence/independence may be at least in part determined by brain dysfunction associated with the alcoholic process.

There is also in the general alcoholism literature a picture of relative failure with regard to establishing a clear description of an "alcoholic personality." This "failure" has been documented in numerous studies such as those of Sutherland, Schroeder, and Tordella (1950), Syme (1957), Dahlstrom and Welsh (1960) and Lisansky (1960). To quote Dahlstrom and Welsh (1960, p. 322), "None of the test findings indicate sufficient homogeneity in the score or pattern distributions to support such a concept in the etiology of this addiction." One viable, contemporary view of alcoholism is that anybody can become an alcoholic, but once having done so numerous commonalities emerge related to the socio-cultural, psychological, and organic consequences of the alcoholism process itself. In the light of these considerations, the prognosis for finding a unitary predisposing personality factor for alcoholism is poor.

This brief review of some of the models of alcoholic functioning suggests that there is as yet no complete model that is relatively free of deficiencies. Areas identified as in need of research include further direct documentation of the neuropathological processes associated with alcoholism, the question of transient or "state" as opposed to chronic or "trait" symptoms, and the longitudinal evaluation of individuals initiated no later than young adulthood and prior to acquisition of alcoholism. In effect, in order to reach a further understanding of the widely observed cognitive and perceptual difficulties experienced by alcoholics, it is necessary to acquire more information concerning (1) any influences that may predispose the individual, (2) the permanent changes associated with excessive alcohol ingestion, and (3) the changes associated with intoxication and its immediate aftermath.

THE SIGNIFICANCE OF PERCEPTION AND COGNITION IN UNDERSTANDING THE ALCOHOLIC

In view of the incompleteness of attempts to establish an etiological model for alcoholism,[a] it might be more appropriate to try to establish a descriptive model. What consistencies do we see in alcoholics that characterize them as a group and distinguish them from others? As we have pointed out, personality variables do not seem to do the job. Attempts to establish alcoholic personality profiles based on psychometric studies of patients have tended to be unsuccessful with regard to discriminating between alcoholics and psychiatric patients in general. While it is surely of clinical relevance to determine that alcoholic patients suffer from symptoms of depression and anxiety, these symptoms clearly are not unique to the alcoholic. However, when one looks at perceptual and cognitive variables, a somewhat different picture emerges. As pointed out above, with the exception of individuals with documented brain damage, the incidence of extreme field-dependent performance among alcoholics is exceptionally high. The various cognitive deficits, such as impairment of certain aspects of abstraction ability, are generally seen only among alcoholics, brain damaged patients, and certain schizophrenic patients. Studies utilizing batteries of neuropsychological tests give some hope of identifying an ability configuration relatively unique to the alcoholic. Thus, the examination of perceptual-cognitive abilities can at least provide useful diagnostic information.

Hopefully, however, the findings we have been reporting go beyond simply being methods for making diagnostic classifications. After all, the diagnosis of alcoholism is not a difficult problem, and is generally made on the basis of objective evidence of sustained, excessive consumption of alcoholic beverages. The matter requiring further understanding is the psychology of alcoholism,

---

[a]In using the term "etiological model" we do not include, for purposes of the present discussion, those theories that view alcoholism as a metabolic or systemic illness, or as a genetic defect. No opinion as to the status of these theories is implied. They were excluded only because their relevance to the issue of perceptual and cognitive abilities is unclear to the author.

including such issues as the tendency to persist in excessive alcohol consumption despite major organic and socially negative consequences, the apparent inability to profit from experience, and the limited capacity to tolerate stress without resorting to further alcohol consumption. There remains the hope that some of the kinds of tests we have been discussing may aid in providing explanations for these and related phenomena. It is only a hope at present, since the needed research relating test performance to naturally occurring behavior has not been accomplished. If we find some relationship between test performance and behavior, then there is some possibility of building a useful descriptive psychological model of alcoholism.

We can begin with the matter of field dependence. What implications does the presence of field dependence have, not for performance on other tests, but for behavior in natural settings? The research evidence here is fairly minimal. Karp, Kissin, and Hustmeyer (1970) found that the more field-dependent the alcoholic patient, the more likely he has to drop out of psychotherapy. Baekeland and Lundwall (1975) discuss this finding in the context of other studies of dropping out of treatment among alcoholics. It is particularly interesting to note their summarization. "In sum, the composite picture of the alcoholic outpatient who is most likely to drop out of treatment is that of a field-dependent, counter-dependent, highly symptomatic, socially isolated lower class person of poor social stability who is highly ambivalent about treatment and has psychopathic features. The skid row alcoholic is the most extreme example of this kind of patient." (Baekeland and Lundwall, p. 751.) Doing some transposing, if all of these factors are interconnected, it could be suggested that field dependence in alcoholics is associated with the variables cited above including a tendency to drop out of treatment.

Another finding of interest is that field dependent people are more susceptible to suggestion than are field independent people (Linton and Graham, 1959.) It is, of course, necessary to document this kind of speculation in the form of determining amount of shared variance, but we can raise the question as to whether field dependence in alcoholics is associated with degree of symptomatology, social class, extent of social isolation, and other considerations of this kind. Indeed, are skid-row alcoholics more field-dependent than middle-class alcoholics?

To take another dimension, we have discussed the alcoholic's impairment of abstraction ability. To Goldstein (1939) and Goldstein and Scheerer (1941) impairment of the capacity to abstract has crucial consequences for how one comes to terms with the environment. The concretely organized individual has difficulty in planning, organizing, and exercising foresight and good judgment. He is defective in his ability to generalize from experience, and finds it difficult to transcend the demands of the immediate stimulus field. Goldstein and Scheerer (1941) refer to this tendency as being stimulus bound, or in a condition of forced responsiveness. Halstead (1947) also considers impairment of abstract reasoning ability as particularly detrimental, viewing it as a defect in "biological intelligence." Halstead relates the concept of biological intelligence to adaptation, and takes the view that abilities like abstraction have survival value in a Darwinian sense. Reitan refers to Halstead's neuropsychological tests as measures of adaptive abilities.

Unfortunately little research has been done to directly study the relationship between performance on tests of abstraction ability and behavior in natural field settings. Chapman and Wolff (1956) studied individuals who had experienced loss of brain tissue with field follow-up, and Halstead, in some unpublished work, studied the relationship in an industrial setting between supervisors' ratings and performance on neuropsychological tests. A crucial factor appears to be the degree of demand placed upon the individual by the environment. Just as in the test situation, routinized verbal and mechanical tasks continue to be done well, but complex tasks involving conceptualization and problem solving ability are done poorly. There is therefore some evidence to suggest that the alcoholic with impaired abstraction ability, as measured by tests, will have difficulty in coping with the more complex demands of the real world. The direct research evidence for this view is minimal, but it would appear to be a reasonable hypothesis.

The point here is that the perceptual-cognitive deficits of the alcoholic may be an important aspect of a descriptive model. Regardless of whether the field dependence appears before or after the alcoholism, and regardless of whether the poor abstraction ability is a manifestation of brain damage or a character trait, these features appear to distinguish the alcoholic from other psychiatric patients more sharply than do so-called personality variables. Thus, the performance of alcoholics on perceptual-cognitive tests may not be a trivial, esoteric curiosity, but could reflect a core dimension of the psychology of alcoholism.

CLINICAL IMPLICATIONS

There appears to be a world of difference between the present realm of discourse and that of the setting in which the alcoholic is treated. The clinician trying to get the alcoholic patient to control his drinking and reorganize his life may not see much connection between what he is trying to do and his patient's ability to set a luminous rod to vertical in a dark room, or to put blocks together into a design. This apparent gap between the researcher or diagnostician and the treatment team often inhibits the capacity of one side to benefit from the work of the other.

It is our view that the significant connection between the researcher and the clinician in the case of alcoholism is that researchers have documented numerous times that alcoholics tend to have definite, identifiable deficits in their perception and thinking. Ideally, these deficits should have implications for treatment approaches and strategies, but it is most unfortunate that this is not commonly the case. If we were, for example, to venture an opinion as to why field-dependent alcoholics drop out of psychotherapy more frequently than field-independent alcoholics (Karp, Kissin, and Hustmeyer, 1970) it would be that the field-dependent alcoholic lacks the intellectual resources to benefit from a verbal-symbolic form of treatment. Similarly, treatment demands are frequently made of alcoholics without prior consideration of whether or not they possess the level of adaptive capacity needed to meet these demands. Furthermore, the alcoholic with his good verbal facade can deceive the clinician into thinking that he has greater capabilities than he actually possesses.

It might be of interest to attempt to relate some of the clinical phenomena of alcoholism to the presence of perceptual-cognitive deficits. Let us begin with perhaps the cardinal symptom, the tendency to persist in excessive alcohol consumption despite continuing and increasing destructive consequences. While this tendency has been interpreted by some as reflecting some self-destructive tendency in the alcoholic or as a "death-wish," it can also be interpreted as a failure to generalize from past experiences. This latter interpretation at least has the benefit of having been demonstrated in the laboratory, while the "death-wish" notion is little more than a clinical speculation. Thus, we would offer the proposition that the alcoholic continues to drink because he is impaired in his ability to comprehend on a conceptual basis the consequences of his actions.

Another symptom commonly seen in alcoholics is the tendency to resort to excessive drinking under conditions of stress. There are numerous ways of dealing with stressful situations, alcohol consumption being only one of them. The difficulty with the alcoholic appears to be that he uses this particular one to excess. While many nonalcoholics may use alcoholic beverages as a means of relieving tension, they also possess the capacity to deal with stress-inducing situations directly through some form of problem solving. In other words, an effective way of dealing with a stress-inducing situation is that of analyzing the situation, identifying the problem, and solving it. As has been well demonstrated by alcoholism research, the alcoholic frequently has a significant problem solving ability deficit. In view of this lack of ability, the only alternative appears to be some form of escape or avoidance. Alcohol is one way of instrumenting such a maneuver.

Aside from the aspects of alcoholism that relate directly to drinking behavior, there are other aspects of alcoholism having to do with accompanying symptoms or characteristics. Perhaps the term most universally invoked to epitomize these characteristics is dependence. The research we have reviewed has led us to be careful to make a distinction between perceptual dependency and behavioral dependency. There seems little question that many chronic alcoholics are perceptually dependent, but the evidence stands against the view that there is a relationship between this characteristic and behavioral dependency (Goldstein, Neuringer, Reiff and Shelly, 1968). The evidence does support the view that perceptual dependency is associated with various cognitive abilities (Goldstein, Neuringer, and Klappersack, 1970; Tarter, Sheldon, and Sugerman, 1975). In this regard, the researcher seems to be telling the clinician that the alcoholic does not necessarily have a dependent personality, but is likely to manifest the kind of dependent behavior commonly seen in the cognitively impaired.

The aim of alcoholism research, like that of any other area of clinical investigation, should be that of increasing scientific understanding of the condition under study as a means of improving diagnostic, treatment, and preventive procedures. Psychological research in the area of perceptual-cognitive functioning has contributed the finding that many alcoholics exhibit substantial but selective deficits. Whether these deficits are the cause of alcoholism or a consequence of it has not been fully resolved. Thus, an area of research with high priority should be a determination of whether such deficits found in non-alcoholic children or young adults are predictive of later acquisition of alcoholism.

Research studies have also reinforced the view of many clinicians that the "good verbal facade" of many alcoholics masks the presence of substantial underlying intellectual deficit. A contribution of neuropsychological research has been that of developing tests that rapidly and effectively tap the underlying thought processes. Further research is needed to document relationships between test performance and behavior in natural settings, but there seems to be sufficient evidence to caution the clinician against using treatments that are too intellectually demanding for a significant number of alcoholic patients. In a positive way, the research findings should encourage clinicians to develop treatment modalities that are more appropriate than some of those now in vogue.

REFERENCES

Baekeland, F., and Lundwall, L. "Dropping Out of Treatment: A Critical Review." *Psychological Bulletin,* 82 (1975): 738–783.

Bailey, W.; Hustmeyer, F.; and Kristofferson, A. "Alcoholism, Brain Damage, and Perceptual Dependence." *Quarterly Journal of Studies on Alcohol,* 22 (1961): 387–393.

Chapman, L.F. and Wolff, H.G. "Studies in Human Cerebral Hemisphere Function: Adaptive Capacity After Loss of Hemisphere Tissue." *Transactions of the American Neurological Academy* (1956): 175–178.

Chess, S.B.; Neuringer, C., and Goldstein, G. "Arousal and Field Dependency in Alcoholics." *Journal of General Psychology,* 85 (1971): 93–102.

Claeson, L., and Carlsson, C. "Cerebral Dysfunction in Alcoholics: A Psychometric Investigation." *Quarterly Journal of Studies on Alcohol,* 31 (1970): 317–323.

Dahlstrom, W.G., and Welsh, G.S. *An MMPI Handbook.* Minneapolis: University of Minnesota Press, 1960.

Edwards, A.L. *Edwards Personal Preference Schedule.* New York: Psychological Corporation, 1954.

Elliott, R. "Interrelationships Among Measures of Field Dependence, Ability and Personality Traits." *Journal of Abnormal and Social Psychology,* 63 (1961): 27–36.

Fitzhugh, L.C.; Fitzhugh, K.B.; and Reitan, R.M. "Adaptive Abilities and Intellectual Functioning in Hospitalized Alcoholics." *Quarterly Journal of Studies on Alcohol,* 21 (1960): 414–423.

Fitzhugh, L.C.; Fitzhugh, K.B.; and Reitan, R.M. "Adaptive Abilities and Intellectual Functioning in Hospitalized Alcoholics: Further Considerations." *Quarterly Journal of Studies on Alcohol,* 26 (1965): 402–411.

Goldstein, G., and Chotlos, J.W. "Dependency and Brain Damage in Alcoholics." *Perceptual and Motor Skills,* 21 (1965): 135–150.

Goldstein, G., and Chotlos, J.W. "Stability of Field Dependence in Chronic Alcoholic Patients." *Journal of Abnormal Psychology,* 71 (1966): 420.

Goldstein, G.; Chotlos, J.W.; McCarthy, R.J.; and Neuringer, C. "Recovery from Gait Instability in Alcoholics." *Quarterly Journal of Studies on Alcohol,* 29 (1968): 38–43.

Goldstein, G.; Neuringer, C.; and Klappersack, B. "Cognitive, Perceptual and Motor Aspects of Field Dependency in Alcoholics." *Journal of Genetic Psychology,* 117 (1970): 253–266.

Goldstein, G.; Neuringer, C.; Reiff, C.; and Shelly, C. "Generalizability of Field Dependency in Alcoholics." *Journal of Consulting and Clinical Psychology,* 32 (1968): 560–564.

Goldstein, G., and Shelly, C. "Field Dependence and Cognitive, Perceptual and Motor Skills in Alcoholics: A Factor Analytic Study." *Quarterly Journal of Studies on Alcohol,* 32 (1971): 29–40.

Goldstein, G., and Shelly, C.H. "Statistical and Normative Studies of the Halstead Neuropsychological Test Battery Relevant to a Neuropsychiatric Hospital Setting." *Perceptual and Motor Skills,* 34 (1972): 603–620.

Goldstein, K. *The Organism.* New York: American Book, 1939.

Goldstein, K., and Scheerer, M. "Abstract and Concrete Behavior: An Experimental Study with Special Tests." *Psychological Monographs,* 53, 2 (Whole No. 239) (1941).

Grant, D., and Berg, D. "A Behavioral Analysis of Degree of Reinforcement and Ease of Shifting to a New Response in a Weigl-Type Card Sorting Problem." *Journal of Experimental Psychology,* 38 (1948): 404–411.

Grassi, J. *The Grassi Block Substitution Test for Measuring Organic Brain Pathology.* Springfield, Illinois: Thomas, 1953.

Halstead, W.C. *Brain and Intelligence.* Chicago: University of Chicago Press, 1947.

Heath, S.R., Jr. "Rail-Walking Performance as Related to Mental Age and Etiological Type Among the Mentally Retarded." *American Journal of Psychology,* 55 (1942): 240–247.

Jacobson, G. "Reduction of Field Dependence in Chronic Alcoholic Patients." *Journal of Abnormal Psychology,* 73 (1968): 547–549.

Jacobson, G.R.; Pisani, V.D.; and Berenbaum, H.L. "Temporal Stability of Field Dependence Among Hospitalized Alcoholics." *Journal of Abnormal Psychology,* 76 (1970): 10–12.

Jones, B.M., and Parsons, O.A. "Alcohol and Consciousness: Getting High, Coming Down." *Psychology Today,* 8 (1975): 53–58.

Jones, B.M., and Parsons, O.A. "Impaired Abstracting Ability in Chronic Alcoholics." *Archives of General Psychiatry,* 24 (1971): 71–75.

Jones, B.M., and Parsons, O.A. "Specific *vs.* Generalized Deficits of Abstracting Ability in Chronic Alcoholics." *Archives of General Psychiatry,* 26 (1972): 380–384.

Jonsson, C.; Chronholm, B.; and Izikowitz, S. "Intellectual Changes in Alcoholics: Psychometric Studies on Mental Sequelae of Prolonged Intensive Abuse of Alcohol." *Quarterly Journal of Studies on Alcohol,* 23 (1962): 221–242.

Karp, S.A.; Kissin, B.; and Hustmeyer, F.E. "Field Dependence as a Predictor of Alcoholic Therapy Dropouts." *Journal of Nervous and Mental Disease,* 150 (1970): 77–83.

Karp, S.A., and Konstadt, N. "Alcoholism and Psychological Differentiation: Long Range Effects of Heavy Drinking on Field Dependence." *Journal of Nervous and Mental Disease,* 140 (1965): 412–416.

Karp, S.A.; Poster, D.; and Goodman, A. "Differentiation in Alcoholic Women." *Journal of Personality,* 31 (1963): 386–393.

Karp, S.A.; Witkin, H.; and Goodenough, D. "Alcoholism and Psychological Differentiation: Effect of Achievement of Sobriety on Field Dependence." *Quarterly Journal of Studies on Alcohol,* 26 (1965): 580–585.

Karp, S.A.; Witkin, H.; and Goodenough, D. "Alcoholism and Psychological Differentiation: Effect of Alcohol on Field Dependence." *Journal of Abnormal Psychology,* 70 (1965b): 262–265.

Klove, H. "Validation Studies in Adult Clinical Neuropsychology." In R.M. Reitan and L.A. Davison (eds.), *Clinical Neuropsychology: Current Status and Applications.* Washington, D.C.: Winston-Wiley, 1974.

Linton, H., and Graham, E. "Personality Correlates of Persuasibility." In C.I. Hovland and I.L. Janis (eds.), *Personality and Persuasibility.* New Haven: Yale University Press, 1959.

Lisansky, E.S. "The Etiology of Alcoholism: The Role of Psychological Predisposition." *Quarterly Journal of Studies on Alcohol,* 21 (1960): 314–341.

Matarazzo, J.D. *Wechsler's Measurement and Appraisal of Adult Intelligence.* (5th ed.). Baltimore: Williams & Wilkins, 1972

McCarthy, R.J. "A Study of the Effect of Rail Walking on Improvement of Rod and Frame Performance of Alcoholics." Master's thesis, University of Kansas, 1967.

Milner, B. "Effects of Different Brain Lesions on Cart Sorting." *Archives of Neurology,* 9 (1963): 90–100.

Neuringer, C.; Goldstein, G.; and Gallaher, R.B. "Minimal Field Dependency and Minimal Brain Dysfunction." *Journal of Consulting and Clinical Psychology,* 43 (1975): 20–21.

Pisani, V.D.; Jacobson, G.R.; and Berenbaum, H.L. "Field Dependence and Organic Brain Deficit in Chronic Alcoholics." *The International Journal of the Addictions,* 8 (1973): 559–564.

Pishkin, V.; Fishkin, S., and Stahl, M. "Concept Learning in Chronic Alcoholics: Psychophysiological and Set Functions." *Journal of Clinical Psychology,* 28 (1972): 328–334.

Reinking, R.; Goldstein, G.; and Houston, B.K. "Cognitive Style, Proprioceptive Skills, Task Set, Stress, and the Rod-and-Frame Test of Field Orientation." *Journal of Personality and Social Psychology,* 30 (1974): 807–811.

Reitan, R.M. "The Relation of the Trail Making Test to Organic Brain-Damage. *Journal of Consulting Psychology,* 19 (1955): 393–394.

Reitan, R.M. "A Research Program on the Psychological Effects of Brain Lesions in Human Beings. In N.R. Ellis (ed.), *International Review of Research in Mental Retardation,* Vol. 1. New York: Academic Press, 1966.

Reitan, R.M. "The Validity of the Trail Making Test as an Indicator of Organic Brain Damage." *Perceptual and Motor Skills,* 8 (1958): 271–276.

Reitan, R.M., and Davison, L.A. *Clinical Neuropsychology: Current Status and Applications.* Washington, D.C.: Winston-Wiley, 1974.

Rotter, J. "Generalized Expectancies for Internal *vs.* External Control of Reinforcement." *Psychological Monographs,* 80, 1 (Whole No. 609) (1966).

Schaie, K.W., and Strother, C.R. "A Cross-Sequential Study of Age Changes in Cognitive Behavior." *Psychological Bulletin,* 70 (1968): 671–680.

Sutherland, E.H.; Schroeder, H.G.; and Tordella, C.L. "Personality Traits and the Alcoholic: A Critique of Current Studies." *Quarterly Journal of Studies on Alcohol,* 11 (1950): 547–561.

Syme, L. "Personality Characteristics and the Alcoholic: A Critique of Current Studies." *Quarterly Journal of Studies on Alcohol,* 18 (1957): 288–302.

Tarter, R.E. "Psychological Deficit in Chronic Alcoholics: A Review." *International Journal of the Addictions,* 10 (1975): 327–368.

Tarter, R.E. "A Neuropsychological Examination of Cognition and Perceptual Capacities in Chronic Alcoholics." Doctoral dissertation, University of Oklahoma, 1971.

Tarter, R.E., and Jones, B. "Motor Impairment in Chronic Alcoholics." *Diseases of the Nervous System,* 32 (1971): 632–636.

Tarter, R.E.; Jones, B.M.; Simpson, C.D.; and Vega, A. "Effects of Task Complexity and Practice on Performance During Acute Alcohol Intoxication." *Perceptual and Motor Skills,* 33 (1971): 307–318.

Tarter, R.E., and Parsons, O.A. "Conceptual Shifting in Chronic Alcoholics." *Journal of Abnormal Psychology,* 77 (1971): 71–75.

Tarter, R.E.; Sheldon, J.; and Sugerman, A.A. "Correlates of Perceptual Field Orientation in Alcoholics." *Journal of Clinical Psychology,* 31 (1975): 364–366.

Teuber, H.L., and Mishkin, M. "Judgment of Visual and Postural Vertical After Brain Injury." *Journal of Psychology,* 38 (1954): 161–175.

Vega, A., and Parsons, O.A. "Cross-Validation of the Halstead-Reitan Tests for Brain Damage." *Journal of Consulting Psychology,* 31 (1967): 619–625.

Vivian, T.N.; Goldstein, G.; and Shelly, C. "Reaction Time and Motor Speed in Chronic Alcoholics." *Perceptual and Motor Skills,* 36 (1973): 136–138.

Wechsler, D. *The Measurement of Adult Intelligence.* Baltimore: Williams and Wilkins, 1974.

Wechsler, D. *The Measurement of Adult Intelligence.* (3rd ed.) Baltimore: Williams and Wilkins, 1944.

Wechsler, D. *Wechsler Adult Intelligence Scale.* New York: The Psychological Corporation, 1955.

Welch, R.B.; Goldstein, G.; and Shelly, C.H. "Perception of the Auditory Midline and Visual Vertical in Brain-Damaged and Non-Brain-Damaged Humans. *Perceptual and Motor Skills,* 37 (1973): 626–634.

Witkin, H.A. "The Problem of Individuality in Development." In B. Kaplan and S. Wapner (eds.) *Perspectives in Psychological Theory: Essays in Honor of Heinz Werner.* New York: International Universities Press, 1960.

Witkin, H.A.; Dyk, R.B.; Faterson, H.F.; Goodenough, D.R.; and Karp, S.A. *Psychological Differentiation.* New York: Wiley, 1962.

Witkin, H.A.; Goodenough, D.R.; and Karp, S.A. "Stability of Cognitive Style from Childhood to Young Adulthood." *Journal of Personality and Social Psychology,* 7 (1967): 291–300.

Witkin, H.A.; Karp, S.; and Goodenough, D. "Dependence in Alcoholics." *Quarterly Journal of Studies on Alcohol,* 20 (1959): 493–504.

Witkin, H.A.; Lewis, H.; Hertzman, M.; Machover, K.; Meissner, P.; and Wapner, S. *Personality Through Perception: An Experimental and Clinical Study.* New York: Harper, 1954.

Zubin, J. "Vulnerability—A New View of Schizophrenia." *The Clinical Psychologist,* 29 (1975): 16–21.

※ Chapter Six

Neuropsychological Studies of Alcoholic Korsakoff Patients

Nelson Butters and
Laird S. Cermak

At the time of diagnosis the average Korsakoff patient is in his late 40s or early 50s and has had a twenty to thirty year history of chronic alcoholism and poor nutrition. This combination of alcoholism and nutritional deficiency (especially the lack of thiamine) results in an atrophy of the dorsal medial nucleus of the thalamus and in most cases of the mammillary bodies (Victor, Adams, and Collins, 1971). The most striking cognitive deficit seen in the Korsakoff patient is his severe memory deficit. The alcoholic patient seems unable to learn and remember any new information such as the name of the hospital or his physician. Also his recall of important historical events that have occurred during the past ten or twenty years is extremely poor. In contrast to his severe recent memory defect, the patient is quite capable of recalling with detailed accuracy events that occurred during his childhood (e.g., names of schools attended and of close childhood friends) and early adulthood (e.g., war experiences). This amnesic gradient, which is so apparent during the clinical examination, has also been confirmed in recent experimental studies of the Korsakoff patients' retrograde amnesia (Seltzer and Benson, 1974; Marslen-Wilson and Teuber, 1975).

During recent years the focus of most investigations of the Korsakoff patients' memory problems has shifted from clinical description to the identification of information processing deficits contributing to this patients'

The research reported in this chapter was supported in part by grants AA-00187 from the NIAA and NS-06209 from the NICDS. The authors wish to thank Drs. Emile Rothstein and David Goodenough of the Brockton VA Hospital and Dr. Ira Sherwin of the Bedford VA Hospital for the use of their hospital's patients and facilities.
Special thanks to Drs. A. Pomfret and R. Furman of the New England Rehabilitation Center for the opportunity to test their encephalitis and right hemisphere patients.

amnesic disorder. George Talland first (1965) described the performance of alcoholic Korsakoff patients on a multitude of perceptual, motor, and learning tasks and these results served as the major impetus for future studies. Warrington and her collaborators and the present authors have also published extensive reviews of information processing analyses performed on these patients (Warrington and Weiskrantz, 1973; Cermak and Butters, 1973; Butters and Cermak, 1975). This chapter will briefly review some of these findings, but will place its greatest emphasis on the several investigations that have been completed since these reviews.

All the Korsakoff patients employed in our studies are drawn from a total population of 23 male alcoholic Korsakoffs treated at the Boston, Brockton and Bedford VA Hospitals. The mean age of this patient population is now 57 years and the full-scale IQs (WAIS) of all the patients are within normal limits (range: 90–120.) Most of the patients belong to a single ethnic group (Irish-Catholic) and socioeconomic status (working class) and the average educational level attained by these patients is 11 years. The alcoholic and nonalcoholic control subjects used in the studies were matched with the Korsakoffs for both IQ and age.

STUDIES OF ANTEROGRADE AMNESIA

Short-Term Memory, Proactive Interference and Encoding

It has now been demonstrated in a number of studies (Samuels et al., 1971; Cermak, Butters, and Goodglass, 1971; Cermak and Butters, 1972; Butters et al., 1973; Kinsbourne and Wood, 1975) that alcoholic Korsakoff patients have a severe short-term memory (STM) deficit as measured by the Peterson distractor technique (Peterson and Peterson, 1959). These patients are unable to recall or recognize meaningful (i.e., three words) or nonmeaningful (i.e., consonant trigrams) verbal materials nine or 18 seconds after presentation, if the delay period has been filled with an activity that prevents or hinders the rehearsal of the materials (e.g., counting backwards from 100 by two's). Figure 6–1 shows the performance of Korsakoff patients, alcoholic, and nonalcoholic controls on the Peterson short-term memory test when consonant trigrams were employed as the stimulus materials.

A second series of studies (Cermak and Butters, 1972) has suggested that at least part of the Korsakoff patients' STM deficit is related to an increased sensitivity to proactive interference (PI). When the experimental conditions were manipulated (e.g., distributed vs. massed presentation of stimuli) to reduce the amount of interference between preceding and new stimuli, the Korsakoffs' performance on the Peterson tasks showed significant improvement. In fact, the Korsakoff patients recalled more items with distributed presentation than the control patients did with massed presentation.

Figure 6-1. Mean Number of Correct Responses for Korsakoff (K), Alcoholic (A), and Normal (N) Groups During Recall of Consonant Trigrams.

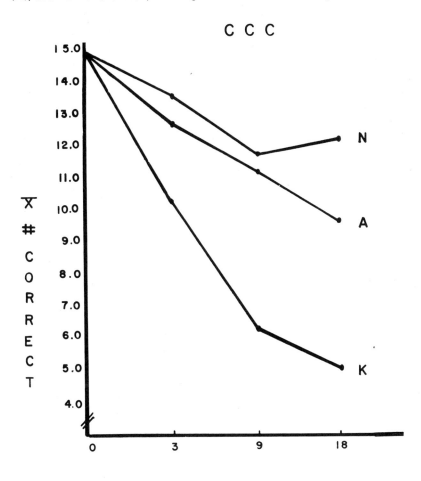

C C C

RETENTION INTERVAL

Since other investigators (Warrington and Weiskrantz, 1970, 1973) had also cited increased sensitivity to interference as a primary contributor to the amnesic syndrome, it became reasonable to ask why these patients have such difficulty in insulating old information from new. A plausible explanation existed within the recent work of theorists of normal memory who have proposed that the ability to differentiate items in memory is largely a by-product of the extent to which individuals initially analyze and categorize the information. It is believed that normals analyze and store (i.e., encode) information on the basis of its physical, phonemic, associative, and semantic features. The greater the extent to which the individual encodes the information, i.e., the more features he can analyze and store, the more easily he will be able to differentiate that material from other stored information during retrieval (Cermak, 1972; Craik and Lockhart, 1972). Of course all levels of encoding are not equivalent. Semantic feature analysis produces more permanent memory traces than does physical or phonemic encoding (Craik and Tulving, 1975). In fact, the more an individual uses semantic encoding in addition to his physical and phonemic analyses, the more likely it is that information will be successfully stored and retrieved since materials stored only on the basis of their physical or phonemic characteristics are more susceptible to the effects of proactive interference (Cermak and Youtz, 1976).

Given this new emphasis on the role of encoding in the memory process, we initiated a number of studies that focused upon the encoding capacities of alcoholic Korsakoff patients. In the initial investigation (Cermak and Butters, 1972) patients and their controls were read an eight-word list in which four semantic categories (e.g., animals, vegetables, professions, and proper names— were represented by two words each. The subjects were then asked either to re-call the list with no cues from the examiner (i.e., free recall) or with the aid of the category names (e.g., "What were the two animal names that appeared on this list?"). Since the control patients recalled more words with cued than with free recall, it was assumed that they had encoded the words on the basis of this semantic feature. The alcoholic Korsakoff patients, on the other hand, performed in exactly the opposite manner; they recalled more words with free than with cued recall. The presentation of the semantic cues to the Korsakoff patients during retrieval seemed to force them to employ a cognitive strategy that they had not used at the time of storage. At any rate, it appeared that the Korsakoff patients had not employed a semantic encoding strategy to the same extent as had the control subjects.

This suspected deficit in semantic encoding was confirmed in a second study also employing a cueing technique (Cermak, Butters, and Gerrein, 1973). In this investigation patients were presented a list of words and then cued for the recall of specific words in the list. Under one condition the patients were asked to recall the word in the list that rhymed with the cue or "probe" word; in a second condition the patients had to recall what word in the list was an exemplar (e.g., dog) from the semantic category indicated by the probe word (e.g., animal). Again the results for the control subjects showed that semantic cues facilitated recall more than did the phonemic cues. However, the Korsakoff patients again failed to perform better with semantic than with phonemic cues. Both groups showed the same level of recall with phonemic cues, but the Korsakoffs recalled significantly fewer items than the alcoholic controls when semantic cues were provided.

Results from a study using a completely different procedure, the false recognition technique, also suggested, like the cueing studies, that Korsakoff patients rely more extensively than normals upon their phonemic, rather than semantic, analysis in attempting to retain verbal materials (Cermak, Butters, and Gerrein, 1973). On this test a sixty-word stimulus list was shown to the patients at the rate of one word every two seconds and the patients had to indicate for every word whether or not the word had appeared previously on the list. Some words were actually repeated, but the list also contained words that were phonemically related (homonyms like *bear* and *bare*), or associatively related (*cigarette* and *match*), or semantically related (synonyms like *ship* and *boat*). It was found that while Korsakoffs and controls did not differ significantly in the number of repetitions they detected, the Korsakoff patients made significantly more false recognitions of the homonyms and associates. This seemed again to be due to their failure to analyze the material on the basis of higher order, nonautomatic, levels that permit differentiation of verbal items in memory.

A final confirmation of this hypothesis came from the results of a feature detection task devised by Cermak and Moreines (1976). This task required that the patient listen to a list of words read at a constant rate (e.g., one word every second) and detect when a word was repeated; or, in another condition of the task, detect when a word rhymed with a previous word; or, in yet another condition, detect when a word was a member of the same category as a previous word in the list. The patient did not have to indicate the previously presented word, rather he had only to raise his hand whenever a match occurred. Memory for particular features of words was then determined by plotting the number of correct matches detected as a function of the number of words intervening between the initial and probe member of each match. As might by now be anticipated, the Korsakoff patients performed normally on the repetition and rhyme conditions, but as soon as more than one word intervened between the critical pair of words on the semantic condition, the Korsakoff patients' detection became dramatically impaired. Thus, it could again be concluded that their memory deficit is, at least in part, due to their inadequate analysis of the semantic features of verbal information.

Having now seen that Korsakoff patients are sensitive to proactive interference and also deficient in the depth of their encoding, it was reasonable to ask whether a causal link exists between those two impairments. While it seems logical that failures in semantic encoding could contribute to increased sensitivity to PI, no direct empirical demonstration of this relationship in amnesic subjects has yet been presented in this paper. However, by employing Wickens' (1970) release from PI technique, Cermak, Butters, and Moreines (1974) have successfully demonstrated just such a relationship between these two factors for alcoholic Korsakoff patients.

Wickens had previously shown that for normals the accumulation of PI over a series of Peterson STM trials was restricted to the semantic category of the words employed. When three animal names were presented on each of four trials, PI specific for this category of information was manifested by a decrement in recall with each succeeding trial. However, when three vegetable names were submitted for the animal names on the fifth trial (i.e., a taxonomic shift), the subjects' recall improved sharply. This release from PI depended upon the subjects' ability to differentially encode the verbal stimuli on the basis of its semantic features. It was predicted that the Korsakoff patients might show a similar release phenomenon for stimuli that were simple and did not tax their defective semantic processing (e.g., consonant trigrams and three-digit numbers) but would show little to no release when abstract taxonomic materials (e.g., animals and vegetables) were used.

Figures 6–2 and 6–3 show that, in fact, the control subjects did demonstrate a release from PI following alphanumeric shifts (from three letters to three numbers or vice versa) and following taxonomic shifts (from three animal names to three vegetables or vice versa). The alcoholic Korsakoff patients, as predicted, also showed a release from PI following the alphanumeric shift (fig. 6–4).

Figure 6-2. Probability of Recall Following an Alphanumeric Shift for Alcoholic Controls.

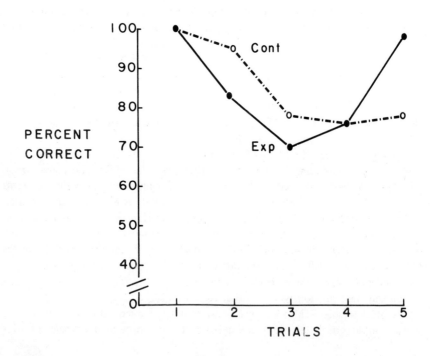

TRIGRAM– NUMERAL   SHIFT
CONTROL GROUP

Figure 6-3. Probability of Recall Following a Taxonomic Shift for Alcoholic Controls.

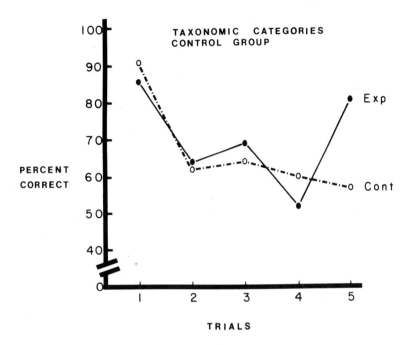

However, when the change on the fifth Peterson trial involved a taxonomic shift, no such release was found (fig. 6–5). Since the Korsakoff patients did not fully encode the semantic differences between vegetables and animals, the PI was not limited to a single category of material but rather affected all of the stimulus materials employed in the taxonomic shift condition. Thus, it can be concluded that these patients' failure to encode the semantic features of verbal material is directly responsible for their increased sensitivity to interference and consequent retrieval deficit.

A General Limitation in Information Processing

Given the Korsakoff patients' severe limitations in their ability to process verbal information, we next sought to determine whether or not processing restrictions exist in other areas as well. It could be that these patients' deficits in semantic encoding are simply one example of a general limitation in the amount of information they are capable of processing in any given period of time. In order to test this possibility Oscar-Berman (1973) has evaluated Korsakoff patients' ability to form and modify problem solving strategies. In her experiment four groups of patients (Korsakoffs, alcoholics, aphasics, and normals) were presented a series of 16-trial, two-choice, visual discrimination problems. The stimuli varied in color, size, form, and position, with the patients

Figure 6-4. Probability of Recall Following an Alphanumeric Shift for the Korsakoff Patients

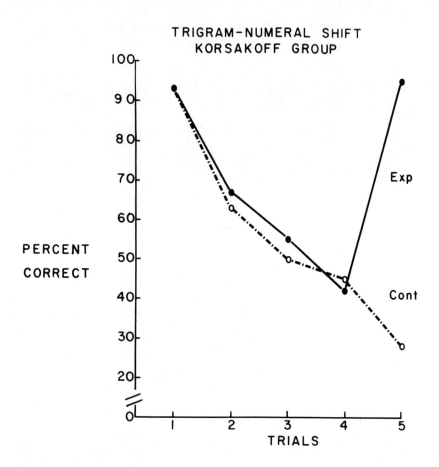

instructed to choose the stimulus dimension the experimenter had preselected as correct. Feedback was provided on two of the 16 trials by the experimenter saying "correct" and on two trials by saying "wrong" regardless of the stimulus dimension chosen by the patient. On the remaining 12 trials no feedback was provided. Then, by analyzing the patients' performance on the 12 blank trials it was possible to determine the strategy or hypothesis they had adopted by observing the dimensions of the stimuli they continued to choose. Also, one could observe whether or not they changed their hypotheses following a negative reinforcement. The results showed that the Korsakoff patients, like the other patient groups, adopted strategies or hypotheses in solving the discrimination problems, but they did not shift hypotheses (e.g., color to form) following a negative reinforcement. Evidently, once the Korsakoff patient adopted a

Figure 6-5. Probability of Recall Following a Taxonomic Shift for the Korsakoff Patients

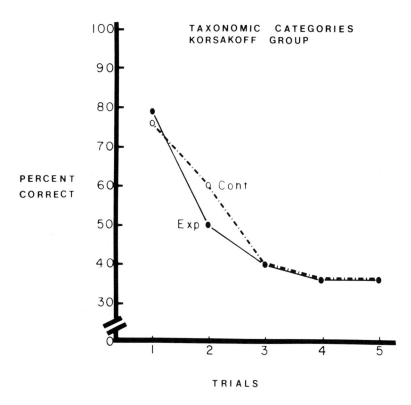

TRIALS

particular strategy he perseverated this hypothesis regardless of the reinforcement contingencies.

Oscar-Berman and Samuels (1976) investigated whether the Korsakoff patients' perseverative tendencies were related to a specific failure to process all of the features of the stimuli. In their experiment the patients were trained on a two-choice visual discrimination task with the stimuli again differing in form, color, size, and position. Following training, the patients were given several test trials designed to determine which stimulus dimensions had become relevant for them. As anticipated the alcoholic Korsakoff patients had utilized fewer stimulus dimensions than did the other brain damaged patients or the normal controls. In fact, many Korsakoffs focused upon the color differences between the two stimuli and failed to notice the differences in form, size, and position. From this finding it could be inferred that the Korsakoff patients' tendency to perseverate on the previously described card sorting task might be related to their failure to analyze more than one feature of a multidimensional stimulus.

To further this hypothesis of restricted processing, as well as to determine whether it also applies to verbal materials, Glosser, Butters, and Samuels (1976) employed a modified version of the dichotic listening technique with alcoholic Korsakoff patients, chronic alcoholics, and normal controls. Their dichotic technique involved a simultaneous presentation of two single digits to the patients; one to his right, one to his left, ear. The patient was instructed to press a response key whenever the digit pairs had certain preselected spatial and/or identity features.

Under the first preselection condition, the patients were instructed to press the response key if the number "10" was presented to their right (or left) ear. In the second condition, the patients were to respond if the critical number "10" appeared in either ear. The third condition required that the patients respond only when the digit pair "9–10" appeared simultaneously in his two ears. If one of the two critical digits was paired with a noncritical digit (e.g., "7"), the patients were instructed not to respond. The fourth condition required that the patients respond only when the digit "9" occurred in the right (left) ear and "10" in the left (right) ear. For all these conditions the interval between successive pairs of digits was 1.2 seconds. For a fifth and sixth condition (virtually repeats of the third and fourth conditions) the interpair interval was increased from 1.2 seconds to 2.0 seconds.

Results for all conditions are shown in figure 6–6. As can be seen the alcoholic Korsakoffs do not differ significantly from the normal controls on Conditions 1 and 2, but on Conditions 3 and 4 the differences between these two groups were significant. It might also be noted that except for their unexplainable difficulty with Condition 1, the alcoholics showed the same pattern of deficits as the Korsakoff patients. As more and more features of the dichotic stimuli had to be processed, the Korsakoffs and the chronic alcoholics became increasingly impaired. On Conditions 5 and 6, both alcoholics and Korsakoff patients improved their performance, but they continued to make more errors than did the normal controls.

The pattern of commission errors made by the Korsakoff patients and the chronic alcoholics in Condition 4 serves to suggest the nature of their difficulty on these dichotic tasks. Here each group made no more errors than the normal controls when both dichotically presented digits were noncritical (e.g., "3" in the right ear, "8" in the left ear). However, when only one of the critical digits was present, or when the ear placement of the two critical digits was inverted, Korsakoffs and alcoholics made many more errors than did the normal controls. It appeared that when the decision processes became complicated, the Korsakoff and alcoholic patients did not fully analyze all the incoming information. They failed to process both channels of inputs and/or they failed to process both dimensions (phonemic, spatial).

The alcoholic Korsakoffs' impairments on the third and fourth conditions of this experiment further confirm the hypothesis that they have a general deficit in analyzing or processing all the dimensions of new information. Whether the

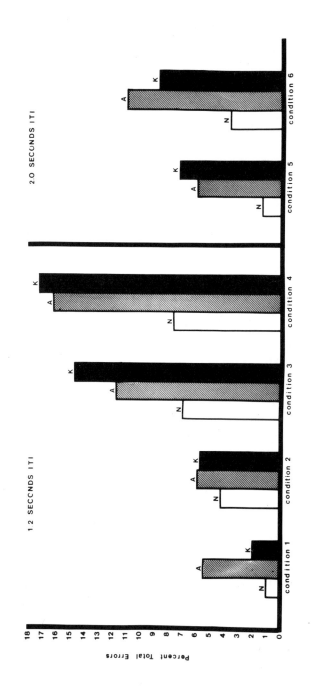

Figure 6-6. Mean Percentage of Errors on the Six Dichotic Conditions for the Korsakoffs (K), Chronic Alcoholics (A), and Normals (N)

stimuli be visual patterns (Oscar-Berman and Samuels, 1976), names of common items (Cermak, Butters, and Gerrein, 1973), or digits presented dichotically (Glosser, Butters, and Samuels, 1976), the alcoholic Korsakoff has difficulty processing all of the features of the stimuli. The present experiment also suggests that what processing a Korsakoff patient can perform takes more than the normal amount of time. Given additional time to process information (Conditions 5 and 6), the alcoholic Korsakoff's performance does improve. This fact had also been observed previously (Cermak, Butters, and Moreines, 1974) in a task in which patients were required to determine whether or not an "A" and an "a" had the same name. Under these conditions Korsakoff patients took longer to respond than did controls.

Finally, the deficits of the chronic alcoholics on the dichotic task indicate that some continuity exists between chronic alcoholics and alcoholic Korsakoff patients, a possibility that has been expressed elsewhere (Cermak and Ryback, 1973, 1976). Most neurological teaching treats the Wernicke-Korsakoff Syndrome as an acute neurological illness related primarily to thiamine deficiency in chronic alcoholics (Victor, Adams, and Collins, 1971). However, the present findings suggest that chronic alcoholics may manifest some of the identical cognitive defects as Korsakoff patients even prior to the onset of Wernicke symptoms. In fact, it is conceivable that these defects in alcoholics' processing of information may be the first indicator of an impending Wernicke-Korsakoff breakdown. It is also interesting to note in retrospect that while Korsakoff patients always perform below chronic alcoholics on tests of STM, the performance of the alcoholics has consistently been inferior to that of normal controls (Cermak and Butters, 1973).

VISUOPERCEPTIVE IMPAIRMENTS

In addition to their difficulties in the analysis of verbal materials we have now seen that alcoholic Korsakoff patients are also limited in the number of dimensions they utilize when analyzing complex visual stimuli (Oscar-Berman, 1973; Oscar-Berman and Samuels, 1976). This finding suggests that the patients may have an impairment in nonverbal memory that parallels their deficit in verbal analysis. In the present section we shall, therefore, review several investigations that explore this possibility as well as describe a study designed to assess the factors underlying the Korsakoffs' only significant deficit on standardized tests of intelligence. This latter experiment involved an investigation of the reduced ability of Korsakoffs to perform the digit-symbol task, a test that involves both visuoperceptive analysis as well as memory for this analysis.

Nonverbal Memory Deficits

The initial study of nonverbal STM processes (Butters et al., 1973) emanated from our findings concerning the patients' problems with verbal encoding. It was felt that if a failure in semantic encoding was the primary factor underlying the

Korsakoffs' verbal memory deficit, then memory for nonverbal materials might be relatively intact under these same conditions. Since the retention of nonverbal materials may require the use of cognitive strategies other than phonemic, associative or semantic encoding, such retention might remain intact in the face of verbal interference from tasks like counting backward. Milner's (1970, 1971) demonstrations that verbal and nonverbal retention are differentially affected in patients with right and left hemisphere damage strengthened the possibility that such a dichotomy might exist for alcoholic Korsakoff patients.

The results of this first study (Butters et al., 1973) confirmed that when Korsakoff patients are tested on verbal and nonverbal STM tasks following verbal distraction they have much more difficulty retaining verbal than nonverbal material (fig. 6–7). However, even under these conditions nonverbal

Figure 6-7. Mean Number of Errors Made by the Korsakoffs (K), Alcoholics (A), and Normals (N) on the Delay (9, 18 Sec.) Trials of the Visual, Auditory and Tactile Memory Tasks

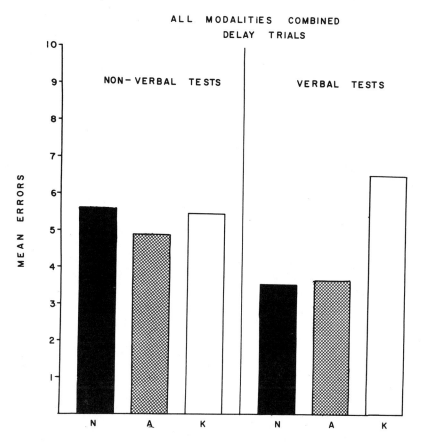

memory was not completely normal. Following an 18 second delay the Korsakoff patients had more difficulty recognizing nonverbal visual and tactile stimuli than did the controls although the difference was only significant for the haptic condition.

Our second study (DeLuca, Cermak, and Butters, 1975) focused on the retroactive interference generated by verbal and nonverbal distractor tasks. Since verbal distraction had been used exclusively in the initial investigation, we were concerned that the findings might not generalize to circumstances employing nonverbal distraction. Consequently, in the DeLuca et al. (1975) study, verbal and nonverbal stimuli were paired with verbal and nonverbal distractor activity. This design allowed us to make a full assessment of the Korsakoff patients' ability to retain both types of materials in the presence of similar or dissimilar distraction. In all, Korsakoff patients and their controls were administered eight variations of the Peterson STM task. The to-be-remembered materials were visually presented consonant trigrams (verbal) or computer generated random shapes (nonverbal). Two auditory distractor tasks (one verbal and one nonverbal) and two visual distractor tasks (one verbal and one nonverbal) were paired with these two types of material making a total of eight separate conditions.

During test session I, retention of both verbal and nonverbal materials was measured following the two auditory distractor tasks. Patients saw the stimuli, then either counted backwards from 100 by two's (verbal distractor) or tracked musical tones (nonverbal distractor) for a duration of twenty seconds. During test session II verbal and nonverbal retention was evaluated again, but this time the distractor activity was visual. Patients saw the stimuli then either scanned a list for the presence of particular words (verbal distractor) or for particular "snowflake" figures (nonverbal distractor) for twenty seconds (fig. 6-8). At the end of the delay period a second stimulus was presented and the patient had to indicate whether it was the "same" as or "different" from the to-be-remembered stimulus.

Figure 6-9 shows the major results for this study. With a 20-second delay the Korsakoffs again retained less verbal than nonverbal material when the distraction was verbal. However, when distraction was nonverbal, the Korsakoffs performed more poorly with nonverbal than with verbal materials. Actually, the Korsakoffs' verbal retention was most affected by changes in distraction; recognition of verbal stimuli was nearly perfect following nonverbal distraction, but approached chance level following verbal distraction. In contrast, the Korsakoff patients' ability to remember the random shapes (nonverbal material) was relatively unaffected by the nature of the distraction. It was later discovered that these patients' nonverbal retention is even impaired when no distraction occurs during the retention interval (also DeLuca et al., 1975). Apparently, whatever encoding strategy normals use to retain nonverbal materials (perhaps some form of imagery) it is either not used by, or unavailable to, Korsakoff patients.

In view of these results it was surprising to discover that Korsakoff patients could use imagery as a technique to aid their learning and retention of a simple

Figure 6-8. Example of the Snowflake Figures Employed on the Nonverbal Visual Distractor Task. The Patient Must Locate Within the 5x5 Matrix of Patterns the Snowflake Design at the Top of the Page

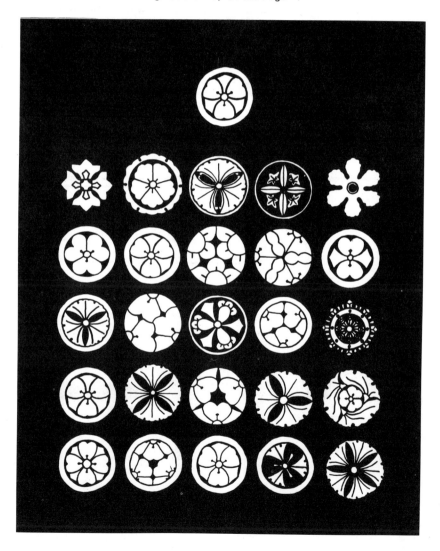

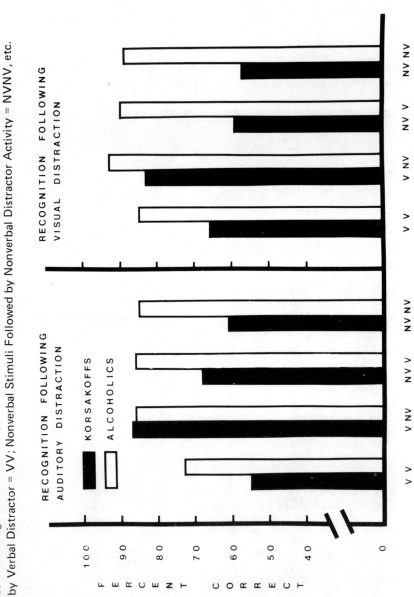

Figure 6-9. Percentage of Correct Responses by Both Groups on Each of the Eight Recognition Conditions. Verbal Stimuli followed by Verbal Distractor = VV; Nonverbal Stimuli Followed by Nonverbal Distractor Activity = NVNV, etc.

paired-associate list of nouns. Cermak (1975) found that suggesting plausible images to the patients during each presentation of the paired-associated combinations resulted in an access route during retrieval. The difficulty that remained was that the Korsakoff patients failed to remember to utilize the image and had to be reminded of its existence. Once they were reminded that they had formed a picture involving both the stimulus as well as a second object, they were relatively successful in retrieving the object. Thus, imagery does appear to be available to the patient, but just as in the case of semantic analysis, he fails to utilize it effectively. Furthermore, when imagery is not suggested to the Korsakoffs, as was the case in the DeLuca et al. study, they do not spontaneously use the technique.

Analysis of Deficits on the Digit Symbol Subtest

While the full-scale, verbal, and performance IQs of the Korsakoffs used in our studies have never differed significantly from those of their matched controls (Butters and Cermak, 1974), these Korsakoff patients have consistently been impaired on one subtest of the WAIS. Table 6–1 shows the 11 WAIS

Table 6–1. Mean Performance (Scaled Scores) of Alcoholic Korsakoffs (*N* = 9) and Nonalcoholic Controls (*N* = 9) on the WAIS

	Korsakoffs	*Nonalcoholic Controls*
Age	53.4	53.2
Years of Education	10.77	10.88
Full Scale WAIS	102.55	99.22
Verbal IQ	105.33	99.77
Performance IQ	98.55	97.22
Information	10.66	10.55
Comprehension	11.55	9.00
Arithmetic	9.66	9.55
Similarities	10.55	9.44
Digit Span	9.44	8.77
Vocabulary	10.77	9.77
Digit Symbol	3.44	6.88
Picture Completion	9.55	9.77
Block Design	8.22	7.77
Picture Arrangement	7.77	7.77
Object Assembly	8.66	6.55

subtest scores for the nine alcoholic Korsakoffs and the nine nonalcoholic controls used in the Butters et al. (1973) study. The two groups were matched for age (53 years), socioeconomic status (working class), and educational background (10 to 11 years of school) and, as can be seen, the only significant group difference in this table is on the digit symbol subtest where the Korsakoff patients are impaired in comparison to the normal controls. While this finding is not new, it does confirm Talland's (1965) observations with a similar population of alcoholic Korsakoff patients.

Glosser, Butters, and Kaplan (in preparation) have questioned whether or not this deficit is due to a visuoperceptive deficit. They administered a modified version of the digit symbol test to 12 alcoholic Korsakoffs, 12 chronic alcoholics, 12 normal nonalcoholic controls, and 11 patients with damage to the right hemisphere. Instead of the nine symbols used on the WAIS, two sets of nine symbols differing in their verbalizability were employed. Nine symbols were known to evoke verbal associations with little difficulty while the other nine (nonverbal) symbols had very low association values. Each set of symbols was then paired with a single digit number in the same manner as on the WAIS. These pairings were each administered under two different conditions. In the standard administration, the task was identical with the WAIS digit symbol. That is, the patient was presented with four rows of numbers and had to copy (substitute) the symbol associated with each number (as indicated in the code at the top of the page). In a second condition, the relationship between the digits and symbols was reversed. The patients were presented with four rows of symbols and had to copy the digit associated with the symbol. Figure 6-10 shows the various digit-symbol (standard) and symbol-digit (reversed) pairings used in the study.

The major rationale behind using the reversed digit symbol and the nonverbal symbols was to increase the perceptual demands of the task. The reversed digit symbol required more perceptual search of the symbols than did the standard format of presentation. In the standard format the subject must simply locate a familiar digit (e.g., 2) in an ordered sequence (1 through 9) and then copy the symbol associated with the indicated digit. However, in the reversed format the subject must search a series of unrelated and unordered symbols in order to locate a single symbol and the digit associated with it. The verbalizability or familiarity of the symbols further complicated the perceptual processes needed to perform these tasks since the more verbalizable and familiar the symbol the more quickly the subject could analyze and process the symbol. It was felt that if the alcoholic Korsakoff patients, like patients with right hemisphere damage, were impaired in their visuoperceptive capacities then both of these groups should be more affected by these digit symbol modifications than should be the normal controls.

The results of this study are shown in table 6-2. The measure employed, substitution or processing time (in seconds), is corrected for differences in the speed with which subjects could copy digits and the two types of symbols. Therefore, it reflects the amount of time needed to process a single digit-symbol or symbol-digit pair. While reversing the task and using unfamiliar symbols did produce small but significant increments in the processing time of the normal controls, these procedures had far greater effects on the processing times of the three patient populations. The alcoholic Korsakoffs and right hemisphere

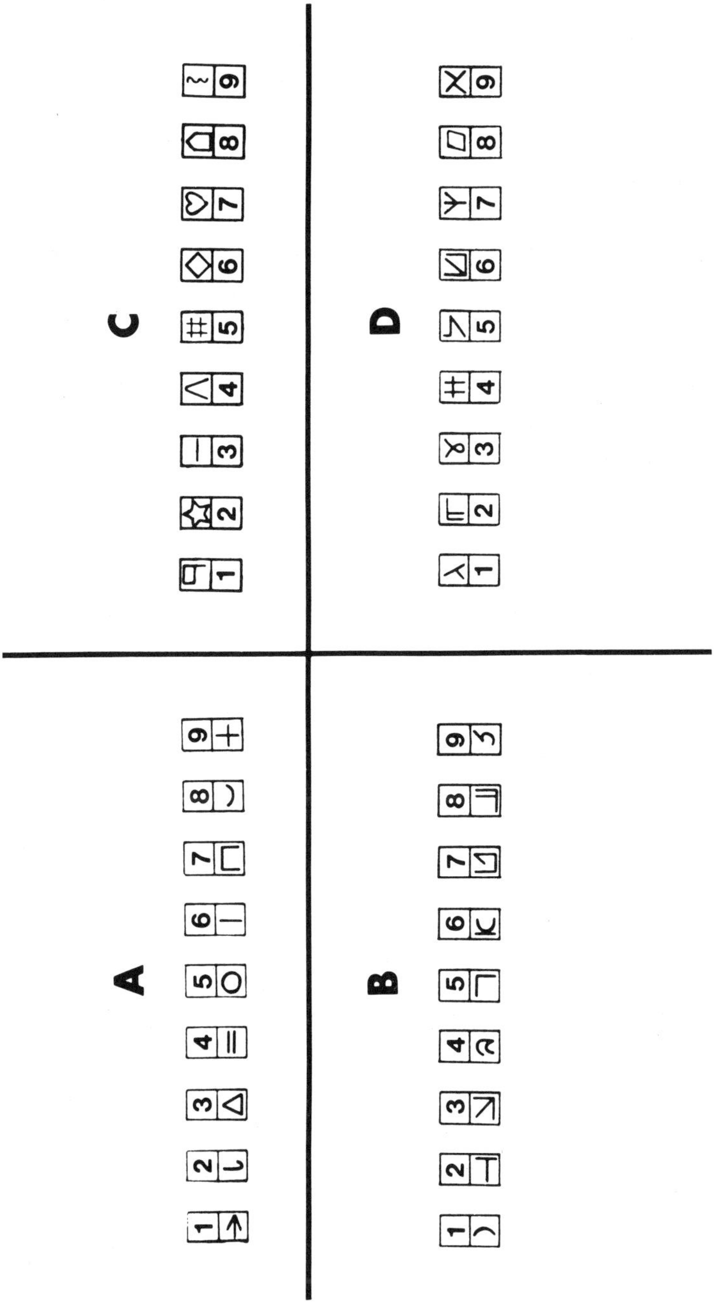

Figure 6-10. The Standard Digit-Symbol (A and B) and Reversed Symbol-Digit (C and D) Pairings. A and C Use Highly Verbalizable Symbols, B and D Unfamiliar Symbols

Table 6-2. Mean Processing Times (Seconds) on Substitution Tests

	Symbol Substitution (Standard Administration)		Digit Substitution (Reversed Administration)	
	Familiar Symbols	*Unfamiliar Symbols*	*Familiar Symbols*	*Unfamiliar Symbols*
Normal Controls	1.086	1.351	1.324	1.685
Alocholic Controls	1.365	1.455	1.693	2.392
Korsakoffs	1.789	1.993	2.296	3.847
Right Hemisphere	3.251	3.078	5,432	6.762

patients were most affected by the perceptual demands of the task, but the alcoholic controls also needed more time to process the materials than that needed by normal controls.

Glosser et al. (in preparation) also correlated performance on the digit symbol tasks with performance on a verbal paired-associate test and on a visual embedded figure test. Substitution time on the digit symbol tasks did not correlate (rho = −.08) with correct responses on the paired-associate task, but there was a significant high correlation (rho = −0.57) between performances on the embedded figure test and processing times on the digit symbol tasks. Consequently, while it was true that the Korsakoff patients were severely impaired on both the embedded figures and paired-associate tasks, only the former appeared to be related to the patients' digit symbol performance. It seems then that the alcoholic Korsakoffs, like the patients with right hemisphere damage, have some visuoperceptive defect that impairs their performance on the digit symbol and probably on other perceptual memory tasks. It should also be noted that, as in the Glosser, Butters, and Samuels (1976) study, the chronic alcoholics showed cognitive defects that mimicked the impairments of the Korsakoff patients. Although their perceptual deficits are not as severe as those of the Korsakoffs, the patterns of impairment are qualitatively similar. Perhaps the processing deficits of the Korsakoffs do not develop acutely but may be found in subdued form in chronic non-Korsakoff alcoholics.

The studies reviewed in this section have all tended to support the hypothesis that alcoholic Korsakoff patients may be impaired in their analyses of complex visual stimuli. This deficit was apparent in the patients' difficulties in remembering computer generated random shapes (DeLuca et al., 1975) and in their problems with the digit symbol subtest (Glosser et al., in preparation). These visuoperceptive impairments may be similar to the perceptual and spatial problems that characterize the performance of patients with damage to the association cortices (Benton, 1969; Warrington, 1969; Dee, 1970; Dee and

Benton, 1970). Patients with damage restricted to the posterior sector of the right hemisphere are known to be severely impaired on the digit symbol subtest and on tests involving the short-term retention of visual stimuli (Butters et al., 1970; Samuels et al., 1971). In fact, two papers (Samuels et al., 1971; Samuels, Butters, and Goodglass, 1971) dealing specifically with comparisons of the memory deficits of Korsakoff patients and patients with right hemisphere damage have found that the two groups have very similar forgetting curves for visually presented geometric patterns with one qualitative exception. The patients with right hemisphere damage forgot almost all of the material exposed initially to the left visual field but retained in normal fashion materials presented to the right field while the Korsakoff patients showed no such field specificity in their forgetting. In fact, Korsakoffs were equally impaired in retention of materials exposed to their left and right visual fields.

The similarities and parallels in the perceptual deficits of Korsakoffs and right hemisphere patients may have important implications for the neurological basis of the Korsakoffs' behavioral syndrome. While there is much evidence to link the patients' STM and encoding difficulties to atrophy of diencephalic and limbic structures (for review, see Victor et al., 1971), the visuoperceptive impairments may have their origin in the atrophy of cortical association areas. A number of neurological and neuropsychological studies of chronic alcoholics also support this conclusion. Pneumonencephalographic studies (Ferrer, 1970; Brewer and Perrett, 1971) have reported a high incidence of bilateral cortical atrophy in long-term chronic alcoholics, and there are many reports (for reviews, see Kleinknecht and Goldstein, 1972; Parsons, 1975; Goodwin and Hill, 1975) linking chronic alcoholism with visuoperceptive and conceptual deficits known to be evident after damage to association cortex.

In summary, it appears that the Korsakoff patients may have two separate neuropsychological syndromes. One is characterized by their anterograde amnesia, STM deficits, and limitations in their analysis of verbal materials. This memory syndrome is due to a severe thiamine deficiency that leads to atrophy of diencephalic and limbic structures (Victor et al., 1971). The second syndrome is characterized by the Korsakoff patients' deficits on a number of perceptual tasks that involve the analysis of complex unfamiliar visual stimuli. This visuoperceptive difficulty is likely related to the direct toxic effects of alcohol on association cortex (Freund, 1973). It should be noted that the patients' perceptual difficulties are only a single indicator of their bilateral cortical atrophy. If the pneumonencephalographic studies are correct, the alcoholic Korsakoffs should also demonstrate other cognitive defects related to anterior and posterior association cortices. Oscar-Berman's (1973) demonstration that alcoholic Korsakoff patients, like patients with frontal lobe damage (Milner, 1964), have difficulty in inhibiting dominant response tendencies on a card-sorting task is consistent with this expectation. Similarly, Parsons and his associates (Tarter and Parsons, 1971; Parsons, Tarter, and Edelberg, 1972;

Parsons, 1975) have emphasized the links between the performance of chronic alcoholics and frontal lobe patients on concept formation and motor tasks.

MOTOR MEMORY

Since it has been shown that Korsakoff patients have impairments in both verbal and nonverbal retention, it seemed likely that they might also be impaired in their ability to retain a motor movement. What needed to be investigated, however, was the question of whether or not such a deficit, if it did exist, was secondary to either a verbal or a nonverbal deficit. In order to determine which of these alternatives was correct, three experiments were performed: a finger-maze task, a rotary-pursuit task, and a STM motor movement task.

For the finger-maze task (Cermak et al., 1973), nine alcoholic Korsakoff patients and nine matched alcoholic controls were instructed to find the correct pathway through a four or six choice-point maze with their index finger. Visual tracking was prevented by imposing a black cloth screen between the patient and his hand on the maze. When the end of the maze was reached, the patients' finger was returned to the start position and a new trial begun. Trials continued until two consecutive errorless trials were achieved, with a limit of sixty trials given to any one patient on either maze.

The Korsakoff patients made a total of 93.0 errors before achieving criterion on the four choice-point maze and 131.1 errors on the six choice-point maze. The controls, on the other hand, made only 25.8 errors and 33.0 errors on the four and six choice-point mazes respectively. Clearly the Korsakoff patients were impaired in their ability to learn mazes, probably beeause their retention of the correct choices made on one trial were forgotten by the time of the next trial. This may have been due to an inability to retain a verbal code (e.g., right-left-left-etc.) to mediate their learning, to an inability to form and retain an image of the maze, or simply to an inability to acquire any motor skill regardless of the level or type of cognitive mediation involved. In order to evaluate this latter possibility a pursuit-rotor task was administered to the same patients. This task probably does not involve verbal mediation or imagery, but rather would seem to be a rather pure motor-skill acquisition task.

On this task (Cermak et al., 1973), patients had to learn to maintain contact between a stylus and a small metallic disc on a turntable. The table rotated at 45 rpm for 20-second trials. Patients were given eight trials a day, four with each hand, for five consecutive days. For each trial, the time on target was recorded. An improvement score, indicating the difference between total time on target during the final and initial testing days was also computed for each patient. No significant differences were found between patient groups on this improvement score, nor for that matter were there any differences in performance between groups on either the initial or the final day's performance. Apparently, Korsakoff patients are not impaired in the acquisition of a pure motor skill, but they are impaired when such acquisition involves some form of cognitive mediation. To determine whether this mediation utilizes verbal encoding or not, a task involving short-term retention of a simple motor movement with or without verbal distraction was performed (Cermak and Uhly, 1975).

Ten Korsakoff and ten alcoholic patients were positioned at the center of a 50-inch board to which a carpenter's sliding tape measure had been attached. The experimenter blindfolded the patient, put his hand on the apparatus, pulled the slide out to a predetermined distance, then returned it and the patient's hand to the starting position. The patient was then asked to try to replicate the distance by pulling the slide out to the same position as that just reached by the experimenter. Following ten nondelay trials of this sort, a delay interval of either 10 or 20-seconds was introduced between the target demonstration and the patients' attempt to replicate the distance. During this interval, the patient either counted backward by two's or used his index finger to perform an alternating tapping task. It was hypothesized that if the Korsakoff patients used some form of verbal mediation (i.e., such as retaining approximate length estimates), then verbal distraction should cause more forgetting than would the "motor" distraction. However, if the patients used some other means of retaining the distance, then either both types of distraction would be equal or the motor distraction would produce the most forgetting.

The results, which are shown in figure 6–11, revealed a motor memory deficit for the Korsakoff patients not apparent when no delay intervened between target demonstration and replication. This deficit was larger at twenty seconds than at ten seconds and was not dependent upon the type of interference employed. Since verbal and motor interference proved to be equivalent, it appeared that the Korsakoff patients' observed deficit in motor memory was not a direct result either of their ability to perform motor skills or of their known deficit in utilizing verbal mediation.

OLFACTORY DEFICITS

Although neuropsychological interest has focused upon the Korsakoff's striking amnesic symptoms, there are neuroanatomical grounds for the investigation of olfaction in this syndrome. The thalamic (n. medialis dorsalis) and hypothalamic (Mammillary bodies) structures damaged in Korsakoff's disease have been shown by comparative neuroanatomical studies to be possible relays for olfactory inputs (e.g., Cajal, 1955; Nauta, 1956). Damage to these structures might conceivably impair olfactory discrimination, and in fact Talland (1965) reported that nine of his Korsakoff patients "seemed to have no capacity for olfactory discrimination." In order to investigate this possibility Jones, Moskowitz, and Butters (1975) investigated the simple discrimination of odors by alcoholic Korsakoff patients. Besides evaluating basic discriminatory capacities, they also assessed STM for odors since Korsakoff patients' retentive abilities in this ancient modality had never been tested.

Three groups of male subjects were assessed: 14 alcoholic Korsakoff patients,

Figure 6-11. Mean Absolute Error for the Korsakoff and Alcoholic Groups After No Delay and Following 10-Sec. and 20-Sec. Delays Filled with Either Verbal or Motor Distraction

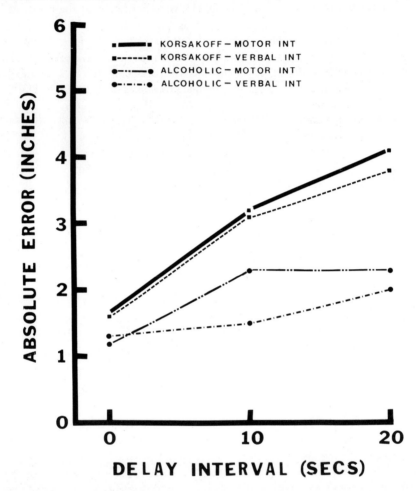

14 alcoholic controls, and 14 nonalcoholic controls. The olfactory test used ten relatively unfamiliar odorants—food essences and chemical compounds—in a sniff-bottle technique. There were two bottles of each odorant, and twenty pairs were used, each odorant matched once with itself and once with another odorant. For each pair the subject judged whether the second odorant was the same as, or different from, the first. The twenty pairs were presented once with zero seconds, and once with thirty seconds, between the two members of each pair. For the thirty-second delay task the Peterson and Peterson distractor technique was employed to prevent the rehearsal of any possible verbal labels. For both delay tasks there was a thirty-second interpair interval.

An analysis and subsequent *t* tests on the mean total errors showed a significant group effect, with Korsakoffs performing significantly worse than both control groups while the latter two did not differ. The mean performance of the Korsakoffs on both delay tasks did not even exceed the chance level. Thus, it was apparent that alcoholic Korsakoffs have a striking impairment of odor quality discrimination.

There are two possible explanations for the olfactory impairment found in this initial study. One, alcoholic Korsakoffs may have elevated intensity thresholds for the perception of odors; two, their ability to discriminate among odor qualities may be selectively impaired although thresholds for odor perception remain normal. In order to evaluate the first hypothesis, Jones et al. (1975) tested the patients' scaling of olfactory intensities. This method provided a broader view of the range of the patients' perceptual deficits. In addition, this investigation also assessed the patients' ability to discriminate stimulus intensity in two other sensory modalities, vision and audition, to determine whether alcoholic Korsakoff patients might have a general discriminative impairment rather than one specific to olfaction.

There were three groups of ten subjects each in this experiment: Korsakoffs, alcoholic controls, and nonalcoholic controls. Each subject judged the intensity of stimuli in three modalities: vision with shades of gray, audition with loudness, and olfaction with the intensity of butanol varied. The procedure in all three modalities utilized two scaling methods, *magnitude estimation* and *category scaling*. The mode of response of the subject for all scaling tasks was nonverbal in order to minimize the problem of verbal perseveration in the Korsakoff patients. For *category scaling* the patients were presented with a chart of numbers corresponding to the number of stimuli in the set, from 1 to *n*, and were asked to point to the appropriate number in response to each stimulus. For *magnitude estimation* the subjects responded by adjusting the length of an unmarked metal spring-loaded tape measure which had been embedded in the end of a four-foot wooden beam. The subject was instructed to make the length of the tape measure correspond to his perception of the intensity of the olfactory, visual, or auditory stimulus presented on a given trial. The greater the perceived intensity of the stimulus, the longer the tape measure. Two variations of the task were used in order to control for the possibility that the memory impairment of the Korsakoff patients would interfere with scaling since they might not be able to remember the standard stimulus presented by the experimenter prior to the actual scaling task. In one variation the standard stimulus was presented only once, at the beginning of the scaling task. In the second variation the standard stimulus was presented before each test stimulus.

Materials for the assessment of grayness were eight Munsell neutral gray cards ranging from values 2 through 9 on the Munsell scale. For auditory assessment six levels of white noise ranging from 45 to 95 decibels were used. The olfactory stimuli were six concentrations of butanol from 0.6 percent saturation to 20 percent saturation presented with the use of an air dilution olfactometer.

The judgments of the subjects were analyzed by means of a computer and plotted in the form of intensity functions for brightness, loudness, and odor intensity. Figure 6–12 shows the intensity function for shades of gray. Functions for all three groups are superimposable for both types of magnitude estimation (with a single standard and with multiple standard) and for category scaling. The form of the intensity function for the Munsell scale of grays is characteristically concave downwards, as Stevens and Stevens (1960) have noted. Figure 6–13 shows the intensity functions for audition. Here the Korsakoffs differed from controls on magnitude estimation with a single standard, showing some recruitment or steepening which may have been exaggerated by one Korsakoff who was hard of hearing. However, alcoholic Korsakoffs were indistinguishable from controls on both multiple standard magnitude estimation and category scaling.

Figure 6–14 shows the intensity functions for olfaction. Here the magnitude estimates of the Korsakoff group show that they systematically perceive odors to be less intense than do alcoholic or nonalcoholic controls. The slope evidence for magnitude estimation of the three lowest concentrations suggests that alcoholic Korsakoffs do not, on the average, smell these levels. Even the three highest concentrations are rated as less intense by the Korsakoffs than these same levels by controls. The steepening slope might be evidence for neural damage and parallels the steepening of the loudness function in patients with neural hearing losses.

The conclusion that this olfactory deficit is due to damage to olfactory nerves, bulbs, or tracts from head trauma does not seem plausible since the alcoholic controls would be equally likely to have suffered head trauma, yet they performed significantly better than Korsakoffs on all olfactory tasks. Of the central structures damaged in Korsakoff's Syndrome the thalamic structures (n. medialis dorsalis) are more likely than the mammillary bodies to be involved in olfaction since five synapses are required for olfactory inputs to reach the mammillary bodies. Further, we administered the test of odor quality discrimination to an amnesic patient (due to trauma) with a diagnosis of bilateral hippocampal damage and found him to be normal in his discriminative capacities. Since the mammillary bodies would receive olfactory inputs via the hippocampus, their contribution to olfactory functions may not be significant. On the other hand, the dorsal medial nucleus of the thalamus, damaged in around 90 percent of Korsakoff patients, and the ventral medial nucleus of the thalamus, damaged in around 60 percent, may play an important role in olfaction. Both receive direct inputs from the paleocortical olfactory area, which may be a relay for olfactory information, and both send projections to neocortex: the medial dorsal nucleus to orbital frontal cortex, and the ventral medial nucleus to frontolateral cortex. It seems possible then that these two thalamic structures may play a vital role in the mediation of olfaction.

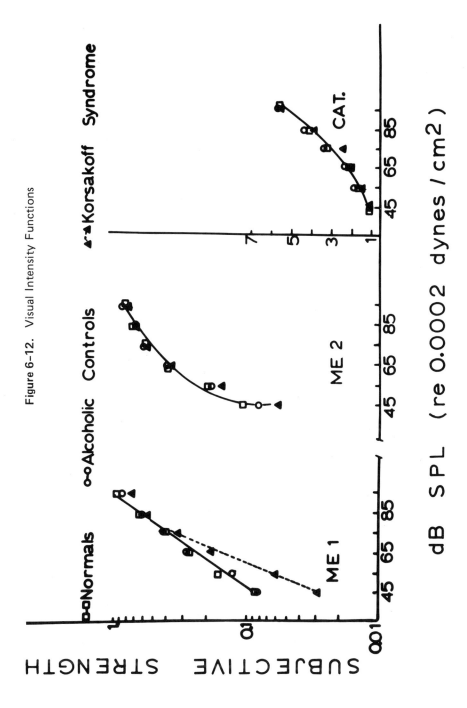

Figure 6-12. Visual Intensity Functions

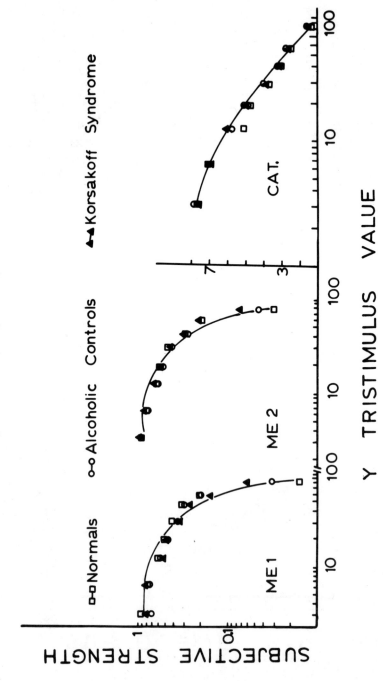

Figure 6-13. Auditory Intensity Functions

Figure 6-14.   Olfactory Intensity Functions

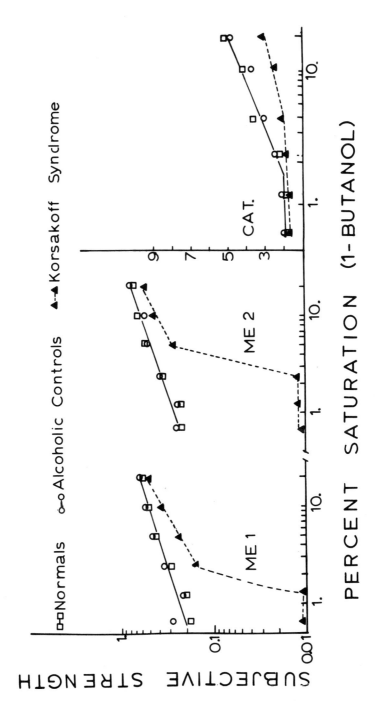

COMPARISONS OF THE MEMORY DISORDERS OF ALCOHOLIC KORSAKOFFS, POSTENCEPHALITICS, AND PATIENTS WITH HUNTINGTON'S DISEASE

This chapter has thus far focused on the neuropsychological characteristics of a particular group of amnesic patients, namely alcoholic Korsakoffs. These patients have been characterized as exhibiting a specific constellation of information processing deficits evidenced by their performance on tests of short-term memory, encoding, and perception. An issue that is germane to such neuropsychological investigations concerns the generality of these findings to other groups of patients with severe memory disorders. It could be asked whether the severe memory problems of alcoholic Korsakoffs, patients with Huntington's Disease, and patients who have survived encephalitis all involve the same information processing deficits or whether these different etiologies result in distinctively different patterns of cognitive impairments.

Memory Performance of Postencephalitic Patients

While it is, of course, possible that the same mechanisms (e.g., increased sensitivity to interference) might be responsible for all forms of amnesia regardless of etiology and locus of lesion, there is now evidence that this view may not be the case. Lhermitte and Signoret (1972) have compared the performance of alcoholic Korsakoff patients with that of postencephalitic patients on four memory tasks. Their tests involved the learning and retention of a spatial array, a verbal sequence, a logical arrangement, and a code. On the first task, the Korsakoff patients showed better retention than the postencephalitic patients. However, on the remaining three memory tests, the postencephalitics were not only superior to the Korsakoff patients, but they did not even differ significantly from normal controls. From these results Lhermitte and Signoret concluded that the memory disorders manifested by amnesics with different etiologies are probably not identical.

Lhermitte and Signoret's empirical differentiation of the alcohol and viral-related amnesias has also received some support from our own investigations. Several memory and information processing tests used with the alcoholic Korsakoffs have now been administered to three patients (S.S., V.J., and N.S.) who survived attacks of herpes simplex encephalitis. One of the patients, S.S., has been described previously (Cermak, 1976) but the results with the other two have not previously been reported. S.S., a 45-year-old optical engineer, V.J., a 53-year-old secretary, and N.S., a 14-year-old high school student, all manifested pronounced anterograde and retrograde amnesia immediately following their attacks of encephalitis. S.S. is still severely amnesic as evidenced by his inability to remember current events and the names of individuals he encounters. Both V.J. and N.S. have improved with regard to their memory capacity, but both still require mnemonic aids (e.g., writing down all appointments and names of people) in their day-to-day lives. V.J. has returned to work on a part-time basis yet still cannot recall many important events in her past (e.g., the death of her parents) and has difficulty in remembering appointments and the specific tasks she has to accomplish in a given day. N.S. has returned to school although she is having difficulty in courses that require the memorization of mathematical or grammatical rules. All three patients have been examined on at least two occasions with no visible change in their psychometric scores or in their performance on our battery of memory and cognitive tasks. All three patients' full-scale IQs have been assessed and are within the normal or superior range (S.S. = 133; V.J. = 96; N.S. = 113).

The most outstanding and consistent feature of these three post-encephalitics' performance is their normal short-term memory. Figure 6–15 shows the performance of these patients on the Peterson distractor task in which

Figure 6-15. Mean Percentage of CCC's Recalled After Delays of 3, 9, and 18 Sec. by Korsakoff (K), Normal (N), and Three Encephalitis Patients (V.J., N.S., and S.S.)

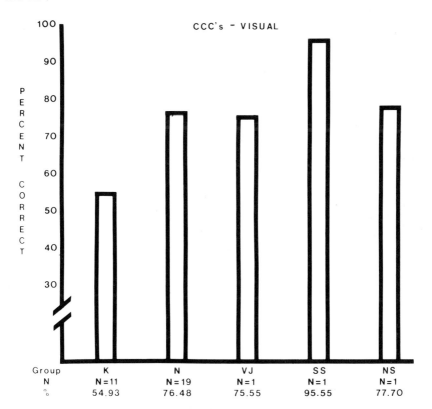

consonant trigrams served as the to-be-remembered materials. For purposes of comparison, the mean performance of 11 alcoholic Korsakoffs and 19 normal controls are also presented. It is evident that all three encephalitis patients have retention scores superior to the mean of the Korsakoff patients. Statistical comparisons show that there is a significant difference between the Korsakoffs and encephalitis patients but not between the normal controls and the encephalitics. Of the three encephalitis patients, S.S., who has the most severe amnesia but also the highest IQ (133), had the best performance on our STM tasks. It should also be noted that V.J. has an IQ score (96) that is less than the mean IQ (102) of the Korsakoff patients and yet her performance on the STM task was superior to that of all 11 alcoholic Korsakoffs.

Conclusions based on this finding should be made cautiously, however, for of the three encephalitis patients only S.S. is still truly amnesic upon clinical examination. V.J. and N.S. still have memory impairments that interfere with their daily lives, but neither of the two can be considered amnesic by the usual clinical criteria. Furthermore, all three encephalitis patients differ from the average Korsakoff patient in educational attainment, IQ, socioeconomic class, and perhaps other factors that may contribute to performance on this STM task. Thus, before definitive conclusions can be drawn concerning these two types of amnesics it will be necessary to study a much larger group of encephalitis patients.

Information Processing Deficits of Patients with Huntington's Chorea

A recently completed study involving patients with Huntington's Chorea (HC) supplies more substantial evidence that different cognitive defects underlie the memory disorders of various brain-damaged populations (Butters et al., 1976). These patients have a genetically transmitted disorder resulting in a progressive atrophy of basal ganglia and cerebral cortex. Their most common behavioral symptoms include involuntary choretic movements and a progressive dementia with severe memory problems as part of the general intellectual decline. In order to assess the nature of this memory deficit in patients with HC two tests of STM, two tests of sensitivity to PI, and two tests of encoding were given to six patients with HC. These HC patients were judged to be demented by clinical and psychometric evaluation (mean verbal IQ = 75) and all evidenced severe memory deficits during clinical examination or on the Wechsler Memory Scale. For purposes of comparison, the performances of six alcoholic Korsakoffs and six alcoholic controls are again included in the presentation of results.

On tests of STM both the Korsakoff and HC patients performed very poorly. In neither the recall of consonant trigrams (fig. 6–16) nor of single words (fig. 6–17) did the Korsakoffs and HC patients differ from each other significantly.

Figure 6-16. Performance of the Korsakoff (K), Huntington's Chorea (HC), and Alcoholic (A) Patients on the Distractor Task Employing Consonant Trigrams

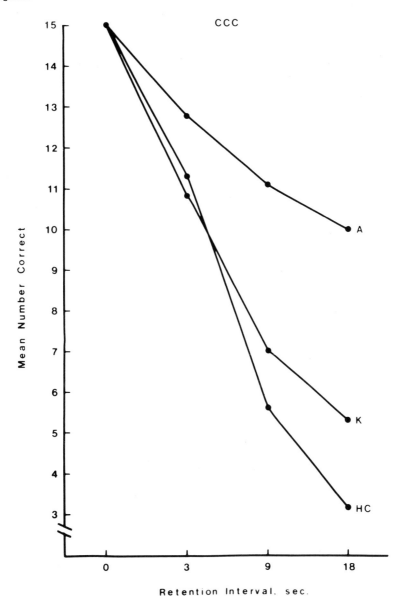

Figure 6-17. Performance of the Korsakoff (K), Huntington's Chorea (HC), and Alcoholic (A) patients on the Distractor Task Employing Single Words

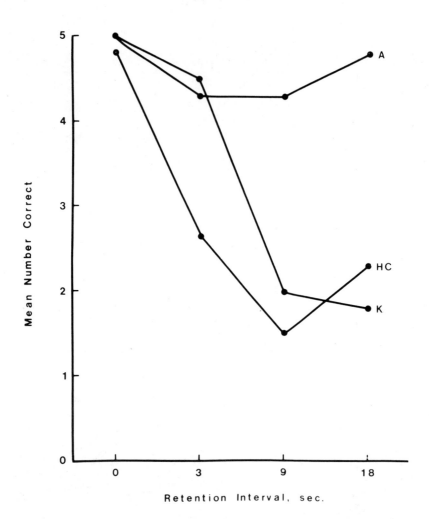

While it has been shown that increased sensitivity to interference plays a prominent role in the STM deficits of Korsakoff patients, the importance of this variable in the memory impairment of the HC patients is not as evident. Figure 6–18 shows the results of a study in which STM was evaluated under massed (high interference) and distributed (low interference) presentation conditions. During massed presentation a six-second rest interval was interspersed between

Figure 6-18. Percentage of Words Recalled by Korsakoff (K), Huntington's Chorea (HC), and Alcoholic (A) Patients Under Massed and Distributed Practice Conditions

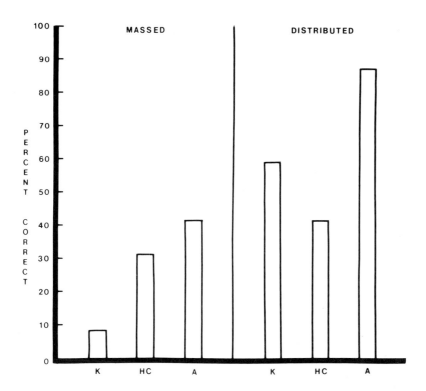

trials and during distributed presentation a one-minute rest interval was allowed between Peterson trials. With distributed presentations the Korsakoffs did significantly better than the HC patients, but with massed presentation there were no significant differences between the Korsakoff and HC patients.

An identical outcome occurred in an experiment manipulating the amount of proactive interference in the learning situation. Here the Peterson trials were divided into blocks of two with a six-second interval between trials. Then simply by varying the similarity of the material presented on the two trials it was possible to manipulate the amount of PI influencing the patient's recall on the second trial of each block. Figure 6–19 shows that, as in the case of massed vs. distributed practice, the alcoholic Korsakoffs performed very poorly under high PI conditions (word triads on both trials) but improved significantly with conditions that minimized PI (consonant trigrams on the first trial, word triads on the second). The HC patients, on the other hand, did not demonstrate a similar improvement. Thus, although the alcoholic Korsakoffs and HC patients

Figure 6-19. Percentage of Words Recalled by Korsakoff (K), Huntington's Chorea (HC), and Alcoholic (A) Patients Under High and Low PI Conditions

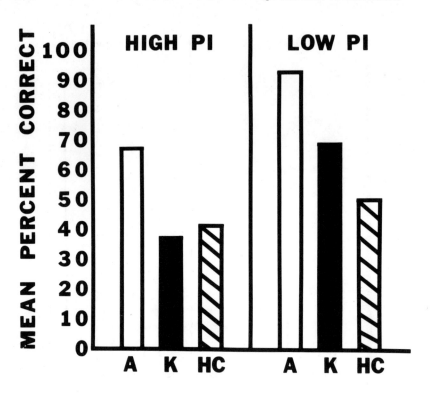

did not differ significantly under high PI conditions, the Korsakoffs recalled more words than did the HC patients under low PI conditions.

The Korsakoffs and the HC patients also performed differently on two encoding tasks. On the previously described test which compared the effects of cued and free recall the Korsakoff patients were impaired with cued but not with free recall, while the HC patients were severely impaired regardless of the method of recall (fig. 6–20). The HC patients recalled significantly fewer words under both free and cued recall than did the Korsakoff or alcoholic control group.

The second encoding task was the false recognition test also described previously in this paper. On this test the patients were instructed to note repetitions of words within a sixty-word list. Some words were repeated while other words were phonetically, associatively or semantically related. As shown in table 6–3, the HC patients and alcoholic Korsakoffs made different types of errors on this task. The Korsakoffs made significantly more false positive errors

Figure 6-20. Mean Number of Correct Responses During Free Recall and Cued Recall by Korsakoff (K), Huntington's Chorea (HC), and Alcoholic (A) Patients

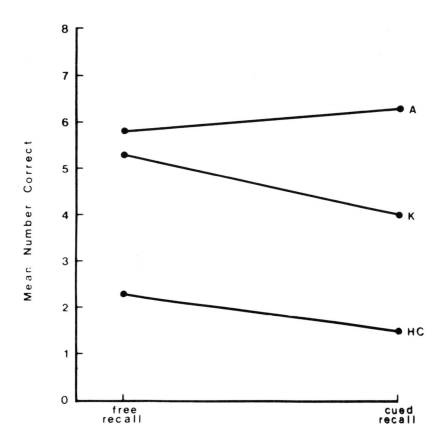

CUEING

Table 6-3. Mean Number of False Recognitions as a Function of the Type of Relationship with a Previously Presented Word, with Repeats Representing Correct Responses

Patient Populations	Homonym	Associate	Synonym	Neutral	Repeats
Korsakoffs	2.3	2.3	0.7	1.0	3.3
Alcoholics	0.5	0.2	0.3	0.0	4.2
Huntington's Chorea	0.3	0.3	0.3	0.2	1.5

(identifying a word as a repeat when it was not presented previously) than did the HC patients or controls, but the HC patients made significantly more false negative errors (failure to identify an actual repetition) than did the other two groups.

The results of these studies strongly suggest that the information processing deficits underlying the HC patients' memory problems are different from those involved in the Korsakoffs' deficits. However, while it is clear that the Korsakoff patients have problems in their encoding processes, the exact nature of the HC patients' processing impairments is not yet clear. Their pattern of deficits may reflect a very severe form of the encoding deficits that characterize the disorders of the Korsakoff patients, but it may also be that HC patients simply cannot store new information (i.e., they fail to consolidate new information).

In summary, the present findings, although fragmentary, suggest that amnesia should not be treated as a unitary disorder. Patients with clinically similar anterograde amnesias can be differentiated on the basis of performance on STM and cognitive tasks. In addition, these patient populations that do have quantitatively similar STM deficits can still be shown to have qualitatively different patterns of impairments on tests of information processing. It seems reasonable, therefore, to postulate that the pattern of memory and cognitive impairments related to chronic alcoholism may be unique and distinguishable from those exhibited by patients with nonalcohol related etiologies and different lesion sites.

REFERENCES

Benton, A.L. "Disorders of Spatial Orientation." In P.J. Vinken and G.W. Bruyn (eds.), *Handbook of Clinical Neurology*. Vol. 3. Amsterdam: North Holland Publishing Company, 1969. Pp. 212–228.

Brewer, C., and Perrett, L. "Brain Damage Due to Alcohol Consumption: An Air-Encephalographic, Psychometric and Electroencephalographic Study." *British Journal of Addiction*, 60 (1971): 170–182.

Butters, N., and Cermak, L.S. "Some Comments on Warrington and Baddeley's Report of Normal Short-Term Memory in Amnesic Patients." *Neuropsychologia*, 12 (1974): 283–285.

Butters, H., and Cermak, L.S. "Some Analyses of Amnesic Syndrome in Brain-Damaged Patients." In K. Pribram and R. Isaacson (eds.), *The Hippocampus*. N.Y.: Plenum Press, 1975. Pp. 377–409.

Butters, N.; Lewis, R.; Cermak, L.S.; and Goodglass, H. "Material-Specific Memory Deficits in Alcoholic Korsakoff Patients." *Neuropsychologia*, 11 (1973): 291–299.

Butters, N.; Samuels, I.; Goodglass, H.; and Brody, B. "Short-Term Visual and Auditory Memory Disorders After Parietal and Frontal Lobe Damage." *Cortex*, 6 (1970): 440–459.

Butters, N.; Tarlow, S.; Cermak, L.S.; and Sax, D. "A Comparison of the Information Processing Deficits of Patients with Huntington's Chorea and Korsakoff's Syndrome." *Cortex*, 1976, in press.

Cajal, S.R. *Studies on the Cerebral Cortex.* London: Lloyd-Luke, 1955.

Cermak, L.S. *Human Memory: Research and Theory.* New York: Ronald Press, 1972.

Cermak, L.S. "Imagery as an Aid to Retrieval for Korsakoff Patients." *Cortex,* 11 (1975): 163–169.

Cermak, L.S. "The Encoding Capacity of a Patient with Amnesia Due to Encephalitis." *Neuropsychologia,* 1976, in press.

Cermak, L.S., and Butters, N. "The Role of Interference and Encoding in the Short-Term Memory Deficits of Korsakoff Patients." *Neuropsychologia,* 10 (1972): 89–96.

Cermak, L.S., and Butters, N. "Information Processing Deficits of Alcoholic Korsakoff Patients." *Quarterly Journal of Studies on Alcohol,* 34 (1973): 1110–1132.

Cermak, L.S.; Butters, N.; and Gerrein, J. "The Extent of the Verbal Encoding Ability of Korsakoff Patients." *Neuropsychologia,* 11 (1973): 85–94.

Cermak, L.S.; Butters, N.; and Goodglass, H. "The Extent of Memory Loss in Korsakoff Patients." *Neuropsychologia,* 9 (1971): 307–315.

Cermak, L.S.; Butters, N.; and Moreines, J. "Some Analyses of the Verbal Encoding Deficit of Alcoholic Korsakoff Patients." *Brain and Language,* 1 (1974): 141–150.

Cermak, L.S.; Lewis, R.; Butters, N.; and Goodglass, H. "Role of Verbal Mediation in Performance of Motor Tasks by Korsakoff Patients." *Perceptual and Motor Skills,* 37 (1973): 259–262.

Cermak, L.S., and Moreines, J. "Verbal Retention Deficits in Aphasic and Amnesic Patients." *Brain and Language,* 1976, in press.

Cermak, L.S., and Ryback, R. "Reversible and Irreversible Effects of Alcohol Upon Memory." Eastern Regional VA Seminar and Workshop on Alcoholism, May 1973.

Cermak, L.S., and Ryback, R. "Recovery of Verbal Memory in Alcoholic Patients." *Quarterly Journal of Studies on Alcohol,* 1976, in press.

Cermak, L.S., and Uhly, B. "Short-Term Motor Memory in Korsakoff Patients." *Perceptual and Motor Skills,* 40 (1975): 275–281.

Cermak, L.S., and Youtz, C. "Retention of Phonemic and Semantic Features of Words: Differential Decay or Differential Interference?" *Memory and Cognition,* 1976, in press.

Craik, F.I.M., and Lockhart, R.S. "Levels of Processing: A Framework for Memory Research." *Journal of Verbal Learning and Verbal Behavior,* 11 (1972): 671–684.

Craik, F.I.M., and Tulving, E. "Depth of Processing and Retention of Words in Episodic Memory." *Journal of Experimental Psychology, General,* 104 (1975): 268–294.

Dee, H.L. "Visuoconstructive and Visuoperceptive Deficit in Patients with Unilateral Cerebral Lesions." *Neuropsychologia,* 8 (1970): 305–314.

Dee, H.L., and Benton, A.L. "A Cross-Modal Investigation of Spatial Performances in Patients with Unilateral Cerebral Disease." *Cortex,* 6 (1970): 261–272.

DeLuca, D., Cermak, L.S., and Butters, N. "An Analysis of Korsakoff Patients' Recall Following Varying Types of Distractor Activity." *Neuropsychologia,* 13 (1975): 271–280.

Ferrer, S. *Complicationes Neurologicas Cronicas Del Alcoholismo.* Editorial Universitaria, S.A., 1970.

Freund, G. "Chronic Central Nervous System Toxicity of Alcohol." *Annual Review of Pharmacology,* 12 (1973): 217–227.

Glosser, G.; Butters, N.; and Kaplan, E. "An Analysis of the Digit Symbol Substitution Test and Brain Damage." Paper in preparation.

Glosser, G.; Butters, N.; and Samuels, I. "Failures in Information Processing in Patients with Korsakoff's Syndrome." *Neuropsychologia,* 1976, in press.

Goodwin, D.W., and Hill, S.Y. "Chronic Effects of Alcohol and Other Psychoactive Drugs on Intellect, Learning, and Memory." In J. Rankin (ed.), *Alcohol, Drugs and Brain Damage.* Ontario: Addiction Research Foundation, 1975. Pp. 55–69.

Jones, B.P.; Moskowitz, H.R.; and Butters, N. "Olfactory Discrimination in Alcoholic Korsakoff Patients." *Neuropsychologia,* 13 (1975): 173–179.

Jones, B.; Moskowitz, H.; Butters, N.; and Glosser, G. "Psychophysical Scaling of Olfactory, Visual, and Auditory Stimuli by Alcoholic Korsakoff Patients." *Neuropsychologia,* 13 (1975): 387–393.

Kinsbourne, M., and Wood, F. "Short-Term Memory Processes and the Amnesic Syndrome." In D. Deutsch and J.A. Deutsch (eds.), *Short-Term Memory.* New York: Academic Press, 1975. PP. 258–293.

Kleinknecht, R.A., and Goldstein, S.G. "Neuropsychological Deficits Associated with Alcoholism." *Quarterly Journal of Studies on Alcohol,* 33 (1972): 999–1019.

Lhermitte, F., and Signoret, J.L. "Analyse neuropsychologique et differenciation des syndromes amnesiques." *Revue Neurologique,* 126 (1972): 161–178.

Marslen-Wilson, W.D.; and Teuber, H.L. "Memory for Remote Events in Anterograde Amnesia: Recognition of Public Figures from Newsphotographs." *Neuropsychologia,* 13 (1975): 347–352.

Milner, B. "Some Effects of Frontal Lobectomy in Man." In J.M. Warren and K. Akert (eds.), *The Frontal Granular Cortex and Behavior.* New York: McGraw-Hill, 1964. Pp. 313–334.

Milner, B. "Memory and the Medial Temporal Regions of the Brain." In K.H. Pribram and D.E. Broadbent (eds.), *Biology of Memory.* New York: Academic Press, 1970. Pp. 29–50.

Milner, B. "Interhemispheric Differences in the Localization of Psychological Processes in Man." *British Medical Bulletin,* 27 (1971): 272–275.

Nauta, W.J.H. "An Experimental Study of the Fornix System in the Rat." *Journal of Comparative Neurology,* 104 (1956): 247–270.

Oscar-Berman, M. "Hypothesis Testing and Focusing Behavior During Concept Formation by Amnesic Korsakoff Patients." *Neuropsychologia,* 11 (1973): 191–198.

Oscar-Berman, M., and Samuels, I. "Stimulus-Preference and Memory Factors in Korsakofff's Syndrome." *Neuropsychologia,* in press.

Parsons, O.A. "Brain Damage in Alcoholics: Altered States of Unconsciousness." In M. Gross (ed.), *Alcohol Intoxication and Withdrawal II.* New York: Plenum Press, 1975. Pp. 569–584.

Parsons, O.A., Tarter, R.E.; and Edelberg, R. "Altered Motor Control in Chronic Alcoholics." *Journal of Abnormal Psychology,* 80 (1972): 308–314.

Peterson, L.R., and Peterson, M.J. "Short-Term Retention of Individual Verbal Items." *Journal of Experimental Psychology,* 58 (1959): 193–198.

Samuels, I.; Butters, N.; and Goodglass, H. "Visual Memory Deficits Following Cortical and Limbic Lesions: Effect of Field of Presentation." *Physiology and Behavior,* 6 (1971): 447–452.

Samuels, I.; Butters, N.; Goodglass, H.; and Brody, B. "A Comparison of Subcortical and Cortical Damage on Short-Term Visual and Auditory Memory." *Neuropsychologia,* 9 (1971): 293–306.

Seltzer, B., and Benson, D.F. "The Temporal Pattern of Retrograde Amnesia in Korsakoff's Disease." *Neurology,* 24 (1974): 527–530.

Stevens, S.S., and Stevens, J.C. "The Dynamics of Visual Brightness." Report PPR246. Harvard University Laboratory of Psychophysics, Cambridge, Massachusetts, 1960.

Talland, G. *Deranged Memory.* New York: Academic Press, 1965.

Tarter, R.E., and Parsons, O.A. "Conceptual Shifting in Chronic Alcoholics." *Journal of Abnormal Psychology,* 77 (1971): 71–75.

Victor, M.; Adams, R.D.; and Collins, G.H. *The Wernicke-Korsakoff Syndrome.* Philadelphia: F.A. Davis, 1971.

Warrington, E.K. "Construction Apraxia." In P.J. Vinken and G.W. Bruyn (eds.), *Handbook of Clinical Neurology, Vol. 4.* Amsterdam: North Holland Publishing Company, 1969. Pp. 212–228.

Warrington, E.K., and Weiskrantz, L. "Amnesic Syndrome: Consolidation or Retrieval," *Nature,* 228 (1970): 628–630.

Warrington, E.K., and Weiskrantz, L. "An Analysis of Short-Term and Long-Term Memory Defects in Man." In J.A. Deutsch (ed.), *The Physiological Basis of Memory.* New York: Academic Press, 1973. Pp. 365–395.

Wickens, D.D. "Encoding Categories of Words: An Empirical Approach to Meaning." *Psychological Review,* 77 (1970): 1–15.

 **Chapter Seven**

An Empirically Derived Typology of Hospitalized Alcoholics

Carolyn H. Shelly and
Gerald Goldstein

The term alcoholism is used in two major senses. In the first case, it is used in a global way to define the effects of abuse of alcoholic beverages. Thus, a number of general definitions have been offered, which usually have elements related to excessive use of alcohol and to some concept of damage, either to the individual or society. Jellinek (1960) defines alcoholism as "... any use of alcoholic beverages that causes any damage to the individual or society or both," (p. 35). The general definition offered by Keller and Efron (1955) is:

> Alcoholism is a chronic illness, psychic or somatic or psychosomatic, which manifests itself as a disorder of behavior. It is characterized by the repeated drinking of alcoholic beverages to an extent that exceeds customary dietary use or compliance with the social customs of the community, and that interferes with the drinker's health or his social or economic functioning. (In *Aspects of Alcoholism*, Vol. 1, p. 9).

The second way in which the term alcoholism is used is as a clinical diagnosis. It is a term applied to a particular individual on the basis of an evaluation, often including both medical and psychological examinations. A course of treatment is usually prescribed, based on the information contained in this diagnostic evaluation.

This proposed distinction is made not to criticize one type of definition or the other, but to point out that they have different kinds of usefulness. For

Indebtedness is expressed to the University of Pittsburgh Computation Center for a grant of computer time, and to Mr. William T. Bowen and Mrs. Loraine Boutwell of the Topeka VA Hospital for providing the follow-up data.

example, the more global definitions may be useful in legal matters or in epidemiological surveys of the incidence of alcoholism. They may be useful in certain kinds of research in which the investigator wishes to define the population to which he wants to generalize. They may be useful in conveying one's philosophy or beliefs concerning alcoholism in general. Note, for example, that Keller and Efron specifically define it as an illness, while Jellinek does not. On the other hand, the usefulness of the general definitions in the area of diagnosis is quite limited. The diagnosis of alcoholism is generally not sufficiently specific to allow for formulation of a treatment program. While all alcoholics may share the attributes contained in the general definitions, it is nevertheless clear that alcoholism is not a single clinical entity, but rather that it covers a wide variety of conditions. For this reason, it has been useful to think in terms of types of alcoholics, and numerous attempts have been made to develop an alcoholism typology. It is the purpose of this chapter to review some of these attempts, and to present some original data reflecting a new approach to the problem.

It may be pointed out that both Jellinek (1960) and Keller and Efron (1955) not only present general definitions, but go on to discuss subtypes. Thus, the definition presented by Keller and Efron continues:

> Many special categories of alcoholics have been identified, including "alcohol addicts," who cannot control their drinking, and "alcoholics with complications." The latter are those whose excessive drinking has led to recognizable physical or mental sequels" (p. 9).

Jellinek has developed a rather elaborate typology, which will be discussed shortly. Despite these attempts, and others to be reviewed, there does not appear to be some satisfactory, universally agreed upon typology of alcoholism. While everyone would agree with the existence of alcoholic subtypes, there is no general agreement regarding a typological system.

Modern typology appears to have progressed beyond the stage of mere clinical taxonomy, and has become more objective and quantitative. By contemporary standards, typologies should be governed by certain principles of measurement. First, the procedures used for making classifications should be objective and clearly defined. Second, the classificatory rules for deciding the type to which some individual subject belongs should be explicit. Third, in the clinical area, the typology developed should not be merely descriptive, but ideally should be related to differential treatment and management plans. For example, in general medicine it is often found that some patients with a particular illness do well with some drug while others do not. Thus, we have a kind of typology; good responders and poor responders. Subsequent research would then be devoted to finding objective tests sensitive to differences between good and poor responders, and establishment of explicit rules to distinguish, on an individual basis, one type from the other. Assuming these considerations represent some of the contemporary standards for adequate typologizing, a sample of proposed alcoholism typologies will be very briefly reviewed in terms of these standards.

A kind of gross typology is implied in the *American Handbook of Psychiatry* (Arieti, 1959) by its having separate chapters covering alcohol addiction (Zwerling and Rosenbaum, Chapter 31) and acute and chronic alcoholic conditions (Thompson, 1959, Chapter 58). The former chapter is listed under "Psychopathic Conditions, Deviations, Addictions," while the latter is listed under "Organic Conditions." Thus, there is the alcoholic for whom personality variables are the major consideration and the alcoholic who has sustained some acute or chronic pathological effect involving the brain.

In clinical parlance, we hear of alcoholics with and without "organic brain syndromes." In the case of the organic alcohol conditions, there is a typology that has been in existence for a long time. As indicated, it is roughly divided into acute and chronic states. The acute states generally have to do with the immediate aftereffects of intoxication and according to Thompson (1959) include delirium tremens, acute alcoholic hallucinosis, alcoholic pathological intoxication, and alcoholic epileptic states. Under the chronic conditions, Thompson (1959) lists chronic mental deterioration, chronic alcoholic psychosis, paranoid type, Korsakoff's psychosis, Wernicke's encephalopathy, nicotinic acid deficiency encephalopathy, Marchiafava-Bignami disease, and hepatogenic alcoholic encephalopathy. He adds polyneuritis as a symptom that frequently accompanies several of the organic alcoholic conditions.

The organic conditions are generally diagnosed by the particular, unique symptoms they present, with the underlying pathology reflecting differences in location of the lesions in the brain, the role of nutritional factors, and the nature of the toxic agent producing the syndrome. Generally, these conditions, at least the more frequently occurring ones, are relatively easy to diagnose. The picture of delirium tremens is quite clear, as is the memory disorder and confabulation of the patient with Korsakoff's syndrome.

These conditions will not be described in detail here, as they are well described by Thompson (1959) and in many standard neurological references. Victor (1962), for example, also has written a catalog of the various organic conditions. He adds a number of types to the list provided by Thompson (1959) including under the acute heading, coma and in the chronic category, alcohol amblyopia, pellagra, cerebellar degeneration, and central pontine myelinolysis. While certain of the chronic syndromes are relatively irreversible end stages of the alcoholism process, there are a number of established treatments. These treatments include vitamin therapy, psychotropic medications of various sorts, and liver function aids.

In many ways, the organic alcoholic conditions are well typed by current standards. The diagnostic procedures, while largely based on clinical observation, are reasonably objective; the rules for classification are clearly stated, and there are some treatment implications. For example, differentiating out nicotinic acid deficiency would normally lead to a relatively specific course of vitamin therapy. Delirium tremens or impending delerium tremens respond well to established hospital treatment regimes. The remaining diagnostic problems lie mainly in the area of chronic mental deterioration, and involve the kind of chronic alcoholic patient discussed in detail in the chapters by Drs. Tarter and Goldstein. As indicated, the clearly identifiable alcohol related organic conditions tend to be end-state phenomena following a severe episode of intoxication or a lengthy history of alcohol abuse and malnutrition.

Possibly the most sophisticated and widely known alcoholism typology is that of Jellinek (1960). He uses the Greek letters alpha, beta, gamma, delta, and epsilon to denote his five types or species of alcoholism. They will be described briefly. Alpha alcoholism reflects sustained, but purely psychological dependence upon alcohol to relieve pain. Drinking is undisciplined, but there is no loss of control or inability to abstain. Beta alcoholism occurs when there are alcoholic complications such as polyneuropathy, gastritis or cirrhosis. There is no physical or psychological dependence, and the major damage is the nutritional deficiency diseases. Jellinek lists four criterai for Gamma alcoholism: (1) increased tissue tolerance (2) adaptive cell metabolism (3) physical dependence (4) loss of control. Delta alcoholism is similar to Gamma, except that instead of "loss of control," there is "inability to abstain." There is the ability to control the amount consumed on any occasion, but attempts at abstinence are always followed by withdrawal symptoms. Epsilon alcoholism is not fully defined, but has to do with periodic or episodic alcoholism.

The formulation of Jellinek's types are apparently based on the observation of alcoholics and patterns of alcoholism throughout the world. Attempts are also made, through appropriate research and clinical observation, to define terms such as "tolerance" and "loss of control." However, if our criteria of objective procedures, explicit rules, and clinical relevance are applied, the Jellinek types are lacking in many respects. Perhaps the essence of our criticism revolves around the fact that, to the best of our knowledge, no one has performed a study in which alcoholics were actually typed according to Jellinek's definitions. We suspect that if an attempt were actually made to classify a sample of miscellaneous alcoholics in accordance with Jellinek's typology, numerous difficulties would arise concerning how one assesses the presence or absence of certain of the differentiating characteristics, and also what decision rules would be used to tell one type from the other. The clinical usefulness of the Jellinek types is also questionable, since again there appears to be an absence of data demonstrating differing efficacies of various treatment modalities among types. Thus, Jellinek's species of alcoholism remains an interesting descriptive categorization, but it is not a working typology.

Tähkä (1966) presented a brief review of attempts to type and classify alcoholics. The distinction is first made among chronic alcoholism, alcoholic addiction, and dipsomania. Chronic alcoholism generally refers to the case in which there are lasting physical or psychological consequences, while addiction refers to the irrestible craving for alcohol and loss of control. Thus, one can be an addict without being a chronic alcoholic. Dipsomania, in current usage, refers only to periodic bouts of drinking. A distinction between real dipsomania and pseudodipsomania was offered by Wingfield (1919), the distinction being whether or not the craving appears spontaneously (real) or after previous drinking (pseudo.) Tahka (1966) also reviews some early attempts to classify alcoholics, which we might describe as being of primarily historical interest. Kehrer and Kretschmer (1924) distinguished between pyknic-cyclothymic alcoholics, in whom the drinking habit evolved out of a gregarious disposition, and leptosomic-schizoid alcoholics who drink to find relief from internal conflicts. Cimbal (1926) distinguished four types: (1) Decadent drinkers who are degenerated people who require alcohol as a stimulus (2) Impassioned drinkers, or belatedly matured, embittered people who drink to relieve emotional conflicts (3) Stupid drinkers who are feeble minded, passive individuals who use liquor as the cheapest and simplest form of enjoyment (4) Self-aggrandizing drinkers, who try to find an illusion of power and grandiosity in intoxication.

Further studies include those of Stockert (1926) who distinguished between *"Stammtischdrinkers"* and true addicts. The true addicts were further divided into schizoid and psychopathic types. Strecker and Chambers (1938) proposed eight types; mentally sick, mentally defective, psychopathic inferior, aggressive, unstable, adynamic, primitive, and psychoneurotic. Allen distinguished between psychopathic and psychoneurotic alcoholics (cited in Tahka, 1966), while Kent (1954) postulated three personality types: (1) the dependent, emotionally immature, (2) the insecure, self-conscious, and tense, and (3) the self-aggrandizing.

Keller and Efron (1955) make a widely accepted distinction between "alcoholic addicts," who cannot control their drinking and "alcoholics with complications," or those with recognizable physical or mental sequels. Another commonly made distinction is between the categories of habitual excessive symptomatic drinking and addiction. The former category includes those alcoholics who drink as a symptom of a social situation, while the latter category includes those who have a compulsion to drink based on an underlying psychological abnormality. In their chapter, Drs. Neuringer and Clopton mention Schafer's (1948) distinction between essential and reactive alcoholics.

Taking a somewhat different approach, Thompson (1959) arrives at eight subtypes of alcoholism, based on different personality patterns. Thus, there is "primary alcoholism," normal drinkers, alcoholism in cyclothymic personality disorders, alcoholism in schizophrenic reactions, alcoholism in chronic depressive reactions, alcoholism in paranoid personalities, alcoholism in psychoneurotic personalities, and alcoholism in sociopathic personalities and character disorders. Thompson (1959) briefly describes the role of alcohol in each of these personality patterns, utilizing several case examples. The term "primary alcoholism" refers to those who are given to excess, but do not have other causes for their alcoholism. Wallerstein and Chotlos (1957) anticipated Thompson's formulation, by suggesting that if one views alcoholism as a symptom, many subgroups can be constructed, utilizing the gamut of psychiatric nosology.

This sample of attempts to typologize alcoholism appears to indicate that with the possible exception of the organic syndromes, there is little unanimity regarding the classifications to be used. Perhaps a more significant aspect of the literature reviewed is the absence of any apparent attempt to marshal scientific evidence for some particular system, based on data obtained from alcoholic subjects. It is clear that most of the typologies suggested are of the post hoc, descriptive type, and are structured within the various theoretical orientations of the typology makers. The language used in some of the systems would hardly pass scientific muster under contemporary standards. There is generally a lack of description of the procedures used by the writer to arrive at his system, and when such description is available, the procedure generally appears to amount to subjective judgments made by single or small groups of clinicians. We have found no evidence for a typology constructed on the basis of the criteria of objective procedures, explicit rules, and clinical relevance. Thus, amidst widespread difficulty in evaluating alcoholism research because of a lack of clarity in defining alcoholic samples used in research studies, there is no standard, objective procedure for typing alcoholics.

The need for a strong typology would appear to be particularly acute in the area of treatment program evaluation. Vast discrepancies in the success rate of some particular modality among different settings and groups of investigators are often explainable on the basis of substantial variation in type of alcoholic patient used in the various investigations. However, there appears to be no generally acceptable way of describing the type of alcoholic used in a study, except perhaps through the listing of demographic and diagnostic information that may or may not be pertinent.

In building a typology, there is always the question of where one begins. The practice of categorizing clinical subgroups usually involves working with symptoms or symptom groups. The Jellinek system is clearly based on the use of symptoms, e.g., "loss of control," increased tissue tolerance." However, other systems of alcoholism categorization work with other characteristics such as drinking pattern (chronic alcoholics vs. dipsomaniacs) or personality characteristics (dependent vs. insecure vs. self-aggrandizing.) Systems such as that of Thompson (1959) do not use symptoms directly, but the diagnostic categories are derived from the interpretation of symptom patterns. Thus we have psychoneurotic alcoholics, sociopathic alcoholics, etc.

In principle, there should be no inherent correctness or incorrectness in any particular basis of classification. As indicated elsewhere, however, some consideration is needed concerning the objectivity and replicability of the procedures employed to evaluate the characteristic in question. Thus, while cirrhosis of the liver may be a readily observable, objectively documented symptom, we cannot say the same thing for loss of control. Does loss of control mean that the person says he has lost control or that some observer infers this to be the case on the basis of his behavior? What if the person and the observer disagree, one way or the other? To what extent can judgments concerning whether or not an individual does or does not have loss of control be influenced by prejudices concerning alcohol and alcoholics, or by practical considerations of the moment? The point is that the use of symptoms, in and of itself, is not objectionable, but while certain symptoms can be clearly and objectively defined, others have not reached that status.

In order to avoid this variability in objectivity, we elected to choose a realm of data in which all variables would be more or less equally objectively determined. Psychological tests constitute such a realm, especially those tests that have clearly described quantitative scoring systems. We felt it would be possible to construct a data base consisting of psychological test scores from which a typology could be derived for alcoholism.

The related task in typology construction has to do with the decision rules used to classify individuals. The problem with the systems reviewed is that these rules were rarely made explicit. It is apparent, however, that in most cases, the basis was post hoc subjective judgment. For example, the clinician after having seen many alcoholic patients may judge that some of them were "psychoneurotic" while others were "psychopathic." An alternative to this procedure involves allowing the data themselves to provide the decision rules. Through correlational statistical analyses it is possible to determine what variables are and are not related to each other. When the matrix of variables becomes large and unwieldy, we have available the technique of factor analysis as an aid in clarifying the major relationships.

In the case of typology, however, we are interested in the relationships among individuals rather than among measures. For this purpose, a factor-analytic-like technique is available, called cluster analysis. Cluster analysis, then, is a statistical technique by means of which subjects can be classified into groups, or clusters, on the basis of similarities and differences among patterns of performance on a number of variables. It has the advantage of typing subjects in a completely objective way, based entirely on internal relationships among variables in the data base. With this advantage comes the disadvantage of questionable relevancy. While essentially any set of data can be cluster analyzed, not every cluster analysis yields groups that have any external reference. If one resorts to this sort of procedure, there seems to be the obligation of determining whether or not the obtained groups have any meaning beyond the mathematics that produced them. It is therefore necessary to anchor the obtained clusters to markers external to the variables that went into the cluster formation.

This method being proposed, in essence, involves identifying clusters based on psychological test performance, and then attempting to relate these clusters to some significant parameters of alcoholism. If some relationship between these clusters and nontest parameters are found, then we may have the basis for a preliminary working typology. If it is not found, then the cluster analysis may provide little more than a mathematical exercise.

What are these parameters? There is certainly no one answer to this question, nor is there a complete answer. We elected to choose some of the variables commonly used to describe the alcoholic patient. These include such matters as length of time drinking, presence of structural damage to the brain, presence of seizures, other diagnoses, and marital, socioeconomic and employment status. Age and amount of education were also considered to be important factors. In other words, we used as our markers diagnostic and demographic data commonly obtained from alcoholic patients. Although the sample will be described in greater detail below, it may be noted now that our work only involved alcoholic patients who at some time required inhospital treatment, during which the diagnosis of alcoholism was made or noted. Thus, the typology to be evaluated is for alcoholic patients, and not necessarily for alcoholics in general.

The choice of psychological tests included in the cluster analysis admittedly reflects a series of biases on the part of the authors, which we shall attempt to justify. Considering the vast number of tests available, some choices had to be made. We, first of all, had a preference for objective tests with clear administration procedures and quantitative scoring systems. Thus, the so-called "projective techniques" and related procedures were ruled out. We were nevertheless still left with a variety of objective personality and ability tests. Our assessment of the objective personality test area left us with the impression that, despite major efforts to do so, little success had been attained with regard to discriminating alcoholics from psychiatric patients in general on the basis of personality testing. On the other hand, we were impressed with the work of Witkin and his collaborators (Witkin, Karp, and Goodenough, 1959), and of Fitzhugh, Fitzhugh, and Reitan (1960; 1965), who were able to demonstrate apparently meaningful differences among alcoholics, normals and brain damaged patients on tests of various cognitive, perceptual, and motor abilities.

Based on these considerations, we elected to utilize various objective ability measures as our test battery. In addition to the procedures used, we would have liked to have had Witkin Rod and Frame Test results, but this was not feasible. It should be added that in addition to the promising research findings, implicit in our choice to use ability measures was the belief that a crucial component of the condition of the alcoholic is his capacity to adapt to and cope effectively with a normal environment. His ultimate fate may frequently be determined less by his psychodynamics than by his capacity to survive in a competitive world.

To review, a survey of numerous attempts to typologize alcoholism had indicated that no current system meets contemporary standards for typologizing, particularly with regard to the issues of objectivity of procedures, explicitness of decision rules used to classify, and relevance. It was argued that pertinent objective procedures could be found within the realm of psychological tests, and that the statistical technique of cluster analysis could classify subjects with complete objectivity on the basis of mathematical rules. Since such a classification is made only on a mathematical basis, it is necessary to test its clinical and theoretical meaningfulness through seeking systematic relationships between the cluster structure obtained and a number of external marker variables. Variables pertinent to alcoholism were felt to include such areas as length of time drinking, acquisition of detectable neurological damage, employment status, marital status, and related considerations. It was further argued that ability-oriented objective tests had more potential for achieving meaningful results than did other types of psychological tests. It may be added, however, that the proposed system for establishing a typology is an open one; additional test and nontest markers may be added to the system at any time.

METHOD

Subjects

Main Study. Subjects for the main study consisted of 150[a], right-handed male patients at a Veterans Administration hospital. All subjects had received the diagnosis of alcoholism at some time or other in their recorded medical history. The diagnosis may have been worded in a number of alternate forms, (e.g., chronic alcoholic addiction, habitual excessive drinking, alcoholic encephalopathy, etc.), but the available historical material had to document some significant abuse of alcoholic beverages. Subjects for the study had all completed a battery of neuropsychological tests. These tests were done on a referral basis and thus do not technically represent a random sample of alcoholics. However, the presence of established or possible alcoholism was commonly used as a reason for referral, and so we customarily evaluated a large proportion of alcoholic patients admitted to the hospital. Referrals were accepted from all sections of the hospital, which included an active neurology service, a medical service, a large psychiatry service, and a number of specialized programs for alcoholic patients.

While all subjects were evaluated during a period of hospitalization, the reason for the hsopitalization need not have been alcoholism. Many of the subjects were in fact in the hospital for direct treatment for alcoholism, but others were there for treatment of a related condition, while still others were there for apparently unrelated conditons. The mean age of the subjects was 46.65 years (SD=8.42), with a mean education of 11.0 years (SD=3.53). None of the subjects in the sample was a patient in one of the specialized alcoholism

---

[a]The initial sample put into the cluster analysis described below consisted of 150 subjects. However, six of them were assigned to a number of very small clusters, consisting of one or two subjects each. These small clusters were dropped from subsequent analyses, and so the sample size for everything but the initial cluster analysis was 144 subjects.

programs at the time of evaluation, although many of them were in such programs previously or subsequently.

Follow-up Study. Subjects for the follow-up study consisted of fifty right-handed male alcoholics randomly selected from patients in the specialized alcoholism treatment programs at the hospital. These subjects are described in greater detail in the results section of this report.

In order to complete the necessary statistical analyses of the data, only subjects who had complete data for the 21 test variables utilized could be included in either part of the study. Patients with missing data were therefore not considered as eligible for selection as subjects.

Procedure:

Psychological Testing. Each subject was individually administered the tests indicated in the list below. In general, all tests were given in the same order.

Tests Administered

(1-11)	(1)	Wechsler Adult Intelligence Scale (WAIS) (11 subtests)
(12)	(2)	Halstead Category Test
(13)	(3)	Tactual Performance Test—Total Time
(14)	(4)	Tactual Performance Test—Memory
(15)	(5)	Tactual Performance Test—Location
(16)	(6)	Speech Sounds Perception Test
(17)	(7)	Seashore Rhythm Test
(18)	(8)	Trail Making Test—Part B
(19)	(9)	Finger Tapping Test
(20)	(10)	Aphasia Screening Test
(21)	(11)	Perceptual Disorders Examination

Since the 11 Wechsler scale subtests were treated separately, there was a total of 21 test variables. These tests comprise a reasonably comprehensive battery for evaluation of perceptual, motor and cognitive skills. They are well described in many places (Matarazzo, 1972; Reitan, 1966; Reitan and Davison, 1974; Russell, Neuringer, and Goldstein, 1970), and space will not be taken to re-describe them here. The tests were all scored in the manner described in the above references. In the cases of the Aphasia Screening Test and the Perceptual Disorders Examination, the scoring system described in Russell, Neuringer, and Goldstein (1970) was employed. These scores were designed to reflect degree of aphasia and of impairment of elementary perceptual skills, in a global manner.

Diagnostic and Demographic Variables. Medical histories varying in completeness from brief notes to extensive narratives were available for each subject.

These records were screened and it was determined that data could be obtained for all subjects on the following items.

1. Age in Years
2. Years of Education
3. Marital Status—Single, Married, Divorced, Widowed or Separated
4. Employment status at time of hospitalization—Employed, Unemployed or Retired
5. Socioeconomic Status—as determined by a modified Hollingshead-Redlich procedure, based on present or previous occupation.

   1 =High Executives, Large Proprietors, and Major Professionals

   2 =Business Managers, Medium Sized Business Proprietors, and Lesser Professionals

   3 =Administrative Personnel, Small Business Owners, and Minor Professionals

   4 =Clerical and Sales Workers, Technicians, Little Business Owners

   5 =Skilled Manual Employees

   6 =Machine Operators and Semi-Skilled Employes

   7 =Unskilled Employees and Never Worked.
6. Primary Diagnosis—Usually the diagnosis for which the patient was being treated when the patient received his research testing. It was scored as Alcoholism, Medical, Neurological or Psychiatric.
7. Alcoholic Organic Brain Syndrome—Any diagnosis made prior to testing with any of the following alternative wordings: (a) Chronic Brain Syndrome: Alcoholism; (b) Alcoholic Encephalopathy; (c) Organic Brain Syndrome: Alcoholism; (d) Nonpsychotic Organic Brain Syndrome: Alcoholism. This variable was scored as present or absent.
8. Other Brain Damage—Any diagnoses involving structural brain damage other than those directly associated with alcoholism were also scored as present or absent.
9. Seizures—Any history of a seizure disorder was recorded as present.

The authors were reticent about including any variables relating to quantitative aspects of the drinking history. While it is undoubtedly of great import to know for how long and in what quantities the patient drinks, the sketchiness and unreliability of this information as obtained either from the alcoholic patient or a relative is well known to most clinicians who work with alcoholics. We were therefore reluctant to provide what might be only pseudo-quantitative data. As a compromise, we adopted the following procedure. The records were screened for those cases in which there was some quantitative estimate of length of time of significant drinking. Based on these cases, it was determined that the median length of time was 15 years. With this reference point in mind, we went back to the cases, and classed those subjects with 15 or more years of drinking history as long-term drinkers, while those with less than 15 years of drinking history were classed as short-term drinkers. In this manner, we were able to obtain what we feel is reasonably reliable data for 108 of the 150 subjects. Thus, we do not have complete data for this variable.

In summary, the data for the main study consisted of 21 test variables and ten "marker" variables. The 21 test variables were derived from the subtests of the Wechsler Adult Intelligence Scale, and a battery of neuropsychological tests, developed by Halstead (1947) and Reitan (1966). The ten marker variables consisted of various pieces of diagnostic and demographic information obtained from the medical records of subjects. Complete data were obtained for each subject, with the exception of the length of drinking variable.

Treatment of Data. The major analysis performed involved the clustering of the 150 subjects in the main study, based on the 21 test variables. For this purpose, the "*k*-means" process was used (MacQueen, 1967), which is one of many methods for classification of multivariate material. The purpose of the procedure is that of partitioning multidimensional data into a number of sets in a reasonably efficient manner. By a process of collapsing means when they do not differ by an assigned value, and separating them when they differ by another value, the process eventually arrives at a reasonably optimal partition. Then all points (in this case, subjects) are classified on the basis of nearness to the final means. In other words, each subject is "clustered" on the basis of the mean from which he is least distant. The computer program that accomplishes this analysis prints out the mean test scores for each of the clusters derived, as well as some identification of the series of subjects that were placed into that cluster. Thus, we get a picture of what the average cluster member looks like on the tests, as well as a list of who belongs to the cluster. Because of the apparently reasonable approach to the classification problem, and the convenience of the computer printout with regard to the needs of the present study, the *k*-means method appeared to be quite suitable.

A major purpose of the study was that of determining whether or not the cluster analysis generated groups could be anchored to the diagnostic and demographic variables. The statistical method utilized to evaluate this relationship was multiple regression, with the ten marker variables as the predictors and the assigned cluster as the criterion variable. Two analyses were actually performed, since length of drinking history was not obtained for all subjects. Therefore one multiple regression analysis was performed for all subjects, while a second one was done with just those subjects for whom length of drinking history was available. Tables containing diagnostic and demographic descriptive data were also prepared, to allow for inspection of similarities and differences among the clusters.

The purpose of the follow-up portion of the study was that of making a preliminary assessment of the clinical relevance of the typology obtained by cluster analysis. Data obtained from the fifty alcoholism treatment program patients mentioned above were used for this part of the study. Assignment of each of these subjects to one of the previously established clusters was made by means of a discriminant function analysis. The discriminant function weights obtained for the original 144 subjects were applied to the test scores of these fifty subjects, on the basis of which a prediction of cluster membership was made for each subject. In other words, cluster assignment was made by means of what would ordinarily be a cross-validation procedure. In this way we could determine whether or not a specialized program catered to some particular type of alcoholic. More importantly, however, follow-up data were available for 32 of the fifty subjects, and so the relationship between cluster membership and treatment outcome could be evaluated, at least on this preliminary basis. Statistical treatment of this part of the study proved to be unfeasible because of the spottiness of the data and the small number of subjects. However, tables containing descriptive data were prepared.

RESULTS

The Main Study Sample
This section contains data that provide a description of the main study sample as a whole. Table 7–1 contains means and standard deviations for each of

Table 7-1. Means and Standard Deviations of the Psychological Test Scores for All Subjects in the Main Study (*N*=150)

Name of Test	Type of Score	Abbreviation	Mean	SD
WAIS Information	Scaled Score	I	10.09	2.84
WAIS Comprehension	Scaled Score	C	11.00	3.52
WAIS Arithmetic	Scaled Score	A	9.91	3.13
WAIS Similarities	Scaled Score	S	9.40	3.44
WAIS Digit Span	Scaled Score	D	9.03	2.95
WAIS Vocabulary	Scaled Score	V	10.10	3.09
WAIS Digit Symbol	Scaled Score	DS	6.25	2.70
WAIS Picture Completion	Scaled Score	PC	9.35	2.68
WAIS Block Design	Scaled Score	BD	8.11	2.64
WAIS Picture Arrangement	Scaled Score	PA	7.95	2.70
WAIS Object Assembly	Scaled Score	OA	8.41	3.01
Halstead Category Test	# Errors	CAT	80.89	29.82
Tactual Performance Test-Time	Time in Seconds	TPT-T	20.82	7.36
Tactual Performance Test-Memory	# Recalled	TPT-M	5.91	2.17
Tactual Performance Test-Location	# Located Correctly	TPT-L	2.47	2.10
Speech Sounds Perception Test	# Errors	SSP	12.20	8.62
Seashore Rhythm Test	# Errors	RHY	7.29	4.03
Trail Making Test-Part B	Time in Seconds	TR-B	142.03	84.45
Finger Tapping Test	Average # Taps	TAP	45.45	10.74
Reitan Aphasia Screening Test	# Errors	APH	7.89	5.69
Perceptual Disorders Examination	# Errors	PD	18.71	15.49

the 21 psychological test variables. Table 7–2 presents the diagnostic and demographic data for all subjects in major clusters, either in the form of means or of percentages.

Table 7-2. Diagnostic and Demographic Data for All Subjects in the Major Clusters

Variable	N	Score	
Mean Age in Years	144	46.65	(SD = 8.42)
Mean Education in Years	144	11.02	(SD = 3.53)
Mean Socioeconomic Status	144	4.52	(SD = 1.71)
% Employed	144	55.1%	
% Married	144	49.8%	
% Short Term Drinkers	102	22.5%	
% Alcoholic Brain Syndrome	144	55.4%	
% Other Organic Brain Syndrome	144	32.2%	
% Subjects with Seizure History	144	22.1%	
% Primary Diagnosis of Alcoholism	144	42.4%	

The Cluster Analysis

The k-means process generated ten clusters. However, five of them were trivial, containing only one or two subjects each. These small clusters were dropped from further consideration, and so the remaining analyses were based on the 144 subjects grouped into five major clusters. The means for each of the test scores in each of the clusters, along with the number of subjects in each cluster are presented in table 7–3. In order to provide a clearer picture of the cluster structure, data were also put in graphic form. The profile patterns of various clusters for the WAIS are presented in figure 7–1. In the case of the other tests, the scores had to be converted into standard score form before profiling could be accomplished. A T-Score conversion was made of the ten neuropsychological test variables, with a mean of fifty and a standard deviation of ten. Some of the scores were reflected so that a T-Score of over fifty always represents an above average score. A set of profiles consisting of the converted mean scores for each cluster is presented in figure 7–2.

The Diagnostic and Demographic Variables

Data for these variables are presented in table 7–4 in the same form as they were in table 7–2. However, in this case the information is broken down by cluster, and frequency distributions are presented for employment status, marital status, length of time drinking and primary diagnosis.

Cluster Descriptions

Cluster 1–N=10 (6.7% of sample). These subjects are below average in verbal and performance intelligence. They exhibit severe retardation of motor speed and impairment of elementary perceptual skills. On the neuropsychological tests they exhibit severe, generalized deficit. Length of drinking history was not known for many of them, but none of those for whom we could obtain information had short histories. They tend to be single and of low socio-economic status. Half of them were employed at time of hospitalization. They average 8½ years of education. Less than half of them were in the hospital with a primary diagnosis of alcoholism, but 70 percent of them carried an alcoholic organic brain syndrome diagnosis. Only one of them had a seizure disorder, but half of them had organic brain syndromes related to processes other than alcoholism. They are the oldest cluster, averaging 58 years in age.

Interpreting these findings, this cluster appears to consist of relatively elderly men of low socioeconomic status, many of whom have medical and neurological

Table 7-3. Means and Standard Deviations of the Psychological Test Scores for Each Major Cluster

Test*	Cluster Number									
	1		2		3		4		5	
	Mean	SD	Mean	SD	Mean	SD	Mean	SD	Mean	SD
I	8.10	1.60	10.02	2.33	6.53	1.06	9.72	1.94	14.00	1.71
C	8.80	1.69	10.08	2.57	7.00	1.77	11.20	2.55	15.83	2.66
A	7.10	1.79	9.02	2.27	6.27	1.75	10.93	2.40	13.52	2.19
S	6.20	1.62	8.88	2.88	4.53	2.42	10.43	2.22	13.30	2.20
D	5.90	2.88	8.08	2.61	6.80	2.14	9.80	1.56	12.35	2.44
V	7.80	2.10	9.74	1.87	6.33	1.40	10.17	2.39	14.13	2.34
DS	0.70	1.34	5.52	1.76	4.33	1.18	7.28	1.52	9.52	2.13
PC	5.10	1.37	8.60	1.90	6.67	1.95	10.63	1.82	12.26	1.57
BD	4.50	1.84	7.14	1.69	5.00	1.77	9.56	1.29	10.83	2.39
PA	3.80	2.35	7.16	1.58	5.87	1.60	8.98	1.99	11.04	2.40
OA	4.10	2.18	7.36	2.27	5.87	2.26	10.26	2.03	10.70	2.40
CAT	127.20	12.43	91.96	22.65	95.47	20.79	66.39	24.29	55.26	25.95
TPT-T	27.24	8.52	24.74	5.32	24.71	5.32	16.87	6.38	15.03	5.70
TPT-M	3.90	1.85	4.76	1.96	5.47	2.45	6.87	1.47	7.61	1.73
TPT-L	0.70	0.82	1.72	1.53	1.13	1.06	3.11	2.18	4.04	2.08
SSP	29.20	10.23	11.26	5.14	21.20	8.17	9.78	6.80	5.26	2.45
RHY	11.90	4.41	7.26	4.03	9.67	3.60	6.46	3.31	5.13	3.20
TR-B	316.00	53.83	153.36	63.34	247.20	68.84	93.15	36.29	75.91	25.56
TAP	36.90	14.07	41.08	10.47	48.93	8.21	49.21	8.59	49.13	8.99
APH	16.30	8.01	8.04	3.65	15.53	5.95	5.76	3.26	3.13	3.12
PD	40.90	15.20	20.58	12.23	19.20	8.18	12.54	10.04	12.61	12.94
# of Ss	10		50		15		46		23	

*For full names of tests, see table 7-1.

Figure 7-1. WAIS Scaled Score Patterns for the Five Clusters

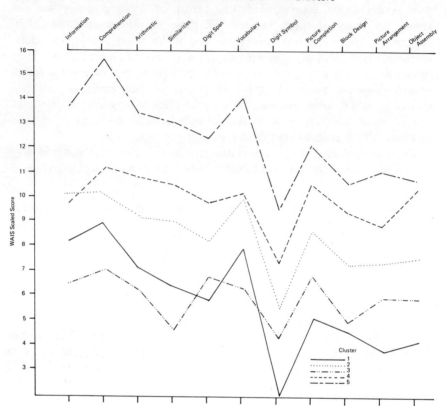

problems other than those directly relatable to alcoholism. Relative to the other clusters and to normative standards, they are severely and globally impaired. Indeed, all but one of them had diagnosed organic brain syndromes associated with alcoholism or some other process. Clinically, the psychological test findings for the cluster as a whole would be commonly interpreted to mean that these individuals are sufficiently impaired to be highly disabled with regard to adapting to a normal environment and engaging in independent living. They would require some form of structured environment in order to achieve some reasonable adjustment.

Cluster 2—N=50 (33.3% of sample). This cluster is the largest one, constituting one-third of the sample. They tend to be younger, more educated and of higher socioeconomic status than Cluster 1 members. Over half of them are married, and while most of them have long drinking histories, there are some short-term alcoholics among them. Slightly over half of them are unemployed. On psychological tests, they have average level language related skills and only

Figure 7-2. T-Scores of Neuropsychological Test Variables for the Five Clusters

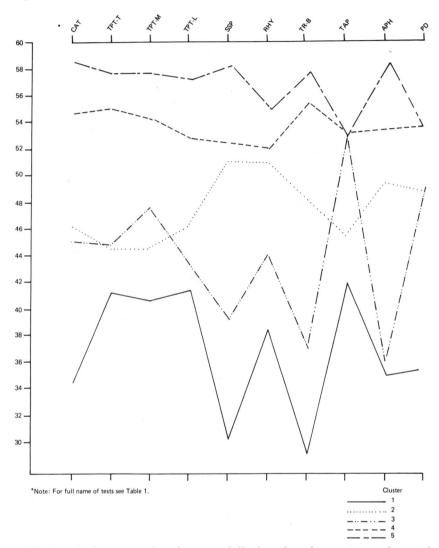

*Note: For full name of tests see Table 1.

Cluster
——————— 1
··············· 2
—··—··— 3
———— 4
——— — 5

mildly impaired perceptual and motor skills, but they demonstrate substantial impairment on tests requiring various complex abilities such as abstract reasoning, novel problem solving and perceptual-motor coordination. The degree of impairment is not as severe as that of the Cluster 1 group, but still reflects significant disability relative to the normal person. Diagnostically, almost two-thirds of the subjects carry the diagnosis of alcoholic organic brain syndrome, while 38 percent of them have organic brain syndromes related to other causes. Twenty percent of them have a combination of alcoholic and other

Table 7–4. Diagnostic and Demographic Data Arranged by Cluster

Variable	Cluster Number				
	1	*2*	*3*	*4*	*5*
Mean Age in Years	58.0	47.5	44.5	44.4	43.8
SD	7.3	7.7	9.4	7.7	7.4
Mean Education in Years	8.5	11.0	8.3	10.1	15.6
SD	2.5	2.6	2.8	2.7	3.1
Mean Socioeconomic Status	5.9	4.6	5.1	4.7	2.9
SD	1.1	1.5	1.5	1.4	2.0
Employment Status					
% Employed	50.0%	46.0%	60.0%	54.3%	65.2%
% Unemployed	20.0%	48.0%	20.0%	28.3%	26.1%
% Retired	30.0%	6.0%	20.0%	17.4%	8.7%
Marital Status					
% Single	60.0%	8.0%	13.3%	2.2%	8.7%
% Married	20.0%	56.0%	60.0%	69.6%	43.5%
% Widowed	20.0%	2.0%	0.0%	2.2%	0.0%
% Divorced	0.0%	32.0%	20.0%	17.4%	43.5%
% Separated	0.0%	2.0%	6.7%	8.7%	4.3%
Length of Drinking					
% Long Term	49.0%	56.0%	53.3%	45.7%	30.4%
% Short Term	0.0%	14.0%	26.7%	28.3%	43.5%
% Don't Know	60.0%	30.0%	20.0%	26.1%	26.1%
Presence of Brain Syndrome					
% Alcoholic Brain Syndrome	70.0%	64.0%	66.7%	41.3%	34.8%
% Other Organic Brain Syndrome	50.0%	38.0%	64.7%	21.7%	4.4%
% Subjects with Seizure History	10.0%	26.0%	26.7%	26.1%	21.7%
Primary Diagnosis					
% Alcoholism	40.0%	46.0%	40.0%	50.0%	34.8%
% Medical	30.0%	2.0%	20.0%	10.9%	13.0%
% Neurological	20.0%	30.0%	13.3%	21.7%	8.7%
% Psychiatric	10.0%	22.0%	26.7&	17.4%	43.5%
Number of Subjects	10	50	15	46	23

etiology organic brain syndromes. Somewhat less than half of them received a primary diagnosis of alcoholism, and about a quarter of them have seizure disorders. Eighty percent of the subjects in this cluster have diagnosed organic brain syndromes, if one combines the alcoholic and nonalcoholic etiology cases.

This cluster would appear to constitute a group of men in early middle age who have already experienced substantial intellectual deterioration. Most of them are unemployed, long-term drinkers. Many of them have experienced some difficulty in brain function, either in the form of a seizure disorder or an organic brain syndrome. Based on the findings that only one case in this cluster had a primary medical diagnosis, and that only one-third of them had organic brain syndromes associated with causes other than alcoholism, there is a strong implication that members of this cluster have alcoholism as their major difficulty, rather than as ancillary to other disorders. While the finding that less than half of the subjects had a primary diagnosis of alcoholism might appear to contradict this inference, it may be pointed out that in many cases, their primary diagnoses reflected various consequences or correlates of alcoholism. For example, in psychiatry, the examining physician may have chosen to give priority to the underlying psychiatric disorder (e.g., anxiety reaction). Many of the neurological diagnoses involve head trauma associated with periods of intoxication. The one primary medical diagnosis in this cluster was diabetes, a condition commonly associated with alcoholism.

An important clinical feature of this group would be what is commonly characterized as a good verbal facade. The preservation of normal verbal intelligence provides this group with the capacity to give the appearance of mental intactness, despite the existence of substantial underlying impairment of cognitive abilities. The impairment, however, becomes manifest on psychological tests and in life situations that require sound judgment, good organizing ability, and the capacity to cope with problems of a complex and novel nature. This group is marked by a considerable degree of deterioration for its mean age. As will become clear when the other groups are discussed, while Cluster 2 members tend to be slightly older than members of some of the other clusters, the degree of deterioration appears to be disproportionate to the relatively small difference in mean age levels. While Cluster 2 members would not appear to require the degree of structure thought to be optimal for the Cluster 1 members, the impairments noted would be likely to have consequences for performance at work, and for the ability to cope effectively with problems as they arise in everyday life.

Cluster 3—N=15 (19% of sample). This cluster consists of a small group of individuals in early middle age who tend to be relatively low in years of education and socioeconomic status. Most of them are married, and about three-quarters of them are long-term alcoholics. Diagnostically, they are quite similar to Clusters 1 and 2. Twelve out of 15 of them have diagnosed organic brain syndromes, either because of alcoholism or for some other reason. Again, substantial impairment is seen on the psychological tests. The pattern appears to reflect a combination of Clusters 1 and 2. They are more like Cluster 1 than like Cluster 2 on language related tests, but more like Cluster 2 than Cluster 1 on tests of complex cognitive abilities. Put another way, they show the same level of moderate intellectual impairment as does Cluster 2, but in their case, verbal abilities are not spared. Indeed, the mean scores on the WAIS verbal subtests tend to be even worse than those attained by the Cluster 1 group. However, relative to the Cluster 1 group, they have good preservation of pure motor speed and relatively good performance on tests of elementary perceptual skills.

There is some clinical research evidence that the pattern described fits the individual with a developmental history of cognitive deficit. This kind of condition may be described in numberous ways and one might see terms such as borderline mental retardation, borderline mental functioning, congenital brain maldevelopment, and mental deficiency in the histories of these individuals. An inspection of the records available for the 15 subjects in the cluster revealed that terms of this type were used to describe four of the subjects. However, the neuropsychological test reports, written without knowledge of the case history, suggested some developmental component in 11 of the 15 cases. Thus, there is something about the cluster pattern that suggests at least to the clinical neuropsychologist the possibility of early childhood or congenital brain dysfunction. Furthermore, Russell, Neuringer, and Goldstein (1970) found a significant amount of concordance between essentially this same test pattern and neurological diagnosis of congenital brain damage.

When the "Process Key" developed by these authors was applied to the present data, the findings were quite striking. This "Key" is a set of objective rules applied to esentially the same psychological test battery as the one used in the present study. The "Key" makes a prediction as to whether the test performance reflects no brain damage, or acute, static or congenital brain damage. When applied to the present data, 0 percent of Cluster 1, 18 percent of Cluster 2, 4.4 percent of Cluster 4 and 0 percent of Cluster 5 were called "Congenital" by the "Key." However, 60 percent of Cluster 3 was placed in the "Congenital" category. Thus, both clinical interpretation and objective classification of neuropsychological test patterns suggest a relatively high incidence of early childhood or congenital brain damage in Cluster 3.

The finding that only four of the 15 cases received confirmation of this condition from the records is not particularly supportive, but without special inquiry there is generally little reason for diagnosticians to address themselves to this area, particularly when the patient is generally presenting with complaints involving his alcoholism or his current psychiatric or physical status. Further research involving direct inquiry into the developmental history of the patient appears to be needed. Elsewhere in this volume, Dr. Tarter reviews evidence for antecedent neurological and neuropsychological impairment in alcoholics. Possibly, Cluster 3 represents a group of alcoholics who display this phenomenon. In any event, it is interesting to note that the cluster anlysis yielded a clinically recognizable pattern.

If indeed Cluster 3 does reflect neuropsychological deficit occurring prior to acquisition of alcoholism, then the clinical implication is that this type of alcoholic has been perceptually and cognitively handicapped for virtually all of his life. Perhaps the alcoholism and other organic and psychiatric conditions add to the degree of impairment, but there may have been significant academic and other adaptive difficulties before these other conditions existed. In summary, the Cluster 3 subject tends to be an individual with limited general intelligence, a moderate degree of impairment of complex problem solving and conceptual skills, and relative intactness of basic motor and perceptual abilities.

Cluster 4—N=46 (30.7% of sample). This large cluster also consists of men who tend to be in early middle age. They average ten years in education and almost 70 percent of them are married. Length of drinking history was available for 34 of the subjects in the cluster: of this number 21 had long histories and 13 short histories. Their socioeconomic status of 4.72 is quite close to what was found for Cluster 2 (4.62) and 54.35 percent have primary diagnoses of alcoholism; 41.3 percent have alcoholic organic brain syndromes, 21.74 percent have organic brain syndromes owing to other causes, and 26.1 percent have seizure disorders. Exactly half of the subjects have organic brain syndromes when one combines the alcoholic and nonalcoholic etiologies. It would appear that this group is healthier than the ones previously mentioned on the basis of there being fewer organic brain syndromes, but there is not a corresponding decline in incidence of seizure disorders.

Psychological test performance is characterized by generally superior performance relative to what was found for Clusters 1, 2, and 3. The WAIS verbal subtests all fall within the average range for the general population as do several of the performance subtests. Psychomotor slowness is still present, but not to the degree found in Clusters 1, 2, and 3. On the neuropsychological tests, measures of elementary perceptual and motor abilities are performed within the normal range. Tests of complex problem solving and abstraction abilities tend to be only slightly deviant from normal, but markedly superior to performance levels of the previously discussed clusters. Overall, none of the mean neuropsychological test scores could be called markedly deficient, but relative to available norms, most of them are slightly below average.

Interpretation of what this cluster constitutes would appear to be relatively straightforward. The average cluster member can be characterized as a mildly impaired individual. Clinical interpretation of the pattern would reflect the impression of mild brain damage. One would suspect that these are alcoholics who are still functioning reasonably well, but who are beginning to show the inroads of deterioration. In everyday life such deterioration is probably only seen in subtle ways, and on examination these individuals are less likely to receive diagnoses of organic brain syndrome than are members of Clusters 1, 2, and 3.

It may be of interest to contrast Clusters 2 and 4 at this point. These groups are quite similar with regard to age, years of education and socioeconomic status. A higher percentage of the subjects in Cluster 4 are married and employed, but the magnitude of the differences are not impressive. The difference in length of drinking, however, may be of importance. The percentage of short-term drinkers in Cluster 4 is twice as high as in Cluster 2. What appears to be of particular significance are the large discrepancies between percentages of organic brain syndrome and between performance levels on the psychological tests. Combining alcoholic and nonalcoholic organic brain syndromes, 80 percent of Cluster 2 carries this diagnosis, while only 50 percent of Cluster 4 does so. Correspondingly, Cluster 2 members tend to do substantially worse on the psychological tests overall than do Cluster 4 members. The interesting point is that while these two groups are of comparable age, educational level, and socioeconomic status, there is a marked discrepancy in their neurological and neuropsychological status.

The only variable we considered that could be related to this discrepancy is length of time drinking. Looking at these data more closely, we find the following. Of the fifty subjects in Cluster 2, drinking histories were available for 35 subjects. Of these 35, there were seven (20 percent short-term drinkers. Of the 34 subjects in Cluster 4 for whom histories were available, 13 (38 percent) were short-term drinkers. Thus, differences in length of time drinking could account for a portion of the discrepancies between Cluster 2 and 4 in regard to test performance and diagnostic variables, but probably do not provide a complete explanation. In any event, these data do appear to rule out age, education, and socioeconomic status as major contributors to differences between the two largest clusters.

Cluster 5—N=23 (15.3% of sample). With regard to the demographic variables, this cluster is characterized by its relatively high socioeconomic status and educational level. Marital status, at 43.5 percent married, is a lower proportion married than found in any of the other groups with the exception of Cluster 1. Further examination of this variable may be of some interest. In Cluster 1, six of the ten subjects report themselves as single, while none of the remaining four report themselves as being divorced or separated. Thus, 21 of the 23 Cluster 5 subjects were married at one time, while, apparently, only four of the ten Cluster 1 subjects were ever married. Thus, there is some suggestion that the reported high incidence of divorce among alcoholics may be relatively concentrated among those with high educational and socioeconomic levels.

On the diagnostic variables, the incidence of organic brain syndrome, alcoholic or otherwise, is lower than in the case of the other clusters. The incidence of primary diagnosis of alcoholism is also relatively low. Of the 15 primary diagnoses that are not alcoholism, ten are psychiatric, three medical, and two neurological. The proportion of primary psychiatric diagnosis is substantially higher in Cluster 5 (43.5 percent) than it is in any of the other clusters. It would appear that Cluster 5 is characterized by a high incidence of psychosocial disruption, as reflected in the relatively elevated divorce and psychiatric diagnosis rates.

The mean scores on the psychological tests reflect almost uniformly normal or better than normal performance. On the basis of available norms, 19 of the 21 tests were performed at an average or better level. With regard to mental abilities, these appear to be normally functioning alcoholics. On the WAIS, the pattern of performance in this group is characterized by superior verbal ability, but performance ability that only hovers around average for the general population. Thus, mean subtest scores on the WAIS range from 15.83 for Comprehension, a superior range score, to 9.52 for Digit Symbol, a score that is slightly below average for the general population. On the psychological tests, all of the tests were performed within the normal range, with two exceptions; the Category Test and the Location component of the Tactual Performance Test. Thus, even within this context of good to excellent performance, the Cluster 5 alcoholic still appears to have some difficulty with abstract reasoning and complex memory abilities.

Despite the generally normal level of performance, the question may be raised as to whether there is any sign of impairment in this group. When dealing with bright, well-educated people, it is often useful to compare present performance with some estimate of former potential; that is, the individual is compared with himself at another time, rather than with the average for the population. Obviously, the best way to do this is to get previous test results, but since this is usually not possible, ways have been devised to make estimates from the current test pattern. Various attempts have been made to construct deterioration indices, most of which are based on the concept of scatter. Thus, a uniform level of performance across tests is felt to be indicative of lack of deterioration, while the opposite is concluded when there is a great deal of scatter. Examining the results for Cluster 5 (see Figs. 7–1 and 7–2), it can be seen that the pattern of performance is quite ragged. It is most apparent on the WAIS, but it is also present in the case of the neuropsychological tests, where the relatively poor performance on the Category Test and Tactual Performance Test-Location contrasts sharply with the relatively excellent performance on the Speech Perception and Trail Making Tests. It is therefore possible that even Cluster 5 may be showing some early signs of deterioration. Indeed, a small number of them have received organic brain syndrome diagnoses.

Cluster 5 thus appears to consist of a group of talented individuals with significant problems of a psychosocial nature. There is a relatively high incidence of short-term drinkers in the cluster as compared with other groups. A relatively small number of members of this cluster have run into alcohol associated medical or neurological difficulties. However, there is some evidence for early deterioration, despite generally good to excellent performance on the psychological tests. One is tempted to speculate that the Cluster 5 member represents the type of upper middle class alcoholic commonly seen in psychotherapy or in other verbally oriented, community based treatment forms.

Relationship between the Clusters and the Diagnostic and Demographic Variables

In order to determine whether or not the relationship between the clusters and the diagnostic variables reached statistical significance, the technique of multiple regression was used. In this case, a stepwise multiple regression analysis was performed, utilizing a computer program found in Dixon (1973) (BMD02R). The stepwise procedure provides information regarding the contribution of the individual variables and variable combinations to the overall multiple correlation coefficient. The predictor variables were the ten diagnostic and demographic indices, while cluster number served as the criterion variable. Since we did not have data on length of drinking for all subjects, two analyses were performed, one with length of drinking excluded and another, with a reduced *n*, (102 subjects) with length of drinking included. In order to help resolve scaling problems associated with some of the diagnostic and demographic indicators, all of them were treated as ordinal or dichotomous variables. This procedure necessitated converting three variables. Marital status was changed to "married-not married," primary diagnosis was converted to "alcoholic-not alcoholic," and employment status was changed to "employed-unemployed." The remaining variables were already ordinal or dichotomous.

Results for both analyses are presented in table 7–5. The final multiple *R* in each case reflects the strength of the relationship between the entire set of predictor variables and the criterion. The probability value associated with the *F*

Table 7-5. Stepwise Multiple Regression Analyses with Diagnostic and Demographic Variables as Predictors and Cluster Membership as the Criterion

A.	Length of Drinking Variable Excluded (N=144)	
Step Number	*Variable Entered*	*R*
1	Education	.439
2	Age	.496
3	Alcoholic Brain Syndrome	.536
4	Other Organic Brain Syndrome	.565
5	Socioeconomic Status	.587
6	Marital Status	.589
7	Primary Diagnosis	.590
8	Employment Status	.591
9	Seizure History	.591 (*p* < .001)

B.	Length of Drinking Variable Included (N=102)	
Step Number	*Variable Entered*	*R*
1	Education	.385
2	Length of Drinking	.483
3	Alcoholic Brain Syndrome	.532
4	Other Organic Brain Syndrome	.560
5	Socioeconomic Status	.567
6	Age	.574
7	Seizure History	.576
8	Marital Status	.578
9	Primary Diagnosis	.580
10	Employment Status	.581 (*p* < .001)

ratio obtained from the analysis of variance performed at the final variable entrance in the stepwise procedure indicates whether or not the obtained multiple R is significantly different from zero. In the case of the analysis with length of drinking excluded, the final multiple R was equal to 0.59 and the final F was equal to 8.0. With 9 and 134 degrees of freedom, this value is significant at the 0.001 confidence level. The final multiple R for the analysis with length of drinking included was equal to 0.58 and the final F value was equal to 4.63. With 10 and 91 degrees of freedom, this value is also significant at the 0.001 level.

These results indicate the cluster membership is associated with a linear combination of demographic and diagnostic variables. Thus, we have established a statistical basis for the typology generated by the cluster analysis; that is, the clustering obtained is associated with external marker variables in the sample studied. As indicated above, the approach employed here involves demonstrating that the typology obtained has some meaning beyond the test scores and mathematics that produced it. We feel that this additional meaningfulness has been demonstrated.

The utilization of a stepwise procedure allows us to examine for which variables had the stronger and which the weaker relationship with cluster membership. The relevant data are presented in table 7–5. The ordering differs somewhat between the analysis in which length of drinking was not included and the one in which it was included. In both cases, however, education seems to be the most important variable. In the analysis in which length of drinking was included, it is the second most important variable. In the analysis in which it was not included, age became the second most important variable. In both analyses, marital status, primary diagnosis, employment status, and seizure history are relatively less crucial. The presence or absence or an organic brain syndrome took an intermediate position in both analyses.

The Follow-up

This portion of the study represented a preliminary attempt to evaluate the clinical relevance of the typology system developed here. The major question we attempted to answer was, "Is there any relationship between cluster membership and treatment outcome?" However, in order to answer this question it was necessary to develop procedures for assigning new subjects to clusters. Thus, the first part of this section is devoted to presenting the results of the procedures utilized. The sample for this part of the study consisted of fifty inpatients in a specialized, time limited, psychiatric treatment program for alcoholics. None of the fifty patients was included in the cluster analysis used to establish the typology. Attempts were made to do social work follow-up on all of these patients one year after discharge, but only 32 of the fifty received such follow-ups. The treatment outcome results were based on thirty of these 32 patients.

Characteristics of the 50 Follow-up Study Subjects. Table 7–6 contains the results of the psychological tests for the fifty subjects. The mean age was 45.26 years (SD=7.48) with 11.7 years of education (SD=2.71). The brevity of the inhospital stay and the structure of the treatment program did not allow time for evaluation for organic brain syndrome or seizure disorder on a routine basis.

Table 7–6. Means and Standard Deviations of the Psychological Test Scores for the 50 Subjects Follow-up Sample*

Name of Test	Mean	SD
WAIS Information	10.90	2.18
WAIS Comprehension	11.38	3.10
WAIS Arithmetic	10.48	2.41
WAIS Similarities	10.04	2.70
WAIS Digit Span	9.90	3.23
WAIS Vocabulary	10.74	2.62
WAIS Digit Symbol	7.54	2.22
WAIS Picture Completion	9.90	2.60
WAIS Block Design	8.98	2.61
WAIS Picture Arrangement	7.94	2.26
WAIS Object Assembly	8.84	2.99
Halstead Category Test	74.72	26.83
Tactual Performance Test-Time	19.04	6.72
Tactual Performance Test-Memory	6.68	1.83
Tactual Performance Test-Location	3.18	2.50
Speech Sounds Perception Test	8.12	4.55
Seashore Rhythm Test	5.42	2.79
Trail Making Test-Part B	114.02	68.46
Finger Tapping Test	51.30	10.77
Reitan Aphasia Screening Test	5.24	3.82
Perceptual Disorders Examination	12.04	9.41

*Type of score and abbreviations are described in table 7–1.

However, the following general information can be provided. Alcoholism was always the primary diagnosis in these cases. Patients admitted to the program who were found on preliminary examination to have major general medical, neurological or psychiatric disorders were transferred shortly after admission to some more appropriate hospital facility. For this reason, it can be assumed that the sample was not likely to contain patients with major physical illnesses, psychiatric disturbances or neurological disorders. Patients who required medical or neurological treatment of acute alcoholic conditions were also not retained in the program, and so such patients were not included in the sample. The mean socioeconomic status was 4.76 (SD=1.73). Using the same criteria as applied in the main study, 54 percent of the subjects were employed, 14 percent retired, and 32 percent unemployed. Fifty-two percent of the subjects were married, 28 percent divorced, 8 percent single, 2 percent widowed, and 10 percent separated.

The problem of assigning new subjects was treated by means of discriminant analysis. A stepwise discriminant analysis (Dixon, 1973) was computed for the original 144 subjects, with the new fifty subjects included as a "cross-validation" group. In this way, the weights used in separating the 144 subjects into clusters were assigned to the test scores of the new group of fifty, and a cluster assignment was made for each of them based on these weights. If the original cluster analysis was stable, then the discriminant function should be highly accurate with regard to assigning individual subjects to clusters. The classification matrix presented in table 7–7 attests to this high level of accuracy; 92.7 percent of the cases were correctly classified. The bottom row of table 7–7 gives the distribution of cluster membership in the follow-up group. It will be noted that almost half of the fifty subjects were assigned to Cluster 4; the remainder,

Table 7–7. Classification Matrix Based on Discriminant Analysis of 150 Subjects with "Cross-Validation" Utilizing 50 Follow-up Study Subjects

	Number of Cases Classified into Group				
			Cluster		
Cluster	*1*	*2*	*3*	*4*	*5*
1	10	0	0	0	0
2	0	47	1	2	0
3	0	0	15	0	0
4	0	0	0	46	0
5	0	0	0	2	21
Follow-up Group	2	12	0	24	12

with the exception of two subjects in Cluster 1, were evenly distributed between Clusters 2 and 5. For readers who wish to calculate cluster membership on the basis of their own data, table 7–8 contains the constants and weights for each variable and cluster. For purposes of clarification, it may be pointed out that the high level of agreement obtained by the discriminant analysis is largely artifactual, since the discriminant analysis and the original cluster analysis were both based on the same data. The high level of agreement obtained only suggests that the cluster analysis is stable, since an independent statistical procedure (discriminant analysis) yields about the same grouping of subjects. The main objective of performing this analysis was that of obtaining the weights needed to classify new cases, since the k means clustering procedure provides no direct way of accomplishing this task.

Looking at the data in another way, we can say that the follow-up group is located somewhere in multivariate space, and that its location may be closer to that of some of the established clusters than to that of others. In order to view the findings in this manner, coefficients of the canonical variables were computed and the means of the first two of these were plotted on a scattergram.

Table 7–8. Discriminant Function Coefficients and Constants for Each of the Five Clusters

Name of Test*	Discriminant Functions				
	Cluster				
	1	2	3	4	5
I	2.09911	2.31971	1.81641	1.93217	2.81132
C	−0.02521	0.45457	−0.02884	0.68563	1.40191
A	2.91719	2.65824	2.76515	3.08040	3.36949
S	−0.06560	−0.18204	−0.41358	0.07079	−0.10823
D	0.70735	1.38143	1.17946	1.92603	2.50016
V	1.10056	0.54970	0.69828	0.23897	0.29235
DS	1.70037	2.93497	2.80669	3.36302	4.23502
PC	−0.31459	1.00605	0.19776	1.58517	2.07347
BD	1.75864	2.33367	1.57610	3.02770	3.47197
PA	1.52615	1.64681	1.80295	1.19532	0.89954
OA	1.18078	1.20801	1.19434	1.19090	0.06427
CAT	0.18463	0.13859	0.14987	0.09090	0.06427
TPT-T	1.10026	1.10625	1.16308	0.93213	0.90038
TPT-M	1.57770	1.85742	2.47318	2.68807	2.60702
TPT-L	1.57770	1.85742	2.47318	2.68807	2.60702
SSP	0.04631	0.18079	−0.29210	0.00919	0.28280
RHY	0.55490	0.31349	0.35762	0.33148	0.29351
TR-B	0.15834	0.09045	0.13522	0.06801	0.06283
TAP	0.51685	0.44980	0.59203	0.54554	0.49539
APH	1.63217	1.18051	1.64438	0.91821	0.88107
PD	0.00475	−0.02039	−0.07161	0.00707	0.00225

Constants				
−131.27523	−115.61269	−122.04669	−134.56694	−175.63293

*Abbreviation key is given in table 7–1.

The results are presented in figure 7–3. In this figure, the first canonical variable is plotted along the horizontal axis, and the second along the vertical axis. The picture is quite clear; the follow-up group lies closest in space to Cluster 4. It is therefore not surprising that almost half of the fifty follow-up subjects were classed into Cluster 4.

Relationships with Treatment Outcome. The findings here do not lend themselves to statistical analysis because of the smallness of the sample size and the spottiness of the data. Of the fifty subjects, 32 completed a follow-up interview one year after discharge from the treatment program. Of these 32, two were in Cluster 1, seven in Cluster 2, 14 in Cluster 4, and nine in Cluster 5. Because of the small number of subjects, Cluster 1 was dropped from further consideration. Therefore, the evaluation was based on thirty subjects distributed among three of the clusters.

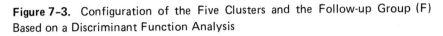

Figure 7-3. Configuration of the Five Clusters and the Follow-up Group (F) Based on a Discriminant Function Analysis

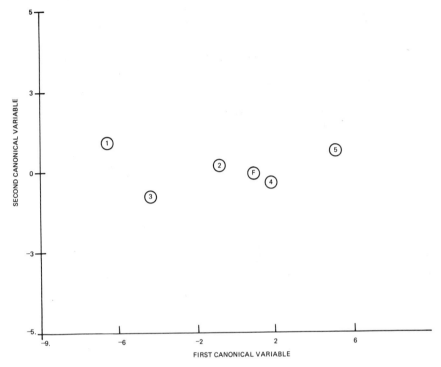

There is some reason to suspect that the ability to locate a patient for follow-up is associated with treatment outcome. The patient who is doing poorly may be reluctant to submit to a follow-up interview, while the patient who cannot be found may be more alienated and itinerant than the patient with a home address at which he can be located. It is therefore interesting to note that while only 25 percent (3 of 12) of the Cluster 5 subjects did not receive follow-up, 41.7 percent of both Cluster 2 (5 of 12) and Cluster 4 (10 of 24) patients did not receive follow-ups.

Another index of treatment outcome is whether or not the expatient is working. The data available indicate that 57 percent of the Cluster 2, 54 percent of the Cluster 4, and 67 percent of the Cluster 5 subjects were working. Thus, there is again a slight tendency for the Cluster 5 subjects to do better. With regard to level of employment, the Cluster 2 group had a mean socioeconomic status of 5. The mean for Cluster 4 was 5.1, and for Cluster 5, the mean was qual to 3. A rating of 5 denotes the socioeconomic level of skilled manual employees, while 3 includes administrative personnel, small businessmen, and minor professionals. It would therefore appear that there is a tendency for more

Cluster 5 members to be working, and working at higher level occupations, than is the case for the other clusters.

As part of the follow-up, the interviewer asks the following two questions: (1) "In the last year, what is the longest length of time you have gone without taking a drink?" (2) "Suppose you look at it another way. In the last year how many months altogether have you gone without taking a drink? Remember, these months do not have to be consecutive." Responses to these questions, by cluster, are presented in table 7–9. One may draw varying inferences from these

Table 7–9. Percentages of Longest Time without a Drink and Total Months of Abstinence in the Follow-up Group Presented by Cluster

		Cluster		
A. *Longest Time without a Drink*		*2*	*4*	*5*
	Whole Year	14.3%	21.4%	22.2%
	10–11 Months	28.6%	7.1%	0.0%
	8–9 Months	0.0%	14.2%	22.2%
	6–7 Months	0.0%	7.1%	0.0%
	4–5 Months	0.0%	7.1%	11.1%
	2–3 Months	28.6%	7.1%	44.4%
	0–1 Month	14.3%	7.1%	0.0%
	Drinking All Year	14.3%	28.6%	0.0%
B. *Total Months of Abstinence*				
	Whole Year	14.4%	21.4%	22.2%
	10–11 Months	0.0%	7.1%	0.0%
	8–9 Months	0.0%	7.1%	0.0%
	6–7 Months	14.3%	0.0%	11.1%
	4–5 Months	14.3%	21.4%	0.0%
	2–3 Months	28.6%	7.1%	44.4%
	0–1 Month	14.3%	28.5%	0.0%
	Drinking All Year	14.3%	28.5%	0.0%

data, but it is perhaps most striking that all of the Cluster 5 subjects had a period of abstinence, even if it was only for one month. A relatively high percentage of the Cluster 5 subjects had a two- to three-month abstinence period. We cannot discern a trend differentiating the Cluster 2 from the Cluster 4 subjects. There are percentage differences, but they appear to be random in nature.

The conclusions that can be reached from this very preliminary analysis are as follows. There appears to be a tendency toward more satisfactory outcome among Cluster 5 subjects. A higher proportion of them were employed relative to members of the other clusters, and employment tended to be at a higher socioeconomic level. Employment, of course, is a questionable outcome variable, unless one knows whether or not there is a higher incidence of employment after treatment than there was before. It will be recalled that in the main study,

Cluster 5 members had a relatively high employment rate, and tended to be of high socioeconomic status prior to hospitalization. Based on the available data, 16.7 percent of the follow-up subjects who were not working prior to hospitalization were employed at the time of the one year follow-up. There were no differences among the clusters, the figure of 16.7 percent holding for Clusters 2, 4, and 5. It would appear that employment status may be more of a predictor of outcome than an indicator of its success or failure.

With regard to the matter of abstinence, there were no complete treatment failures in Cluster 5. No member of that cluster who was followed up did not have a period of abstinence, albeit a brief one, during the year following discharge. The highest incidence of drinking throughout the entire year occurred in Cluster 4 (28.5 percent). On the other hand, the incidence of total abstinence did not vary greatly among the three clusters. Perhaps all of this material can be summarized in the statement that employed patients with relatively high socioeconomic status and good performance on tests of mental abilities are less likely to be complete treatment failures than are patients who do not meet these criteria. This formulation may provide a partial explanation for the great diversity in rate of success reported for various alcoholism treatment programs. These differing rates of successful treatment may be associated more with the type of alcoholic patient treated than with the particular treatment modality.

DISCUSSION

This research has led to the establishment of an objectively derived typology of hospitalized alcoholics based on psychological test performance. It was shown that an association existed between the statistically generated types or clusters and a number of diagnostic and demographic variables generally considered to be indices of some important dimensions of alcoholism. A very preliminary attempt to evaluate the usefulness of this typology in clinical prediction showed some relationship between type and treatment outcome. Considering these findings, the most useful discussion would appear to involve the development of methods to refine the system and extend its usefulness. As indicated previously, the goal is a practical, generally accepted working typology that has applicability in clinical settings.

There are first of all practical matters to consider. The neuropsychological test battery used in this study is lengthy and not universally available. Thus, while we may be tempted to refine the clustering by adding procedures such as personality and additional perceptual-cognitive measures, it would probably be more useful to do the opposite. A reduction in the number of tests used could make the typologizing operation more accessible from the point of view of material available and of time. It would therefore be useful to look for the minimum number of measures needed to make an accurate prediction of the cluster. There is nothing magical about the 21 measures used in the present study; a smaller number may do just as good a job. Once the number of variables is brought to a minimum, another practical matter would involve the preparation of tables that would expedite computations needed to arrive at the cluster membership of individual subjects. Presently, this can only be accomplished through solution of a lengthy set of equations.

There are numerous other problems that can be pursued, particularly in the area of clinical prediction. Typologizing is ultimately an arbitrary procedure of dividing up some given entity. It is therefore crucial that the usefulness of the division scheme selected be evaluated along with the internal adequacy of the scheme itself. In the case of alcoholism we have defined usefulness in terms of ability to predict treatment outcome and eventually to have the capability of selecting the most appropriate treatment for the patient on the basis of his type. type.

The present study was admittedly retrospective, and we had to make do with the data available. It would be important to do a planned study in which one can be assured of obtaining sufficient follow-up data for each type. Studies should also be accomplished in which a variety of treatment modalities are used with members of the various types in order to establish whether or not there is a relationship among outcome, type, and the kind of treatment offered. For example, it might be reasonable to expect that our Cluster 1 and 3 subjects would be relatively poorer candidates for verbal psychotherapy than the Cluster 5 subjects. On the other hand, the Cluster 1 and 3 subjects may be relatively more responsive to an activity-oriented program in which a great deal of support and shelter is offered. These speculations could be evaluated by follow-up in a planned study.

Despite the diversity in level and pattern of test performance produced by subjects in the present study, it is highly likely that the entire spectrum of alcoholism was not sampled. At one extreme, there were no subjects with active Korsakoff-Wernicke's syndromes in the sample, while at the other, there were few, if any, alcoholics who were functioning so well that they did not require hospitalization. It would be important to include cases in these extreme groups in future refinements of the typology. Since the present study only utilized male patients, it would also be important to repeat the entire procedure with females.

One question of theoretical, but perhaps also of practical interest has to do with the nature of the typology established here. The question concerns whether we established a number of discontinuous types, or simply described points on a continuum of mental deterioration. It is true that as one goes from Cluster 1 to Cluster 5, the test scores tend to get better. Figures 7–1 and 7–2 indicate differing patterns to some extent, but they also clearly show a distinct change from cluster to cluster in performance level. On the other hand, when one examines the entire set of characteristics of each cluster, including the test, diagnostic, and demographic variables, one gets some impression of discontinuity. There are subjects who apparently functioned at low levels throughout their lives, and never made successful academic or vocational adjustments. These individuals contrast sharply with another group of subjects with extensive educational backgrounds and successful careers in business or the professions. There is also the Cluster 1 subject, who tends to have alcoholism as one of several physical and mental problems.

These vignettes constructed from test and historical data give the impression of discontinuity, and suggest that members of one cluster may indeed be very different kinds of people from members of another. It may be suggested that while there is a thread of continuity among the clusters, when one considers the test, medical and demographic information available, there are strong indications of discontinuity, at least among some of the clusters. In other words, it seems to be more than a matter of the Cluster 1 subjects being the very deteriorated ones and the Cluster 5 subjects being the very intact ones, with the others positioned between these extremes. The differences may be qualitative as well as quantitative.

SUMMARY

Utilizing a sample of 150 hospitalized alcoholic patients, an attempt was made to establish an objectively derived typlogy of alcoholism through cluster analysis of a series of psychological tests. The tests included the WAIS and the Halstead Neuropsychological Test Battery. Five major clusters were extracted, accounting for 144 members of the original sample. It was shown by means of a multiple regression analysis that cluster membership was associated with a linear combination of diagnostic and demographic variables obtained from medical records. These variables included age, education, employment status, marital status, length of time drinking, and a number of diagnostic indices including type of primary diagnosis, presence or absence of brain damage associated with alcoholism and with other causes, and presence or absence of a seizure disorder.

A follow-up study utilized fifty additional subjects, all of whom were patients in a specialized alcoholism treatment program. Through the use of discriminant analysis, each of these subjects was assigned to one of the previously established clusters, and the group's pattern of cluster membership was determined. Most of them fell into a cluster that was described as containing members with mild mental impairment who were possibly showing early signs of alcoholism associated brain damage. The remaining subjects distributed themselves evenly into a cluster whose members were described as alcoholics with normal mental functioning, and another cluster that was characterized as containing members with substantial intellectual deterioration. Follow-up data were available for thirty of the fifty subjects, and so it was possible to examine in a preliminary way the relationship between cluster membership and treatment outcome. The general conclusion reached was that patients who were employed immediately before hospitalization in a relatively high socioeconomic status occupation and who performed in the normal range on the psychological tests, were less likely to be without a period of abstinence during the follow-up year than were other patients.

The need to make the typology more usable through shortening of the test battery and simplifying the cluster assignment procedure was discussed, as was the desirability of including a broader range of alcoholics in future studies. The need for planned as opposed to retrospective follow-up research was also expressed.

REFERENCES

Allen, E.B. "Alcoholism as a Psychiatric Medical Problem." In V. Tähkä (ed.), *The Alcoholic Personality*. Finland: Maalaiskuntien Liiton Kirjapaino Helsinki, 1966.

Arieti, S. (ed.). *American Handbook of Psychiatry* (2 vols.). New York: Basic Books, Inc., 1959.

Aspects of Alcoholism (2 vols.). Philadelphia: J.B. Lippincott Company, 1963.

Cimbal, W. "Trinkerfursorge als teil der verwahrlostenfursorge." *Allgemeine Zeitschrift für Psychiatrie,* 84 (1928): 52.

Dixon, W.J. (ed.). *BMD Biomedical Computer Program.* Berkeley: University of California Press, 1973.

Fitzhugh, L.C.; Fitzhugh, K. B.; and Reitan, R.M. "Adaptive Abilities and Intellectual Functioning in Hospitalized Alcoholics." *Quarterly Journal of Studies on Alcohol,* 21 (1960): 414–423.

Fitzhugh, L.C.; Fitzhugh, K.B.; and Reitan, R.M. "Adaptive Abilities and Intellectual Functioning of Hospitalized Alcoholics: Further Considerations." *Quarterly Journal of Studies on Alcohol,* 26 (1965): 402–411.

Halstead, W.C. *Brain and Intelligence.* Chicago: University of Chicago Press, 1947.

Jellinek, E.M. *The Disease Concept of Alcoholism.* New Haven, Conn.: Hillhouse Press, 1960.

Kant, F. *The Treatment of the Alcoholic.* Springfield Ill.: Thomas, 1954.

Kehrer, F., and Kretschmer, E. *Die Veronlagung zu Seelischen Storungen.* Berlin: J. Springer, 1924.

Keller, M., and Efron, V. "The Prevalance of Alcoholism." *Quarterly Journal of Studies on Alcohol,* 16 (1955): 619.

MacQueen, J. "Some Methods for Classification and Analysis of Multivariate Observations." *Proceedings of the 5th Berkeley Symposium on Mathematical Statistics and Probability.* (Vol. 1). University of California, 1967.

Matarazzo, J.D. *Wechsler's Measurement and Appraisal of Adult Intelligence.* (5th ed.). Baltimore: Williams & Wilkins, 1972.

Reitan, R.M. "A Research Program on the Psychological Effects of Brain Lesions in Human Beings." In N.R. Ellis (ed.), *International Review of Research in Mental Retardation* (Vol. 1). New York: Academic Press, 1966.

Reitan, R.M., and Davison, L.A. *Clinical Neuropsychology: Current Status and Applications.* Washington, D.C.: V.H. Winston & Sons, 1974.

Russell, A.; Neuringer, C.; and Goldstein, G. *Assessment of Brain Damage: A Neuropsychological Key Approach.* New York: Wiley-Interscience, 1970.

Schafer, R. *The Clinical Application of Psychological Tests.* New York: International Universities Press, 1948.

Stockert, F.G. "Zur frage der disposition zum alkoholismus chronicus." *Zeitschrift für die Gesamte Neurologie und Psychiatrie,* 106 (1926): 379.

Strecker, E.A., and Chambers, F.T., Jr. *Alcohol–One Man's Meat.* N.Y., Macmillan, 1938.

Tähkä, V. *The Alcoholic Personality.* Finland: Maalaiskuntien Liiton Kirjapaino, 1966.

Thompson, G.N. "Acute and Chronic Alcoholic Conditions." In S. Arieti (ed.), *American Handbook of Psychiatry* (Vol. 1). New York: Basic Books, Inc., 1959.

Victor, M. "Alcoholism." In A.B. Baker (ed.), *Clinical Neurology,* (Vol. 2). New York: Harper & Brothers, 1962.

Wallerstein, R.S., and Chotlos, J.W. *Hospital Treatment of Alcoholism.* New York: Basic Books, 1957.

Wingfield, H. *The Forms of Alcoholism and Their Treatment.* London: Hodder & Stoughton, 1919.

Witkin, H.; Karp, S., and Goodenough, D. "Dependence in Alcoholics." *Quarterly Journal of Studies on Alcohol,* 20 (1959): 493–504.

✳ Chapter Eight

Neuropsychological Investigations of Alcoholism

Ralph E. Tarter

INTRODUCTION

A comprehension of the consequences of alcohol abuse in man must necessarily incorporate empirically derived information from the various levels of biological organization. Through an understanding of the morphological, neurochemical, and physiological alterations of the central nervous system, one can then better appreciate the significance of behavioral and psychological disturbances that may originate after chronic ingestion of this potentially toxic substance. Conversely, by systematic investigations of behavioral and psychological capacity of alcoholics, it may be possible to infer underlying neurophysiological dysfunction. By deriving a perspective of the brain-behavior relationships involved, it is hoped that knowledge of the intrinsic processes of alcoholism will ultimately facilitate overall efforts in developing precise forms of therapeutic intervention. For example, it has already been found that treatment perseverance (Kissin, Platz, and Su, 1970) and outcome (Kissin, Rosenblatt, and Machover, 1968) depend to a large extent on psychological factors. Hence, the importance of pursuing neuropsychological research should not be underestimated insofar as it adds to our awareness of the pathological process, and can assist in implementing more effective rehabilitation techniques.

A primary issue in alcoholism research concerns the presence or absence of brain damage in afflicted persons. Assuming that alcohol, if consumed in a chronic and unrestrained manner, does indeed cause neurological injury, then a host of secondary but nonetheless vital questions also remain to be answered. Severity and localization of brain damage, duration of alcoholism history before impairment is clinically manifest, as well as the role played by other variables such as age, nutrition, genetics, and premorbid competency must all be taken into consideration in evaluating the effects of ethanol abuse. While a concluding statement cannot be advanced regarding the contribution and interaction of all these factors at this time, there is nonetheless an accumulating body of information which over the last decade or so has substantially added to our understanding of the neuropsychological sequelae of alcoholism.

Practical problems also exist which make it difficult to draw generalizations about the neuropsychological competence of alcoholics. Sampling characteristics and the problems in defining alcoholism are two obvious examples. The most commonly accepted definition of alcoholism is one advocated by Keller (1960), and identifies the alcoholic in terms of personal and interpersonal difficulties resulting from abusive drinking. However the possibility exists that neuropsychological disruption may occur prior to this stage in the alcoholism process. The lack of an accepted definition of alcoholism in which competency characteristics are included has also added to our difficulties in deriving measures of alcoholism severity, duration and categorical subtypes of drinkers. Furthermore, the absence of behavioral criteria in categorizing alcoholic individuals other than simply an appraisal by self or other that he drinks too much has invariably led to problems in sampling, thereby making it risky to generalize results from investigations in which subjects have been drawn from different populations.

Another variable to be researched concerns the potential for recovery. Are any or all of the impairments reversible after a period of sobriety? Are the deficits that have been found merely the transient effects of prolonged intoxication and withdrawal? These latter questions emphasize the critical importance of time of testing as a factor in deriving conclusions about the existence and extent of neuropsychological disruption.

The objective of this presentation is therefore to describe the psychological and neurological competency of chronic alcoholics. Research pertaining to patients with amnesic syndromes will be dealt with in another chapter (Butters and Cermak). Studies are reviewed in which the basic aim was to delineate the capacity and efficiency of functioning of persons seeking treatment for alcohol abuse.

While it will be demonstrated in this chapter that alcoholics suffer from a detectable neurological pathology and psychological deficit, it should be emphasized beforehand that one must view such findings with caution and perhaps even with an attitude of healthy skepticism insofar as investigations of this aspect of alcoholism have only recently aroused much curiosity in scientists.

PSYCHOLOGICAL CAPACITY

Intelligence

Alcoholics do not exhibit an intellectual disturbance as measured by standardized tests of intelligence. Repeatedly, they have been observed to function within the average (Bauer and Johnson, 1957; Fitzhugh, Fitzhugh, and Reitan, 1960, 1965; Goldstein and Shelly, 1971; Murphy, 1953; Peters, 1956; Wechsler, 1941, 1958) to superior ranges (Halpern, 1946; Kaldegg, 1956; Malerstein and Belden, 1968; Plumeau, Machover, and Puzzo, 1960) on such tests as the WAIS and Wechsler-Bellevue. However, apart from summary IQ scores, there is suggestive evidence for a neuropsychological disturbance. Teicher and Singer (1946) found superior verbal IQ scores relative to performance IQs in their alcoholic sample. Wechsler (1941) also reports a similar subscale difference and concluded that it was the product of alcoholism and not other factors, such as aging. With the exception of two studies by Fitzhugh, Fitzhugh, and Reitan (1960, 1965) all of the investigations cited above also found a relative depression in performance IQ. While there is some consistency to this observation and its possible neuropsychological implications are apparent, it should be noted that the differences in subscale IQs are of small magnitude and typically less than ten points.

On other measures, Tarter and Jones (1971a) and Kish (1970) were unable to observe differences between alcoholics and normals or psychiatric patients on the Shipley Institute of Living Scale. It was also found that no association between conceptual quotient (an index of intellectual deterioration) and duration of alcoholism existed (Tarter and Jones 1971a). On the Raven's Progressive Matrices, a test of general intelligence and perceptual organization, Jones (1971a) found impaired performance in alcoholics which increased with progressive duration of alcoholism. On a battery of 23 factorially pure tests of cognition, Tarter, Buonpane, and Wynant (1975) found comparable performance in alcoholics and psychiatrics. Alcoholics have also been tested on the General Aptitude Test Battery (Kish, 1970; Kish and Cheney, 1969) and when contrasted to the standardization sample performed more poorly on the Numerical, Motor coordination, Finger dexterity, and Manual dexterity subtests. General intelligence, and the Verbal, Spatial, Perceptual, and Clerical aptitudes were unimpaired.

It is apparent that traditional psychometric measures of intelligence have not been particularly useful in elucidating the type and degree of impairment in alcoholics. On the other hand, several investigators have found evidence for a disturbance using the Halstead-Reitan Battery, a measure of biological intelligence. The concept of biological intelligence was first advanced by Halstead (1947) in an effort to quantify neurological efficiency; and after further modification and validation by Reitan (1955) this test battery has proven to be exceptionally valuable in the identification and localization of brain damage. On this instrument, alcoholics have been observed to obtain an impairment index score that implicates neurological impairment (Fitzhugh, Fitzhugh, and Reitan, 1960, 1965; Vivian, Goldstein, and Shelly, 1973). The severity of deficit is less than that found in the acutely brain damaged, but overall performance is poorer than nonalcoholic and normal individuals.

In conclusion, alcoholics do not exhibit an intellectual deterioration as measured by standard psychometric tests. The concept of biological intelligence as quantified by the Halstead impairment index on the other hand suggests that alcoholics do suffer from a neuropsychological deficit. But which specific psychological capacities are impaired that lead to reduced neurobehavioral efficiency? We shall now turn our attention to the various aspects of psychological functioning: perception, cognition, motor skill, learning, and memory in an attempt to answer this question.

Perception

A variety of perceptual tasks have been applied to alcoholics with mixed results. Perceptual speed as measured by the Stroop Test (Goldstein and Chotlos, 1965) was not different in alcoholics and normals. Claeson and Carlsson (1970), administered two of Thurstone's tests of perceptual speed and likewise found no evidence for impairment on the Figure Identification Test and Street Gestalt Test.

Perceptual-motor coordination is also intact as measured by such tests as the Bender-Gestalt (Hirschenfang, Silber, and Benton, 1967, 1968; Kates and Schmolke, 1953; Hirschenfang, Silber, and Benton, 1968). Reinehr and Golightly (1968) reported that only 10 percent of their alcoholic subjects performed in the critical or impaired ranges. In contrast to these findings is the observation by Kaldegg (1956) that 11 of 18 subjects demonstrated signs of impairment. On other measures of perceptual-motor functioning it has been reported that alcoholics were deficient on a star tracing task (Vivian, Goldstein, and Shelly, 1973) and Purdue Pegboard (Tarter and Jones, 1971b), but in the latter investigation, the impairments disappeared after approximately three months of sobriety.

Alcoholics exhibit deficits on tasks of a perceptual-motor nature that require a high level of spatial appreciation. For example, several researchers have observed deficient performance in alcoholics on such tests as the Block Design subtest of the WAIS (Goldstein, Neuringer, and Klappersack, 1970) and Wechsler-Bellevue (Fitzhugh, Fitzhugh, and Reitan, 1960, 1965). Similar impairments were noted on the Grassi Block Substitution Test (Gordon, 1957; Grassi, 1953; Jonsson, Cronholm, and Izikowitz, 1962). Claeson and Carlsson (1970) reported that their alcoholic sample tended towards impairment on the Kohs Block Design Test, but the exclusion of a control group make interpretation of their data difficult.

Fitzhugh, Fitzhugh, and Reitan (1960) also found inferior performance by alcoholics on the time measure of the Tactual Performance Test of the Halstead-Reitan Battery. This test requires subjects while blindfolded to place simple geometric shaped objects in their appropriate places in a form-board. After adding another 18 subjects to the original sample they found that the alcoholics were also deficient on the time and location measure. These findings indicate that alcoholics have difficulty in conceptualizing spatial relations where visual input is unavailable.

One aspect of perceptual functioning that has been the subject of extensive research concerns perceptual field orientation. The capacity to articulate elements of a perceptual field by adjusting a rod to its vertical position despite distractions from the surrounding frame and body position which are both in various degrees of tilt was shown to be impaired in alcoholics (Witkin, Karp, and Goodenough, 1959). The inability of alcoholics to perform comparably to normals on the rod and frame test indicates that as a group that they are perceptually field dependent. Other investigations have confirmed the observations of Witkin and his colleagues in both alcoholic men (Bailey, Hustmeyer, and Kristofferson, 1961; Goldstein and Chotlos, 1965; Karp and Konstadt, 1965; Karp, Witkin, and Goodenough, 1965a, 1965b) and alcoholic women (Karp, Poster, and Goodman, 1963). The perceptual field dependency is not affected by duration of drinking history (Karp and Konstadt, 1965), length of sobriety (Bailey, Hustmeyer, and Kristofferson, 1961; Karp, Witkin, and Goodenough, 1965a) or acute administration of alcohol (Karp, Witkin, and Goodenough, 1965b).

Although there is an impressive amount of evidence which demonstrates a dependent mode of perceptual functioning in alcoholics, there is much controversy as to the source of this orientation. Witkin and coworkers (Witkin et al., 1954) have interpreted their findings as reflective of a dispositional personality trait, while others (Bailey et al., 1961; Goldstein and Chotlos, 1965) have suggested that brain damage may be responsible for the perceptually dependent style in alcoholics. Evidence in favor of either of these two conflicting positions is equivocal; while rod and frame performance is not correlated with personality measures of dependency (Goldstein et al., 1968), there is on the other hand no significant association between alcoholism duration and perceptual dependency (Karp et al., 1965c). There is however a significant positive correlation between rod and frame performance and several cognitive variables. Tarter, Sheldon, and Sugerman (1975) found that general reasoning ability was able to account for over 25 percent of RFT variance. By combining four other cognitive tests that also correlated with RFT performance (length estimation, sensitivity to problems, mechanical knowledge, and speed of closure), over 52 percent of the variance could be accounted for.

Related to perceptual field orientation is another widely tested capacity—perceptual closure. This latter skill involves identifying a simple geometric figure that is hidden within a complex design as for example, in the Embedded Figures Test. Correlations between the rod and frame test and Embedded Figures Test are significant. Rudin and Stagner (1958) observed a correlation of 0.55 while Goldstein et al. (1970) reported a correlation of 0.63. However, unlike the rod and frame test, measures of perceptual closure have not always been found to differentiate normals from alcoholics (Jones and Parsons, 1971b; Rhodes, Carr, and Jurji, 1968; Rudin and Stagner, 1958). Other tests of closure have similarly not been useful in differentiating alcoholics from normals. Tarter (1971) observed no impairments on the Copying Test and Claeson and Carlsson (1970) found no deficit on the Gottschaldt Test.

Two important considerations present themselves in light of the above findings. First, although significant correlations between the rod and frame and Embedded Figures Test are typically observed, this fact does not of itself mean that the latter measure alone can be employed as a substitute test of field orientation. There is sufficient residual variance to suggest that differing psychological functions are measured by each test. Thus while most investigators (e.g., Karp and Konstadt, 1965; Karp et al., 1965a, 1965b; Witkin et al., 1954) have combined several tests to derive a perceptual index, other researchers have relied solely on the Embedded Figures Test to infer perceptual orientation (Burdick, 1969; Rhodes et al., 1968). The correlation of any two tests with appreciable residual variance should under any circumstances be evaluated cautiously and for spurious effect, and in no such circumstance is it justified to substitute one test for another in the naive belief that they measure the same psychological function.

Given this correlation, the second question can then be raised: What characteristics are shared between these two tests? To shed some light on this problem, Goldstein et al. (1970) observed positive correlations between the Embedded Figures Test and Object Assembly, Block Design and Picture Completion subtests of the WAIS. Witkin et al. (1954) have also reported that the perceptual index (a composite score of the rod and frame, Embedded Figures, and Body Adjustment Tests) correlated with the performance subtests of the WAIS. These latter findings suggest that certain components of spatial functioning are measured by all of these tests.

What these specific components are still remains unclear. Jacobson (1968) found that alcoholics shifted toward the field-independent orientation after a one-hour period of sensory deprivation. He interpreted the results as implicating an impairment of kinesthetic and proprioceptive functioning in alcoholics under conditions of body disorientation. The period of sensory deprivation enabled the subjects to focus on body sensations not normally attended to, and from this increased experience of awareness they could then perform more efficiently when in a condition of bodily tilt. While this hypothesis is intriguing, and may account for some of the deficits in rod and frame test performance, it does not explain why many alcoholics are impaired at judging rod verticality when the body is in the upright position (Goldstein and Chotlos, 1965).

On another task, Thurstone's Figure Turning Test, in which the subject must select one of seven geometric designs which upon orientation would be identical to a sample figure, Claeson and Carlsson (1970) found that 70 percent of their alcoholics were unable to perform competently. It thus appears that the disturbance in spatial capacity is not solely an impairment of bodily cue utilization, but probably also entails an inability to process environmental input requiring conceptualization, integration, and transformation of disparate elements of the perceptual field.

Disturbances in other spatial tasks have also been reported. In addition to impairments on the Tactual Performance Test previously noted, alcoholics have also been found to perform inferior to normals on the Trail Making Test of the Halstead-Reitan Battery (Fitzhugh et al., 1965; Goldstein and Chotlos, 1965). Tarter (1971) found that alcoholics performed more poorly than normals on another maze task, the Maze Tracing Speed Test. Jonsson et al. (1962) noted a similar impairment in their alcoholic sample, but the deficits disappeared after a period of sobriety. From these studies it appears that alcoholics manifest deficits on spatial tasks that require a certain degree of planning in the visual guiding of a sequence of responses through a complex array. Whether or not these impairments are reversible, as suggested by Jonsson et al. (1962), merits further investigation and will be discussed more fully in a subsequent section of this chapter.

Where a cognitive component is part of the overall task demand alcoholics have also manifested impairments. For example, Jones and Parsons (1972) found deficient performance on only subtest IV of the Halstead-Reitan Category Test. This test requires the subject to identify a spatial or positional type of concept. On the Wisconsin Card Sorting Test, Tarter (1971) noted a tendency for the alcoholics to perseverate their responses according to the place or physical location of a stimulus instead of the intrinsic dimensional qualities of the stimulus.

Although the state of knowledge pertaining to perceptual functioning in alcoholics is incomplete, it has been shown that impairments are reflected on some tasks and not on others. On the tasks where deficits are found, it is not yet known whether or not they are reversible. Systematic investigations of this problem are unfortunately lacking and until efforts are directed toward this problem, the tentative conclusion advanced at this time is that disturbances in perceptual-spatial functioning are extant but not universally reflected on every task.

Motor Efficiency

Peripheral neuropathy of small and large nerve fibers has been reported in alcoholics (Appenzeller and MacGee, 1962). Both axonal (Walsh and McLeod, 1970) and segmental (Denny-Brown, 1958) nerve degeneration has been observed and found to be correlated with the duration and severity of alcohol abuse (Mandsley and Mayer, 1965). At the physiological level, nerve conduction velocities are reduced in both the sensory (Casey and LeQuesne, 1972) and motor (Wanamaker and Skillman, 1966) systems as a probable result of degeneration of the myelin sheath. Damage to the nerves themselves can also be inferred from the fact that the amplitude of nerve action potentials are also reduced (Bischoff, 1971; Casey and LeQuesne, 1972).

Muscular atrophy has been inferred on the basis of the fact that alcoholics suffer from muscle weakness (Carlsson et al., 1969; Ekbom et al., 1964; Tarter and Jones 1971b). Thus there is a substantial body of evidence to implicate a pathology to the skeletal muscles and peripheral nervous system from pathophysiological investigations. Neurological examination of afflicted persons also suggest neuromuscular pathology in the form of symptoms such as ataxia, paresthesia, disturbances of vibratory and position sense as well as pain, numbness, and hyperesthesia. While any or all such symptoms need not be manifested in the alcoholic, their progression when manifest is from the distal to proximal extremities in a symmetrical fashion, and usually appearing first and most severely in the lower limbs.

Behavioral measurement of motor function revealed deficits in finger tapping speed. In one study, Tarter and Jones (1971b) noted impairments in finger and manual dexterity as well as motor coordination in alcoholics on the General Aptitude Test Battery. Mixed results on the other hand have been found for reaction time. Talland (1963) reported reduced reaction times but he was unable to establish for certain if the alcoholics were detoxified at the time of testing. Vivian et al. (1973) also found that alcoholics were slower than normals in a discrete trial reaction time procedure. Contrary to these results, Callan, Holloway, and Bruhn (1972) were unable to detect decrements in a continuous reaction time paradigm that required sustained attention. On another motor task, alcoholics were found to be impaired on the knob turning test. This task requires the subject to rotate a knob as slowly as possible through 180° arc and is presumed to be a measure of motor inhibition. The fact that their knob turning behavior was significantly faster than controls suggests that they are motorically disinhibited (Parsons, Tarter, and Edelberg, 1972). Their inability to regulate motor functioning also indicates that they are deficient in the capacity of *antrieb* or skill in executing a response regardless of the time requirements (Zangwill, 1966).

In conclusion, there is strong evidence for a muscular and motor disturbance in chronic alcoholics, but here, too, the elicitation of a deficit depends on the particular test and task demands. Furthermore, while impairments are found in laboratory settings, the percentage of alcoholics exhibiting clinically apparent peripheral neuropathy and myopathy is rather small, with estimates ranging from 0.3 percent (Janzen and Balzereit, 1968) to 5 percent (Neidermeyer and Prokup, 1959).

Abstracting Ability

If a hierarchy of man's psychological functions could be constructed, it would probably be agreed that it is his superior capacity to form symbolic representations, to reason and hence solve problems that distinguish him from other animals. In a complex technological society such as ours, it can readily be seen how the loss or reduction of this capacity would have deleterious consequences to the individual. Studies of alcoholics have provided us with some very interesting data about their conceptual capacity.

Impairments have been reported (Fitzhugh et al., 1960, 1965; Jones and Parsons, 1971) on the Halstead-Reitan Category Test. In a further investigation, Jones and Parsons (1972) found that the impairments were due to a deficiency in performing on subtest IV, where a visual-spatial concept must be identified. Goldstein and Chotlos (1965) also administered this test but departed from the standard procedure by utilizing a correction procedure and by inserting a three-second delay between the subject's response and feedback. No impairments were observed in their alcoholic sample with these variations in procedure.

A cognitive deficit has also been noted on other tasks as well. Reinehr and Golightly (1968) reported that nine of their thirty subjects performed in the impaired ranges on the Organic Integrity Test. Lovibond and Holloway (1968) observed that, nondeteriorated alcoholics performed more poorly than normals on the Query Brain Damage Scale, a modification of the Goldstein Object Sorting Test, and deteriorated alcoholics performed at a level inferior to the other two groups. In one study (Jonsson et al., 1962) it was found that alcoholics were deficient in appreciating the intrinsic meanings ot proverbs.

Negative findings have however been reported from a variety of sources. Pishkin, Fishkin, and Stahl (1972) employed a sophisticated rule-learning paradigm, but were unable to detect impairments in the identification of either simple or complex concepts. The identification of synonyms is similarly intact in alcoholics (Claeson and Carlsson, 1970; Jonsson et al., 1962; Tarter and Jones, 1971a). Thurstone's Figure Classification Test was administered in one study by Claeson and Carlsson (1970), who concluded that there is no indication for a disturbance in inductive reasoning. More recently, Tarter et al. (1975) found no sign for an abstracting deficit as measured by a battery of factorially pure tests of induction, syllogistic reasoning, verbal comprehension, semantic flexibility and fluency.

On the Wisconsin Card Sorting Test, a performance-oriented cognitive task, this author (Tarter, 1971, 1973; Tarter and Parsons, 1971) attempted to further elucidate the nature of the abstracting deficit in alcoholics. It was found that alcoholics were not impaired in their initial acquisition of simple concepts of color, shape or number, but they were quite deficient in shifting a response set after criterion had been achieved on the previous concept. It was also noted that they tended to perseverate along a positional or spatial concept independently of the stimulus dimensions of the discriminanda. Thus it appeared that the alcoholics were more susceptible than normals to the buildup of perseverative interference. Furthermore, the alcoholics were less capable than normal controls in persisting with or sustaining a correct mode of responding as indicated by the fact that a positively reinforced sequence of responses was more likely to be interrupted by an error. Learning to learn or interset improvement was similar for both alcoholics and normals. However, the alcoholics did demonstrate an impairment in utilizing the information contained in an erroneous response to achieve a subsequently correct one.

One important observation to emerge from these studies is the role played by alcoholism history. Impairments in set shifting and error utilization were manifest most frequently by subjects whose alcoholism history was longstanding and usually exceeding ten years. Set impersistence was however observed in short- and long-term alcoholics, but was most severe in those persons with a longstanding history. The fact that deficits on this test were found in alcoholics also provides additional support for the presence of a cognitive impairment. It must be pointed out that the manifest deficits may be task-specific, insofar as intact performance was exhibited by alcoholics on a verbal variation of this test (Jone, 1971b).

As in the case of intelligence, alcoholics do not demonstrate general and pervasive impairments on all tasks that tap abstracting ability (Jones, 1971a; Jones and Parsons, 1972). Deficiencies of performance are test related and in some instances are observed on only some components of the overall task requirements as for example in the Wisconsin Card Sorting Test. One variable that remains to be elucidated concerns the relationship between alcoholism duration and cognitive competency. From the data accrued by Tarter (1971, 1973) on the WCST and Jones (1971a) on the Raven's Progressive Matrices, it appears that a positive association may indeed exist. Furthermore, the findings of Lovibond and Holloway (1968) also implicate a progressive decline in capacity of abstracting ability with increasing duration of alcoholism as measured by the Query Brain Damage Scale.

Learning and Memory

Memory capacity in alcoholics has not been fully researched. While it has often been observed that alcoholics exhibit "blackouts," that is, memory loss for events that occured while in the intoxicated state, there is a dearth of information pertaining to storage and retrieval competency while in a sober condition. In a dichotic memory task, Chandler, Vega, and Parsons (1973) noted that alcoholics suspected of being brain damaged were more apt to give confabulated and repetitive answers in recall. Alcoholics not suspected of neurological injury were unimpaired in their performance.

Tests of memory have led to conflicting results in alcoholics. Jonsson et al. (1962) found that alcoholics performed well on a paired-associate task but were deficient in remembering a display of common objects. Claeson and Carlsson (1970) noted a moderate learning deficit but no retentive impairment on a paired-associate test. On the Benton Visual Retention Test, they found that 65 percent of their alcoholic subjects performed in the impaired ranges. Intact performance has on the other hand been observed on the Memory for Designs

Test (May, Urquhart, and Watts, 1970) and on the memory measure of the Halstead-Reitan Tactual Performance Test (Fitzhugh et al., 1960, 1965). In another study (Weingartner, Faillace, and Markley, 1971) it was found that alcoholics learned more slowly than controls on free recall and serial learning tests but this declined after three weeks of sobriety.

Experiments with animals have been more conclusive. Freund (1973, 1975) found impairments in learning and memory in mice after a period of continuous ethanol consumption. Although these results cannot be readily generalized to humans, they do show that under strict laboratory conditions where the pertinent variables can be controlled, especially nutrition, alcohol may cause permanent neurological damage.

One particular aspect of memory functioning which has been receiving increasing attention concerns the alcoholic blackout. This phenomenon refers to the inability by the individual while in a sober state to recall events that took place during intoxication. Goodwin and his colleagues, in a series of experiments (1969, 1970, 1973), have substantially added to our understanding of this peculiar form of amnesia and concluded that the memory loss reflects a deficit in short-term memory which becomes manifest after a threshold quantity of alcohol has been consumed. Similar conclusions have been drawn by Ryback (1969a, 1969b). Tarter and Schneider (in preparation) investigated the memory capacity of alcoholics and related it to the onset and frequency of the blackout. They were unable to detect a relationship between memory capacity and blackout frequency when the alcoholics were tested in the sober condition. The blackout was, however, found to be tied to specific drinking characteristics such as drinking to intoxication, craving, tolerance to alcohol, and loss of control. The blackout was also most frequently observed in persons who became alcoholic at a comparatively younger age than those persons reporting few or no periods of amnesia from drinking. From these investigations it appears that the acute manifestations of a blackout are tied to memorial capacity during inebriation, but short-term memory during the sober state is unrelated to frequency of blackouts. On the other hand, the blackout is related to specific drinking characteristics and alcoholism history.

From these studies and those previously discussed, it is apparent that alcoholics manifest psychological and behavioral deficits. Although personality and motivational factors may be a factor, the possibility also exists that the pattern of impairments implicate a central neurological disruption. The next section of this chapter is an attempt to integrate the psychological and neurological data into a meaningful perspective in order to clarify the brain-behavior relationships that may be disrupted from chronic ethanol consumption.

NEUROPSYCHOLOGICAL INTEGRATION

Historically two distinct trends and traditions have evolved which attempt to explicate brain-behavior relationships. First, there developed out of the medical sciences techniques of direct observation such as the arteriogram and pneumoencephalogram. The testing of reflexes and recording brain electrical activity have also provided us with a wealth of information about brain functioning and added methods by which pathological processes can be identified to our arsenal of tools. The second and relatively more recent approach is based upon psychological and behavioral measurement. From systematic examination of the pattern of deficits in individuals with known neurological pathology, test batteries with standardized administrative procedures and norms have been devised which have proven exceptionally useful in the diagnosis of brain damage. The Halstead-Reitan Battery (Reitan 1955) is but one example of a neuropsychological test.

Do chronic alcoholics exhibit an impairment on neuropsychological tests? Two sources of evidence support the hypothesis of a neurological disruption. On the Halstead-Reitan Battery, an instrument capable of discriminating normal from neurologically impaired persons (Reitan, 1955, Vega and Parsons, 1969), alcoholics have been found to perform in the impaired ranges (Fitzhugh et al., 1960, 1965; Goldstein and Shelly, 1971). Second, on certain psychological functions there is a progressive decline in capacity with increasing duration of alcoholism. Thus Tarter (1973) and Tarter and Parsons (1971) found that certain aspects of cognitive ability declined as drinking abuse became more prolonged. Similar results were reported by Lovibond and Holloway (1968), who found increasing impairment on the Query Brain Damage Scale as deterioration progressed. On tests of speed and strength, the recovery of function after almost three months of sobriety was less in alcoholics who have been chronic alcoholics for more than ten years as compared to less chronic drinkers (Tarter and Jones 1971b). Considering these findings and those previously discussed, the conclusion can be tentatively advanced that alcoholics suffer from a neurological impairment.

What then is the nature of this impairment and how severe are its manifestations? It has been known for quite some time from clinical neurological research that excessive alcohol consumption can lead to several types of neuropathies such as dementia, Korsakoff Psychosis, cerebellar degeneration and, less frequently, pontine myelinosis and corpus callosum degeneration (Marchiafava-Bignami Disease). These conditions are typically observed in the advanced stages of alcoholism so that the patient under scrutiny usually exhibits quite severe limitations in functioning. How severe are the deficits in the intact alcoholic, one who can function adequately in everyday activities, maintain a job, and does not present obvious neurological pathology? Unfortunately, this issue has not yet been thoroughly studied, but several investigations have been conducted which lend themselves to interpretation. The results of these studies suggest that the neuropsychological capacity of alcoholics is less than in normals, but better than the acutely brain damaged (Fitzhugh et al., 1960, 1965). Where impairments have been quantified the extent of performance decrement has ranged from the mild to moderate.

Given that detectable deficits exist, but are not severely debilitating to the individual, another question of vital importance can be posed; namely, does the pattern of deficits implicate a specific neurological involvement or is the central pathological process diffusely generalized throughout the brain? To date, four neuropsychological hypotheses have been put forward. While not mutually exclusive, each states rather explicitly the presumed neurobehavioral mechanisms that are involved. These hypotheses are:

1. Chronic alcohol abuse results in premature aging of the brain.
2. Chronic alcohol abuse leads to global or generalized CNS deterioration.
3. Chronic alcohol abuse differentially disrupts the right hemisphere of the brain.
4. Chronic alcohol abuse exerts its greatest detrimental effect on the anterior-basal regions of the brain.

With respect to the first hypothesis there is evidence from psychological and pathological research which indicates that alcoholism leads to an acceleration of the senescent process. Kish and Cheney (1969) found on the GATB that alcoholics in their 30s performed comparably to nonalcoholics in the fifth decade of life. On the Halstead-Reitan Battery, Fitzhugh et al. (1965) concluded that there is premature aging in terms of adaptive abilities or biological intelligence. This finding was confirmed by Jones and Parsons (1971), who analyzed Category Test performance of alcoholics and found that while young normal controls and alcoholics were of comparable ability, older alcoholics were differentially impaired. A similar conclusion was reached by Goldstein and Shelly (1971).

Corroborative evidence for an accelerated aging process was provided by Courville (1955), who after extensive examination of alcoholics at autopsy concluded that "that body and brain of the habituated individual becomes prematurely old" (p. 90). In one EEG study, Smith, Johnson, and Burdick (1971) observed that the sleep pattern of alcoholics appeared similar to that found in aged individuals and similar to persons suffering from diffuse cerebral pathology. Thus the available evidence supports the notion of an insidious effect of alcohol when considered in terms of the aging process, both from direct observation of the brain itself (Courville, 1955) and also as inferred from standardized psychological test performance (Kish and Cheney, 1969; Fitzhugh et al., 1965).

The second neuropsychological hypothesis states that the primary manifestation of chronic alcoholism is diffuse CNS pathology (Brosin, 1967). A functional decline of surviving brain cells may lead to a global loss of cognitive and intellectual capacity indicative of a senescent state in the very advanced stages of alcoholism and such a process is not infrequent in older persons. One may therefore observe deficits in problem-solving, memory, storage and retrieval, and so forth. However from the information presented in this chapter so far, it is apparent that alcoholics in their third, fourth or fifth decade of life are not usually so pervasively deteriorated. Nonetheless, diffuse cerebral atrophy may be extant in the alcoholic which is not detectable by psychological or neurological measurement until the sixth or seventh decade of life.

A third neuropsychological hypothesis that has been advanced on the basis of the pattern of psychological impairments exhibited by alcoholics is that there is a differentially greater disruptive effect of chronic alcohol abuse on right than left hemispheric functioning (Jones and Parsons, 1972; Parsons et al., 1972). Whether the right hemisphere has a greater predilection to disruption than the left hemisphere, or alternatively, whether impairments reflective of right hemisphere functioning are easier to detect is not clear. Attempts have not yet been made to clarify this point. In any event, behavioral evidence has been obtained that implicates a greater deficit in those capacities that are presumably mediated or subserved by the right hemisphere. On the Wechsler scales there have been reported, in the majority of studies, lower performance than verbal IQs, with the difference being larger than one would expect from chance alone (Wechsler, 1941). Inferior performance IQ relative to verbal IQ has often been considered a diagnostic factor in lateralizing brain damage (Vega and Parsons, 1969). Another source of evidence is derived from the observation that decrements are frequently manifest on spatial types of tasks which are known to be mediated by the right hemisphere, whereas verbal-linguistic functions are innervated by the left hemisphere. Thus, when both the verbal and spatial forms of the Wisconsin Card Sorting Test are administered, impairments have been noted on only the spatial test form (Jones, 1971b). In addition, the literature reviewed on spatial capacity in a previous section of this chapter strongly pointed to a dysfunction of the right hemisphere, especially the findings by Fitzhugh et al. (1965) on the Tactual Performance Test, where alcoholics performed in the impaired ranges, suggesting perhaps a right parietal focus of damage.

On motor tasks, alcoholics have been observed to be deficient in left handed performance. Parsons et al. (1972) found on a test of motor regulation that alcoholics were impaired only in left hand but not right hand performance when compared to normals. Tarter and Jones (1971b) observed a nonsignificant trend in this direction as well. On the dichotic memory test, Goodglass and Peck (1972) found that information presented to the left ear was recalled more poorly by alcoholics than controls, while right ear recall was not deficient. Hence, there is evidence from psychological research to implicate a right hemispheric involvement in chronic alcoholism. However, because very little has been done to systematically test this hypothesis, the present findings must be considered as preliminary. In addition, it should be recognized that not all test results point to a lateralized disorder. For example, on several spatial taks, most notably the Embedded Figures Test and Bender-Gestalt, there has been no consistent decrement reported. Thus, while the intriguing possibility remains that the right hemisphere might be more vulnerable than the left to the chronic effects of alcohol, or that alcohol adversely disrupts primarily right hemispheric functioning, the evidence to date is still far from conclusive.

A fourth hypothesis has been advanced by Tarter (1971, 1973, 1975a, 1975b), which in essence proposes that alcoholics are neurologically impaired in the anterior-basal regions of the brain. Specifically frontal-limbic-diencephalic structures are presumed to be deleteriously affected by longstanding alcohol abuse. That these structures of the brain do indeed comprise a morphological and functionally integrated system has been known for many years (Brutkowski, 1965; Fulton, 1952; Marsala and Grofova, 1962; Nauta, 1964; Pribram, 1958). The fact that lesions in various parts of this system result in similar behavioral deficits (Brutkowski, 1965) indicates that within the intact organism common behaviors are mediated by the frontal-limbic-diencephalic system.

Evidence in support of this hypothesis has been accumulated from neurological as well as psychological research. Haug (1968) and Brewer and Perrett (1971) observed from pneumoencephalographic measurement that the third ventricle was dilated, indicating an atrophic process in this brain region. Segal et al. (1970) reported after intensive clinical study that alcohol withdrawal leads to symptoms similar to those exhibited by persons with diencephalic lesions. EEG measurements have also been obtained with at least two groups of investigators reporting a frontal focus of pathology (Brewer and Perrett, 1971; Lereboullet, Pluvinage, and Anstutz, 1956). There have also been reported findings from two neuropathological inquiries that alcoholics are differentially most atrophic in the anterior part of the brain (Alexander, 1941, Courville, 1955). Furthermore frontal-diencephalic tracts have been found in one investigation to be disrupted in alcoholics (Creutzfeldt, 1928). Thus while the number of neurological studies is somewhat limited, there is nonetheless support for the notion that alcoholics suffer from an anterior-basal focus of pathology.

The pattern of psychological deficit also points to an anterior-basal focus of pathology. In a comprehensive review of the literature, Tarter (1975b) has demonstrated that the pattern of impairments exhibited by chronic alcoholics is similar to that in persons suffering from acute brain damage and also experimental animals with lesions to these regions of the brain. Some of the deficits found in alcoholics include an inability to temporally organize behavior (Tarter, 1973), poor error utilization (Tarter, 1973), spatial perseveration (Tarter, 1973), set perseveration (Tarter, 1973), deficient spatial scanning (Fitzhugh et al., 1960, 1965; Goldstein and Chotlos, 1965; Tarter, 1971), and disrupted motor regulation (Parsons et al., 1972). However, not all tests that supposedly tap anterior-basal integrity result in impairment. For example no decrements were noted on a serial alternation task (Tarter, 1971), even though it has been stated by Luria (1966) that this is a prime characteristic exhibited by frontally damaged individuals. In addition, alcoholics are not impaired in "learning to learn" (Tarter, 1973), despite the fact that many studies have been conducted which demonstrate impairments of this capacity in animals (Warren and Akert, 1964) with anterior brain lesions.

In another test of the anterior-basal hypothesis, Smart (1965) preselected two groups of alcoholics on the basis of their WAIS performance. Subjects whose Verbal IQ exceed the Performance IQ by more than 18 points were assigned to one group and those persons where the IQ difference score was less than 5 points were placed in another group. It was subsequently observed that the former group obtained a significantly higher extraversion score on the Maudsley Personality Inventory. The tendency towards extraversion associated with presumed neurological injury, as measured by the WAIS, was interpreted as reflective of a personality change with brain damage. That frontal lobe injury does indeed result in changes toward extraversion had already been documented by several investigators (Meyer, 1961; Petrie, 1949; Tow, 1955).

In summary, it can be seen that active efforts have been made by a number of researchers to integrate neurological and psychological findings in alcoholics. Although the exact nature of the neuropsychological disruption is as yet not fully understood, the weight of the available evidence does suggest a deleterious effect of chronic alcohol intake. Thus, while we can cautiously conclude at this time that a neuropsychological impairment exists in chronic alcoholics, we must also consider the potential for recovery or reversibility of the observed deficits.

Reversibility of Impairment

A vital issue and one which has received comparatively little attention is whether the observed deficits in alcoholics are permanent and hence irreversible. Does sobriety lead to a recovery of function? Several studies have been conducted which tend to indicate that improvement does occur for at least several important psychological and behavioral capacities. While dramatic improvements are often seen as the alcoholic passes through withdrawal, the present discussion will focus only on post-withdrawal changes.

In one study, McLachlan and Levinson (1974) reported increased WAIS Block Design Performance to the point where no detectable impairment was manifest after one year of abstinence from alcohol. In another investigation Long and McLachlan (1974) observed a significant improvement on several of the WAIS subtests as well as on the Halstead-Reitan Battery. After a one-year interval of sobriety there were performance increments on the Category Test and Finger Tapping Test.

The summary score of all tests or impairment index also showed significant improvement. No improvement in Trail Making Test performance was observed. Tarter and Jones (1971b) found that alcoholics, especially those with less than a ten-year history of excessive drinking, improved in finger tapping speed and perceptual-motor coordination. Muscle strength also showed recovery after approximately ten weeks of sobriety. Goldstein et al. (1968) found that gait instability decreased with sobriety and that this process could be facilitated by practice on the part of the subject. Page and Linden (1974) administered the WAIS, Bender-Gestalt, Shipley Institute of Living Scale, Trail Making Test, and Halstead-Reitan Battery. They noted improvements after two weeks of sobriety but with no further changes occurring after an additional two months of abstinence. The authors concluded that "abstract reasoning, short-term memory and coding, sequencing ability, and general mental flexibility are depressed in alcoholics to a severely disruptive extent for about a week, after which partial recovery occurs rapidly and remains essentially asymptotic for at least two months" (p. 105).

Clarke and Haughton (1975) tested alcoholics on the Similarities, Vocabulary, Block Design, Object Assembly subtests of the WAIS and Visual Reproduction subtest of the Wechsler Memory Scale. Compared to a matched control group, they found that the alcoholics were still deficient in visual-spatial and visuomotor coordination as well as visual reproduction and abstract reasoning after ten weeks of abstinence. Smith, Johnson, and Burdick (1971) reported improvement from test to retest on the Shipley Institute of Living Scale, Embedded Figures Test, and Hidden Figures Test. Similar results have also been obtained for memory functions. Allen, Faillace and Reynolds (1971) observed in serial and free recall paradigms that it took up to two weeks for recovery of memory capacity to take place. Retentive decrements exhibited by alcoholics upon hospital admission also disappeared after approximately three weeks (Weingartner, Faillace, and Markley, 1971). Greiner (1961) also reported no significant memory loss in alcoholics sober from 2 to 11 years.

Improvements on a variety of psychometric measures have been reported also by Jonsson, Cronholm, and Izikowitz (1962), who evaluated alcoholics on admission and again after withdrawal effects had subsided. In addition to psychological measures, there is at least one study (Bennett, 1960) in which initial abnormal EEG tracings were observed to change toward the direction of normality with sobriety. However, in this latter study, only slightly more than half the subjects exhibited disturbed EEG tracings in the first place.

Contrary to the above cited studies, other researchers have not observed dramatic recovery of capacity. Carlsson, Claeson, and Pettersson (1973) reported only slight differences in performance on several perceptual and cognitive tests from the first week of hospitalization to at least two weeks thereafter. Unfortunately, methodological limitations and the brief interval between test and retest make it difficult to generalize their findings. They did observe, however, that on a battery of eight tests, there was evidence for cerebral impairment in 83.6 percent of their subjects on at least three of the tests. In one well-designed animal study, Freund and Walker (1971) found that mice were still deficient in an avoidance learning task after 4-1/2 months of sobriety. An impairment in timing behavior was exhibited by rats after thirty days of alcohol abstinence (Walker and Freund, 1973). Thus in at least one human and two animal studies, no reversibility of neuropsychological deficit was noted. While the animal studies are important insofar as they can control for extraneous variables, the results are unfortunately not capable of extrapolation to the human condition, since different recovery rates in man and animals probably take place. Nonetheless, the results of the animal investigation implicate a neurological impairment from ethanol which in terms of the life span of the animal lasts an appreciable amount of time.

In conclusion, the information available to date indicates that there is improvement on a variety of psychological and behavioral capacities as the individual progresses from inebriation through withdrawal and into a state of sobriety. During abstinence there appears to be continued improvement, but the extent and course of recovery at this time is not well understood. Some investigators have reported recovery after two months. Further research will hopefully clarify this important issue by determining the relationship of drinking history to recovery; and second, by delineating the type of functions which are most readily recoverable by sobriety alone and which might require more direct modes of therapeutic intervention.

Antecedent Neuropsychological Impairment

Up to this point the discussion has been confined to the effects of alcohol abuse on psychological capacity and neurological integrity consequential to alcohol abuse. However, in recent years there has been an accumulating body of evidence which suggests that many alcoholics may have minimal brain damage (MBD) and/or exhibited symptoms of hyperactivity as children prior to drinking onset. While not all children manifesting such characteristics show obvious organic impairment, such behavioral characteristics as impulsivity, distractibility, aggressiveness, dyslexia, and antisocial inclinations are often considered "soft" signs of a central neurological disruption.

In four studies to date, it has been shown that an alcoholic parent more frequently than one would expect on a chance basis (or compared to a nonalcoholic parent) has an offspring who is either hyperactive or diagnosed as suffering from MBD (Cantwell, 1972; Goodwin et al., 1975; Morrison and Steward, 1973a, 1973b; Tarter et al., in preparation). In two of the studies (Goodwin et al., 1975; Morrison and Stewart, 1973a), a genetic interpretation seemed most feasible in light of the fact that the MBD children were reared apart from their biological alcoholic parents. Thus, there appears to be an association between parental alcoholism and childhood minimal brain damage.

The question then arises, what becomes of such children? In one study (Mendleson, Johnson, and Stewart, 1971), it was found that 15 percent of minimally brain damaged children between the ages of 12 and 16 were already exhibiting excessive drinking. In a recently completed investigation, Tarter et al. (in preparation) found that the most severe drinkers as adults also retrospectively reported more childhood symptoms of MBD than less severe drinkers. Severe drinkers were defined by such features as increased tolerance to alcohol, withdrawal symptoms, positive psychic effect from their first drinking experience, positive psychic effect from their first drink after a period of abstinence, absence of social drinking in their history, loss of control, and alcohol related problems prior to the age of forty. The severe drinkers (tentatively identified as primary alcoholics) reported over four times as many MBD symptoms as the less severe drinkers (secondary alcoholics). They also reported a significantly greater incidence of parental alcohol abuse. Furthermore, their general clinical condition as revealed by MMPI profiles suggested normality when compared to the secondary alcoholics, except for the MacAndrew Alcoholism Scale, in which they scored significantly higher.

From these studies, which at this time must still be considered preliminary, there is mounting evidence to implicate a central neurological disturbance in some alcoholics of an yet undetermined nature that exists prior to drinking. This disturbance appears to be due to an inheritance factor which when phenotypically expressed is in the form of a minimal brain syndrome and/or hyperactivity. The notion that childhood MBD is related to adult alcoholism is an intriguing possibility, but not altogether unexpected in light of the fact that it has already been shown to be related to sociopathic and hysterical disorders in other adult pathological manifestations (Guze, 1975).

IMPLICATIONS FOR TREATMENT

Does psychological deficit have any bearing on treatment outcome? Certainly one would presume that the processes of therapy would be influenced by the psychological competence of the individual. Reduced abstracting abilities for instance would seem to make it difficult for the person to respond to the "insight" modes of therapy, where the person must utilize cognitive strategies in redirecting his life style and asserting control over his drinking.

Standardized measures of intelligence and neuropsychological competency have however not been useful in predicting treatment outcome. Plumeau, Machover, and Puzzo (1960) administered the Wechsler-Bellevue and Goldstein (1970) tested alcoholics on the Halstead-Reitan Battery and all were unable to identify those persons responsive to treatment on the basis of these measures. Other tests, on the other hand, have proven more useful. Karp, Kissin, and Hustmeyer (1970) found that perceptual field independence may be a prerequisite to successful rehabilitation. They also observed that the more differentiated and sophisticated alcoholics responded best to psychotherapy, while the less competent alcoholics benefited most by a more structured form of treatment intervention.

From these preliminary findings, the possibility exists that a comprehensive appraisal of the psychological status of the alcoholic may have important therapeutic implications. Unfortunately, conspicuously little is known about the intrinsic processes of therapy and specific manifestations of psychological impairment outside the laboratory to enable a derivation of those factors responsible for successful rehabilitation. However, the type of studies by Kissin et al. (1968, 1970) cited at the outset of this chapter may provide us opportunities to integrate the findings on psychological deficit with other clinical information to devise more successful treatment programs.

REFERENCES

Alexander, L. "Neuropathological Findings in the Brain and Spinal Cord of Chronic Alcoholics." *Quarterly Journal of Studies on Alcohol,* 1 (1941): 798.

Allen, R.; Faillace, L.; and Reynolds, D. "Recovery of Memory Functioning in Alcoholics Following Prolonged Alcohol Intoxication." *Journal of Nervous and Mental Disease,* 153 (1971): 417–423.

Appenzeller, O., and MacGee, L. "Gas-Liquid Chromatographic Analysis of Sural-Nerve in Peripheral Neuropathics." *Journal of the Neurological Sciences,* 7 (1962): 593–603.

Bailey, W.; Hustmeyer, F.; and Kristofferson, A. "Alcoholism, Brain Damage, and Perceptual Dependence." *Quarterly Journal of Studies on Alcohol,* 22 (1961): 387–393.

Bauer, R., and Johnson, D. "The Question of Deterioration in Alcoholism." *Journal of Consulting Psychology,* 21 (1957): 296.

Bennett, A. "Diagnosis of Intermediate Stage of Alcohol Brain Disease." *Journal of American Medical Association,* 172 (1960): 1143–1146.

Bischoff, A. "Die alkoholische polyneuropathie (alcoholic polyneuropathy)." *Deutsch Medizinische Wochenschrift,* 96 (1971): 317–322.

Brewer, C., and Perrett, L. "Brain Damage Due to Alcohol Consumption: An Airencephalographic Study." *British Journal of Addictions,* 66 (1971): 170–182.

Brosin, H. "Acute and Chronic Brain Syndromes." In A. Friedman and H. Kaplan (eds.), *Comprehensive Textbook of Psychiatry.* Baltimore: Williams and Wilkins, 1967. Pp. 708–711.

Brutkowski, S. "Functions of Prefrontal Cortex in Animals." *Physiological Reviews,* 45 (1965): 721–746.

Burdick, J. "A Field Independent Alcoholic Population." *Journal of Psychology,* 73 (1969): 163–166.

Callan, J.; Holloway, F.; and Bruhn, P. "Effects of Distraction Upon Reaction Time Performance in Brain-Damaged and Alcoholic Patients." *Neuropsychologia,* 10 (1972): 363–370.

Cantwell, D. "Psychiatric Illness in the Families of Hyperactive Children" *Archives of General Psychiatry,* 27 (1972): 414–417.

Carlsson, C.; Claeson, L.; and Pettersson, L. "Psychometric Signs of Cerebral Dysfunction in Alcoholics." *British Journal of Addictions,* 68 (1973): 83–86.

Carlsson, C.; Dencker, S.; Grimby, G.; and Tichy, J. "Muscle Weakness and Neurological Disorders in Alcoholics." *Quarterly Journal of Studies on Alcohol,* 30 (1969): 585–591.

Casey, E., and LeQuesne, P. "Electrophysiological Evidence for a Distal Lesion in Alcoholic Neuropathy." *Journal of Neurology, Neurosurgery, and Psychiatry*, 35 (1972): 624–630.

Chandler, B.; Vega, A.; and Parsons, O. "Dichotic Listening in Chronic Alcoholics With and Without a History of Possible Brain Injury." *Quarterly Journal of Studies on Alcohol*, 34 (1973): 1099–1109.

Claeson, L., and Carlsson, C. "Cerebral Dysfunction in Alcoholics: A Psychometric Investigation." *Quarterly Journal of Studies on Alcohol*, 31 (1970): 317–323.

Clarke, J., and Haughton, H. "A Study of Intellectual Impairment and Recovery Rates in Heavy Drinkers in Ireland." *British Journal of Psychiatry*, 126 (1975): 178–184.

Courville, C. *Effects of Alcohol on the Central Nervous System*. Los Angeles: San Lucas Press, 1955.

Creutzfeldt, R. "Hirnveranderunzen bei bewhonheitstrinkern." *Zeitschrift fur die Gesante Neurologie und Psychiatrie*, 50 (1928): 321–324.

Denny-Brown, D. "The Neurological Aspects of Thiamine Deficiency." *Federation Proceedings*, 17 (Suppl. 2), (1958): 35.

Ekbom, K.; Hed, R.; Kirstein, L.; and Astrom, K. "Muscular Affections in Chronic Alcoholism." *Archives of Neurology*, 10 (1964): 449–458.

Fitzhugh, L.; Fitzhugh, K.; and Reitan, R. "Adaptive Abilities and Intellectual Functioning in Hospitalized Alcoholics." *Quarterly Journal of Studies on Alcohol*, 21 (1960): 414–423.

Fitzhugh, L.; Fitzhugh, K.; and Reitan, R. "Adaptive Abilities and Intellectual Functioning of Hospitalized Alcoholics: Further Considerations." *Quarterly Journal of Studies on Alcohol*, 26 (1965): 402–411.

Freund, G. "Chronic Central Nervous System Toxicity of Alcohol." *Annual Review of Pharmacology*, 13 (1973): 217–227.

Freund, G. "Impairment of Memory after Prolonged Alcohol Consumption in Mice." In M.M. Gross (ed.)' *Alcohol Intoxication and Withdrawal*. New York: Plenum Publishing Corp., 1975.

Freund, G., and Walker, D. "Impairment of Avoidance Learning by Prolonged Ethanol Consumption in Mice." *Journal of Pharmacology and Experimental Therapeutics*, 179 (1971): 284–292.

Fulton, J. *The Frontal Lobes and Human Behavior*. The Sherrington Lectures. Liverpool: Liverpool University Press, 1952.

Goldstein, G. "Brain Damage as a Factor in Treatment Outcome of Chronic Alcoholic Patients." Paper presented at the Annual Meeting of the *American Psychological Association*, Miami Beach, Florida, September 1970.

Goldstein, G., and Chotlos, J. "Dependency and Brain Damage in Alcoholics." *Perceptual and Motor Skill*, 21 (1965): 135–150.

Goldstein, G.; Chotlos, J.; McCarthy, R.; and Neuringer, C. "Recovery from Gait Instability in Alcoholics." *Quarterly Journal of Studies on Alcohol*, 29 (1968): 38–43.

Goldstein, G.; Neuringer, C.; Reiff, C.; and Shelly, C. "Generalizability of Field Dependency in Alcoholics." *Journal of Consulting and Clinical Psychology*, 32 (1968): 560–564.

Goldstein, G.; Neuringer, C.; and Klappersack, B. "Cognitive, Perceptual and Motor Aspects of Field Dependency in Alcoholics." *Journal of Genetic Psychology,* 117 (1970): 253–266.

Goldstein, G., and Shelly, C. "Field Dependence and Cognitive, Perceptual and Motor Skills in Alcoholics: A Factor-Analytic Study. *Quarterly Journal of Studies on Alcohol,* 32 (1971): 29–40.

Goodglass, H., and Peck, E. "Dichotic Ear Order Effects in Korsakoff and Normal Subjects." *Neuropsychologia,* 10 (1972): 211–217.

Goodwin, D.; Crane, J.; and Guze, S. "Phenomenological Aspects of the Alcoholics 'Blackout'." *British Journal of Psychiatry,* 115 (1969): 1033–1038.

Goodwin, D.; Hills, S.; Powell, B.; and Viamontes, J. "Effect of Alcohol on Short Term Memory in Alcoholics." *British Journal of Psychiatry,* 122 (1973): 93–94.

Goodwin, D.; Othmer, E.; Halikas, J.; and Freemon, F. "Loss of Short Term Memory as a Predictor of the Alcoholic 'Blackout.' *Nature,* 227 (1970): 201–202.

Goodwin, D.; Schulsinger, F.; Hermansen, L.; Guze, S.; and Winokur, G. "Alcoholism and the Hyperactive Child Syndrome." *Journal of Nervous and Mental Disease,* 160 (1975): 349–353.

Gordan, K. *Grassis Kubsubstitutions test.* (Grassi's Block Substitution Test). Unpublished dissertation; Stockholm, 1957.

Grassi, J. *The Grassi Block Substitution Test for Measuring Organic Brain Pathology.* Springfield, Illinois, Thomas, 1953.

Greiner, D. "Selective Forgetting in Alcoholics." *Quarterly Journal of Studies on Alcohol,* 22 (1961): 1358–1360.

Guze, S. "The Validity and Significance of the Clinical Diagnosis of Hysteria (Briquet's syndrome)." *American Journal of Psychiatry,* 32 (1975): 138–141.

Halpern, F. "Studies of Compulsive Drinkers: Psychological Test Results." *Quarterly Journal of Studies on Alcohol,* 6 (1946): 468–479.

Halstead, W. *Brain and Intelligence,* Chicago: University of Chicago Press, 1947.

Haug, J. "Pneumoencephalographic Evidence of Brain Damage in Chronic Alcoholics." *Acta Psychiatrica Scandinavica,* 203 (1968): 135–143.

Hirschenfang, S.; Silber, M.; and Benton, J. "Comparison of Bender-Gestalt Reproductions in Patients with Peripheral Neuropathy." *Perceptual and Motor Skills,* 24 (1967): 1317–1318.

Hirschenfang, S.; Silber, M.; and Benton, J. "Personality Patterns in Peripheral Neuropathy." *Diseases of the Nervous System,* 29 (1968): 46–50.

Jacobson, G. "Reduction of Field Dependence in Chronic Alcoholic Patients." *Journal of Abnormal Psychology,* 73 (1968): 547–549.

Janzen, R., and Balzereit, F. "Polyneuropathie bei alkoholabusus (Polyneuropathy in alcohol abuse.)" *Internist (Berline),* 9 (1968): 260–263.

Jones, B. "Verbal and Spatial Intelligence in Short and Long-Term Alcoholics." *Journal of Nervous and Mental Disease,* 153 (1971a): 292–297.

Jones, B. "Performance of Chronic Alcoholics on the JVAT: A Test of the 'Temporal Sequencing Deficit Hypothesis Using a Verbal Abstraction Task.' Paper presented at the Southwestern Psychological Association Meetings. San Antonio, Texas, April 29–May 1, 1971b.

Jones, B., and Parsons, O. "Impaired Abstracting Ability in Chronic Alcoholics." *Archives of General Psychiatry*, 24 (1971): 71–75.

Jones, B., and Parsons, O. "Specific vs. Generalized Deficits of Abstracting Ability in Chronic Alcoholics." *Archives of General Psychiatry*, 26 (1972): 380–384.

Jonsson, C.; Cronholm, B.; and Izikowitz, S. "Intellectual Changes in Alcoholics; Psychometric Studies on Mental Sequels of Prolonged Intensive Abuse of Alcohol." *Quarterly Journal of Studies on Alcohol*, 23 (1962): 221–242.

Kaldegg, A. "Psychological Observations in a Group of Alcoholic Patients." *Quarterly Journal of Studies on Alcohol*, 17 (1956): 608–628.

Karp, S.; Kissin, B.; and Hustmeyer, E. "Field Dependence as a Predictor of Alcoholic Therapy Dropouts." *Journal of Nervous and Mental Disease*, 150 (1970): 77–83.

Karp, S., and Konstadt, N. "Alcoholism and Psychological Differentiation: Long-Range Effect of Heavy Drinking on Field Dependence." *Journal of Nervous and Mental Disease*, 140 (1965): 412–416.

Karp, S.; Poster, D.; and Goodman, A. "Differentiation in Alcoholic Women." *Journal of Personality*, 31 (1963): 386–393.

Karp, S.; Witkin, H.; and Goodenough, D. "Alcoholism and Psychological Differentiation: Effect of Achievement of Sobriety on Field Dependence." *Quarterly Journal of Studies on Alcohol*, 26 (1965a): 580–585.

Karp, S.; Witkin, H.; and Goodenough, D. "Alcoholism and Psychological Differentiation: Effect of Alcohol on Field Dependence." *Journal of Abnormal Psychology*, 70 (1965b): 262–265.

Kates, S., and Schmolke, M. "Self-Related and Parent Related Verbalizations and Bender-Gestalt Performances of Alcoholics." *Quarterly Journal of Studies on Alcohol*, 14 (1953): 38–48.

Keller, M. "Definition of Alcoholism." *Quarterly Journal of Studies on Alcohol*, 21 (1960): 104–111.

Kish, G. "Alcoholics GATB and Shipley Profiles and Their Interrelationships." *Journal of Clinical Psychology*, 26 (1970): 482–484.

Kish, G., and Cheney, T. "Impaired Abilities in Alcoholism Measured by the General Apitude Test Battery." *Quarterly Journal of Studies on Alcohol*, 30 (1969): 384–388.

Kissen, B.; Platz, A.; and Su, W. "Social and Psychological Factors in the Treatment of Chronic Alcoholism." *Journal of Psychiatric Research*, 8 (1970): 13–27.

Kissen, B.; Rosenblatt, S.; and Machover, S. "Prognostic Factors in Alcoholism." *APA Psychiatry Research, Rep.*, 24 (1968): 22–43.

Lereboullet, J.; Pluvinage, R.; and Anstutz, D. "Aspects cliniques et ilectroencephalographiques des atrophies cerebrales alcooliques." *Revue Neurologique*, 94 (1956): 674–782.

Long, J., and McLachlan, J. "Abstract Reasoning and Perceptual-Motor Efficiency in Alcoholics: Impairment and Reversibility." *Quarterly Journal of Studies on Alcohol*, 35 (1974): 1220–1229.

Lovibond, S., and Holloway, I. "Differential Sorting Behavior of Schizophrenics and Organics." *Journal of Clinical Psychology*, 24 (1968): 207–311.

Luria, A. *Human Brain and Psychological Processes.* New York, Harper and Row, (1966): Pp. 412–466.

McLachlan, J., and Levinson, T. "Improvement in WAIS Block Design Performance as a Function of Recovery from Alcoholism." *Journal of Clinical Psychology*, 30 (1974): 65–66.

Malerstein, A., and Belden, E. "WAIS, SILS and PPVT in Korsakoff's Syndrome." *Archives of General Psychiatry*, 19 (1968): 743–750.

Mandsley, C., and Mayer, R. "Nerve Conduction in Alcoholic Polyneuropathy." *Brain*, 88 (1965): 335–356.

Marsala, J., and Grofova, I. "Connections of the Frontal Cortex with the Basal Ganglia, Thalamus, Hypothalamus and Mesencephalon." *In Theses of the Czechoslovakian Medical Congress.* Prague: State Health Publications House, (1962): 56–57.

May, A.; Urquhart, A.; and Watts, R. "Memory for Designs Test–A Follow-Up Study." *Perceptual and Motor Skills*, 30 (1970): 753–754.

Mendelson, W.; Johnson, N.; and Stewart, M. "Hyperactive Children as Teenagers: A Follow-Up Study." *Journal of Nervous and Mental Disease,* 153 (1971): 273–279.

Meyer, V. "Psychological Effects of Brain Damage." In H.J. Eysenck (ed.), *Handbook of Abnormal Psychology*, New York: Basic Books, 1961.

Morrison, J., and Stewart, M. "The Psychiatric Status of the Legal Families of Adopted Hyperactive Children." *Archives of General Psychiatry*, 28 (1973a): 888–891.

Morrison, J., and Stewart, M. "Evidence for Polygenetic Inheritance in the Hyperactive Child Syndrome." *American Journal of Psychiatry*, 130 (1973b): 791–792.

Murphy, M. "Social Class Differences in Intellectual Characteristics of Alcoholics." *Quarterly Journal of Studies on Alcohol*, 14 (1953): 192–196.

Nauta, W. "Some Efferent Connections of the Prefrontal Cortex in the Monkey." In J. Warren and K. Akert (eds.), *The Frontal Granular Cortex and Behavior*, New York: McGraw-Hill, 1964, Pp. 397–409.

Neidermeyer, E., and Prokop, H. "Ueber die alkoholpolyneuritis and deren stellung im Rahmen chronischer alkoholschaden des gesamten nervensystems." (On alcohol polyneuritis and its place among chronic alcohol injuries of the entire nervous system.) *Wiener Klinische Wochenschrift*, 71 (1959): 267–268.

Page, R., and Linden, J. "Reversible Organic Brain Syndrome in Alcoholics: A Psychometric Evaluation." *Quarterly Journal of Studies on Alcohol*, 35 (1974): 98–107.

Parsons, O.; Tarter, R.; and Edelberg, R. "Altered Motor Control in Chronic Alcoholics." *Journal of Abnormal Psychology*, 72 (1972): 308–314.

Peters, G. "Emotional and Intellectual Concomitants of Advanced Chronic Alcoholism." *Journal of Consulting Psychology*, 20 (1956): 390.

Petrie, A. "Personality Changes After Pre-Frontal Leucotomy." *British Journal of Medical Psychology*, 22 (1949): 200–207.

Pishkin, V.; Fishkin, S.; and Stahl, M. "Concept Learning in Chronic Alcoholics: Psychophysiological and Set Functions." *Journal of Clinical Psychology*, 28 (1972): 328–334.

Plumeau, F.; Machover, S.; and Puzzo, F. "Wechsler-Bellevue Performances of Remitted and Unremitted Alcoholics and Their Normal Controls." *Journal of Consulting Psychology*, 24 (1960): 240–242.

Pribram, K. "Comparative Neurology and the Evolution of Behavior." In A. Roe and G. Simpson (eds.), *Behavior and Evolution*. New Haven, Connecticut: Yale University Press, 1958.

Reinehr, R., and Golightly, C. "The Relationship Between the Bender-Gestalt and the Organic Integrity Test." *Journal of Clinical Psychology*, 24 (1968): 203–204.

Reitan, R. "Investigation of the Validity of Halstead's Measures of Biological Intelligence." *Archives of Neurology and Psychiatry*, 73 (1955): 28–35.

Rhodes, R.; Carr, J.; and Jurji, E. "Interpersonal Differentiation and Perceptual Field Differentiation." *Perceptual and Motor Skills*, 27 (1968): 172–174.

Ryback, R. "State-Dependent or 'Dissociated' Learning with Alcohol in the Physical and Social Stimuli." *Journal of Psychology*, 45 (1958): 213–225.

Ryback, R. "State-Dependent or Dissociated Learning with Alcohol in the Goldfish." *Quarterly Journal of Studies on Alcohol*, 30 (1969a): 598–608.

Ryback, R. "The Use of Goldfish as a Model for Alcohol Amnesia in Man." *Quarterly Journal of Studies on Alcohol*, 30 (1969b): 877–882.

Segal, B.; Kushnarev, V.; Urakov, I.; and Misionzhnik, E. "Alcoholism and Disruption of the Activity of Deep Cerebral Structures: Clinical-Laboratory Research." *"Quarterly Journal of Studies on Alcohol*, 31 (1970): 587–601.

Smart, R. "The Relationships Between Intellectual Deterioration, Extraversion and Neuroticism Among Chronic Alcoholics." *Journal of Clinical Psychology*, 21 (1965): 27–29.

Smith, J.; Johnson, L.; and Burdick, J. "Sleep, Psychological, and Clinical Changes During Alcohol Withdrawal in NAD-Treated Alcoholics." *Quarterly Journal of Studies on Alcohol*, 32 (1971): 982–984.

Talland, G. "Alcoholism and Reaction Time." *Quarterly Journal of Studies on Alcohol*, 24 (1963): 610–621.

Tarter, R. "A Neuropsychological Examination of Cognition and Perceptual Capacities in Chronic Alcoholics." Doctoral Dissertation, University of Oklahoma, 1971.

Tarter, R. "An Analysis of Cognitive Deficits in Chronic Alcoholics." *Journal of Nervous and Mental Disease*, 157 (1973): 138–147.

Tarter, R. "Brain Damage Associated with Chronic Alcoholism." *Diseases of the Nervous System*, 36 (1975a): 185–187.

Tarter, R. "Psychological Deficit in Chronic Alcoholics: A Review." *International Journal of the Addictions*, 10 (1975b): 327–368.

Tarter, R.; Buonpane, N.; and Wynant, C. "Intellectual Competence of Alcoholics." *Quarterly Journal of Studies on Alcohol*, 36 (1975): 381–386.

Tarter, R., and Jones, B. "Absence of Intellectual Deterioration in Chronic Alcoholics." *Journal of Clinical Psychology*, 27 (1971a): 453–454.

Tarter, R., and Jones, B. "Motor Impairment in Chronic Alcoholics." *Diseases of the Nervous System*. 32 (1971b): 632–636.

Tarter, R.; McBride, H.; Buonpane, N.; and Schneider, D. "Differentiation of Alcoholics According to Childhood History of Minimal Brain Dysfunction, Family History and Drinking Patterns." (In preparation).

Tarter, R., and Parsons, O. "Conceptual Shifting in Chronic Alcoholics." *Journal of Abnormal Psychology*, 77 (1971): 71–75.

Tarter, R.; Sheldon, J.; and Sugerman, A. "Correlates of Perceptual Orientation in Chronic Alcoholics." *Journal of Clinical Psychology*, 31 (1975): 364–366.

Tarter, R., and Schneider, D. "Blackouts: Relationship with Memory and Alcoholism History." (In preparation).

Teicher, M., and E. Singer. "A Report on the Use of the Wechsler-Bellevue Scales in an Overseas General Population." *American Journal of Psychiatry*, 103 (1946): 91–93.

Tow, P. *Personality Changes Following Frontal Leucotomy*, Oxford: Oxford Medical Publications, 1955.

Vega, A., and Parsons, O. "Relationships Between Sensory-Motor Deficits and WAIS Verbal and Performance Scores in Unilateral Brain Damage." *Cortex*, 5 (1969): 229–241.

Vivian, T.; Goldstein, G.; and Shelly, C. "Reaction Time and Motor Speed in Chronic Alcoholics." *Perceptual and Motor Skills*, 36 (1973): 136–138.

Walker, D., and Freund, G. "Impairment of Timing Behavior After Prolonged Alcohol Consumption in Rats." *Science*, 182 (1973): 597–598.

Walsh, J., and McLeod, J. "Alcoholic Neuropathy; An Electrophysiological and Historical Study." *Journal of the Neurological Sciences*, 10 (1970): 457–469.

Wanamaker, W., and Skillman, T. "Motor Nerve Conduction in Alcoholics." *Quarterly Journal of Studies on Alcohol*, 27 (1966): 16–22.

Warren, J., and Akert, K. (eds.), *The Frontal Granular Cortex and Behavior*, New York: McGraw-Hill, 1964.

Wechsler, D. "The Effect of Alcohol on Mental Activity." *Quarterly Journal of Studies on Alcohol*, 2 (1941): 479–485.

Wechsler, D. *The Measurement and Appraisal of Adult Intelligence*, Baltimore: Williams and Wilkins, 1958.

Weingartner, H.; Faillace, L.; and Markley, H. "Verbal Information Retention in Alcoholics." *Quarterly Journal of Studies on Alcohol*, 32 (1971): 293–303.

Witkin, H.; Karp, S.; and Goodenough, D. "Dependence in Alcoholics." *Quarterly Journal of Studies on Alcohol*, 20 (1959): 493–504.

Witkin, H.; Lewis, H.; Hertzman, M.; Machover, K.; Meissner, P.; and Wapner, S. *Personality Through Perception: An Experimental and Clinical Study*, New York: Harper and Bros., 1954.

Zangwill, O. "Psychological Deficits Associated with Frontal Lobe Lesions." *International Journal of Neurology*, 5 (1966): 395–402.

Author Index

Subject Index

✳ About the Authors

Gerald Goldstein – Dr. Goldstein is Chief of Neuropsychology Research at the Veterans Administration Hospital, Highland Drive, Pittsburgh, PA and assistant professor of Psychiatry at the University of Pittsburgh School of Medicine. He was formerly director of the neuropsychology research program at the Topeka Veterans Administration Hospital and a consultant to the Menninger Foundation. His major interests are clinical neuropsychology, alcoholism research, and cognitive processes.

Charles Neuringer – Dr. Neuringer is Professor of Psychology and Director of Undergraduate Studies at the University of Kansas. He received his Ph.D. degree in clinical psychology from the University of Kansas in 1960. He is interested in prediction of suicidal risk, neuropsychology, and computer applications in diagnostic evaluation.

ABOUT THE CONTRIBUTORS:

Nelson Butters – Dr. Nelson Butters received his Ph.D. from Clark University in 1964. Following a two year postdoctoral position at the Neuropsychology Laboratory at N.I.M.H. he joined the Psychology Research Service at the Boston VA Hospital. Dr. Butters is currently Associate Chief of the Psychology Research Service at the Boston VA and is Professor of Neurology (Neuropsychology) at the Boston University School of Medicine. He also holds academic appointments at Clark University and the University of Massachusetts (Boston).

Laird S. Cermak – Laird Cermak received his Ph.D. from The Ohio State University in 1968. He was an assistant professor at Tufts University from 1968 to 1972 and is presently a research psychologist at the Boston Veterans Administration Hospital. In addition, Dr. Cermak holds appointments as an associate professor at Boston University School of Medicine, Sargent College, Clark University and Tufts University.

James R. Clopton – James R. Clopton is assistant professor of clinical psychology at Texas Tech University in Lubbock, Texas. Dr. Clopton received his Ph.D. from the University of Kansas in 1974, and he completed an internship in clinical psychology at the Veterans Administration Hospital in Topeka, Kansas. In addition to psychological testing, Dr. Clopton's major professional interests are family psychotherapy and applied research in clinical psychology.

Douglas R. Denney – Douglas R. Denney, Ph.D., is an associate professor of psychology at the University of Kansas. He obtained his doctorate degree in the area of clinical psychology from the University of Washington in 1970. After serving two years on the faculty at the State University of New York College at Buffalo, Dr. Denney joined the faculty at the University of Kansas in 1972. His research has focused upon two major areas: outcome studies of behavior therapy and cognitive development in children.

Raymond L. Higgins – Raymond L. Higgins is an assistant professor of psychology at the University of Kansas. He received his Ph.D. from the University of Wisconsin, Madison, in 1973, and joined the University of Kansas staff in 1974. He is currently acting as the assistant director of the Clinical Psychology program. Dr. Higgins' research has focused primarily on the etiological processes underlying the development of problem drinking, with specific emphasis on tension-reduction models of alcoholism.

Carolyn Shelly – Ms. Shelly is a Psychology Technician at the Veterans Administration Hospital, Highland Drive, Pittsburgh, PA and an instructor in psychiatry at the University of Pittsburgh School of Medicine. She received her master's degree in experimental psychology from the University of Kansas in 1971. Ms. Shelly's major interests are clinical neuropsychology, statistical methods and computer applications.

Ralph E. Tarter – Dr. Tarter is a research psychologist at the Carrier Clinic Foundation in Belle Meade, New Jersey. He received his Ph.D. degree in physiological psychology from the University of Oklahoma in 1971. His major research interests are in neuropsychology and alcoholism.